ADVANCES IN
LIBRARY ADMINISTRATION
AND ORGANIZATION

Volume 3 • 1984

ADVANCES IN LIBRARY ADMINISTRATION AND ORGANIZATION

A Research Annual

Editors: GERARD B. McCABE
Director of Libraries
Clarion University of Pennsylvania

BERNARD KREISSMAN
University Librarian
University of California, Davis

VOLUME 3 • 1984

 JAI PRESS INC.

Greenwich, Connecticut　　　　　　　　　　*London, England*

CONTENTS

v

INTRODUCTION

The late W. Carl Jackson was the founding editor of Advances in Library Administration and Organization. Carl, so concerned about our profession and its literature, saw a need for an annual which would provide space for deeper analysis of current issues in our profession; space to explore new developments and space to encourage more librarians and others to write for a broad library interested audience, not just librarians but for administrators, trustees, and others as well, and not for academic libraries only but all kinds of libraries. Separate and apart from Carl's efforts, our publisher asked me if I was interested in working on publications and after some reflection I replied affirmatively. Our publisher asked Carl if he was interested in having me as an assistant and Carl very graciously accepted me as assistant editor. When tragically, Carl was lost at sea, I was left with this heavy responsibility. Very briefly, Warren Boes, a good friend from library school days joined me only to die suddenly, accidentally. Bernard Kreissman then came to join me and together we have been preparing these volumes for the last several years.

In keeping with the original plan, many of the articles that appear in this annual are solicited by the editors, some very specifically. We have asked knowledgeable librarians to prepare their articles in some depth. Some articles have been volunteered. Our overall objective is to develop or find and publish very long articles, too long usually to be of interest to professional journals. This hasn't always been the case. Some of our articles have been much shorter and some of the articles in this volume are short. Nevertheless, they appear to have pertinence to the profession and so are worthy of publication here. As part of our general objective and again one of the original objectives, efforts are made to find good, new authors who haven't necessarily published before or who may have only thesis or dissertation credit or one or two short articles to their credit elsewhere. Some experienced authors have asked to select their own topics but always with the approval of the editors. Overseas authors are being sought. Some have agreed to write and we await their manuscripts for future volumes.

As originally conceived by Carl Jackson and refined by Bernard Kreissman and myself, ALAO must be devoted to the publication of library research and to the provision of comprehensive reports of economic, political, social and administrative developments in the library field. Another objective included the publication of outstanding historical and conceptual papers covering the theoretical and pragmatic aspects of library management. In the future we anticipate ranging into the fields of high technology, into publication of articles on the history of publishing, and articles on other subjects whether of a historical nature or even on the cutting edge of library science.

The editors are aware, because they both are academic librarians, that many potential authors and readers will view ALAO as a publication intended for academic librarians. That is not the case. We are actively interested in articles from authors who work in other library fields and have solicited librarians in other areas of our profession. Articles from administrators and from those in the information field have also been solicited. Eventually, a very broad range of authorship should appear in our successive volumes.

One of our editorial objectives is to publish a comprehensive bibliography which appears to be of some use and which may otherwise not appear or otherwise not be readily accessible. In Volume II we published a bibliography on children's authors of the 19th century, hoping to stimulate further work in that area. In this volume, we are publishing a bibliography of the writings of a pioneer in the field of renal transplantation, Dr. David M. Hume. With the current interest in transplantation of human organs and the heroic ordeal of the late Dr. Barney Clark in 1983 and the thrilling stories of successful organ transplantations in young infants, also occurring in 1983, it seemed timely to publish such a bibliography.

At the Association of Research Libraries 50th anniversary meeting, some very good papers were presented and four of those papers appear in this volume. Short though they are, they are significant for what they contribute to our literature. All of the articles in this volume are presented for your professional interest and reading enjoyment. We believe they will be useful to you, beneficial to working librarians, and to those who are not librarians but who are administrators or people who work in fields associated with libraries and that they will help your further understanding of the library profession and needs of all our libraries.

Gerard B. McCabe
Editor

INTERNATIONAL EXCHANGE AND CHINESE LIBRARY DEVELOPMENT

Priscilla C. Yu

INTRODUCTION

This study seeks to demonstrate the importance and utility of international exchange to library development, especially for developing Third World countries.

Countries of the Third World of Africa, Asia and Latin America share a common desire to modernize, to acquire new skills and knowledge, including modernizing their libraries. However, most of these countries are faced with a multitude of problems, foremost of which is the shortage of foreign exchange; an obstacle which, among others, deters the developing countries from purchasing the necessary books and journals on the international market. This applies to all fields of knowledge—from the contemporary and classical works of the West to the latest scientific and technological publications. A question, therefore, confronting the devel-

Advances in Library Administration and Organization, Volume 3, pages 1–24.
Copyright © 1984 by JAI Press Inc.
All rights of reproduction in any form reserved.
ISBN: 0-89232-386-8

oping Third World nations is how to gain access to the new knowledge and skills required to achieve the goal of modernization despite the financial constraints. A conventional method for Third World countries to partially resolve the problem has been to utilize international exchange, acquiring new knowledge and skills from the developed world via barter. Out of necessity, international exchange has become a method of obtaining many basic publications.

However, the meaning of international exchange should not be limited to the modernization of library collections. Third World countries also require education in the areas of general and specific library organization and developments and the training of library professionals, without which overall library development would be greatly constrained. Thus, when discussing international exchange in the context of the Third World, we mean exchange not only in the traditional sense of publications acquisition, but exchange to include the transfer of library technical knowledge and skills, organizational know-how and exchange of library personnel in the context of total library development. Given the level of library development in most Third World countries, only this "total" approach to international exchange makes sense.

In light of the vital function and great importance of international exchange to libraries in the Third World, an examination of one developing country's experience with and attitudes and practices toward exchange can provide some lessons for other Third World nations. At a minimum, the study can point to some basic problems confronting libraries in that one country.

China is a case in point. Like most Third World nations, it has had a great desire to modernize, to gain access to new scientific and technological knowledge. In recent years, a lack of material wealth and underdevelopment was evident in many sectors of the country, including education, industry and others. Given China's economic conditions as a developing nation and the goals of modernization, acquiring current scientific, technological and other literature was extremely urgent. It sought international exchange, the flow of information and ideas whether in the sciences or humanities. As the primary depository and channel through which new knowledge could be disseminated, Chinese libraries were a focus of modernization. The leaders in China have recognized the importance of library development and Vice–Premier Fang Yi, in charge of China's scientific and technical and cultural programs, declared that libraries in China were very much underdeveloped and needed to gain knowledge in areas such as automation, management, library planning and design.[1] Library modernization thus was a vital component of China's total development.

This study will be divided into three sections. First we will begin by historically examining library development, principally research and university libraries, from the establishment of the People's Republic of China in 1949 until 1981—its growth and problems, it objectives and functions. The purpose of the section is to provide a general background to China's library development and the role of international exchange. Second, we will examine the contemporary attitudes and practices of the Chinese toward exchange. And third, based upon the Chinese experience, the study will conclude with some thoughts on how to further international exchange and improve library services. It is an assumption of this work that international exchange serves a key role in national development, of which library development plays a major function, particularly for Third World countries in the process of modernization, a situation where trained professionals and material resources are scarce.

HISTORICAL BACKGROUND, 1949–1980

The Period of Soviet Influence

Following the founding of the People's Republic of China in 1949, Soviet influence was strong, dominating all sectors of the country, including the libraries. The Chinese depended heavily upon the Soviet Union, which became the primary source of economic and technical assistance.

From 1949–1954 the Chinese introduced the theories and practices of Soviet libraries. China accepted Lenin's views on mass education with the help of the libraries as a way of raising the literacy level of the populace so the country could achieve the goals of socialism. In addition, Soviet library science books and articles were translated and many Soviet library experts were invited to lecture in China; Chinese librarians also were sent to the Soviet Union to study library science.[2]

Beginning in 1956 there was a strong push to move forward in the sciences, part of the First Five–Year Plan (1953–1957) drive toward modernization. A goal was to make more science materials available in order to increase productivity as well as find ways to strengthen scientific research. Thus in the fifties, libraries and research institutes in China were developing to their fullest as well as being keenly aware of the need to gain access to foreign scientific materials. The impetus upon launching the "March to the Sciences Movement" in 1956 was especially apparent in national and large research libraries. There was an urgent need to obtain technical documents and other scientific materials from abroad. Since purchase of foreign publications was very costly, exchange was utilized widely.

The Soviet Union aided China extensively in the procurement of publications. For example, the Soviet All–Union Institute of Scientific and Technological Information (VINITTI) sent vast quantities of scientific publications to China, while the Chinese Academy of Sciences established a flourishing exchange program with its Soviet counterpart. This was indispensable to strengthen Chinese scientific research. The Chinese Academy of Sciences utilized international exchange as a means to supplement their acquisition program; in 1958, for example, 46,132 titles were received from the Soviet Academy of Sciences in exchange for 29,831 Chinese items.[3] Not to be overlooked was the National Library of China.* From 1949, the National Library established exchange programs with three of the largest libraries in the Soviet Union: Lenin State Library (Moscow), Library of the Academy of Sciences of the USSR (Leningrad), and the Fundamental Library or the Social Science Library of the Academy of Sciences of the USSR (Moscow).[4] Through mid-1957, the National Library of China received over 200,000 volumes of exchange books and periodicals from the Soviet Union.[5] A large portion of the publications received dealt with modern technology, agriculture, and biology which were especially useful in aiding China's economic development.

International exchange was not limited to the Soviet Union during the 1950s, though for the most part the greatest support came from that country. China also received on exchange great quantities of scientific publications from countries throughout the world. Soon after the founding of the People's Republic of China, the National Library of China established exchange relations with major foreign libraries. By 1956 it had exchange relations with 563 institutions in 64 countries, including countries in Europe, Asia, Africa, Australia, South and North America. Books were received from Moscow, Berlin, Warsaw, Prague, London, Paris, New York, Calcutta, Tokyo and many other places. From 1950–1956 the National Library of China sent out 301,615 volumes of books and periodicals and received 182,162 volumes—an average each year of 50,000 volumes sent out and 30,000 volumes received.[6] For the year 1960 alone, the exchange program had expanded tremendously; the National Library received on exchange 110,000 books and periodicals and sent out more than 135,000 items—three times the amount received and approximately twice the number sent out during the years of the early to mid fifties.[7] The Library kept several copies of each publication it received on international exchange and distributed the duplicates to universities and colleges, government agencies, public libraries, factories and mines.[8] Exchange during the fifties was thriving in China. It was evident that to stimulate development in science and technology, strong exchange contacts were necessary.

At this time, various means to promote library development at the research and higher education level were undertaken. In December 1956, a conference was held in Beijing on Higher Educational Institution Library Work. Addressing the meeting, former Deputy Minister of Higher Education, Liu Gaifeng, stressed the importance of scientific research in college and research libraries. He encouraged each library to "periodically reorganize the collection of books and periodicals; strengthen foreign exchange on scientific and technical materials; and increase the circulation of books to its fullest extent."[9]

Other conferences were also held by various educational units in China to encourage the development of library science toward a more progressive scientific level. For example, in 1956 library representatives from 11 provinces met in Nanjing to participate in the first scientific scholarly meeting in library science since the founding of the People's Republic in 1949. At the meeting papers were read on various basic theoretical issues on library science and cataloging which would serve as a path for discussions in the future. The following year the library science departments of Peking University and Wuhan University also held various meetings on fundamental problems of library science.[10]

Even the late Premier Zhou Enlai in his 1956 "Report on the Question of Intellectuals," emphasized the importance of library development and the procurement of scientific publications:

> We must prepare all the necessary conditions for the development of scientific research. In this connection, a matter of the foremost significance is to provide the scientist with the necessary textbooks and facilities to carry out their work, and make available to them reference materials on file in archives and the required technical materials . . . Strenuous efforts should be made to improve the method of importation of foreign books and periodicals, and to work out a system for the equitable distribution of what books and periodicals we have on hand.[11]

Thus during the first decade of the People's Republic of China, great stress was made to secure Soviet and other foreign scientific and technical resources to serve China's developmental needs.

Proliferation of Libraries, 1949–1959

As previously mentioned, Soviet assistance and influence very much dominated library development in China during the fifties. As an illustration, China adopted the Soviet three-tier library system: the public library system (under the direction of the Ministry of Culture), the Academy of Science libraries (under the Chinese Academy of Sciences), and the academic libraries (under the Ministry of Higher Education).[12] Similar to the Soviet Union, libraries of all types were considered important and vital institutions in the life and development of Chinese society. Libraries were "to serve politics, production, workers, peasants, soldiers and scientific studies."[13]

During the 1950s, rural and labor libraries proliferated rapidly. Towards the end of 1956, there were 182,960 village libraries; by 1958, 35,000 labor union libraries had been established. Rural and labor libraries were to reach the peasants and workers in order to popularize scientific and technological knowledge and promote production. The primary purpose of the rural libraries was to disseminate knowledge on socialism and farming techniques. The reading material consisted mainly of popular pamphlets on current events and general and scientific information. A common slogan was "to deliver books to the readers," and incite enthusiasm to the masses.[14] Thus rural libraries took an active role in adult education. Labor union libraries were to use books, periodicals and newspapers to help staff members and workers interpret national policies and raise their political and scientific awareness level. Not only did rural and labor libraries flourish, but the public library system as a whole was rapidly developing. Statistically the number of public libraries above the county level increased from 55 in 1949 to 83 in 1952, 96 in 1955, 375 in 1956, 400 in 1957 and 848 in 1959.

College and research library systems also proliferated during the 1950s. For example, college libraries increased from 132 in 1949 to 229 in 1958, an increase of 73 percent within a nine year span.[15] The major university libraries included those of Peking University, the Chinese People's University and Qinghua University in Beijing; Nankai University in Tianjin; Fudan University and Jiaotong University in Shanghai; Nanjing University in Nanjing; Wuhan University in Wuhan; and Zhongshan University in Canton.[16] Towards the end of the 1950s there were approximately 300,000 libraries in China at all levels with a total cumulation of 260 million books,[17] of which 40 million or 15 percent were in university library collections.

As an example of how vast and how fast the university collections grew, let us examine Peking University Library. Peking University Library was one of the largest university libraries in the country. It was established in 1902 with a main collection of 78,000 volumes. In 1950 when Peking University absorbed Yanjing University, the collection grew to 1,128,115 volumes; by the end of 1961 Peking University Library had accumulated more than 2,000,000 volumes.[18]

With the proliferation of libraries and growth of collections came greater attention to and study of the problems of library development, including areas such as library organization and preservation, readers' service, and the staff development of library workers. Among the major issues studied were problems relating to classification and cataloging. There were many classification schemes in China and between 1949–1957 more than 30 new classification tables were devised by individual libraries.[19] Due to the great increase in the different types of classification, at the end of the 1950s and early part of the 1960s, many libraries began to reorganize their catalogs and scholars conducted research in Chinese language cataloging. A result was to simplify and romanize the Chinese characters. Some libraries changed from cataloging according to the radicals of Chinese characters to cataloging according to Chinese pronounciation. In addition, increased research was conducted along the lines of organizing a more comprehensive cataloging system. However, in the 1960s these research studies were challenged and labeled as bourgeois.[20]

Late in 1957, Chinese libraries made a leap in development by organizing a program for library coordination. The official title for the betterment of library service was the National Book Coordination Act of 1957. Its main aim was to attain a controlled library system in the country whereby scientific research could be conducted. The act clearly stipulated two immediate goals: (1) To establish national and regional library network centers; and (2) to compile union catalogs covering the holdings of the entire country. From this act two main library centers (Beijing and Shanghai) were established. Nine regional library network centers were set up in Tianjin, Liaoning, Heilongjiang, Shaanxi, Gansu, Sichuan, Hubei, Guangdong, and Jiangsu. These centers were set up to coordinate and assist the library programs in local libraries at all levels, to expand the acquisition of foreign materials mainly in the scientific and technical fields, the international exchange of publications (to be conducted by certain library network centers), planning and coordinating the preparation of union catalogs in various fields and in training librarians. Specifically, the main responsibilities of each library network center were (1) to oversee the planning of union catalogs in various fields and in training librarians, (2) to plan the distribution of responsibilities among member libraries in the network regarding acquisition, distribution, exchange and interlibrary loan, (3) to plan in the compilation of union catalogs and checklists of new publications, and (4) to study ways of improving the quality of work among library personnel.[21]

The decade of 1949–1959 was one of general achievement in China. Higher education was fostered and libraries and research institutes were progressing rapidly. However, in spite of these developments, China was still beset with internal and external problems. The problem of insufficient foreign currency to buy the necessary books and materials for scientific studies, let alone material goods, still plagued the country. The fact that China had cut herself off from contacts with many countries of the developed Western World was a hindrance to development.

The break with the Soviet Union in the early 1960s was another blow to China's progress. As noted, the assistance and influence of the Soviet Union in all areas of China's development was very strong. During the 1950s, China had depended heavily upon the Soviet Union for the organization and planning of library work. The Soviets had aided China in procuring much needed scientific books and periodicals at a reasonable cost as well as by exchange. However, by the early 1960s relations between the two countries waned and finally deteriorated to the point where the Soviet Union withdrew all scientific and technical assistance to China, including library development. Hence China began a movement toward self-reliance; access to new scientific and technological developments from abroad was limited and the population was discouraged from foreign interaction, including reading foreign publications.

The Cultural Revolution, 1966–1976

Beginning in 1966 and lasting until the mid-1970s, there was a sharp change in the policies of the Chinese government, which had dire consequences for the nation. This was the catastrophic period of the Cultural Revolution. It affected all areas of the country, economically, politically, socially, and culturally. Led by Mao and the Gang of Four, fanatic Red Guards rampaged over the country, downgrading the intelligentsia class and all cultural activities. The slogan of the Cultural Revolution was to smash the four olds—old thoughts, old culture, old customs, and old habits of the bourgeois classes. Government doctrines propagating Mao's ideas were the sole source of materials allowed to be published and read—this included subject matters relating to politics, technology, and science. Scientific and technological books published before the Cultural Revolution were not available for usage.

The movement had a profound effect on the furtherance of library development. Some libraries were destroyed and others were closed for certain periods; those that did remain open were allowed to collect only materials used to propagate government policies. The number of libraries decreased. For example, in 1965, there were 1,100 public libraries above the county level; by 1976 the number had decreased to 851, a 23% decrease.[22] The Cultural Revolution actually moved China's development clock backwards by at least 20 years, not only in terms of library development but in all phases of the country's growth.

The universities and academic libraries suffered the worst toll. The acquisition of most foreign publications via purchase was halted as well as the acquiring of materials through foreign exchange. The harm done to the educational system during this period was very deep. Undergraduate and graduate training ceased. University students were required to spend several years in the countryside or in factories as manual workers. The principle of education during this period was to learn by doing. Formal education ceased, including the training of new library personnel. The two famous schools of library science in China (Wuhan University and Peking University) ceased taking in new students. Research in library science was temporarily halted, and no journals were published in the field of library science. After 1972, however, the library science departments of Peking and Wuhan accepted new students once again and library science research resumed. The Library of the Chinese Academy of Sciences and the library science departments of Peking University and Wuhan University undertook a series of translations of articles on the modernization of foreign libraries around 1973.[23]

The Impact of the Cultural Revolution

With the fall of the Gang of Four, Mao Zedong's death, and the end of the Cultural Revolution in 1976, China was in shambles and disarray. The harm done during 1966–1976 was extremely detrimental. Realizing the impact of the Cultural Revolution and the many years of isolation, China was keenly aware that it needed to regain access to the developed nations if it were to modernize. A shift in policy occurred. The new policy was to accomplish the goals of the four modernizations—industry, agriculture, defense, and science and technology, first spelled out by the late Zhou Enlai in 1975 and subsequently pursued by Deng Ziaoping and his followers. Thus a new era began for China.

The policy of self-reliance and limiting foreign interaction was replaced with international cooperation. The modernization of libraries in China was now seen as a prerequisite to the four modernizations. In 1978 former Chairman Hua Guofeng stated in his report to the First Session of the 5th National People's Congress: "Libraries of all types should be promoted so that a network serving the masses and scientific research can be established."[24] This official pronouncement was the directive for libraries to start their plans for modernization. In 1979, Deng Ziaoping, a pragmatist, admitted that China lagged behind the West in development by twenty to thirty years; he confessed that China was backward and needed to seek scientific and technical aid from abroad.[25]

Once more libraries regained their places in society. The long prohibited books in libraries were made accessible; methods for cataloging books and periodicals, especially foreign materials, were improved. Book and periodical exchanges with foreign countries were increased.[26] For example, libraries in Shanghai, Tianjin, Jiangsu, Hubei, Guangdong, Sichuan, Shaanxi, Gansu, Liaoning and Heilongjiang began to renew and re–establish exchanges with libraries in foreign countries.[27] An example of the revival of library development in China after the Cultural Revolution was demonstrated in China's modernization of library collection methods, rebuilding of libraries, training of new professionals and the establishment of library organizations. There was now an urgency for expansion and growth in the library field.

An immediate requirement for library development was the securing of resources. University libraries had suffered the most during the Cultural Revolution. Some were demolished and books were destroyed. As a result, collections of Western sources and serial publications deteriorated. Consequently, there was a dire need for new textbooks and scientific periodicals. The government requested all university libraries to undertake a textbook development program. At the same time, each university was encouraged to develop an exchange program.[28]

At the public library level during 1979, 395 new public libraries were constructed. At the end of the year (1979), there were a total of 1,651 public libraries above the county level.[29] By 1980 there were 1,732 public libraries in China, with a collection totalling close to 200 million volumes.[30] Table I shows the development of Chinese public libraries from 1949 to 1980. There was a notable drop, 44 percent, in public library growth during the period between 1965 and 1970. This was attributed to the Cultural Revolution when libraries were destroyed and closed.

An equally urgent problem in the modernization of Chinese libraries was the demand for trained library personnel. The shortage of trained personnel can be clearly seen in a survey of the age levels and educational background of head librarians in China (Tables 2 and 3). As the tables indicate, there was a scarcity of head librarians under the age of 40, with fifty percent of the heads in the 51 to 60 age bracket. Furthermore, in 1981 only 92 or 8.5 percent out of 1,085 head librarians had received

Table 1.   Chinese Public Library
Development 1949–1980

Year	Number of Libraries
1949	55
1957	400
1965	577
1970	323
1975	629
1978	1,256
1979	1,651
1980	1,732

Source: "Libraries, Archives and Museums," in *Zhongguo Nianjian, 1981* (China Yearbook, 1981), (Hongkong: Kingsway, 1981), pp. 534–535.

Table 2. Age Distribution of Chinese
Head Librarians in 1981

Ages		Numbers	Percentage
Below 40		14	1.29
41–50		222	20.46
51–60		543	50.05
Above 60		306	28.20
	TOTAL	1,085	100.00

Source: Adapted from "A Survey of Chinese University and
Colleges Libraries," *Tushu Qingbao Gongzuo* (English title: *Library and Information Service*), No. 1
(1982): 33.

professional training in librarianship.[31] Without trained personnel,
Chinese library development faced a difficult future.

In the post–1976 period, China took steps to overcome the personnel
problem through greater attention to library science education. Historically, library education in China began sixty years ago. As early as 1920,
Boone Library School in Wuhan had offered courses in Library Science
and later in 1928 developed into a library school. Before 1949, there were
four institutions offering library science education in China (see Table 4).
Most of the older Chinese librarians were trained in these schools. After
1949, Boone Library School became part of Wuhan University. During
this time, Peking University also offered a library science program. Most
library science education ceased during the tumultuous time of the Cultural Revolution. Since 1978, many new library science departments have
been founded in institutions of higher learning. As of 1980 there were 27
universities and colleges offering programs in library science, as indicated
in Table 4.

Table 3. Educational Levels of Chinese
Head Librarians in 1981

Educational Level		Numbers	Percentage
University		720	66.36
Senior High		256	23.59
Junior High		109	10.05
	TOTAL	1,085	100.00

Source: Adapted from "A Survey of Chinese University and
College Libraries," *Tushu Qingbao Gongzuo* (English title: *Library and Information Service*), No. 1
(1982): 33.

Table 4.   Chinese Institutions
Offering Formal Education in
Library and Information Science

Years	Numbers
Before 1949	4
1949–1957	4
1958–1962	6
1962–1978	2
1978–1979	17
1980	27

Source: Huang Zongzhong, "Thirty Years of Library
Services in New China," *Wuhandazue Xuebao* (Eng-
lish title: *Wuhan University Journal,* Philosophy and
Social Sciences *Edition*), No. 5 (1979):68–76.
Zhang Junyan, Lu Huihong and Zhang Jinfang, "Ex-
ploring the Management of the Educational Institu-
tions of Library Science," *Tushuguanxue Tongxun*
(English title: *Bulletin of the China Society of Library
Science*), No. 2 (1981):79–84.
Huang Zongzhong and Zhang Qiyu, "Education in Li-
brarianship: Retrospect and Prospects," *Tushu-
guanxue Tongxun* (English title: *Bulletin of the China
Society of Library Science*), No. 3 (1980):16–25.

Another example of library development in China was demonstrated
when the new China Society of Library Science held its first meeting in
July 1979 at Taiyuan, in Shanxi Province. Liu Jiping, the director of the
National Library of China, was elected President of the Society. The
objectives of the organization were to strengthen the role of libraries in
China and provide a basis for library cooperation and coordination at
home and abroad. Specifically, the association was charged with the directives: "To organize research to produce publications, to conduct academic exchanges with foreign libraries and librarians, and to introduce
achievements in library science in China and abroad."[32]

As the China Society of Library Science became established, other
provinces, municipalities and autonomous regions set up their own library
societies. The local library societies were member associations of the
China Society of Library Science. These library societies and those of
the Association of University Libraries in Beijing, the central government
departments and other research institutes comprised a sum of 28 library
societies in China, with a total membership of 4,551.[33] Thus with the
founding of academic organizations and the holding of academic conferences, library science in China was ushered into a new era.

CHINESE ATTITUDES AND PRACTICES TOWARD INTERNATIONAL EXCHANGE

We have examined China's library development from 1949 to the early 1980s and have seen how domestic and international events have affected the development of libraries in China. The Soviet Union was used as a model for China's library development from the establishment of the People's Republic in 1949 until the early 1960s. With Soviet assistance, China marched toward scientific and technological modernization. However, with the Sino–Soviet split and Cultural Revolution, China was left with few linkages with the developed world. For China's libraries, as we have seen, the series of events were devastating. To rectify past mistakes and to re–embark upon a policy of modernization, China's policy since 1976 has been to reopen linkages with the outside world, especially the West, and expand and develop in areas of education and technology. China now recognizes that it must gain access to foreign educational resources and scientific know–how if it is to surge ahead. Therefore, international exchange has once again become indispensable, similar to the 1950s. This section will discuss the post–1976 attitudes and practices of Chinese librarians toward exchanges, principally with the developed nations of the West. Chinese librarians and library science professors assigned a high value to international exchange after 1976. Generally speaking, Chinese library specialists considered exchange both important and beneficial. It was a method of obtaining materials not otherwise for sale and a way of procuring foreign materials economically. International exchange was also perceived as a method of collection development, enriching a library's general collection and for building and filling hiatuses in special collections. The more avenues opened to obtain printed materials, the better it was for China. The librarians also felt that the concept of international exchange carried with it the lessening of tensions between nations and the idea of friendship and cooperation with the United States and other developed countries. There was also the desire to learn as much knowledge as possible from the West and to have more contacts with foreign countries through exchange of publications as well as exchange of librarians and scholars.

To gain some idea as to Chinese attitudes and outlook regarding specific issues on international exchange, interviews were conducted in 1981 with Chinese library professionals at the University of Peking Library, Beijing; the National Library of China, Beijing; Wuhan University Library, Hubei Province; Wuhan University Library School, Hubei Province; Hubei Provincial Library, Wuhan, Hubei Province; and Zhongshan University Library, Guangzhou (Canton).[34] In the interviews, questions were posed concerning five primary areas: (1) What are the goals of international exchange? (2) What were the immediate expectations? (3) How did the Chinese libraries seek to operationalize their exchange program? (4) What were the patterns of the exchange relationships? (5) What were some of the problems in acquiring materials on exchange and what suggestions could be made to improve the process?

First, let us examine the question of goals. The ultimate goal for the Chinese is the modernization of their libraries. The Chinese library professionals who were interviewed felt especially strongly that they needed to acquire materials in the areas of science and technology, given China's ten "lost" years (the Cultural Revolution) and the resulting developmental lag. Optimistically, the Chinese hope to reach by 1985 the level of the late 1970s in Western technology. By the end of the 20th century, the Chinese plan to be completely modernized.[35] Gaining access to current Western scientific sources and expanding their exchange program is absolutely essential if China is to achieve these goals. Exchange, therefore, was conceived as a means of receiving first hand knowledge of a particular field. The goal is to acquire more up–to–date material in the scientific fields by expanding China's exchanges with developed countries.

An example of achieving the goal of acquiring new materials can be seen in the case of the National Library of China. The National Library of China, the equivalent of the Library of Congress, is the largest library in China and is a depository for all books published in China. It was the only library whose collection was least affected by the Cultural Revolution. In 1949, the National Library housed approximately 1.4 million volumes. In 1981, 10 million volumes were in the Library, one–third of which were received through exchange. By that time, all languages and subjects were represented.[36] At the time of the interview, the National Library maintained the largest international exchange program in China. From the founding of the People's Republic of China in 1949 until 1981, the National Library established exchange relations with over 3,000 institutions in 120 countries and regions. In 1981, it maintained exchanges with more than 300 partners in the United States, followed by Japan, Great Britain and Australia. The National Library received over 3,000 periodical titles and approximately 10,000 monographic and pamphlet titles on exchange. Table 5 compares the percentage of periodicals received on exchange to that of purchased periodicals from 1966–1980. At the start of the Cultural Revolution in 1966, more exchange periodicals were received than those purchased. During the Cultural Revolution exchange continued to be utilized, notwithstanding the increase in numbers of purchased periodicals during the years 1971–1980. The results of Table 5 indicate that during the period of the Cultural Revolution through 1980, there was a strong reliance on exchange of periodicals to supplement the

Table 5. Periodicals Received on Exchange by the National Library
of China 1966–1980

Year	Received on Exchange	Purchased	Percentage on Exchange
1966	4,852	4,617	105
1969	2,613	3,368	78
1971	2,267	3,452	66
1973	3,038	4,680	65
1974	2,473	5,169	48
1980	3,693	9,209	40

Source: Adapted from Li Zhenming, "On Seventy Years of Building the Foreign Language Collection in the National Library of China," *Tushuguanxue Tongxun* (English title: *Bulletin of the China Society of Library Science*), No. 2 (1982):21–32.

purchased items. An average of 67% of the foreign language periodicals was obtained through exchange during the period.

Concern with improving library service was stated as an equally important Chinese goal by the interviewees. Libraries in China are basically underdeveloped in operational techniques and use many old–fashioned and manual methods in their operations. In 1978 at the National Science Conference, Vice Premier Fang Yi stated that by 1985 "a preliminary national automated science and technical information and library network be established."[37] Thus the modernization of libraries can be seen as a prerequisite for the modernization of industry, agriculture, defense, and science and technology. As previously discussed, the goal of strengthening scientific knowledge actually began in the 1950s when scientific research was encouraged and library science reached a new stage in development. However, most scientific research came to a halt during the Cultural Revolution and all seats of higher learning were closed during the ten years. After the Cultural Revolution, these institutions were once again opened. In the 1980s, there is a sense of urgency to make up for lost time, to rebuild libraries and library collections as well as to upgrade the training of librarians.

Improving library service is strongly manifested by the Wuhan University Library Science Department, one of the oldest library schools in the country. Founded in 1920, it graduated over 100 students annually (1981) as part of a four–year bachelor's degree program. The school had seventeen graduate students and twenty–five faculty in 1981. According to Deputy Director Ms. Sun Binyang, Chinese libraries should learn new technologies in library operations and management from foreign libraries. The exchange of books and journals in advanced scientific management is much desired in order to modernize and improve the level of teaching— that is in order to integrate theoretical knowledge with practical working experiences. At the time of the interview, Wuhan Library Science Department had made an effort to offer more Scientific–Tech Information courses. However, they were still weak in gaining access to source materials on information retrieval and scientific management techniques. Since computer technology is related to China's push to modernize, a great deal of emphasis has been made at Wuhan to develop up–to–date courses in fields such as library automation, information retrieval and machine indexing.

With the long–range goals of modernization defined, concern was with the immediate needs and expectations of Chinese libraries. Historically some libraries in China had a long tradition of international exchange, while others had felt no need to engage in exchange with foreign partners but rather centered their attention on domestic exchange. For example, prior to 1966 Wuhan University Library had not engaged in international exchange. Its exchange with foreign partners began in 1979 and by 1981 Wuhan had 23 international exchanges because its immediate concern was to expand and develop more exchange relations outside China to secure foreign materials.

The effects of the Cultural Revolution had a profound effect upon Chinese attitudes and outlook toward the utility of international exchange. The Cultural Revolution was highly damaging to China's development, as we have earlier noted. Realizing how underdeveloped they are as a result of a decade of suppressed education, China now admits it has to do a great deal of catching up with the developed world. Libraries which seemingly had no interest in international exchange in the past now appreciate the utility of international exchange as a means of acquiring modern scientific and technical knowledge and keeping in contact with library developments in the West.

International exchange serves a major function not only in obtaining current materials as a supplement to purchasing, but also in filling gaps in collections, general and specific. The gaps can be defined in two ways. First there is a gap of non–Chinese materials published during the period of the Cultural Revolution—a void exists in Western serial holdings and books published between 1966–1976. Second, there is a gap in specialized subject areas. For example, there is a noticeable hiatus in the Western languages Reference Collection at Zhongshan University Library for the years 1966–1976. Acquiring reference tools from this period such as bibliographies, catalogs, and annuals is one of Zhongshan University Library's immediate goals. Another library which has serious gaps in specific subject areas is the National Library of China. Though the National Library was closed during the Cultural Revolution, nevertheless, exchange functions continued. However, since the National Library had little to offer at that time other than political tracts, certain foreign libraries discontinued their exchange. As a result, the National Library's serial runs were interrupted and obtaining some back issues has been a problem.[38]

Chinese libraries also see international exchange as an economical way of building a particular collection. This form of collection development is common in Third World countries where they simply cannot afford to purchase all the books they desire or to fill all the gaps in subject coverage. Consider, for example, social sciences. In China many fields in the social sciences have not been fully developed, such as sociology, demography and anthropology. At the time of the 1981 interview, Zhongshan University Library was an example of a library which needed to update social science materials. Since it had not actively engaged in international exchange in the past, only after the Cultural Revolution did it cultivate exchange relations with foreign countries. Exchange developed steadily and freely and in 1981, Zhongshan had exchanges with 63 foreign universities and academic institutions in 9 countries. It developed close ties with the University of California Library at Los Angeles, which sent books on exchange in the fields of sociology, anthropology and law. In return, Zhongshan sent books and journals published by the University such as the *Zhongshan University Bulletin* (social sciences and natural sciences editions), as well as commercially produced texts. Zhongshan even managed to obtain out–of–print books for exchange partners. As with other libraries, Zhongshan's budget was not sufficient to buy all the books and journals required. With the high costs for foreign materials and with the scarcity of foreign exchange funds in China, exchange was seen as a most expedient way of obtaining essential Western materials in areas of concern.

Another example of collection development in special areas was Peking University Library. It sought to further expand its exchange program in the humanities and social sciences, which included philosophy, economics, sociology and all of the other social sciences. Gaining access to current materials in these fields was one of their primary concerns in 1981. Unlike many of the other libraries which did not engage in international exchange until recently, exchange began at Peking University Library in 1953. However, during the Cultural Revolution exchange temporarily ceased; international exchange resumed after 1976. In 1981 Peking had exchanges with over 300 institutions, mainly academic, in 50 countries. The majority of exchanges were with Japan, the United States, and West Germany.

The question of how Chinese libraries operationalized their exchange relationships produced varied responses. Many of the Chinese libraries

which had recently established an international exchange program had
formulated no hard and fast rules. Exchange was very flexible: the main
concern was procuring the required foreign materials. On the other hand,
libraries which had long–standing programs proposed, in principle, a title
for title exchange for serials; piece for piece for monographs, but in actual
practice were extremely generous in offering exchange materials—many
times sending more than receiving. As an example, exchange with the
United States was further strengthened in the Fall of 1979 when a group
of 12 American Delegation of Librarians went to visit China. The group
represented the American Library Association, the Association of Research Libraries, the Association for Asian Studies, and the Library of
Congress. The trip reinforced the U.S. – People's Republic of China Cultural Agreement signed in 1979 which in turn led to a formal publication
exchange program between the National Library of China and the U.S.
Library of Congress. The agreement stated that beginning January 1980,
the Library of Congress would send a full set of U.S. Government publications (approximately 20,000 pieces per year) to the National Library
of China. In exchange, the National Library of China agreed in July 1981
to send to the Library of Congress one copy of all titles they received
amounting to 10,000 pieces a year which included all types of material.[39]
It was reported at the 1982 Annual American Library Association meeting
that the number of Chinese materials received by the Library of Congress
had expanded enormously. Since October 1981, LC received 18,476 titles
which was 8,000 titles more per year than what was expected. As a result
more funds have been requested to hire additional catalogers at LC to
keep up with the new Chinese materials.[40]

Similar. to the National Library of China, Peking University Library
officials said they maintained a liberal title for title and piece for piece
exchange. They sent lists of their own university publications for partners
to select. They also sent subject catalogs; for example, in the area of
Chinese history, foreign partners interested in that field may procure the
publications through exchange. Many of these publications are not for
sale.

Regarding the operationalization patterns of libraries which have lately
established exchange relations, Hubei Provincial Library constitutes one
such example. Hubei Provincial Library's program in international exchange only began in the 1980s and operates very arbitrarily. The Provincial Library sends books and journals published in Hubei province.
Their interest is in receiving science publications which could supplement
their purchased items. A major reason for stressing materials related to
scientific research is that Wuhan, the capital of Hubei Province, is a major
Chinese industrial center. A modern library building solely for Scientific
Research was constructed in the late 1970s to serve scholars and scientists

of the region. The library building is situated adjacent to Hubei Provincial Library. The Scientific Research Library receives current scientific books and journals in Chinese, Western languages, Russian and Japanese.

The last questions discussed during the interview were some of the problems in acquiring materials on exchange and what suggestions could be made to improve the process. The questions generated a variety of responses. Comments ranged from the length of time publications were delivered, cost of postage and ways of gaining access to bibliographic information and recommendations of other countries' publications to problems of obtaining certain materials, a desire to gain more knowledge in administrative management, greater selectivity of materials received on exchange and the problem of maintaining a cost balanced exchange. One of the common problems expressed by several Chinese libraries was the slow mail service which takes three to six months for items sent by surface mail, a perennial problem in international exchange. However, this problem was not restricted just to exchange publications but applied to book trade and paid sources as well.[41] For example, the difficulty of the time lag in shipment of materials can be seen in the case of the National Library of China. Before July 1981, the National Library of China had only been able to send 20 to 40 percent of the titles from the *Quan Guo Xinshumu* (National Bibliography of the People's Republic of China) and their monthly exchange lists to the Library of Congress. The problem was that by the time the title appeared in the *Quan Guo Xinshumu*, the items had already been in print six months. Added to that, there was the delivery time by the National Library to send the *Quan Guo Xinshumu* to the Library of Congress, plus the time for the Library of Congress to select, search, make requests and then transmit their reply. By then, the title was difficult to obtain because of the delay. The solution as previously mentioned was that henceforth the National Library would automatically send one copy of all titles received for processing to the Library of Congress.[42] During the course of the interview, Peking University offered another suggestion to improve the slow mail service and that was to schedule more frequent shippings. In connection with shipping, the problem of postage came up—that is who was to bear the responsibility of costs for delivery. Peking University Library felt the recipient should not assume all costs, but that each side be responsible for its own shipment.

Peking University Library also expressed a concern for gaining access to current materials being published by other countries, as well as acquiring a greater knowledge in selecting foreign publications. It would be helpful, for example, for Chinese academic libraries to know what were some of the current, basic Western works used for classroom teaching and research. A possible solution put forth was to have faculty members and research scholars from various foreign exchange institutions study

and learn the Chinese library's profile—its strengths and weaknesses—
and recommend current works from publishers' book lists and announce-
ments appropriate for the specific Chinese library in question. Another
problem expressed by Peking University Library was the difficulty in
acquiring pre–1911 and pre–1949 materials for exchange partners. Other
problems included the need to gain more knowledge in administrative
management, since it was felt that Chinese libraries were not strong in
that area; and that exchange should not be limited to acquiring source
materials, but that international library exchange should also be expanded
to include the exchange of library professionals. Consideration of the
latter problem would hasten the process of China's library modernization
as well as foster international friendship.

In regard to the problem of selectivity, Zhongshan University Library
expressed concern that greater care should be given to the choice of
publications. Libraries, Chinese and foreign, should not send out un-
wanted, outdated or throwaway material. The research quality of the
exchange item and its use in academic libraries should be the criteria. To
improve the situation, Zhongshan believed in sending out duplicate books
and journals lists so that partner institutions could select what they
wanted. This would alleviate unnecessary duplication. Finally the issue
of how to maintain a balanced price to price exchange was raised by the
National Library of China. It was felt that China's currency and book
prices were on the whole stable, but in other countries prices fluctuated
and were generally high. For instance, regarding exchanges with the
United States, it was an impossibility to observe a strict price to price
exchange, for the value of the dollar was high and book prices constantly
increasing. Exchange, therefore, should be carried out on the basis of
title for title or piece for piece, with the understanding that the materials
were useful in collection development for both the donors and recipients.

CONCLUSION

The 1980s was a time of accelerated development in China. Schools, universities and research institutes once again were revived and there was
now a place in society for intellectual growth. The government's policy
was one of expansion in education and cultural affairs. This included
library development. The government, however, could only support limited library development, including the purchase of foreign materials
within budgetary constraints. Publishers prices of books and periodicals
have escalated and have been a tremendous burden to Third World countries. Throughout the world, book prices in the past ten years have risen
50%, 100% and even 250%. Thus international exchange has become a

method with which to supplement the purchase of those highly sought materials. In addition, international exchange has been a means of acquiring additional scientific and technical materials from research institutes and universities which were not available in the commercial market. In order to further the growth of libraries in China, the demands of scientific and other such publications have become a necessity.

The question is often asked, ''Why utilize international exchange when donations of books and journals from developed nations would do as well?'' The answer is that Third World countries abhor dependency and want to be able to give as well as receive. China's pride, self–esteem, and recognition in what the country has and can contribute are important; only then can it confidently seek assistance from developed nations. The concept and practice of exchange—a two–way process—without question created a basis of friendship, equality, and understanding, so essential for a successful exchange relationship. Furthermore, the flow of exchange materials from China not only enables developed countries to be aware of China's needs and achievements, but also enhances the reputation of Chinese scholars, researchers, and scientists so that personal contacts can be made with their counter colleagues abroad.

In addition to the need for international exchange of materials, there is also a need to train, via exchange, professional librarians and information science specialists. There were a dozen or so library schools in Chinese universities in the early 1980s when last noted, but there was still a scarcity of trained librarians. To educate new professionals, an exchange of librarians should be encouraged, that is, Chinese professionals, be it faculty, library administrators, graduate and research members of the profession, should be sent to study abroad and in return should invite library faculty from abroad to teach in China. In the United States, the Graduate Library School and Information Science of Simmons College and Ohio University Libraries have offered an internship program for the international exchange of librarians with select libraries in China. A corps of professional librarians is essential if modernization of Chinese libraries is to be realized.

Chinese library development within the context of international exchange could be encouraged through workshops, with cooperation and assistance from developed countries. Workshops could pool specialists from various foreign libraries and stimulate thinking and new ideas. Discussions could center around crucial areas of library training, from building a strong library school curriculum, book selection, collection development and the role of efficient scientific management in library administration to the basics in library automation, information retrieval and the establishment of library networks.

In conclusion, this study has demonstrated the importance and utility of international exchange for library development in the Third World, including collection building, expanding various library systems, organization and technical changes, and the training of library personnel. It should be noted that library development is vital to national development. To attain the goal of China's modernization has required the acquisition of science and technology sources; without a strong international exchange program the realization of this goal would have been difficult to achieve. Through the interchange of publications and the direct exchange and contacts of library professionals, international exchange has contributed toward the total modernization of China.

ACKNOWLEDGMENT

I wish to acknowledge the research assistance of Kwok-kan Tam.

NOTES

* The National Library of China was formerly known as the National Library of Beijing.

1. Warren Tsuneishi, "U.S. Librarians Visit the People's Republic of China," *Library of Congress Information Bulletin* 38, No. 48 (November 30, 1979): 487–488.

2. Su hua Zhang, "The Development of the Study of Library Science in Our Country during the Last 30 Years and the Mission Henceforth," *Beijingdaxue Xuebao* (Peking University Journal, Philosophy and Social Science Edition), No. 1 (1981): 85–93.

3. Leslie T. C. Kuo, "Communist China: Restoration and Expansion," *Library Journal* 87, No. 20 (November 15, 1962): 4133–4136.

4. "The National Library of Beijing Exchanged Many Books with Foreign Countries in the Past Four Years," *Guangming Ribao* 24 December 1953, p. 3.

5. Julia Wang, *A Study of the Criteria for Book Selection in Communist China's Public Libraries, 1949–1964* (Kowloon, Hong Kong: Union Research Institute, 1968), p. 99.

6. Zheming Li, "International Exchange of Books and Periodicals in the National Library of Beijing," *Renmin Ribao* (People's Daily), 8 September 1956, p. 7.

7. Nancy Lai–shen Huang, *Library Development in Communist China, 1949–1962* (M. A. Thesis, University of Chicago, 1964), p. 35.

8. K. T. Wu, "China, Libraries in the People's Republic of," in Allen Kent, et al. (ed.) *Encyclopedia of Library and Information Science* 4 (New York: Marcel Dekker, 1970), pp. 627–646.

9. Huang, *Library Development in Communist China*, p. 41.

10. Zhang, "The Development of the Study of Library Science in Our Country during the Last 30 Years and the Mission Henceforth."

11. Committee for the Compilation of the History of Library Service, "Library Service of Our Country during the Last Ten Years," *Beijingdaxue Xuebao-Renwen Kexue* (Peking University Journal, Social Science Edition), No. 4 (1959): 93–107. For an English translation, see *Union Research Service* 19, No. 8 (April 26, 1960): 105–115 and 19, No. 10 (May 3, 1960): 130–149.

12. Lee–hsia Hsu Ting, "Chinese Libraries during and after the Cultural Revolution," *Journal of Library History* 16, No. 2 (Spring 1981): 417–434.

13. Ting, "Chinese Libraries during and after the Cultural Revolution."

14. Wu, "China, Libraries in the People's Republic of."

15. John T. Mah, "Libraries in the People's Republic of China," *Wilson Library Bulletin* 45, No. 10 (June 1971): 970–975.

16. Wu, "China, Libraries in the People's Republic of."

17. Kuo, "Communist China: Restoration and Expansion."

18. Ibid.

19. Mah, "Libraries in the People's Republic of China."

20. Zhang, "The Development of the Study of Library Science in Our Country during the Last 30 Years and the Mission Henceforth."

21. Wu, "China, Libraries in the People's Republic of."

22. Ting, "Chinese Libraries during and after the Cultural Revolution."

23. It is important to note that in the 1970s, a pioneer work on computer cataloging was completed by a senior professor in library science, Professor Liu Guojun (former head of the Department of Library Science, Peking University). Professor Liu Guojun was a scholar in Library Science and introduced Western theories and methods to China. He was an honorary executive member of the China Society of Library Science and Adviser to its Translation and Publication Committee. Professor Liu received his doctorate from the University of Wisconsin and returned to China in 1925. He taught at Beijing University beginning in 1951 and did a great deal of publishing. During the Cultural Revolution period, Professor Liu was tortured by the "Gang of Four." Professor Liu, nevertheless, did not stop writing. In 1972 he began to translate and do research on the question of computers. His first work was a detailed explanation of the Library of Congress' MARC which he translated into Chinese. Later he authored an article "An Introduction to MARC;" he also wrote an essay on "Some Questions Concerning Computer Cataloging." The latter was considered a pioneer work on China's computer cataloging. However, research was at a limited level in the early 1970s; the quality of work was weak. Yet Liu's work was considered important enough to have an impact on the future modernization of Chinese libraries. He died on June 27, 1980. See "Professor Liu Guojun, Famous Expert of Library Science Passed Away," *Tushu Qingbao Gongzuo* (English title: *Library and Information Service*), No. 5 (1980): 38; and Zhang, "The Development of the Study of Library Science in Our Country during the Last 30 Years and the Mission Henceforth."

24. Josephine Riss Fang, "Contemporary Developments in Librarianship in the People's Republic of China," *International Library Review* 13, No. 2 (April 1981): 211–219.

25. Yü-ch'en Ch'en, "Chinese Communist Policy on Science and Technology: Changes and Effects," *Issues and Studies* 15, No. 6 (June 1979): 45–64.

26. "Libraries," in *Zhongguo Baike Nianjian, 1981* (Chinese Encyclopedia Yearbook, 1981), (Shanghai: Xinhua Shudian, 1981), pp. 533–534.

27. "Libraries," in *Zhongguo Baike Nianjian, 1980* (Chinese Encyclopedia Yearbook, 1980), (Shanghai: Xinhua Shudian, 1980), pp. 622–624.

28. Kieran P. Broadbent, *Dissemination of Scientific Information in the People's Republic of China* (Ottawa, Ont.: IDRC, 1980), p. 52.

29. "Libraries," in *Zhongguo Baike Nianjian*, 1980.

30. "Libraries, Archives and Museums," in *Zhongguo Nianjian, 1981* (China Yearbook, 1981), (Hongkong: Kingsway, 1981), pp. 534–535.

31. "A Survey of Chinese University and College Libraries," *Tushu Qingbao Gongzuo* (English title: *Library and Information Service*), No. 1 (1982): 33.

32. "PRC Establishes Library Association," *Library of Congress Information Bulletin* 38, No. 36 (September 7, 1979): 369.

33. *A Brief Introduction to the China Society of Library Science* (Beijing: China Society of Library Science, 1980), pp. 18–21.

34. The visits to the Chinese libraries occurred during October 1981. I wish to thank the

following librarians for their time spent in answering my questions: Mr. Guo Songnian, Deputy Director of the University of Peking Library, Beijing; Mr. Huang Zungui, Head of the Department of Reading Rooms and Lending Service and Jiang Binxin, staff member in the Foreign Relations Department, National Library of China, Beijing; Mr. Wang Lingao, Deputy Director, Wuhan University Library, Hubei Province; Miss Sun Binyang, Deputy Director, Wuhan University Library School, Hubei Province; Mr. Xiong Jin Shan, Deputy Director, Hubei Provincial Library, Wuhan, Hubei Province; Mr. Lien Zhen, Head, Zhong-shan University Library, Guangzhou (Canton).

35.   E. E. David, Jr., "China: Objectives, Contradictions, and Social Currents," *Science* 203, No. 4380 (February 9, 1979): 512–515.

36.   Marianne Tell, *A Note about China's Scientific and Technological Information System* (Stockholm: Stockholm Papers in Library and Information Science, 1980), p. 11.

37.   Yi Fang, "Report to the National Science Conference (excerpt)," *Hongqi* (Red Flag), No. 4 (1978): 19–31.

38.   Broadbent, *Dissemination of Scientific Information in the People's Republic of China*, pp. 13–14.

39.   Library of Congress, Exchange and Gift Division, "Current Status of the Exchange Program with China," September 11, 1981. (Mimeograph), no pagination.

40.   "Division Committee and Discussion Group Reports," *RTSD Newsletter* 7, Nos. 5 and 6 (September/October and November/December 1982): 48–50.

41.   Priscilla C. Yu, "International Gift and Exchange: The Asian Experience," *The Journal of Academic Librarianship* 6, No. 6 (January 1981): 333–338.

42.   Library of Congress, "Current Status of the Exchange Program with China."

REFERENCES

Broadbent, Kieran P., *Dissemination of Scientific Information in the People's Republic of China*. Ottawa, Ont.: IDRC, 1980.

Exchange of Ideas: East and West Meet the Challenge. Tokyo: The National Diet Library, 1958.

Handbook on the International Exchange of Publications, 4th edition. Edited by Frans Vanwijngaerden. Paris: UNESCO, 1978.

Huang, Nancy Lai–shen. "Library Development in Communist China, 1949–1962," M. A. Thesis, University of Chicago, 1964.

The International Exchange of Publications, edited by Maria J. Schiltman. Pullach/Munchen: Verlag Dokumentation K. G. Saur, 1973.

Ruggles, Melvin J. *Soviet Libraries and Librarianship*. Chicago: American Library Association, 1962.

Studies in the International Exchange of Publications, edited by Peter Genzel. Munchen: K. G. Saur, 1981.

Tell, Marianne. *A Note about China's Scientific and Technological Information System*. Stockholm, Sweden: Royal Institute of Technology, 1980.

Wang, Julia. *A Study of the Criteria for Book Selection in Communist China's Public Libraries*, 1949–1964. Kowloon, Hong Kong: Union Research Institute, 1968.

Zhongguo Tushuguan Minglu (English title: *Director of Chinese Libraries*), edited by Wang Enguang, Wu Renyong, Xie Wanruo. Beijing: Chinese Academic Publishers, 1982.

MEASURING PROFESSIONAL PERFORMANCE:

A CRITICAL EXAMINATION

Andrea C. Dragon

Measuring performance in profit–making organizations is much less ambiguous than in nonprofit organizations. This is because of the existence of centuries of traditions, laws, and practices associated with the profession of accounting. Because economic organizations exist to make a profit and because governmental taxing authorities and stockholders are vitally interested in the nature of the organization's profits, accounting for profit–making organizations has become a highly developed art/science. The way an organization calculates its profits is of the utmost concern to more than just the tax collector and the share-owners. Whether profit is determined to be equal to return on investment, earnings per share or after tax net, the success of the organization is measured by the yardstick of profit.

Those familiar with the business world know that success cannot be measured by number of employees, or size of the organization's head-quarters, or favorable public opinion. The only valid criterion for judging

Advances in Library Administration and Organization, Volume 3, pages 25–46.
Copyright © 1984 by JAI Press Inc.
All rights of reproduction in any form reserved.
ISBN: 0-89232-386-8

success in business is profit. Divisions, departments and units in a company are evaluated by measuring the contribution each has made to the "bottom line;" i.e., the overall profit or loss of the company. Individuals working in profit–making organizations understand the motives and objectives of the company and realize that their continued employment depends on whether or not profits are created through the sale and distribution of goods and services.

Measuring performance in nonprofit organizations is far more complicated because of the absence of clearly established accounting procedures for determining noneconomic success. Accounting is concerned with dollars and cents and therefore is of little value in measuring success in nonprofit organizations. It would be most helpful if the accounting profession were inclined to create a methodology for determining "profit" when "profit" is expressed not in monetary terms but in human terms.[1]

This is not to say that accounting as a method of measuring organizational performance is totally useless to nonprofit organizations. There are numerous revenue–producing organizations which are able, at least partially, to judge their success by measuring their income. But orchestras, museums, private schools, associations and other revenue–producing organizations cannot totally measure their success by whether revenues exceeded expenses. These organizations do not exist to generate an economic surplus but rather exist to fulfill nonmonetary objectives. Organizations receiving income directly from the recipients of their offerings may use this income as an indicator of satisfaction with the offering, but organizations sometimes reject income as a measure of success. Certain cultural organizations clearly measure their success in terms of their ability to achieve artistic standards and eschew economic considerations except as necessary to keep the organization minimally functioning.

But many nonprofit organizations generate no revenue. They sell no tickets, admissions, memberships nor charge tuition. These organizations receive funding from public or private sources and are obligated to these funding sources only to perform the activities consistent with their mission and objectives. These organizations exist to do good and their existence is an indication that good is being done. A library, for example, exists to serve the informational needs of the community and its mere existence is often sufficient evidence that the informational needs of the community are being met.

Public service organizations by their very nature resist being defined as failures or successes. It is fashionable to talk of the failure of the public education system in the United States but who has it failed? What has it failed to do? By what criteria is success measured? Compared with public education one-hundred years ago, the schools today are a whopping success.

Often it is exceedingly difficult to quantify the performance of public service organizations. If one organization provides 20 terminally ill patients with daily home visits by counselors, but another performs the same service for 40 patients, is the first less successful than the other? If an organization providing assistance to recovering alcoholics is able to keep only one individual per year from reverting to alcohol dependency, is that organization successful?

One method of measuring social benefit performance is to either observe some desired changes in the individual or group targeted to receive the service or message, or to have a reasonable anticipation that a desired change will occur. Although this method is useful in conceptualizing criteria for evaluating performance, it is not helpful in determining the efficiency with which the organization has converted the public's resources into public goods.

One attempt to address the need that funding sources have to evaluate the performance of the organizations they sponsor is to use so-called output measures. These measures incorporate descriptive statistics and simple enumeration of such activities as total client visits in a given period, attendance at meetings, and enrollment in courses. The assumption underlying the use of output measures is simply that more output per amount of resources invested is better than less. It is therefore better to have more client visits than less, to have more students attend classes than less, and so on. If the objective of a legal aid society is to provide service to the legally indigent in proportion to their numbers in the whole community, then the society would probably aim to serve more clients than fewer. If last year the society was able only to meet a fraction of the demand for services, then an increase of 25 percent in cases handled is an output measure indicating a more successful year.

Output measures have traditionally been the most widely used criteria for evaluating the performance of libraries. These measures were originally developed as "professional standards," i.e., public library standards, academic library standards, etc. The standards were used by library directors to persuade local funding authorities that (a) the library was performing adequately or, (b) the library was not performing adequately, and more resources were needed to "bring it up to standards."

However, judging a library's performance based upon whether or not it meets standards results in an evaluation dependent upon the relationship between funding and the size of the community. The standards equated library success with the quantity of resources the library could marshall. They did not address the quality of service a library produced regardless of its budget.

For these reasons, the concept of library standards is being seriously questioned. The Public Library Association has recently published[2] a description of twelve output measures the association feels are suitable replacements for the old standards. The value of the output measures is that they serve to objectively indicate levels of performance. It is then up to each library to compare the scores on output measures with the library's objectives. If the score indicates progress toward meeting an objective, then the library is successful.

An example of a useful output measure proposed by the Public Library Association is "Library visits per capita." This measure is obtained by dividing the annual number of library visits (obtained by a door count) by the total population in the local jurisdiction. Other examples of output measures are "circulation per capita," "program visits per capita," "references fill rate," and "turnover rate." All these measures have the advantage of being relatively inexpensive to obtain. What they lack in elegance and sophistication they compensate for by being straight-forward and less subject to varieties of interpretation.

HUMAN PERFORMANCE AS A COMPONENT OF ORGANIZATIONAL PERFORMANCE

Although the introduction of output measures into public library performance evaluation is a welcome advancement in the long process of developing accounting–like measures, output measures are not in themselves sufficient to measure library performance because they lack a quality dimension. Quality measures are probably more important in nonprofit organizations than in profit–making ones because there are no market forces acting upon nonprofits to improve or maintain quality. Nonrevenue generating organizations, such as libraries, are insulated from market forces because library users are unable to select alternatives in a way that would have an economic impact on the library. There is no economic mechanism for consumer reaction to the output of libraries. Because there are no market or external forces acting as checks on quality, it behooves libraries to devote considerable attention to the measurement of performance quality.

Because many public libraries have established goals and policies indicating they view themselves primarily as service organizations, it becomes necessary to examine the performance of those engaged in providing the service if the library is to measure performance at all. In comparison with measuring human performance, measuring circulation per capita or cost per circulation is child's play. But, if management is truly desirous of providing quality service, then the control and measurement of human performance is required.

MOTIVATIONAL AND ORGANIZATIONAL VARIABLES AS PERFORMANCE DETERMINANTS

Before reviewing methodology of performance appraisal, a brief review of the major components of organizational behavior is in order.

Motivation

The motivation to work has been studied intensively for several decades. Although it is too early for universal conclusions based on predictive theories, the research evidence to date tends to support those who believe that the motivation to work results from the individual's subjective assignment of value to the various outcomes of performance and the strength of the individual's belief in the likelihood of obtaining those outcomes through his or her own efforts.[3] Put more simply, this expectancy theory of motivation states that an individual will be motivated to work if he or she highly values the outcomes of performance *and* strongly expects to receive those outcomes as a result of his or her performance. The unmotivated worker is one who is:

1. Disinterested in performance outcomes;
2. Does not believe that desired outcomes will result from performance;
3. Does not believe that his or her efforts will result in the required or desired level of performance.

It's important to note that outcomes of performance may be either intrinsic or extrinsic and that the organization has little effect upon the individual's subjective assignment of value to the outcomes. One person may work very hard on a task another may find boring and refuse to do. This is because the first individual places a high value on the outcomes obtained by working alone and quietly on a repetitive task while the second individual perceives those particular outcomes as worthless.

Expectancy theory also helps explain the common phenomena of the competent employee who becomes an incompetent supervisor or manager. The "Peter Principle" may not completely explain why a highly performing cataloger becomes a failure when promoted to Director of Technical Services. If expectancy theory of motivation is correct, then the cataloger placed a higher value on the intrinsic outcomes of cataloging than on the intrinsic outcomes and presumably higher organizational rewards of managing and supervising. Because the newly appointed Director of Technical Services was uninterested in the outcomes he or she was also uninterested in learning to perform in a way that would result in obtaining the rewards.

The Availability of Rewards

One of the key elements in modern motivational theory is the understanding of the methods used by the organization to reward performance. As discussed above, the motivation to work is dependent upon the employee understanding the relationship between performance and rewards. But many employees in libraries and other nonprofit organizations understand clearly that there is no relationship between performance and extrinsic rewards such as salary increases and promotions. An individual who knows that superior performance will not be rewarded will soon be giving the organization mediocre performance. While it is true that the intrinsic rewards for superior performance remain, the research evidence suggests that the availability of extrinsic rewards *based on performance* is a powerful motivating influence.[4] There is also the distinct possibility that an unfair or unequal distribution of organizational rewards will have the effect of lowering motivation.

Although the debate concerning the influence of monetary rewards on motivation has been acrimonious, it is safe to say that the majority of opinion is that monetary rewards are influential but the exact nature of that influential mechanism is unknown.[5] What is known is that individuals vary markedly in the value they place on formal organizational rewards such as salary and promotion. It would be foolhardy, however, for a library manager to believe he or she completely understands the subjective value any particular employee places on extrinsic rewards. The value placed on monetary rewards can change quickly and the wise library manager should assume that such rewards are powerful motivators unless proven otherwise.

In addition to monetary rewards, the organization has at its disposal other kinds of rewards such as travel to professional meetings, special training in new skills or competencies, public praise and recognition, increased autonomy over work design and planning, and increased organizational resources such as equipment, space and clerical staff. Whether or not management recognizes and uses these compensations as part of the formal rewarding system, they are recognized as rewards by the employees and as such they become part of the employee's motivational expectancies.

When an organization attempts to link compensation and performance, it does so with the understanding that certain performance will be rewarded and other performance will not. According to expectancy theory this type of compensation system should have the desired effect of increasing employee efforts in desired performance areas. If employees feel that their performance is adequately measured and if they feel that rewards are directly related to the appraisal of performance then the research evidence tends to support this type of reward system as an effective motivational influence.[6]

Many library managers believe that bureaucratic rigidities, nonconfidential payroll records, union contracts and civil service protections prevent the implementation of performance–based monetary reward systems. Unable to manipulate the monetary reward system, library managers reward performance by promotion into newly–created job classifications or creating changes in the organizational design enabling highly performing workers to enjoy a more favorable working climate. Because these rewards lie outside the formal reward system or union contract, they cannot easily be challenged by passed–over employees.

Although these administrative rewards may be highly valued by the receiving employee, unless he or she understands the relationship between the reward and job behavior, these kinds of nonmonetary administrative rewards may not provide a continuing source of motivation. The employee is left thinking "What did I do to deserve this?" If management distributes rewards to encourage continued desired performance then both parties ought to clearly understand why the reward was presented.

There is another pitfall involved in administering nonmonetary rewards outside the formal performance appraisal system. Expectancy theory states that an individual's motivation is based not only on the value assigned to outcomes of behavior, but also on the strength of the employee's belief that performance is linked to outcome. If the employee believes that high performance will lead not to being rewarded but to being punished; i.e., someone else receiving the new job classification, then in all probability that employee will alter job performance in an attempt to determine what behavior management will reward next time resources or benefits are distributed.

The availability of rewards cannot be overstated in understanding the motivation to work. Performance that is seldom rewarded will become increasingly less important to most workers. Although intrinsic rewards are important in understanding motivation, the fact remains that monetary rewards are powerful factors in the motivation to work.

Managers should understand that the availability of rewards needs to be linked to performance. Employees believing that distributed rewards are unrelated to performance will not expect their efforts and abilities to be rewarded and therefore, will have diminished interest in improving performance.

Ability

Ability refers to someone's capacity to perform a job. It includes manual, psychological and intellectual capacities. Ability is usually a stable characteristic that changes only through long, not completely understood educational and social forces. It is obvious that persons who do not possess certain requisite abilities will be unable to perform as well as those who do. No small amount of skill is required to determine if the candidate possesses the appropriate ability at the time of hire or promotion. There are numerous consulting companies whose sole function is to assess the ability of job aspirants through various testing procedures. Unfortunately, few libraries ever attempt to measure the abilities of a prospective professional employee but prefer instead to estimate ability through an interview or by contacting references. Ability is something that can be determined with minimal expense if the library knows what competencies the candidate will be required to possess as prerequisites and which ones the candidate will be allowed to acquire through job experiences or formal training. Just as the ability of musicians and actors is assessed through auditions, it ought to be possible to assess the ability of a children's reference librarian by having the candidate "audition" at the reference desk for two hours. Similarly, it ought to be possible to assess the ability of a science cataloger by having the candidate demonstrate his or her ability to catalog a few physics monographs.

Training

Training or development is a series of formal experiences with the objective of learning new behavior. Training is perceived by many organizations as a method of manipulating the ability levels of employees. It includes:

1. Identification of the behavioral objectives of the training program;
2. Identification of the content of the training program;
3. Identification of the learning experiences which will facilitate mastery of the content;
4. Assessment of the training needs of employees; and
5. A review of the effectiveness of the training program.

The first three steps can be completed long before the first employee is hired. They then become the core of a training program that is readily available when needed. Too often, libraries have found it difficult, if not impossible, to identify the desired behaviors of professional staff, and therefore have been unable to effectively implement professional training programs.

It is ironic that in most libraries training programs are made available to only the lowest level employees. The more critical a person's role in the library, especially in the delivery of service, the less training he or she is apt to receive. During the last two decades, graduate library education has become more theoretical placing the burden of practical training and inculcation of organizational values on the library. On the whole, libraries have responded to this situation not by implementing training programs but rather by providing professional employees with still more classroom instruction by paying for attendance at "professional development" courses. Although these programs do assist the professional in acquiring additional knowledge, often they do not teach appropriate behavior.

The absence of formal training programs for professionals may be variously interpreted. To some employees it indicates management's satisfaction with performance. To others it indicates a lack of management's understanding of the critical nature of professional tasks. To others it is merely the reaffirmation of the widely held belief that there cannot and should not be norms for professional behavior. The result is uneven service, patron dissatisfaction, and professionals who sincerely believe they are above reproof.

Lack of formal training experiences increases the ambiguity professionals often experience in their relationship to their work. On the one hand the library management says prompt, courteous and accurate service is a high priority, yet the library provides no training in the behavior it considers appropriate to the service function. Also, the amount of training given to professionals varies considerably from one department to another. A cataloger's training is informal but continuous, but someone assigned to outreach services to specific client groups may receive only the most cursory training. How is it possible for a library director to make fair evaluations of performance when one candidate for a middle–management position has had the benefit of on–the–job training and the other has not?

Environmental Factors

Although the primary environmental factor influencing organizational performance is the availability of rewards as has been discussed previously, two other environmental factors, organizational design and leader behavior, need to be mentioned.

There is a belief among corporate managers that some jobs are designed for failure and others are designed for success. The belief is grounded in observations leading to the conclusion that often organizational policies and practices are so rigid or inappropriate that even the most able and motivated employee will be unable to perform satisfactorily. There are other situations in which the organizational design and the task structure are so favorable that any but the most incompetent employee could easily succeed.

The removal of organizational barriers to performance requires a management firmly committed to performance rather than compliance with rules, policies and procedures. Many managers unwittingly impede performance by withholding resources required to achieve high performance. They place additional brakes on performance by creating inefficient channels of communication and irrational department boundaries. An all too typical, but regrettable, example of this situation is the library manager who desires to improve performance through the introduction of expensive computerized systems but does not recognize that an improvement in performance could be achieved through organizational redesign.

What is often incorrectly diagnosed as a lack of motivation and commitment is the manifestation of an employee's attempt to cope with the ambiguity caused by fuzzy job descriptions, capricious policies, task assignment and withheld resources. The discomfort felt by the employee in this situation tends to drain away some of the energy available for creatively and effectively working on a task. When the organizational ambiguity reaches a high level, very little can be accomplished. Anything management can do to increase certainty and reduce ambiguity will have a positive effect upon performance.

We have said so far that organizational performance is determined by:

1. The motivation to work;
2. The availability of rewards;
3. Individual ability;
4. Training;
5. Organizational design.

To this list we will add a sixth determinant, leader behavior. Leaders influence performance by affecting each of the other five performance determinants. Leaders influence motivation because they set performance requirements and either facilitate or impede the awarding of rewards based upon performance. Leaders make not only monetary rewards available but also such rewards as praise, expanded job duties, recognition, and environmental amenities. Leaders determine the abilities required to perform tasks and then select those applicants who possess the requisite abilities. Leaders plan and implement training programs. Leaders design organizations.

An organization will receive the kind of performance from employees its leaders require and reward. But all too often compliance with administrative policies is rewarded and not achievement of service or technical objectives. Employees will be motivated to do those things that management feels are important. Management indicates the relative importance of tasks, policies and objectives by the manner in which it selects, trains and rewards its employees.

The effect of leader behavior upon performance is fairly complex and deserves far more attention than space permits. The salient aspects of leader behavior revolve around the leader's control of rewards, training, selection, and performance feedback. A leader is usually not able to influence the value any particular employee assigns to a performance outcome nor is he or she able to influence inborn abilities. Although these two performance determinants lie outside the leader's sphere of influence, the leader's ability to influence the other determinants of performance is critical and therefore it is certainly appropriate to credit or blame a library's leadership for overall organizational performance.

CONSTRAINTS ON MEASURING PROFESSIONAL PERFORMANCE IN LIBRARIES

Unclear Performance Objectives

Unless performance objectives are clearly understood by both management and employees, any performance appraisal system will fail to distinguish between high and low performing employees. Organizational rewards must then be distributed according to nonperformance criteria. It is unlikely that a system evaluating only personality traits, for example, will effectively assist management in its efforts to reward and encourage appropriate behavior.

The lack of clear performance objectives is certainly not unique to libraries, but its consequences are particularly troublesome to them because to a larger extent users judge the success or failure of a library by the way its staff performs.

In an attempt to address the problem of unclear performance objectives, a number of libraries have implemented "Management by Objectives," or MBO appraisal systems.[7] Both the library literature and the management literature report examples of success and failure of this system. While it is impossible to review all the arguments for and against MBO as an appraisal system, it can be said that many management experts believe MBO is better suited to planning, development and control functions than to performance appraisal. Most agree that the establishment of individual goals is a professionally appealing and beneficial experience for those involved in the process but the very fact that each employee sets individual goals creates a problem for those who must evaluate the acomplishment of those goals in terms of their worth to the library.

It is difficult to attach rewards equitably in an MBO system because there are no standards against which the merit of the goals can be measured. If each cataloger achieves an individualized set of objectives, management faces the difficult task of awarding merit pay increases for the achievement of some objectives but not others. Unless the MBO process involves the establishment of clear performance objectives that apply to all employees engaged in similar tasks, the MBO process ceases to be useful in distinguishing and documenting superior performance.

It is not surprising that when faced with the task of writing performance objectives most librarians substitute a list of ongoing activities. Never having seen or read a list of overall library performance objectives, individual librarians respond to the assignment by jotting down the activities they enjoy and call the completion of them an objective. The value of such activity to the library is not trivial, but is certainly less than an optimal application of MBO as a method of performance appraisal.

Collegiality and Professional Orientation

Another barrier to effective performance appraisal is the concept of collegiality. This is not difficult to understand when one considers that there is no educational preparation or socialization process separating library managers from other professional librarians. Unlike hospital administrators who have educational backgrounds and responsibilities quite unlike those of the nursing and support staff, library administrators and middle managers have received similar educations and possess MLS degrees identical to those they supervise. Except in the largest libraries, the management personnel have specific functional responsibilities in addition to their supervisory ones which necessitate their becoming "one of the workers" for some or most of each day. While this situation is some instances leads to egalitarian feelings among the library staff, it also makes the task of evaluating the performance of colleagues an uncomfortable experience for management and a cause for resentment among subordinates.

Librarians have fought a long battle to achieve professional status and are understandably reluctant to engage in practices that will result in a diminution of that status. To many librarians, professionalism means individual responsibility for adherence to standards transcending the needs of the local institution. To submit to the degradation of performance appraisal would lessen the professional's self–respect and respect for the profession.

It is understandable that professional librarians would be reluctant to participate in formal appraisal systems. Without the assurance that rewards will be distributed according to performance, both management and professional staff have little to gain and much to lose in implementing a formal appraisal system. One major concern is the risk of diminishing the feeling of collegiality among staff. The majority of librarians work in small libraries where they regard each other as co–workers rather than members of a scalar chain of command. The consequences of changing the social dynamic to one having superior/subordinate characteristics is not eagerly anticipated by those involved in the situation. Perhaps this intense feeling of collegiality rather than competition is characteristic of female–dominated organizations. Whatever its origins, the feelings in libraries are those of discomfort with a strong military–type chain of command. A strictly enforced performance appraisal system tends to reinforce the military and therefore alien aspects of the organization.

INDIVIDUAL ORGANIZATIONAL BENEFITS DERIVED FROM PERFORMANCE APPRAISAL

An organization derives four main benefits from measuring performance:

1. Better personnel decisions;
2. More effective training programs;
3. Better utilization of resources;
4. Avoidance of discrimination.

In addition, individuals benefit from performance measurement by receiving clarification of acceptable and unacceptable behavior, obtaining feedback, and understanding the relationship between performance and rewards.

Library administrators make numerous personnel decisions but frequently these hiring, firing, transfer or promotion decisions are based upon inadequate performance information. A system of appraisal in which specific performance areas are evaluated would provide the information with which the administrator could make performance predictions about a candidate.

Without this information, personnel decisions become a matter of intuition or personal preference. Often library managers, lacking suitable information on which to make performance predictions, make promotion decisions solely to reward past performance. While it is true that past performance is a good predictor of future performance, it is not necessarily true that excellent performance as a children's librarian in a wealthy suburb is an indicator of excellent performance as director of children's services in a large urban library.

Training programs may benefit enormously from the implementation of an appraisal system that specifies what behavior the organization feels is indicative of outstanding performance. Training fills the gap between job requirements and the abilities of individuals. No amount of training can be successful unless (1) the job requirements are known, and (2) individual abilities are assessed. In this way, the information provided by a performance appraisal system is analogous to that provided through a selection process. The purpose of a training program is to enable trainees to do something they were unable to do prior to the training experience. Without performance specifications, neither the trainees nor the trainers know what the program is to accomplish.

Because 70 to 80 percent of a library's budget is expended on human resources, husbanding those resources to achieve optimum performance is a vital management responsibility. Without the information provided by a sound performance appraisal system, inventorying the library's human resources becomes a formidable and therefore often postponed task. Instead of utilizing the skills of the library's human resources to continually improve service, the library manager makes staffing decisions based on considerations other than performance. The result is a library staff vulnerable to the anxieties created by ambiguous personnel criteria.

Space does not permit a complete discussion of the legal ramifications of performance appraisal, but several key issues need to be discussed. First, when performance appraisal is used as a basis for making a promotion decision, it clearly falls within the purview of Title VII of the 1964 Civil Rights Act and the subsequent sets of government guidelines on employee selection.[8] Because libraries employ women and members of minority groups, they need to be concerned about assuring the legality of promotion practices, because any practice which adversely affects protected group members is unlawful unless justified by a "business necessity."

Library managers should be aware that in at least seven cases the courts have ruled against employers who used performance appraisal systems to assess vague or subjective characteristics. In *Robinson vs. Union Carbide* (538 F. 2d 652), the characteristics assessed were adaptability, bearing, demeanor, manner, maturity, drive and social behavior. In this case the court ruled that "such high–level subjectivity subjects the ultimate promotion decision to intolerable occurrence of conscious or unconscious prejudice" (p. 662). In a similar case [*Stallings vs. Container Corporation of America.* (73 FRD S11)], the employees were rated on their leadership ability, experience, technical knowledge, general intelligence, general business acumen, and past job performance. The judge in the case stated that "apart from the determination of whether a wage roll employee has the technical knowledge required for the job . . . the remainder of the decision is a 'subjective' judgment call" (p. 516). In another case, *Williams vs. Anderson* (562 F. 2d. 1081), the characteristics assessed for the promotion of an athletic coach (viz, personal appearance, cooperation, dependability, stability, and leadership) were judged unsatisfactory because of their subjective nature.

As in all situations where the law is still evolving, courts differ on the matter of subjectivity in ratings. Some courts have upheld the use of subjective ratings as long as the employer can demonstrate that the methods and procedures used to implement the appraisal criteria are consistent with the intent of the law.

Library managers wishing to avoid charges of discrimination should be scrupulous in basing personnel decisions on job requirements and not on subjective global assessments. A performance appraisal system that documents both the requirements of the job and the abilities of individuals is an excellent way to both avoid legal entanglements and make effective use of human resources.

REVIEW OF APPRAISAL METHODS

Self-Appraisal

In a recent review of research studying self–appraisal systems, Thornton[9] concluded that self–appraisals manifest more leniency, less agreement with other sources, less discriminant validity and less reliability than ratings by supervisors and peers. He stated that he was unable to determine whether this situation was a result of the type of rating scale used, the amount of training in performance appraisal given those doing the rating, or variations in the purpose of the appraisal. He states, "the inescapable conclusion of this review is that individuals have a significantly different view of their own job performance than that held by other people" (p. 268).

Given this rather gloomy presentation of the psychometric failings of self–appraisal, Thornton goes on to discuss possible ways to utilize self–appraisal within a larger appraisal system. He believes that the leniency problem in self–appraisals could be turned into an opportunity to foster an exchange of ideas between subordinate and supervisor over the disagreement in appraisal. However mutually beneficial such healthy conflict might be, it does not resolve the basic issue of determining the correctness of perception in order to allocate organizational rewards.

Peer Appraisal

It has been estimated that nearly 70 percent of terminations are for social–motivational, rather than technical reasons. Many people possess the technical skills and educational qualifications required to perform adequately, but are terminated nevertheless. The phrases "personality conflict," or "professional or artistic differences" are cited as reasons for termination. Whatever reasons are stated, the fact remains that sometimes an individual is fired because the group "chemistry" wasn't right. It would be extremely useful to managers if there were a method that would indicate during the selection process whether or not the chemistry was going to be right. No doubt, application of such a technique would result in reduction of incorrect selection decisions.

Recently, there have been several studies indicating that peer ratings are valuable not only in making technical judgments about job performance, but also in making valid assessments about an individual's ability to work effectively in a group. Kane and Lawler,[10] suggest that for peer ratings to be used effectively three conditions must exist:

1. The existence of peer groups whose members are afforded unique views of salient aspects of each other's behavior.
2. The existence of peer groups whose members are capable of accurately perceiving and interpreting the salient aspects of each other's behavior.
3. A perceived need to improve the effectiveness with which some characteristic or characteristics of peer group members are being assessed.

These three conditions exist in many library organizations, yet peer ratings are rarely used. One reason for this is the difficulty in obtaining a single measure for an individual. Averaging group members' ratings statistically causes problems, and it is also difficult and awkward to make comparisons between members of unequal size groups. Another problem with peer ratings is separating valid judgments of job performance from considerations of friendship. Despite these methodological shortcomings, Kane and Lawler believe that peer rating can be effective when *descriptive* information is desired about each ratee. They suggest that this method is useful for feedback purposes since people can be rated in terms of specific behavior and outcomes. In order to ensure the effectiveness of peer ratings, they state that groups should consist of at least ten members each and that the members be trained in the use of rating scales. They also indicate that for the present, simple averaging is the most practical way of obtaining a score.

In another important review of peer assessment, Lewin and Zwany[11] flatly state:

> Peer evaluations are valid tools for predicting future success and are superior to all other measures available at the time of the rating.[12]

After reviewing many empirical studies of peer assessment, they state that the evidence supports the following propositions:

1. Friendship does not have a biasing effect upon the validity of peer ratings in some situations.
2. Racial prejudices are apparently strong influences upon peer ratings in most situations.
3. Length of acquaintanceship is important only as it provides information relevant to the rating criteria.
4. Interaction relevancy is the crucial variable.
5. Face–to–face interaction is unnecessary so long as relevant behavior is available to the raters.
6. Within very broad limits of group homogeneity, peer evaluations are stable across groups and accurately predict future success in situations where the group composition changes.[13]

Supervisor Appraisal

Despite evidence suggesting certain advantages of peer–appraisal and self–appraisal, most libraries and indeed most other organizations having formal appraisal systems rely on the supervisor to conduct the performance appraisal.[14] The author has collected many appraisal formats from all types of libraries and nearly all of them represent two methods of appraisal: the trait and the global.

In the trait rating method, the superior is asked to rate the employee on a number of personality traits such as: initiative, judgment, dependability, creativity, ability to work with others, appearance, and thoroughness. Even when these personality traits are adjectivally or numerically anchored, it is still quite impossible to be objective when it comes to rating someone's judgment, appearance, creativity, etc. In addition, it may be that several of the personality traits on the list are irrelevant to the job. No one appreciates having one's creativity judged when the job, say, of revising catalog cards, requires very little creativity. In fact, in that particular example, the less creativity the better. In many years of discussions of these trait rating systems with librarians who are evaluated by them, this author has come to the conclusion that they are universally distrusted. Their one advantage is that they are quickly completed and gotten out of the way without too much of an investment in time and energy on the part of the supervisor.

The other type of system used in libraries is termed the "global" in that it attempts to assess all the traits and factors relevant to performance in one single rating. These global ratings can be useful if the supervisor doing the rating has the inclination and the ability to thoughtfully appraise the subordinate's behavior in a manner consistent with the organization's objectives.

But, like trait ratings, global assessments of performance are usually far removed from actual behavior. These kinds of summary reviews of performance lack behavior–specific feedback necessary to improve performance. They are practically useless in providing information that can easily be translated into specific behavioral objectives for training purposes. In addition, because these assessments only review past performance, they are unlikely to assist the individual being reviewed to understand and cope with changes in the job situation.

MEASURING RESULTS AND PROVIDING FEEDBACK

All professional librarians are measured against standards but unfortunately they, either don't know what those standards are or the standards are inappropriate. Notwithstanding the appraisal format, a supervisor has in mind some standard of performance when he or she appraises the performance of a subordinate. The subordinate is measured against the supervisor's image of what the performance should have been. Some measure up, some don't, but because the supervisor withholds the standards, the subordinate is forever trying to determine what it is that the boss wants. A subordinate is forced to guess at appropriate behavior. If he or she guesses correctly, then the result is pleasant for all concerned. Incorrect guesses lead to reprimands, failure to be promoted, failure to receive merit pay, failure to receive tenure, or termination. But in all likelihood, if someone walked into the boss's office and demanded, "What exactly do you want from me?" the boss would be unable to articulate what was wanted. Even if the boss were able to respond honestly, the answer might come out, "I want you to do your job without causing me a lot of bother." When pressed for an explanation of what "my job" entailed, the boss would probably respond, "As a professional it is up to you to determine what your job is." The subordinate would be left guessing at the specific behavior required for the job.

The only way off this frustrating not–so–merry–go–round, is for the management of the library to come to grips with the whole issue of professional behavior. One way to do this would be to simply list the behavior the management feels is appropriate and inappropriate for each job category. Another, probably more useful approach, is for the library management to conduct a series of interviews with professional job incumbents and ask each to respond to the following two questions:

1. What specific behavior indicates to you that someone is performing superiorly as a children's librarian (reference librarian, government documents librarian, etc.)? Remember, behavior is something observable.
2. What specific behavior indicates to you that someone is performing poorly as a children's librarian, etc.?

As a result of these interviews, management might discover that the collective judgment of the staff regarding professional behavior differs substantially from that held by management. In some libraries it may be possible to manipulate the reward system in such a way that the staff will respond by engaging in that behavior deemed appropriate by management even though it is thought inappropriate by the staff.[15]

Whether management bases the appraisal system on a list of behavioral standards gleaned "bottom–up" from the staff, or whether the behavioral standards are imposed from the "top–down," they ought to become the yardstick for measuring professional conduct. Knowing what management considers "good" and "poor" professional conduct, would be a tremendous relief to many librarians. Those who disagree with the behavioral standards could seek employment in libraries having different standards, or they could engage in reasoned debate with management in an attempt to change the standards.

Simply producing a list of behavioral performance standards is not sufficient to ensure a useful appraisal system. Supervisors need to provide feedback to their subordinates frequently enough so that the individual has the opportunity to be reinforced for excellent behavior and has the opportunity to be informed of and can correct inappropriate behavior. This feedback should be behavior specific; frequent; very brief; and informal. The following are examples of this kind of feedback:

1. "I saw how you handled that disturbed elderly gentleman. You were kind but firm and you were nonthreatening when you escorted him out. You did an excellent job."
2. "I think you did an excellent job of reprimanding the page for being late. You told him that the rest of the staff depends on him at certain

times of the day and when he fails to show up, it creates problems for many people. I know it's hard to supervise these highschool pages, but you are doing an excellent job."

3. "This morning you spent 30 minutes on a personal phone call. I wanted to talk to you about this afternoon's meeting, but you were on the phone. I was very upset when I discovered it was a personal call. When you tie up outside lines with personal calls you prevent patrons from reaching us."

4. "Instead of directing that little boy to the shelves where the dinosaur books are, it would have been better if you had accompanied him to the shelves and helped him choose a book that would be suitable for his reading level."

When a librarian first joins a cataloging department and begins to catalog, his or her work is always "revised" or inspected. Mistakes are brought to the fledgling cataloger's attention and corrected. In the library where this author was trained in cataloging, each cataloger wrote her initials on the verso of the main entry. If the reference librarian or anyone else using the catalog had any difficulty with the entry or classification, they knew to whom to bring their questions. As a beginning cataloger, this author was grateful to have a more experienced person revising my work. The accuracy and consistency of the catalog and the ability for it to be used decades in the future were far more important than my feelings about criticism. It was far better to have someone catching my mistakes than to allow errors to be filed in the catalog.

Another reason perhaps why feedback critical of performance is given and received more easily in the technical aspects of librarianship is that the standards for professional conduct are known. Supervisors rarely have to make "judgement calls" concerning rules for main entry, classification, or filing. The correctness of a cataloger's behavior is subject to less debate than the correctness of a children's librarian. The standards for professional performance as a cataloger are not subject to varieties of interpretation. A cataloger does not have to guess at the correct way to catalog to the same extent that a children's librarian must test the consequences of various behavioral responses to particular situations. By establishing standards for professional performance, management not only relieves staff of the anxiety of not knowing the consequences of behavior, but also relieves supervisors of the anxiety of having to provide performance feedback without knowing the difference between "good" and "bad" performance.

In establishing standards for professional conduct, libraries articulate to their consumers the value they place on service. It is no longer true that libraries have a monopoly (if they ever did) on information service and independent learning. The consumer seeking recreational reading has many alternative sources from which to choose. The consumer seeking to upgrade intellectual skills or to increase cultural awareness and sophistication may choose public television programs, community college courses, community–based educational opportunities, museum–sponsored programs or specialized periodical subscriptions. The library is at a distinct advantage in competing for these consumers because the library has the one asset they lack—librarians. The professional librarian is the greatest resource the library has. There is no other institution in the world staffed by people who are trained to be experts in the techniques of acquiring, organizing, and circulating a collection of recorded knowledge and at the same time trained to be experts in assisting people of all ages in the selection and use of that recorded knowledge.

Libraries have succeeded in developing governing codes for the technical aspects of librarianship. These codes are intended to apply universally. The assumption underlying these codes is that all consumers of library service, regardless of local circumstances, are deserving of accuracy and consistency in the organization and management of library collections. The widespread use of computers for monitoring code enforcement indicates that libraries are willing to invest heavily to ensure that technical performance standards are developed, monitored, and controlled.

Unlike technical performance standards which are intended for all libraries, service performance standards need to be developed locally to meet the demands of the local situation. What is appropriate service in a large, research–oriented public library may or may not be appropriate in the reference room of an inner–city community college. Locally developed performance standards, monitored through the use of specific behavioral feedback from the supervisor and evaluated through a continuing process of performance appraisal will bring to public service the same commitment to high performance that has heretofore been reserved for technical service. Performance standards will indicate to library consumers that the library is as concerned about the manner in which information is delivered as it is about the manner in which it is acquired, paid for, and cataloged.

NOTES & REFERENCES

1. For a thorough discussion of this topic, see Robert N. Anthony and Regina E. Herzlinger, *Management Control in Nonprofit Organizations*, Revised (Homewood, Illinois: Richard D. Irwin, Inc., 1980).

2. Douglas Zweizig, *Output Measures for Public Libraries* (Chicago: American Library Association, 1982).

3. Leonard A. Schlesinger, Robert G. Eccles, John J. Garbarro. *Managing Behavior in Organizations: Text, Cases, Readings* (New York: McGraw–Hill, 1983).

4. Wayne F. Cascio and Elias M. Awad, *Human Resources Management: An Information Systems Approach* (Reston, Virginia: Reston Publishing Company, 1981).

5. For a thorough discussion of this topic, see L. L. Cummings and Donald P. Schwab, *Performance in Organizations; Determinants & Appraisal* (Glenview, Illinois: Scott, Foresman and Company, 1973).

6. See Schlesinger, Eccles and Garbarro, *Managing Behavior in Organizations; Text, Cases, Readings*.

7. For a review of MBO and its application to libraries, see Dimity S. Berkner, "Library Staff Development Through Performance Appraisal," *College and Research Libraries* (July 1979), p. 335–344.

Also, Dennis C. Fields, "Library Management by Objectives: The Humane Way," *College and Research Libraries* (September 1974), p. 344–348.

8. For a recent review of the legal aspects of performance appraisal, see Lawrence S. Kleiman and Richard L. Durham "Performance Appraisal, Promotion and the Courts: A Critical Review," *Personnel Psychology* v. 34 (1981), p. 103–121.

9. George C. Thornton, III, "Psychometric Properties of Self–appraisals of Job Performance," *Personnel Psychology* v. 33 (1980), p. 263–271.

10. Jeffrey S. Kane and Edward E. Lawler, III, "Methods of Peer Assessment," *Psychological Bulletin*, v. 85, no. 3 (1978), p. 555–586.

11. Arie Y. Lewin and Abram Zwany, "Peer Nominations: A Model, Literature Critique and a Paradigm for Research," *Personnel Psychology*, v. 29 (1976), p. 423–447.

12. *Ibid*. p. 430.

13. *Ibid*. p. 434–435.

14. For a thorough review of the literature of performance rating by supervisors, see Frank J. Landy and James L. Farr, "Performance Rating," *Psychological Bulletin* V. 87, no. 1 (1980), p. 72–107.

15. For a variation of this type of method, see David V. Mallenhoff, "How to Measure Work by Professionals," *Management Review* (November 1977), p. 39–43.

THE TURNOVER PROCESS AND
THE ACADEMIC LIBRARY

James G. Neal

INTRODUCTION

Turnover is an important measure of the health of an organization. Interest in the turnover process has produced an extensive and diverse record of research, with increasing emphasis on model–building and integrative theory. Each of the three major classes of turnover determinants: individual employee characteristics, work–related factors and economic variables, is closely associated with the concepts of employee–organization linkages and organizational commitment. The extent and quality of these bonds are key elements in understanding work behavior and, in particular, the turnover decision.

The academic library represents a service organization heavily dependent upon its employees, with personnel costs constituting a major portion of operating budgets. The increasing complexity of bibliographic, tech-

Advances in Library Administration and Organization, Volume 3, pages 47–71.
ISBN: 0-89232-386-8

nical and service processes in libraries has thrust greater responsibilities on the shoulders of all employee groups. Skillful management of valuable human resources, especially as pressures for cost containment and accountability mount, is an essential element of library effectiveness and success.

This review of several important features of employee turnover demonstrates that it is a complex phenomenon requiring a systematic view and a concern for many variables within both the organization and the environment. It also emphasizes the need for academic library managers to improve their understanding of the turnover process and its impact on the individual, the work group, the organization and the larger academic and library communities.

EMPLOYEE–ORGANIZATION LINKAGES

Linkages exist in all types of organizations that employ people. The extent and quality of these linkages or connections are jointly important to the individual employee and the employing organization. Two basic categories of linkages can be identified: membership status includes the acts of joining, and staying or leaving; and quality of membership indicates the level of involvement and contribution to the organization. These linkages are operationalized in terms of three factors: employee commitment, absenteeism and turnover (Mowday, Porter & Steers, 1982).

When an individual goes to work for an organization, an exchange relationship or "psychological contract" is created in which each trades something in return for receiving something of value from the other party. For the employee, joining and staying with an employer provides for a source of current economic rewards in the form of wages, and future economic security in the form of retirement benefits. There are also potential psychological advantages in terms of job satisfaction and the support of a congenial work group. Strong organizational connections may have negative consequences as well for the individual, particularly when tenure prevents the employee from obtaining a range of skills that are transferable to a better position with another employer.

For the organization, when indices of nonlinkage, absenteeism and turnover are high, operational costs usually go up. Most employers, therefore, strive to maintain strong membership status links. In addition, strong feelings of attachment to the organization may encourage spontaneous and innovative behavior without the need for role prescriptions or reward incentives. Alternatively, there can be costs to the organization in having employees too strongly linked, especially when marginally effective performers stay on impeding the addition of new employees with better capabilities. These linkages have macro–implications as well, for example, through an impact on higher education or academic librarianship. When both the quality of membership and membership status linkages are deficient throughout a large number of organizations, the level of productivity and the quality of products and services are affected.

Changes taking place in society inevitably affect the kinds and depths of bonds between employees and organizations. Socionormative, demographic, economic and technological changes serve to alter the work environment which in turn affects individual linkages with organizations. Socionormative changes may include revised definitions of success, work ethics, attitudes toward authority, and sex–role stereotypes. The changing composition and characteristics of the labor force, in terms of educational level, average age, and percentage of women, minorities and dual career households are important demographic shifts. The condition of the economy can strongly influence the decision to maintain membership or look for more attractive opportunities. Technology–promoted changes include the creation of rapid obsolescence in many jobs and fields, the information explosion and increasing ability to exchange information, and the increase in specialization of expertise within organizations with a greater need for professionals in various areas. These various changes collectively point to significantly reduced or weakened linkages.

ORGANIZATIONAL COMMITMENT

Organizational commitment has been consistently demonstrated to be an important factor in understanding the work behavior of employees. The topic has received considerable attention because employee commitment to an organization is viewed as a reliable predictor of certain behaviors, especially turnover. In addition, the concept is appealing because it is linked to the notion of loyalty, a traditionally desirable behavior to be exhibited by all employees.

Several researchers have proposed typologies into which various approaches to commitment can be organized. Etzioni (1961) bases his typology on a model of member compliance with organizational directives. The power that organizations maintain is rooted in the nature of employee involvement. This commitment may take three forms: moral involvement which is a positive orientation based on internalization of organizational goals and values and identification with authority; calculative involvement which is a relationship based on a rational exchange of benefits and rewards; and alienative involvement which is a negative orientation found in exploitative relationships. Control mechanisms are implemented for each form of commitment to produce compliance with organizational demands: coercive power in the case of alienative, symbolic rewards in the case of normative, and remuneration in the case of calculative involvement.

Kanter (1968) suggests that different types of commitment result from different behavioral requirements imposed on members by organizations. Three different but interrelated types of commitment are identified: continuance, cohesion and control commitment. Continuance commitment is based on the member's dedication to the survival of the organization, and involves personal sacrifices and investments that make it costly or difficult for the employee to leave. Cohesion commitment is an attachment to social relationships in an organization often promoted by ceremonies and activities that enhance group cohesion and develop psychological attachment to the organization. Control commitment is a member's attachment to the norms of the organization that shape behavior in desired directions and encourage the formulation of self–conceptions in terms of organizational values.

Salancik (1977) distinguishes between the organizational behavior approach and the social psychological approach. With the former, commitment is viewed in terms of strong identification with and involvement in the organization—an attitudinal relationship. With the latter, commitment is viewed in terms of costs invested in the organization that bind the individual to the organization—a behavioral relationship.

On the basis of such typologies, a definition of organizational commitment can be formulated (Mowday, Porter & Steers, 1982): the relative strength of an individual's identification with and involvement in an organization. It is characterized by three factors: a strong belief in and acceptance of the organization's goals and values, a willingness to exert considerable effort on behalf of the organization, and a strong desire to maintain membership in the organization. Another important element of organizational commitment is the notion of exchange. Individuals come to organizations with needs, desires and skills, and expect to find a work environment where abilities can be used and needs satisfied. When an organization provides such a situation, the likelihood of commitment increases (Steers, 1977).

Studies have examined the effects of personal characteristics, role–related characteristics, structural characteristics and work experiences on organizational commitment. Among the personal characteristics investigated, including age, tenure, educational level, gender, race and various personality factors, commitment has been found to be positively related to age and tenure, and inversely related to education (Morris & Sherman, 1981). Three related aspects of the work role have been found to influence commitment: job scope or challenge, role conflict, and role ambiguity. Influences are positive when the employee has a clear and challenging job assignment, and negative when assignments become ambiguous, place the employee in conflict, or provide excessive role stress.

Studies of the influence of organizational structure on commitment have focused on organization size, the presence of unions, span of control and centralization of authority (Stevens, 1978). Other variables have included formalization, functional dependence, worker ownership and occupational groupings. Findings indicate that employees experiencing greater decentralization, greater dependence on the work of others, and greater formality of written rules and procedures, and those employees having a vested financial interest in the organization felt more committed (Morris & Steers, 1980). Work experiences are an important socializing force and influence the degree of attachments formed with the organization. Those variables found to be related to commitment are: organizational dependability, personal importance to the organization, net expectations, perceived pay equity, group norms regarding hard work, leadership style, and social involvement in the organization.

An area of commitment research important to academic librarianship deals with the effects of professional involvement on the compatibility of organizational and professional commitments. Etzioni (1964) notes a basic incompatibility between professionals and organizations which is related to divergent authority patterns. The professional is seen as responding to authority based on expertise, while the organization is characterized by authority based on hierarchical position. The professional entering an organization is seen as having to choose between commitment to profession and commitment to organization. In a study of the compatibility of commitments of college teachers, Thornton (1970) found that professional and organizational commitments can be compatible under certain conditions. The extent to which the professional experiences and perceives an organizational situation as reaffirming and exemplifying principles of professionalism determines the compatibility of the two commitments.

Consequences of organizational commitment may include job performance, tenure with the organization, absenteeism, tardiness and turnover. Commitment does influence the amount of effort put forth by an employee and this effort does determine actual performance. There is a significant correlation between increased tenure and increased commitment, but the causal relationship between these two variables is unclear. Commitment does represent an important influence on attendance motivation and employee tardiness. Highly committed employees would be more motivated to be present to facilitate organizational goal attainment. The strongest and most predictable behavioral outcome of employee commitment is reduced turnover (Angle & Perry, 1981; Steers, 1977).

DEFINITION OF THE TURNOVER PROCESS

Turnover is a dynamic concept, and is best defined as the degree of individual movement across the membership boundary of an organization (Price, 1977). In the work situation, it is the termination of employees and the hiring of new employees to replace them. The decision to leave is the final and anticlimactic event in a process that starts when the employee is selected and hired. The tenure of an employee is punctuated by four critical decision points: postorientation, periodic satisfaction checks, changes in relationships, and warning signs. Employees continuously are asking themselves two key questions: Is this a good job? and Is this an organization I want to continue to work for? The answers to these questions are significantly influenced by trigger events in the work environment (Roseman, 1981).

It is important to distinguish between voluntary and involuntary turnover, as well as avoidable and unavoidable separations. Avoidable separations relate to conditions the employer has some control over such as wages, benefits, hours and working conditions. Unavoidable separations are ones the employer generally has no control over such as retirement, death and pregnancy. Voluntary separations, frequently referred to as quits or resignations, are initiated by the employee while involuntary terminations such as dismissals or layoffs are initiated by the employer. Most turnover research focuses on voluntary separations for three reasons: most turnover is voluntary, theory formation is easier when the phenomenon to be explained is homogeneous, and voluntary turnover is more subject to control by managers.

MEASUREMENT OF TURNOVER

A variety of measures have been developed to help describe levels and patterns of turnover. Only those formulas which have been used extensively in the turnover literature are described. This discussion is aided by two critical reviews of turnover measurement techniques (VanDerMerwe & Miller, 1971; Price, 1977), and covers average length of service, crude turnover rates, stability and instability rates, and survival and wastage rates. These formulas vary significantly in their precision, ease of computation, and control for variables.

The average length of service is computed in two ways, the first based on the existing members or stayers and the second on the leavers. The sum of the length of service for each member of an organization divided by the number of members provides the average length of service (stayers). This formula is relatively easy to compute from available personnel information, it is readily understandable, and it is easy to obtain an adequate size for the average because it is based on the total membership of the organization. A serious disadvantage is the inability of this average to indicate the high turnover rate of low–service members. The average length of service (leavers) is the median length of service of all members who leave during a period. This measure is also easy to compute and understand, and does indicate where, by length of service, turnover is taking place in the organization. There are two disadvantages: it may be difficult to obtain an adequate size for the average because it is based only on the leavers during a specific period, and it does not indicate how much turnover characterizes the organization.

Two types of crude rates are used to measure turnover, one based on accessions to the organization, the other on separations from the organization. The accession rate equals the number of new members added during a period divided by the average number of members during the period; the separation rate equals the number of members leaving during a period divided by the same average. This average number of members is calculated by adding the number of members at the beginning of the period and at the end of the period, usually a month or a year, and dividing by two. The rate is usually multiplied by 100 and expressed as a percentage. The separation rate is the most frequently used measure of turnover in the literature. Crude turnover rates are easy to compute and understand and do indicate the volume of turnover in an organization, but they have no precise meaning, do not control for the lengths of service variable, and are very misleading when the size of the organization is increasing.

Stability and instability rates require data collection during a period of time, the former based on the number of beginning members who leave during the period. Both figures are divided by the total number of members at the beginning of the period to provide the rates. These rates have a fixed range of 100 and are complementary. The most important advantage of these rates is their precise meaning; an instability rate of 50 percent can be attained in only one way: half of the members at the beginning period leave by the end of the period. But these rates are based on membership analysis at two points in time and do not indicate the turnover that takes place during the period. In addition, they do not control for length of service.

Survival and wastage rates focus exclusively on new members, sometimes referred to as a "cohort of new entrants." Two periods of time are required for calculation, the first to define the group of new members, and a second which must pass before the rates can be calculated. The survival rate equals the number of new members who remain during a period divided by the number of new members; the wastage rate equals the number of new members who leave during a period divided again by the number of new members. Usually expressed as percentages, the rates are complementary with a total fixed rate of 100. The concept of half–life corresponds to a survival and wastage rate of 50 and indicates the length of time required for a cohort of new members to be reduced to one half its original size. The survival and wastage rates have a precise meaning and control for length of service by focusing on new members entering during a period. They are somewhat more difficult to compute than the other rates, dealing with new members rather than the total membership, and requiring two periods of time rather than one. Short periods of time are needed to define the cohort of new members making the rates most adaptable to larger units.

It is recommended that multiple measures be used in most turnover research. For the academic library, a productive combination would be the crude separation rate and the average length of service (leavers), both easy to compute. The first would indicate the amount of turnover which is taking place and allow for useful comparisons with other types of organizations and national or regional averages. The second would indicate where, by length of service, turnover is taking place in the library. Use of these complementary measures provides two important types of information about organizational turnover–its location and volume.

CAUSES OF TURNOVER

The literature of organizational behavior and industrial psychology are replete with investigations into the causes of employee turnover, with well over 1,000 studies on the subject having been carried out. A review of this research by Herzberg and others (1955) found evidence of a significant relationship between employee dissatisfaction and subsequent turnover, but noted serious methodological problems. March and Simon (1958) proposed a model of the "decision to participate" influenced by two major components: the perceived desirability of leaving the organization, and the perceived ease of movement from the organization. This inducements–contributions model views an individual's level of job satisfaction and perception of promotion opportunities influencing the desirability of movement. Perceived ease of movement is influenced by extraorganizational alternatives and the personal characteristics of the employee.

Vroom (1964) proposed that the probability of an employee leaving was a function of the difference in strength between two opposing forces: the forces to remain reflected in job satisfaction levels and the forces to leave reflected in the outcomes that an individual cannot attain without leaving the present position. Examining the literature from a clinical psychology perspective, Lefkowitz (1971) found the following influences on turnover: the employee's initial job expectations concerning the nature of the job, job satisfaction, the physical work environment, financial compensation, and supervisory style and workgroup dynamics. Porter and Steers (1973) found job satisfaction, viewed as the sum of an individual's net expectations on the job, to be an important influence on the employee's participation decision. They argue for more emphasis on the withdrawal process in turnover research, and more attention to the role of employee performance levels in turnover.

Price (1977) provides the most comprehensive examination of research on the causes of turnover. In his review, he evaluates various correlates or indicators to which turnover is related. Those with strong support include: employees with low lengths of service usually have higher rates of turnover than those with high lengths of service, younger employees usually have higher rates of turnover than older employees, and periods with high levels of employment usually have higher rates of turnover than periods with low levels of employment. Those correlates with medium support in the literature include: unskilled blue–collar employees usually have higher rates of turnover than skilled blue–collar employees, blue–collar employees usually have higher rates of turnover than white–collar employees, and the United States usually has higher rates of turnover than other highly industrialized countries. Those correlates with weak support include: better–educated employees usually have higher rates of turnover than less–educated employees, nonmanagers usually have higher rates of turnover than managers, and nongovernment organizations usually have higher rates of turnover than government organizations.

Price cites four correlates which are consistently but very weakly supported: time of work—with those working at night experiencing higher rates of turnover, place of birth—with greater turnover for those born in urban areas, the existence of pension plans—with more turnover for those without this benefit, and time of year—with turnover higher during warmer months. He also points out six correlates whose relationship with turnover is unclear: sex, size of community, marital status, amount of work, race, and existence of a union.

Price then proposes several determinants of turnover, analytical variables believed to produce variations in turnover. The first eight determinants are assumed to produce an indirect impact on turnover by acting first through job satisfaction. Higher amounts of pay—the wages and fringe benefits given to employees in return for their services—will produce lower amounts of turnover. Higher amounts of integration or the extent of participation in primary organizational relationships (having close friends at work) and higher amounts of instrumental communication—the extent to which information about role performance is transmitted to the employee (on–the–job training)—will produce lower amounts of turnover. Higher amounts of formal communication the extent to which information is officially transmitted to employees memorandums and training manuals, will produce lower amounts of turnover. Higher amounts of centralization to extent to which power is concentrated in an organization will produce higher amounts of turnover. Higher amounts of routinization the extent to which role performance is repetitive will produce higher amounts of turnover. Higher amounts of distributive justice, the extent to which conformity is followed by the receipt of positive sanctions (a strong relationship between promotion and merit), will produce lower amounts of turnover. Higher amounts of upward mobility, the movement between different status levels in an organization, will produce lower amounts of turnover.

Two key variables are seen as intervening between these eight determinants and turnover. The first is job satisfaction or the extent to which employees have a positive, affective orientation toward membership in the system. Therefore, low pay, few close friends, little formal and job–related information, low participation, inequities and little promotional opportunity produce a decrease in job satisfaction, which will cause an increase in turnover. The second is opportunity, the extent to which alternative occupational roles are available in the environment. High levels of unemployment generally mean low levels of opportunity. Opportunity is not affected by job satisfaction or the determinants, but does influence the relationship between satisfaction and turnover.

Three additional determinants are seen to have a direct impact on turnover rather than through job satisfaction. A high amount of community participation will produce a lower amount of turnover. Work commitment, the extent to which the occupational role constitutes the central life interest of a company's employees, will produce a lower amount of turnover. A high social class position tends to produce a higher amount of turnover.

Muchinsky and Tuttle (1979) reviewed over 150 studies and grouped them on the basis of test–score, biographical, personal, attitudinal and work–related factors. Some of the earliest historical attempts to predict employee turnover involved the use of standardized tests or inventories measuring personality, interest, intelligence or aptitude. Results show that personality differences have a very marginal impact on turnover, a negative relationship between vocational interest and turnover, and there were diverse findings relating intelligence and ability to turnover. Studies of relations between biodata predictors and turnover indicate that biological items can predict turnover reasonably well. Personal factors have included age, tenure, family size and family responsibility. Employee age and length of employment are consistently and negatively related to turnover. Degrees of family responsibility are positively related to turnover. The relationship between family size and turnover depends on whether the employee is the primary (positive relation) or secondary (negative relation) wage earner. Research relating attitudinal factors to turnover is the most pervasive and the results are most consistent: job dissatisfaction is associated with turnover. This finding has been evidenced across various types of samples and across various types of attitudinal measures, including overall satisfaction, facet satisfaction, morale, and need satisfaction.

Many studies have examined the impact of work–related factors on turnover. Workers receiving less feedback and recognition, with less job autonomy and responsibility, working for supervisors with less human relations skills, and who are less subject to pre–employment interventions tended to have higher rates of turnover. Muchinsky and Tuttle emphasize that organizations can facilitate the reduction of employee turnover by providing prospective employees with a preview of what the job will entail in terms of tasks and responsibilities. Pre–employment booklets, job training, work sample measures, and orientation programs help foster realistic expectations in employees regarding their jobs. Muchinsky and Tuttle also cite the effectiveness of the "behavioral intention" approach to turnover prediction and list three employee groups characterized by high rates of turnover: employees whose spouses are members of "temporary systems" such as educational institutions; employees who work as secondary wage earners; and young, highly talented managerial employees of leading organizations.

Economic opportunity factors consistently have been shown to have the strongest impact on turnover (Muchinsky & Morrow, 1980). These factors include: the overall state of the national and local economy, the type of industry and average level of earnings, the state of the labor market in the occupation, the concentration of firms within an industry, the existence of a secondary labor market, and the availability of alternate institutional income sources (unemployment insurance or welfare eligibility).

Roseman (1981) discusses the major areas in which managerial action or nonaction can precipitate and encourage turnover. He cites problems in the following areas: employee selection, work assignment, pay and benefits, promotion, supervision, work environment, and employee development.

The selection process contributes substantially to turnover problems, particularly when employees are selected who are likely to fail or unlikely to stay with the organization. Common deficiencies include: inadequate job specification with obsolete, unrealistic or unclear elements; failure to document selection mistakes; lowering job qualifications and hiring marginal candidates when it is difficult to recruit or there is pressure to fill jobs quickly; emphasis on factors unrelated to performance; reliance on tests as a substitute for judgment; unrealistic job expectations; hiring candidates who interview well; ignoring risk factors contained in candidate messages about goals and expectations; shortchanging the time vested in selection; and limiting the pool and recruitment sources.

The work climate may contribute to employee decisions to leave an organization. Practices that can spoil a work environment are categorized under five headings: values, relationships, inequities, trespasses, and uncertainties. Destructive values include: give only what you must; value groups and ignore individuals; and don't trust employees. The encouragement of adversary relationships, the introduction of sudden change, and the straining of relationships can all contribute to an unhealthy work environment. Whenever employees believe that they are not getting a fair share of rewards, status, workload, or opportunities, the work environment becomes inhospitable.

Employees resent trespassing on their territory. Interference with home life, overlapping assignments, or work responsibility conflicts can all contribute to turnover problems. Employees will feel insecure when they are not kept informed, when inconsistent policies and procedures are issued and changed regularly, and when they are uncertain where they stand.

The hiring manager's desire to "fill a vacancy" and the candidate's desire to "land a job" may interfere with a satisfactory matching of candidate and job. Often this is a result of insufficient attention to job specifications and failure to present all aspects of the job to the applicant. Too abbreviated or prolonged an orientation period, being insufficiently demanding, overdemanding, or overprotective during orientation can create problems. Employees may be right for a job when they are hired, but as they grow personally they may outgrow the job. Similarly, the growth of an employee may not keep pace with the growth of responsibility in the job. Economic shifts, reorganizations, shifts in key personnel, and changes in organization rate of growth may affect demands made on employees. Some employees are readily able to adapt to change, while others view changes in their work assignment as very threatening.

Employee satisfaction often depends on the organization's compensation program and handling of several pay policy issues: equitability, personal needs, automatic/standard increases, cost–of–living increases, minimum and maximum rates, salary spread, market value, government guidelines, nonsalary incentives and benefits. When the number of employees ready for promotion and the number of available openings are not in balance, turnover will increase. This imbalance may be aggravated by inaccurate employee perceptions of their readiness for promotion. Another problem may be the unequal distribution of openings in an organization, concentrated in specific operations, locations or job titles. A valuable employee thrust into a new job prematurely or with misconceptions will encounter difficulties and may feel the price of promotion is too great. Promotions also affect interested onlookers in the organization, with employees often judging the organization on the fairness of its promotions.

Many of the personal reasons employees offer for leaving are actually manifestations of supervisory problems in the organization. Some critically negative characteristics include: preoccupation with self–protection, inflexible work style, indecisiveness, unfairness, noncommunicativeness, inability to handle stress, destructive criticism, negative reinforcement, unwillingness to share credit, and failure to respond to individual desires and needs. Managers must also enable employees to feel a sense of personal growth throughout their careers. Nongrowth may lead to low energy, unenthusiastic, uncommitted, disinterested, and cynical employees and unacceptable levels of turnover.

MODELS OF THE TURNOVER PROCESS

Despite the long and substantive tradition of investigations into the causes of employee turnover, what has been neglected until recently in the literature are serious efforts to construct useful models of the turnover process. We have discussed March and Simon's (1958) literature–based model of the decision to participate, Vroom's (1964) expectancy/valence theory framework, and Price's (1977) model of the process producing voluntary separations composed of structural, economic, and social psychological variables.

Mobley (1977) developed a model concerning the behavioral space between job satisfaction and voluntary separation. This space is a process composed of thoughts of quitting, evaluations of the utility of a job search, intention to search, search, evaluation of alternatives, and intention to quit or stay. In an expanded turnover model, Mobley (1979) explicitly recognizes the role of perceptions, expectations and values, as well as available job alternatives as factors in the turnover decision.

Reviewing these and other existing models, Mowday, Porter & Steers (1982) identify eight shortcomings that should be addressed in future models of voluntary employee turnover. Models must recognize the role of available information about one's job or prospective job in an individual's participation decision. Models must acknowledge the importance of the degree to which an employee's expectations and values surrounding a job are met by organizational experiences. Employee job performance level as a factor influencing desire or intent to leave has been overlooked.

Models concentrate exclusively on one job attitude—job satisfaction—and ignore other attitudes, such as organizational commitment or job involvement. Nonwork influences, such as family or hobbies, are not consistently considered. Current models assume that once an employee becomes dissatisfied with a job, the wheels are set in motion for termination, and ignore the fact the employees may be able to change the current work situation. Models of turnover should clarify the role of available alternative job opportunities. Also, models assume a one–way flow process and ignore important feedback loops that can enhance or reduce the desire to leave or the act of turnover.

Two recent models seek to overcome some of these shortcomings. Steers and Mowday (1981) construct a cognitive model focusing on the processes leading to the decision to participate or to withdraw. Bluedorn (1982) develops a model incorporating three items: a revision of the model developed by Price, Mobley's satisfaction to voluntary separation linkages, and organizational commitment. Organizational commitment is proposed as a consequence of job satisfaction and as an antecedent of job search.

TURNOVER IN THE ACADEMIC LIBRARY

The preceding discussions of employee–organization linkages, organizational commitment, and the measurement, causes and models of turnover emphasize the importance of turnover management to organizational effectiveness. Academic libraries, so heavily dependent upon human resources, stand to gain significantly from an improved understanding of the turnover process. Turnover research has generally focused on manufacturing firms and the blue–collar worker. Only recently have service organizations and white–collar occupations come under increasing scrutiny. Libraries, however, have not been the settings for any systematic investigations of turnover patterns and causes.

Two studies are noteworthy for their preliminary assessment of the turnover process in the academic library. The first (McAnally & Downs, 1973) was prompted by a dramatic increase in the turnover rate among ARL university library directors in the early 1970s. Interviews with twenty–two directors and former directors sought to identify the causes for this trend. Several key environmental factors were cited: growth in enrollments, changes in the presidency, proliferation in university management, expansion of instructional and research programs, fragmentation of traditional academic disciplines, information explosion, hard financial times and inflation, pressure for planning and budgeting systems, technological change, changing theories of management which emphasize the growing role of employees in decision–making, unionization, increasing control by state boards, and the lack of a national system for information management and access. The net results of these conditions were extraordinary pressure on the library director to improve and expand collections and services, but with declining resources, status and voice in university management.

They also identified several developments within the university library. Greatly intensified pressures were being exerted on the director by the president's office, the library staff, the faculty, the students, and state boards of control in public universities. Other factors were: a declining ability of the library to meet the needs of the university community, a lack of goals and planning experience, an inability to quickly accommodate educational changes, a decline in the status of the director, decreasing financial support, renewed questioning of centralized library services, ineffective sharing of resources and automation efforts, and a growing unacceptability of traditional hierarchical and authoritative styles of management. These changes collectively produced a crisis of confidence and a level of frustration which prompted many library directors to deal with their fundamental dissatisfaction by leaving their positions.

Library managers continue to face many of these same problems in the early 1980s. The pressures for accountability, for expanding new technology–based services, and for coping with reduced resources have all fueled anxiety but also prompted greater flexibility. It is this adaptability to change, coupled with improved planning and budgeting techniques, as well as the introduction of new organizational patterns, which has contributed to greater stability in research library executive suites.

A second study (Neal, 1982) reported the results of a survey of university libraries in the Association of Research Libraries on their perceptions and responses to support staff turnover problems. Slightly less than fifty percent of the libraries or their universities actually compute turnover rates on a regular basis. Those that do so utilize the crude separation rate formula and report the results annually. The libraries were asked to provide data on the number of support staff members and the number leaving their positions over a period of a year. Turnover rates were then computed using the crude separation rate formula for the sixty-two libraries able to furnish this information. The resulting voluntary turnover rate of 20.1 percent for support staff in large academic libraries is close to the median rates identified in studies of clerical workers and other service organizations. The surveyed libraries were also asked to indicate the major reasons why it was felt staff members were quitting their positions. The results indicate that in addition to dissatisfaction with salary, the library administrators view the high number of itinerant employees such as student spouses and individuals taking a work break between stages of their education as the major factor contributing to support staff turnover.

Several respondents emphasized the critical problems they were facing with the low rates of turnover among their professional staffs. Studies of turnover patterns and causes among academic librarians must consider several distinctive factors: the role of the national versus the local job market, increasing emphasis on alternative career paths for librarians, the impact of faculty status and tenure for librarians, organizational versus professional commitment, emphasis on continuing education, promotional opportunities, participatory management styles, etc.

Student assistants represent another important employee group in academic libraries. Traditionally assigned to shelving and other routine duties, student workers are increasingly involved in service programs and technical operations. They are staffing the reference desks and providing manpower for retrospective conversion projects; participating in collection evaluation studies and providing programming assistance. Their skills and experience have become critical to the operation of the library and their expanding role involves a greater investment in training. These changes, however, have not produced significant reductions in student employee turnover rates which are high and which are characteristic of a group for which the part–time work assignment is of secondary importance, wages are generally low, alternative employment opportunities in commercial establishments are often more attractive, and job stability is frequently linked to meeting financial qualifications for work–study awards. In addition, student employee turnover is an inevitable by–product of student attrition and graduation.

THE IMPACT OF TURNOVER

The literature dealing with the impact of turnover has focused on the issues of organizational effectiveness and costs. More recently, however, the consequences of turnover have been analyzed at other levels, including the individual employee, the work group, the larger community of which the organization is a part, and society in general.

Studies of the costs of turnover have generally found that the expense is much greater than anticipated, involving both tangible and intangible costs. Zimmerer (1971) groups the fiscal impact into six categories: costs incurred when an individual leaves an organization, costs of advertising the position and recruiting and selecting someone for it, costs of new employee orientation and training, costs of equipment underutilization due to employee absence, costs of lost production because of personnel changing jobs, and costs of lost productivity due to lack of training.

Flamholtz (1973) speaks of positional replacement costs and "the sacrifice that would have to be incurred today to acquire a substitute capable of rendering a set of services equivalent to that provided by a resource presently owned or employed." His taxonomy of costs includes both the outlay and opportunity costs which must be incurred. One of the obvious costs involved is the maintenance of a personnel department in an organization to manage the termination and hiring processes. The separation of an employee may involve an exit interview, severance pay, extra social security payments, and extra unemployment insurance charges. Recruitment may involve job specification, advertising, visits to colleges or conferences, employment agency fees, prizes and awards, organizational literature, public relations activities, and correspondence. The selection and placement of a new employee may involve application forms, interviewing, testing, medical examinations, reference checks, security and credit checks, processing applications, travel expenses, and more correspondence. The management of a vacancy may require the payment of overtime and the hiring of temporary help. There are learning costs involved as well, including formal orientation and training programs, and decreased production and increased supervision during the break–in period.

A number of positive economic and job–related benefits may result from the turnover decision for the person leaving the organization. This is dependent largely on conditions in the job market and the individual's skills and abilities. A new position can be a source of career advancement and increased earnings. Turnover may result in a better fit between an individual's vocational interests and actual work activity, and a reduction in job–induced stress. It may provide opportunities to undertake new challenges, to develop new job skills and to enhance commitment to job and organization. It may involve a move to a more desirable geographic location and closer to (or farther away from) one's family. But there are also costs associated with the decision to change jobs. A move to a new position may mean a loss of seniority and nonvested benefits, may promote transition stress and disrupt social relationships with former co–workers, family and friends.

Turnover also may have a significant impact on those workers who stay with an organization. On the positive side, there may be increased opportunities for advancement and promotion and more favorable job attitudes among the remaining employees. When the person leaving is not well respected or liked, their departure may be a source of satisfaction and hope for improvement in the organization, and may contribute to improved performance, in particular when tasks are highly interdependent. New employees may be a source of stimulation in terms of new approaches to the job and opportunities to develop new friendships. On the negative side, turnover may produce increased workloads and decreased performance, especially when the work is interdependent and the person leaving was a key employee or high performer. When open positions are filled from outside the organization, there may be dissatisfaction among the employees not promoted. When the person leaving is a close friend, co–worker relations may be less satisfying.

Work groups play an important role in an organization and turnover will have unique implications at this level of analysis (Mowday, Porter & Steers, 1982). The composition of a work group is a major determinant of group effectiveness, with performance for many types of tasks controlled by the most competent group member. New members may bring creative ideas, new approaches to solving problems, and needed skills to the group, and may be more willing to question group norms and procedures that impede effectiveness. When the person leaving is a deviant member of the group, cohesiveness may increase among the remaining members, conflict may decrease and group relations may become more harmonious. The burden of increased workloads shared by remaining group members may require higher levels of cooperation and coordination of efforts and thus bring the group closer together.

Turnover may also seriously threaten group effectiveness when the person leaving is a group leader or high performer. The disruption of work and group processes may be heightened in small groups and when turnover is relatively less frequent. Groups with high membership instability tend to cope better. New group members may not consider existing group norms appropriate and the socialization process may generate considerable disagreement. The balance of positive and negative consequences for the work group is thus controlled by several moderating variables: task interdependence, group cohesiveness, characteristics of the leaver, size of the group, predictability of turnover, difficulty of replacement, and characteristics of the replacement.

The consequences of turnover have most frequently been considered at the organizational level of analysis. Although it is recognized that there are both costs and benefits, the negative impact tends to be more visible and to have clearer implications for overall organizational effectiveness. We have already considered the costs of selection and recruitment, training and development, and administrative staff produced by turnover. We have also reviewed the impact of turnover on employee morale, productivity and conflict. The disruption of work can be critical as projects lose continuity and key activities are interrupted. Mistakes may increase as overloaded employees try to fill in until a replacement is hired and trained. This situation is further complicated in organizations facing hiring freezes. Turnover, depending on labor market conditions may be epidemic, causing the remaining employees to question their own situations as the organization grapevine rings with stories of inequities or better job opportunities elsewhere. High rates of turnover may promote negative public relations and discourage prospective employees.

Price (1977) focuses on the impact of turnover on seven organization variables: administrative staff, formalization, integration, satisfaction, innovation, centralization and effectiveness, and states the relationships in the form of propositions based on their support in the research literature. Successively higher amounts of turnover probably produce successively larger proportions of administrative staff members relative to production staff members. With increasing personnel turnover, greater bureaucratization of the organization and greater administrative expenditures are incurred to meet the costs of employee separation, recruitment, placement and training. Successively higher amounts of managerial turnover probably produce successively higher amounts of formalization at a decreasing rate. Formalization is the degree to which the norms of an organization are explicit and involves such rubrics as rules, regulations, procedures and policies. The key variables that mediate this relationship are reduced consensus, decreased interaction, and the decreased likelihood of control.

Successively higher amounts of turnover probably produce successively lower amounts of integration, defined as the degree of participation in primary groups. The key variable in this case is the amount of interaction. When turnover is high, the opportunity to interact declines and fewer close friendships are formed. Successively higher amounts of turnover probably produce successively lower amounts of satisfaction, defined as the degree of affect that members of an organization have toward membership. Turnover tends to lower satisfaction because it lowers group consensus and thereby increases conflict. Successively higher amounts of turnover probably produce higher amounts of innovation but at a decreasing rate. Innovation is defined as the degree to which an organization is a first or early user of an idea among its set of similar organizations. Turnover produces innovation, especially in the case of a new manager, because the main power holders expect and support innovation and because innovation is not constrained by a set of prior obligations.

Successively higher managerial turnover probably produces successively lower centralization, defined as the concentration of power in an organization. Managerial turnover decreases the amount of knowledge that managers have about the organization and without knowledge, power is more difficult to exercise. To some researchers, an increase in the size of the administrative staff and reduced integration are harbingers of reduced effectiveness, the degree of organizational goal achievement. Others, however, have argued that an increased administrative staff improves the organizing capacity, and that increased formalization may help reduce uncertainty and increase effectiveness. Furthermore, researchers are increasingly skeptical over whether increased satisfaction results in increased effectiveness and decreased centralization has been viewed as reducing effectiveness by several investigators. The multiple set of consequences has both positive and negative elements. The critical question is whether there is a net balance of positive or negative consequences. Price concludes that the amount and variety of supporting evidence is in favor of "conventional wisdom" which sees turnover as generally having a negative impact on effectiveness.

Several of the respondents to the ARL survey on support staff turnover cautioned not to overlook the benefits of "higher caliber" though turnover-prone employees. They pointed out that turnover is useful in that libraries are able to maintain a lower salary base and turnover helps to alleviate the problem of employees becoming very frustrated in what they see as dead-end jobs. We have already broached several of the important benefits to the organization of turnover. Rates of pay for new hires are lower and eligibility for some benefits may not occur until seniority is established. To the extent that those who leave the organization are poor performers, turnover presents the opportunity to upgrade the workforce. To the extent that turnover takes place in jobs above entry level, opportunities for upward mobility are created. Turnover also increases personnel staffing flexibility. Turnover encourages management to re-examine the organizational structure and content of jobs. and impetus for creative change often results from the loss of valued employees. Turnover allows people with new ideas, different frames of reference and unique experiences to join the organization and employees who don't fit in well because of deficiencies in skills, temperament, energy or drive will leave the organization. Turnover is one way for an organization to reduce entrenched conflict. In organizations where heavy physical or psychological demands are placed on employees or where job skills rapidly become obsolete, a lack of turnover can be detrimental to organizational productivity.

Muchinsky and Morrow (1980) have done some preliminary evaluation of the consequences of aggregated turnover on a region or economy. They see turnover as "a determinant of the allocative efficiency of a given labor market," that is, the adequacy of fit between individuals and their jobs or the extent to which workers' abilities are being optimally utilized and rewarded at their true market value. This is achieved by allowing individuals not suited for their work to find a more compatible job, with the cumulative effect being a higher rate of productivity in a region or job market than would exist without turnover. The middle and upper level positions in today's organizations are filled by a generation that will not be retiring for some time, thus significantly reducing chances for promotion of younger generations. All professions must carefully monitor this contracting of upward organizational ability, especially in light of a tendency for later retirements. Turnover is also seen as influencing, albeit in a small positive way, the chances of women and minorities to move into the upper administrative ranks of organizations. The role of turnover within the local job market for clerical and other skilled staff and the national job market for professional and managerial staff demands the increased attention of academic librarianship.

THE MANAGEMENT OF TURNOVER

Organizations must attempt to establish a turnover rate which optimizes the need for change and the need for continuity. The management of turnover involves three activities: the measurement and analysis of turnover rates to define the problem, the documentation of the reasons why employees are leaving, and the implementation of appropriate remedial measures to deal with the problem.

The exit interview can be a valuable source of information concerning reasons for employee turnover. Exit interviews also offer opportunities to retain competent employees by exploring the causes of dissatisfaction and seeking solutions to their problems, to clarify complaints against employees who are separated involuntarily, to promote good relations with employees who separate, and to obtain reliable data on problem areas which will enable management to set up corrective programs. It is important that the person conducting the interview be mature, sympathetic and knowledgeable and that the physical setting be comfortable and the atmosphere friendly. Roseman (1981) suggests a productive format for the exit interview: statement of purpose, relevant background information, positive aspects of the job, negative aspects of the job, critical incidents, reasons for leaving, suggested changes, and separation agreements. Employee reluctance to give candid statements during the exit interview may require a telephone interview or postexit questionnaire sent to the former employee several weeks after termination. In the survey of ARL libraries, it was found that only forty–five percent regularly conduct exit interviews. In most cases, the library personnel officer or the university personnel office carry out the interview, but too often the library director or department head is assuming this responsibility.

Mowday, Porter and Steers (1982) identify approaches available to managers for strengthening employee linkages with the organization. Select employees with the propensity to become linked. Create clear and realistic job and organization previews. With a disproportionate amount of turnover occurring among employees with low lengths of service, improve the quality of the early job experience. Provide opportunities for a sense of commitment to develop by allowing individuals the choice of "engaging in work performance acts" beyond the normal, routine job duties. Provide jobs that maximize "felt responsibility" for what is happening in and to the organization. Integrate employees into the social fabric of the organization. And demonstrate a genuine concern for employees' welfare.

Programs aimed at the effective management of turnover have included a variety of elements: improvement of recruitment and selection procedures, the establishment of updated and realistic job requirements, increased opportunities for promotion, effective orientation programs, formal employee training programs, supervisory training, competitive and equitable salaries and fringe benefits, performance appraisals, responsive complaint procedures, consistent application of policies and procedures, corrective disciplinary procedures, greater employee participation in decision–making, improved communication, attractive working conditions, and restructuring of jobs. The respondents to the ARL survey mentioned the following programs most frequently: staff development opportunities, improved salaries, better selection practices, reviews of job classifications, promotional opportunities, supervisory training, and tuition assistance and released time for classes.

The key element in the management of turnover is effective performance by first–line supervisors. They must be informed and knowledgeable about the technical and administrative aspects of their position, and about organizational policies and procedures that affect their subordinates. They must be skillful in applying constructive discipline and effective in interpersonal communication. And they must be able to handle difficulties and people and to respond to the needs of colleagues and subordinates. In assessing the impact of turnover on the organization, managers must recognize the role it can play in effective human resources planning and how it relates to employee satisfaction and organizational vitality.

AN ACTION AND RESEARCH AGENDA

The importance of turnover management to organizational effectiveness and success demands action on the part of individual academic libraries as well as the academic library profession. Library managers should begin to collect and analyze data on turnover patterns for their employees, and to encourage academic administrators to adopt institution–wide turnover monitoring programs. Methodologies should be organized, preferably well–designed exit interviews, to identify those factors which are contributing to turnover problems in the library and remedial programs should be implemented which address these main causes. The following elements will be critical: the promotion of organizational values and goals which can attract and sustain employee commitment, regular evaluations of the equity and competitiveness of salaries and benefits, honest previews of employment, adequate and realistic job specification, on–going supervisory training, expanded efforts to nurture the new employee, greater awareness of the importance of the selection process and improved change and conflict management skills.

The Association of College and Research Libraries must take a leadership position in the promotion of turnover management in academic libraries. The formulation of guidelines for the collection, measurement and reporting of turnover data would enable and encourage the computation of benchmark statistics for groups of employees in academic libraries, for different size institutions, and for geographic regions. Sensitivity to the importance of turnover and improved understanding of its various aspects and related concepts can be cultivated by conference programs and committee consideration of appropriate issues.

The academic library profession must also promote substantive research on turnover–related topics. These studies might include analysis of turnover trends in individual libraries for different employee groups and the testing of the assorted variables related to turnover in academic library settings. Other valuable investigations might include: the professional versus the organizational commitments of academic librarians; the relationship between technological change and turnover, especially as they relate to skill obsolescence and job performance; tenure for academic librarians and the maintenance of organizational vitality; vacancy management in academic libraries and the impact of employment freezes; turnover rates and the achievement of affirmative action goals; salary rates and fringe benefits in academic libraries as compared with regional and national norms; the development of secondary labor markets for librarians; sources of innovation and creativity in the academic library; the impact of the quality of work life movement on turnover patterns and employee retention methods; and the role of other forms of withdrawal as a substitute for turnover.

REFERENCES

Allport, F. H., "A Structuronomic Conception of Behavior: Individual and Collective." *Journal of Abnormal and Social Psychology*, 64(1962): 3–30.

Anderson, B. W., "Empirical Generalizations on Labor Turnover." In *Studies in Labor and Manpower*, edited by R. Pegnetter. Iowa City: University of Iowa: 33–59, 1974.

Angle, H. and Perry, J., "An Empirical Assessment of Organizational Commitment and Organizational Effectiveness." *Administrative Science Quarterly*, 26(1981): 1–14.

Bardo, J. W. and Ross, R. H., "The Satisfaction of Industrial Workers as Predictors of Production, Turnover and Absenteeism." *Journal of Social Psychology* 118(1982): 29–38.

Bluedorn, A. C., "The Theories of Turnover: Causes, Effects, and Meaning." In *Research in the Sociology of Organizations*, Volume I: 75–128. Greenwich, Conn.: JAI Press, 1982.

Cawsey, T. F. and Wedley, W. C., "Labor Turnover Costs: Measurement and Control." *Personnel Journal* 58(1979): 90–95.

Dalton, D. and Tudor, W., "Turnover Turned Over: An Expanded and Positive Perspective." *Academy of Management Review* 4(1979): 225–235.

Etzioni, A., *A Comparative Analysis of Complex Organizations* New York: Free Press, 1961.

Etzioni, A., *Modern Organizations*. Englewood Cliffs, N. J.: Prentice–Hall, 1964.

Farris, G. F., "A Predictive Study of Turnover." *Personnel Psychology* 24(1971): 311–328.

Flamholtz, E. G., "Human Resources Accounting: Measuring Positional Replacement Costs." *Human Resource Management* 12(1973): 8–16.

Gaudet, F., *Labor Turnover: Calculation and Cost*. New York: American Management Association, 1960.

Gellerman, Saul W., *Managers and Subordinates*. Hinsdale, Ill.: Dryden Press, 1976.

Hellweg, S. A., "The Exit Interview—A Potential Management Tool for University Administrators." *Journal of College and University Personnel* 32(1981): 37–38.

Henrichs, J. R., "The Exit Interview." *Personnel* 48(1971): 30–35.

Herzberg, F. *et al.*, *Job Attitudes: Review of Research and Opinion*. Pittsburgh: Pittsburgh Psychological Services, 1957.

Jeswald, T. A., "The Cost of Absenteeism and Turnover in a Large Organization." In *Contemporary Problems in Personnel: Readings for the Seventies*, edited by W. C. Hamner and F. L. Schmidt. Chicago: St. Clair Press: 352–357, 1974.

Kanter, R. M., "Commitment and Social Organization." *American Sociological Review* 33(1968): 499–517.

Kerr, C. and Rostow, J. M. (eds.), *Work In America: The Decade Ahead*. New York: Van Nostrand, 1979.

Lefkowitz, J., "Personnel Turnover." *Progress in Clinical Psychology* (1971): 69–90.

McAnally, A. M. and Downs, R. B., "The Changing Role of Directors of University Libraries." *College and Research Libraries* 34(1973): 103–125.

March, J. G. and Simon, H. A., *Organizations*, New York: Wiley, 1958.

Marsh, R. M. and Mannari, H., "Organizational Commitment and Turnover: A Prediction Study." *Administrative Science Quarterly* 22(1977): 57–75.

Martin, T. N., "A Study on Reducing Turnover Costs." Paper presented at the 37th annual meeting of the Academy of Management, Orlando, Florida, 1977.

Mobley, W. H., "Intermediate Linkages in the Relationship Between Job Satisfaction and Employee Turnover." *Journal of Applied Psychology* 62(1977): 237–240.

Mobley, W. H. *et al.*, "Review and Conceptual Analysis of the Employee Turnover Process." *Psychological Bulletin* 86(1979): 493–522.

Morris, J. and Sherman, J. D., "Generalizability of an Organizational Commitment Model." *Academy of Management Journal* 24(1981): 512–526.

Morris, J. and Steers, R. M., "Structural Influences on Organizational Commitment." *Journal of Vocational Behavior* 17(1980): 50–57.

Mowday, R. T., "Viewing Turnover From the Perspective of Those Who Remain: The Influence of Attitudes on Attributions of the Causes of Turnover." *Journal of Applied Psychology* 66(1981): 120–123.

Mowday, R. T., Porter, L. W., and Steers, R. M., *Employee–Organization Linkages*. New York: Academic Press, 1982.

Muchinsky, P. M. and Morrow, P. C., "A Multidisciplinary Model of Voluntary Employee Turnover." *Journal of Vocational Behavior* 17(1980): 263–290.

Muchinsky, P. M. and Tuttle, M. L., "Employee Turnover: An Empirical and Methodological Assessment." *Journal of Vocational Behavior* 14(1979): 43–77.

Neal, J. G., "Staff Turnover and the Academic Library." In *Options for the 80s. Proceedings* of the Second National Conference of the Association of College and Research Libraries: 99–106. Greenwich, Conn.: JAI Press, 1982.

Pettman, B. O. (ed.), *Labour Turnover and Retention*. London: Wiley, 1975.

Porter, L. W. and Steers, R. M., "Organizational, Work and Personal Factors in Employee Turnover and Absenteeism." *Psychological Bulletin* 80(1973): 151–176.

Price, J. L., "The Effects of Turnover on the Organization." *Organization and Administrative Sciences* 7(1976): 61–88.

Price, J. L., *The Study of Turnover*. Ames, Iowa: Iowa State University Press, 1977.

Roseman, E., *Managing Employee Turnover, A Positive Approach*. New York: AMACOM, 1981.

Salancik, G. R., "Commitment and the Control of Organizational Behavior and Belief." In *New Directions in Organizational Behavior*, edited by B. M. Staw and G. R. Salancik: 1–54. Chicago: St. Clair Press, 1977.

Staw, B. M., "The Consequences of Turnover." *Journal of Occupational Behavior* 1(1980): 253–273.

Steers, R. M., "Antecedents and Outcomes of Organizational Commitment." *Administrative Science Quarterly* 22(1977): 46–56.

Steers, R. M. and Mowday, R. T., "Employee Turnover and Post–decision Accommodation Processes." In *Research in Organizational Behavior*, Volume 3, edited by L. Cummings and B. Staw. Greenwich, Conn.: JAI Press, 1981.

Stevens, J. M., Beyer, J. and Trice, H. M., "Assessing Personal, Role, and Organizational Predictors of Managerial Commitment." *Academy of Management Journal* 21(1978): 380–396.

Thornton, R., "Organizational Involvement and Commitment to Organization and Profession." *Administrative Science Quarterly* 15(1970): 417–426.

Van Der Merwe, R. and Miller, S., "The Measurement of Labour Turnover." *Human Relations* 24(1971): 233–253.

Vroom, V. H., *Work and Motivation*. New York: Wiley, 1964.

Waters, L. K. and Roach, D., "Job Satisfaction, Behavioral Intention, and Absenteeism as Predictors of Turnover." *Personnel Psychology* 32(1979): 393–397.

Zimmerer, T., "The True Cost of Labor Turnover." *Management of Personnel Quarterly* 10(1971): 9–12.

SUBJECT BIBLIOGRAPHERS IN ACADEMIC LIBRARIES:

AN HISTORICAL AND DESCRIPTIVE REVIEW

John D. Haskell, Jr.

In order to address the matter of subject bibliographers, it is necessary to define terms. In the course of researching this article[1] the author encountered a myriad of labels for such individuals, some which are synonymous with "subject bibliographers" and others which are slight variations on that term. The eleven terms encountered were: "librarian selectors/subject specialists/bibliographers," "subject specialists," "specialist bibliographers," "reference–bibliographers," "area specialist bibliographers," "subject consultants," "subject librarians," "professional–specialists," "specialist librarians," "information officers," and "liaison librarians."

The term "subject bibliographer," in this paper, will be used to refer to an individual in an academic library who has responsibility for developing a particular portion or portions of the library's collection. That responsibility may relate to one subject or several subjects, works pub-

Advances in Library Administration and Organization, Volume 3, pages 73–84.
Copyright © 1984 by JAI Press Inc.
All rights of reproduction in any form reserved.
ISBN: 0-89232-386-8

lished in a particular geographic area or areas, works published in a particular language or languages or to an interdisciplinary area such as American Studies. Before examining who our subject bibliographer is and what he does, let us turn to the beginning. The first appearance of what is today's bibliographer can be traced to Germany in the Napoleonic era. What is known as the *Referatsystem* in Germany was implied as early as 1815 at the University of Breslau.[2] The individuals known collectively as *Referenten* were and are members of the library staff with high academic qualifications in whose hands book selection in specific fields is placed. The *Referenten* are members of what is known as the higher service or *Höhere Dienst* and they usually possess a doctorate.

By the mid–1870s, professor–librarians had been replaced by full-time librarians in twelve German universities. By the 1960s, the eighteen German universities employed, on the average, a corps of eight subject specialists. Prior to 1970, *Referenten* would discuss the books they selected in regularly scheduled buying sessions or *Kaufsitzung* but by that date, two out of five libraries had abandoned this practice.[3] By 1975, *Referenten* were the rule of the day in German universities. Stuttgart had eight *Referenten*, Frankfurt had seventeen, Regensburg, with an annual accession rate of 100,000 to 130,000 had twenty–two, and Bremen had twenty–seven. Those who had specific language responsibilities became known as *Sprachreferenten*.

When did subject bibliographers emerge in America? As early as 1897, Alfred C. Potter, of what was then known as the Ordering Department of the Harvard College Library, speaking to the American Library Association in Philadelphia, referred to the faculty as "a body of trained specialists" and observed that ". . . they may fairly be supposed to know better than the librarian can what gaps exist in present collections and what is needed to fill them."[4] He goes on to say, however, that ". . . in practice the ideal is somewhat shattered; it has sometimes seemed to me that almost any other system of selecting books would be better than that usually followed by college libraries."[5] Clearly, Potter was dissatisfied with faculty selection, but stopped short of suggesting that employing librarians as selectors might be a preferable system.

In order for a library to even consider hiring subject bibliographers it would have to be a relatively large operation attempting to be a comprehensive collection of works in many subjects written in many languages. It is this size factor which explains why German universities employed subject bibliographers before such individuals were commonplace in American research libraries. J. Periam Danton has observed that as of 1850, thirteen German university libraries had collections of more than 100,000 volumes. In that year, no American academic library had yet reached that figure; Harvard was at 84,200. By 1875, nine German academic libraries had more than 200,000 volumes while only one American university library (Harvard) had exceeded 200,000 volumes. In the intervening twenty–five years, the number of German libraries with more than 100,000 volumes had risen to twenty while in America, only Yale's collection with 114,000 volumes, exceeded that figure. Between 1850 and 1875, the mean yearly increase in German university libraries was 3,368 volumes while for libraries in the United States the comparable figure was 1,168 volumes. This would explain why most German libraries had inaugurated the *Referatsystem* by the end of the 1920s but no American libraries had yet employed full–time subject bibliographers.

It was not until 1945 that an American library, Harvard, considered subject bibliographers for the library staff. The Librarian at that time, Keyes D. Metcalf, in a memorandum on the financial situation of the library, proposed that since professors were too busy to provide the systematic assistance needed to build the Harvard collections, an alternative method would be to add four to six subject specialists to the staff who would spend at least half of their time on book selection. By 1952, only one specialist, in English literature, had been hired at Harvard and he was unable to devote half of his time to selection. Despite this slow start, Metcalf and his colleague Edwin Williams, as of 1952, were still willing to try to develop a system of subject bibliographers but were unwilling for the cost of the program to be met by reducing the library's book funds. They stated that "If the plan for subject specialists is too expensive, . . . at least one person [should] be added to the staff who could give all his time to book selection."[8] Three years later, in 1955, Andrew Osborn, Assistant Librarian at Harvard, argued that "material must now be collected from countries throughout the world instead of from the relatively few countries that were producing scholarly publications fifty years ago."[9] He went on to reiterate Metcalf's earlier proposal: "The ideal approach to a solution for many of the problems of book selection at Harvard, all things considered, would be through a number of full– or part–time subject specialists on the library staff, officers with an academic background but sufficient library experience to understand the technical problems involved, who could devote their energies to the exacting task of selection. This method has been in use in a number of fields for several years now, and has proved to be entirely satisfactory. The obvious drawback to its extension is the cost."[10]

Others in the immediate post–war period were also recommending and in some cases employing subject bibliographers. Robert B. Downs, speaking to the Western New York Chapter of the Special Libraries Association in 1946, remarked that in order to find properly qualified bibliographers it was necessary to go outside the library profession. He also believed that more success was likely to come from converting subject specialists into library workers than from attempting to convert general library workers into subject specialists.[11]

In England, by the late 1940s, subject bibliographers were also being employed more widely. When introduced at University College London, this institution became the third university, after Oxford and Cambridge, to institute such a system. The major reason for its introduction at London was in order to systematically build up a collection which had suffered disastrous losses as the result of war–time destruction.[12]

By 1949, Herman H. Fussler, then Director of the University of Chicago Library, concluded that:

> The bibliographer working in a broad area of knowledge and advising the director represents, to my mind, the most effective way of achieving the necessary integration and coordination of acquisition policy in a large and complex university library.[13]

Moving into the 1950s one finds the University of Nebraska hiring staff both for subject matter training and competence in librarianship. At Southern Illinois University in 1957 one half of the book funds were allocated to academic departments; three years later only 25% of the book budget was allocated to the fifty–six academic departments.[14]

By the 1960s, the notion and use of subject bibliographers was firmly entrenched. In 1966 the Subject Specialists Section of the Association of College and Research Libraries unsuccessfully petitioned the Committee on Organization of the American Library Association for division status; the section had 2,200 members in 1967 but is now defunct.

The first account in the literature which describes a large number of subject bibliographers in an American academic library is a 1966 article by Cecil K. Byrd. It describes the program at Indiana University where ten individuals had been hired as bibliographers. In doing so, Indiana was attempting to provide university–wide the bibliographical expertise formerly found only in departmental libraries. By 1979, Indiana had fourteen subject bibliographers.[15]

In a 1967 article in *Libri*,[16] J. Periam Danton reported that Columbia, Harvard, Indiana, Michigan, Stanford, and the University of Washington were among the major libraries in which responsibility for book selection was increasingly being placed in the hands of specialists on the library staff. UCLA then had nine specialists responsible for *full–time* book selection. They were responsible not for subjects but for geographical areas. Danton further noted that at UCLA 85% of all purchased titles added to the library were being selected by library staff. He also went so far as to say that "Most Anglo–American university libraries . . . should move as speedily as possible toward a comprehensive plan of book selection by library staff specialists."[17]

A survey[18] was also conducted that year of seventy selected academic libraries ranging in size from three hundred thousand volumes to over a million. Robert Haro concluded that most of the larger academic libraries had bibliographers or subject specialists responsible for book selection and of the libraries with more than a half million volumes, 69% utilized such staff.

Hendrik Edelman and G. Marvin Tatum, in an essay on the development of library collections in American universities, identified Donald Wing at Yale, Felix Reichmann at Cornell, Rudolf Hirsch at Pennsylvania, and Elmer Grieder at Stanford as members of "a generation of uniquely capable bibliographers who made their mark" on the 1960s.[19] By 1969, the University of Chicago had twenty–one librarians responsible for book selection, some of whom were subject specialists and some of the specialists dealt only in materials published in languages other than English.[20]

The seventies continued the trend of the sixties; by 1975 there were twenty British university libraries using some form of subject specialization. The previous year, Ann Coppin concluded that subject specialists had "arrived" when she wrote "The question is no longer whether or not to have subject specialists, it is rather the question of their most effective use."[21]

The above account of developments from 1945 to the seventies has perhaps given the impression that instituting a system of subject bibliographers was accomplished with very little difficulty and with little opposition from faculty members. In fact this was not the case. Certainly the most vocal spokesman for subject bibliographers was Danton although others joined the bandwagon as well. Many reasons had to be presented in order to turn the tide. Herman Fussler argued that faculty selection resulted in lack of continuity of acquisitions policy since the selectors changed from year to year. Cecil Byrd believed that specialists resulted in collections of depth and comprehensiveness. Many proponents of subject bibliographers cited a 1936 study by Douglas Waples and Harold Lasswell in which a comparison was made of the holdings by major research libraries of 500 English, French, and German works in social science fields judged by specialists in those fields to be of scholarly importance. Harvard held 65% while Chicago, California, and Michigan held 49, 40, and 31% respectively. The New York Public Library held 92%. The point, of course, was that all of the selection at the New York Public had been done by subject specialist librarians. Waples and Lasswell concluded that "In terms . . . of the data available, the New York Public Library appears more attentive than the other . . . American libraries to the future needs of American scholars. . . . It pays greater deference to posterity."[22]

One might also wish to use the conclusion drawn by Gayle Evans in his dissertation (see note 20) as an argument for bibliographers if one believes that the use of a book is a measure of its value to a collection. Evans's study set out to determine whether librarians "will be more successful than either faculty or book agents (i.e., approval plans) in selecting titles that will be more useful to the library's patrons as determined by the titles' circulation within the first twelve months after they are made available to the public."[23] He concluded that in three of four institutions studied in which librarians selected books, the librarian selections had a higher percentage of circulated titles than faculty selections and showed that these differences in use were *statistically significant*.

Danton, in addition to agreeing with the Waples study and views of Byrd and Fussler, made other cases for subject bibliographers. He echoed Osborn's concern for global responsibility and stated unequivocally that selection is the most important task performed by librarians. He argued that the quality of a collection is the result of countless selection discussions made over time, and most importantly, since librarians have the ultimate *responsibility* for a collection they, not the teaching staff, should also have the *authority* and funds for book purchases. Danton also pointed out that faculty may engage in special interest purchasing and remarked that such publications as *Bibliographie de Belgique* and *Der Schweizer Buchhandel* cannot be effectively routed to a large number of faculty members. Danton believed that librarian selectors have the time and obligation to develop the collection with a consistency of viewpoint.[24]

Lest one be left with the notion that faculty always wore black hats in the battle for bibliographers, mention should be made of the fact that in some cases faculty were very willing to give the library primary responsibility for collection development. Some even initiated the idea, especially where new area studies programs were being developed and faculty suddenly became aware of the fact that acquiring needed materials would be a monumental task. In other instances, faculty, who moved from a library which had librarian specialists to one which did not, often exerted pressure on the library to appoint such specialists.[25]

Let us next consider what background and training has generally been expected of subject bibliographers. The basic issue seems to have been whether a subject specialist should be required to possess both a degree in a subject and a master's degree in librarianship. Indiana University in the sixties did not insist on library training if an individual with appropriate subject and language skills was available. Generally, libraries have insisted on two master's degrees. Ann Coppin believes that this is because many librarians are unwilling to accept as library colleagues individuals who do not possess the M.L.S., regardless of their other academic qualifications. Robert Downs suggested that library school students be permitted to register for courses in other professional schools while in library school. Certainly an asset for any bibliographer is knowledge of one or more foreign languages particularly in a library in which individual bibliographers are responsible for collecting works in a particular language regardless of the subject matter. It has also been observed that an advanced subject degree combined with foreign language proficiency is helpful in establishing a rapport with teaching faculty.[26]

An economic factor which emerged in the late 1970s had a major impact on the availability of individuals who were qualified subject specialists. No longer did employers have to seek librarians who subsequently pursued further graduate study. Many individuals who completed Ph.D. degrees and then found themselves unable to secure teaching positions in universities immediately enrolled in library schools in order to make themselves more attractive candidates on the job market.

Two accounts in the literature, both by British librarians, take issue with the emphasis found in America on formal academic training in a subject. Writing in 1974, Charles Crossley of the University of Bradford remarked that "the trained librarian is, or can become, a specialist in the *literature* [italics mine] and librarianship of a particular subject which is what subject specialist librarianship is all about."[27] Peter Woodhead, (see note 12) of the University of Leicester, found that the general view of the bibliographers whom he interviewed was that "the need to call on subject knowledge was not great; the important thing was to build up one's knowledge of the subject *literature*" [italics mine].[28]

Perhaps this is the appropriate juncture to answer the question of what bibliographers do. The question is perhaps best addressed by examining typical duties and responsibilities and then identifying varying types of subject responsibility.

The task at which most time is spent is, of course, selection of materials. The most frequently used tools as determined by Géza Kósa, at least at the institution which he surveyed, were bibliographies and publishers' advertisements. Book reviews were considered less productive sources because of the extensive time lag between the appearance of a book and its review. Selection is not limited to newly published materials but also involves purchasing of retrospective materials, particularly as the bibliographer identifies weaknesses and gaps in the areas for which he is responsible. Retrospective purchases are also involved when attempting to replace missing volumes or badly worn or brittle books.

Other duties include establishing contacts with the book trade in foreign countries and in some cases traveling abroad at library expense. The bibliographer may also press for prompt handling of materials which he knows from his contacts with faculty members are urgently needed. In some libraries, bibliographers are also called upon to assist with cataloging and classification and are asked to help formulate cataloging policies within their subject speciality.[29]

Reference and bibliographic instruction may also be included among a bibliographer's duties in a smaller library. In the ideal situation, the bibliographer buys not according to balances in allocated funds but what the library needs. It is precisely in buying what the library needs that the bibliographer has to be particularly careful that his own personal interests are not translated into "what the library needs." Some bibliographers have a tendency to overbuy or to show favoritism for their academic clientele.[30]

Finally, bibliographers are expected to come into close contact with faculty on a regular basis, to communicate library policies to departments, to serve as an ombudsman and "trouble shooter," and to act as coordinator, advocate and apologist for the library's collection policy.[31]

What is the optimum size of a "subject" in the context of subject specialization? Messick found that, in general, a bibliographer is responsible for and works with one, two, or possibly three related subjects. This is the case in large academic libraries, but in smaller ones, the bibliographer may find himself responsible for such "subjects" as all of the humanities, social sciences or sciences.

At Indiana in the 1960s individuals were responsible for such areas as Economics and Government, English, History, Far Eastern Studies, and Modern Foreign Languages (European). In Germany during the same period one found such combinations as Religion/Philosophy, Physics/ Chemistry/Biology/Medicine, and Geology/Mathematics. Currently, in some German libraries, the responsibilities are of monumental and unmanageable proportions. This is often due to a failure on the part of the libraries to divide responsibilities between the *Höhere Dienst* (higher service) referred to earlier, and the *Gehobene Dienst* (literally the "elevated" but in fact the middle service). In some cases one may find rather curious combinations of responsibility. At a British library in the mid 1970s an individual was responsible for Scandinavia and Archeology of the Anglo-Saxon Period while another person was charged with Art, Architecture, Music and Agriculture.

As noted earlier, not all libraries are able to afford full time bibliographers and they often assign them other responsibilities. One unusual example is also at a British library where the specialist responsible for Ancient History, Classics, and Papyrology was also responsible for the Photocopy Room and incoming interlibrary loans.[32]

Bibliographers are not uniformly found in the same place within the organizational structure of the library. There have typically been three areas in which bibliographers are placed in a library. They are acquisitions, reference or an independent status reporting generally to the assistant director of collection development. Haro and Messick believe that the independent arrangement is the best way to prevent the primary responsibility from being diluted by other demands.[33]

Lastly, let us consider the matter of interpersonal relations between subject bibliographers and other members of the library staff. There is general agreement in the literature that subject bibliographers ought to have considerable independence and autonomy. Haro argued that they should also receive higher pay and have greater status than "regular" librarians. Others have maintained that specialists should have job mobility equivalent to that of administrators and that they should be able to move up within subject specialization and not have to decide between management, where they would no longer be specialists, and scholarship.

In some European libraries in the 1960s and 1970s specialists were given privileges far beyond any found in American libraries. In the Royal Library at Copenhagen, bibliographers were allowed to spend two hours each *day* [italics mine] on their own research. In Germany, in order to encourage bibliographers to publish, they were allowed one afternoon each week for private reading. Although this practice was abandoned by 1975 in German academic libraries, the *Lektor* or public library equivalent of the *Referent* still enjoyed the privilege. By the 1970s, the passivity and aloofness which had been the trademark of the German bibliographer disappeared.

Specialists are sometimes permitted to attend meetings related to their specialities. Within the American Library Association there are such groups as the Slavic and East European Section of the Association of College and Research Libraries and the newly formed English and American Literature Discussion Group also within ACRL. Outside of ALA, one finds such groups as the Association for the Bibliography of History which meets at the annual meeting of the American Historical Association. Unfortunately, some administrators are hesitant to send staff members to "non–library" meetings.

According considerable independence and autonomy is not without its dangers and difficulties. An individual who has great freedom in carrying out some of his duties may insist on as much freedom in carrying out other duties. It is this independence which also results in charges of elitism and "prima donna" both of which can have adverse effects on staff morale. Eldred Smith pointed out the pitfalls yet concluded the "If they do, as some have charged, represent an elite in academic librarianship, it is an elite that pays its own way through quality service and hard work."[34]

One recent writer, Dennis Dickinson, in a paper presented in 1978 to the ACRL conference in Boston (see note 34) wonders whether there is a future for subject bibliographers. He implies that the real reason for hiring bibliographers in the 1960s and 1970s was to spend the large sums of money which were available for library materials during those years rather than to achieve "balanced" collections or to relieve overburdened faculty. Perhaps a survey could be conducted to determine whether the creation of bibliographer positions was or was not coincidental with the availability of funds; Dickinson maintains that it was not coincidental. He also believes that the current economic situation has made these positions "largely anachronistic."

The one exception he makes relates to area studies: "There will likely be a continuing requirement for librarian specialists to support area studies collections which present a complex of bibliographic, linguistic, acquisition and processing problems amenable to no other apparent solution."[35] His final conclusion is that approval plans, publication on demand, and resource centers "may begin to make it possible to move away from a system of librarian selectors and toward a more rational and effective means of building collections."[36] One can take issue with whether these methods are more rational and effective than subject bibliographers.

While it certainly cannot be denied that the economic climate of the 1980s is not that of the sixties and seventies, why not, as Eldred Smith has suggested, look for economies in other areas of the library? A statement which he made in 1974 is as valid today as it was then: ". . . the use of subject specialist librarians represents a commitment to service that has long been overdue and from which most library administrators will not willingly back away."[37]

NOTES AND REFERENCES

1. This author would like to thank the libraries of Johns Hopkins University, the University of Tennessee, Virginia Polytechnic Institute and State University, and Virginia Commonwealth University for providing photocopies of journal articles; the University of Virginia also provided a book on interlibrary loan.

2. Peter Biskup, "Subject Specialists in German Learned Libraries," *Libri* 27 (1977): 137; J. Periam Danton, *Book Selection and Collections: A Comparison of German and American University Libraries*, (New York: Columbia University Press, 1963), p. 36.

3. Biskup, 139–140, 142.

4. Alfred C. Potter, "The Selection of Books for College Libraries," *Library Journal* 22 (1897): 40.

5. Ibid.

6. Danton, 20, 32–33.

7. Keyes D. Metcalf and Edwin E. Williams, "Book Selection for the Harvard Library," *Harvard Library Bulletin* 6 (Spring 1952): 200.

8. Ibid., 201.

9. Andrew Osborn, "The Development of Library Resources at Harvard," *Harvard Library Bulletin* 9 (Spring 1955): 199.

10. Ibid., 204–205.

11. Robert B. Downs, "Preparation of Specialists for University Libraries," *Special Libraries* 37 (September 1946): 210–211.

12. Russell Duino, "The Role of the Subject Specialist in British and American University Libraries: A Comparative Study," *Libri* 29 (1979): 5–6; Peter Woodhead, "Subject Specialisation in Three British University Libraries," *Libri* 24 (1974): 31–32.

13. Herman H. Fussler, "The Bibliographer Working in a Broad Area of Knowledge," *College and Research Libraries* 10 (July 1949): 202.

14. Ann Coppin, "The Subject Specialist on the Academic Library Staff," *Libri* 24 (1974): 123; Danton, 80.

15. Cecil K. Byrd, "Subject Specialists in a University Library," *College and Research Libraries* 27 (May 1966): 191–193; Duino, 3.

16. J. Periam Danton, "The Subject Specialist in National and University Libraries, with Special Reference to Book Selection," *Libri* 17 (1967): 42–58.

17. Ibid., 55.

18. Robert P. Haro, "Book Selection in Academic Libraries," *College and Research Libraries* 28 (March 1967): 104–105.

19. Hendrik Edelman and G. Marvin Tatum, Jr., "The Development of Collections in American University Libraries," *College and Research Libraries* 37 (May 1976): 236.

20. Gayle E. Evans, "The Influence of Book Selection Agents Upon Book Collection Usage in Academic Libraries." Ph.D. Dissertation, University of Illinois, 1969, p. 57.

21. Duino, 15; Coppin, 124.

22. Fussler, 201; Byrd, 193; Douglas Waples and Harold D. Lasswell, *National Libraries and Foreign Scholarship*, (Chicago: University of Chicago Press, 1936): 71, 74–75.

23. Evans, 133.

24. Danton, "Subject Specialist," 43, 45, 47; Danton, *Book Selection*, 69, 73, 134.

25. Eldred Smith, "The Impact of the Subject Specialist Librarian on the Organization and Structure of the Academic Research Library." In *The Academic Library: Essays in Honor of Guy R. Lyle*, edited by Evan I. Farber and Ruth Walling. (Metuchen, N.J.: Scarecrow Press, 1974): 72–73.

26. Byrd, 193; Coppin, 126; Downs, 212; Robert P. Haro, "The Bibliographer in the Academic Library," *Library Resources and Technical Services* 13 (Spring, 1969): 166; Robert D. Stueart, "The Area Specialist Bibliographer: An Inquiry Into His Role." Ph.D. Dissertation, University of Pittsburgh, 1971, pp. 101, 156.

27. Charles Crossley, "The Subject Specialist Librarian in an Academic Library: His Role and Place," *ASLIB Proceedings* 26 (June 1974): 238.

28. Woodhead, 38.

29. Géza A. Kósa, "Book Selection Tools for Subject Specialists in a Large Research Library: An Analysis," *Library Resources and Technical Services* 19 (Winter 1975): 13–18; Thomas J. Michalak, "Library Services to the Graduate Community: The Role of the Subject Specialist Librarian," *College and Research Libraries* 37 (May 1976): 259; Haro, "The Bibliographer," 165; Kenneth Humphreys, "The Subject Specialist in National and University Libraries," *Libri* 17 (1967): 32.

30. Fussler, 202; S. A. Cramer, "Management for Change in British University Libraries," *Libri* 27 (1977): 172; Smith, 74; Selby U. Gration and Arthur P. Young, "Reference–Bibliographers in the College Library," *College and Research Libraries* 35 (January 1974): 28.

31. Haro, "The Bibliographer," 169; Frederick M. Messick, "Subject Specialists in Smaller Academic Libraries," *Library Resources and Technical Services* 21 (Fall 1977): 372.

32. Messick, 369; Byrd, 191; Biskup, 146–147; Woodhead, 34–36.

33. Haro, "The Bibliographer," 163; Messick, 368.

34. Crossley, 246; Dennis W. Dickinson, "Subject Specialists in Academic Libraries: The Once and Future Dinosaurs," in Robert D. Stueart and Richard D. Johnson, eds., *New Horizons for Academic Libraries*, (München: K. G. Saur, 1979): 441; Haro, "The Bibliographer," 168; Gration and Young, 34; Biskup, 139, 144, 147–149; Humphreys, 40; Smith, 81.

35. Dickinson, 442.

36. Ibid.

37. Smith, 80.

UNIVERSITY OF CALIFORNIA
USERS LOOK AT MELVYL:
RESULTS OF A SURVEY OF USERS OF THE
UNIVERSITY OF CALIFORNIA PROTOTYPE
ONLINE UNION CATALOG

Gary S. Lawrence, Vicki Graham and
Heather Presley

SUMMARY

Between March and May of 1982, an online questionnaire was adminis-
tered to every 25th user who began a MELVYL session. The content of
this questionnaire was identical to that developed jointly by the project
consortium for the Public Access Project sponsored by the Council on
Library Resources, Inc.[1] MELVYL users completed 1,259 online ques-

Advances in Library Administration and Organization, Volume 3, pages 85–208.
Copyright © 1984 by JAI Press Inc.
All rights of reproduction in any form reserved.
ISBN: 0-89232-386-8

tionnaires during this period. Questionnaire data were supplemented by information from the MELVYL computer transaction logs, permitting analysis of issues like the relationship between actual computer response times and perceived response-time problems, and between the number of records retrieved and the users' reported satisfaction.

We found that MELVYL users are frequent library users and frequent users of both the online catalog (only 9 percent were first-time users) and the card catalog. Over 80 percent discovered the catalog by seeing a terminal in the library, and over half said they learned to use MELVYL from instructions on the terminal screen. A majority of respondents were men, and over 60 percent were undergraduates. MELVYL users come from all academic disciplines, but relative to users of online catalogs at other participating libraries, more MELVYL users appear to come from scientific disciplines and engineering. The characteristics of the MEL-VYL user population are apparently strongly influenced by the specific locations of the limited number of MELVYL terminals and the characteristics of the libraries in which those terminals are placed (Section III).

Most users come to the catalog with subject-related information, and most conduct subject searches (Section IV). MELVYL users report that their most serious problems in using the system include remembering what is included in the catalog, using truncation, reducing large retrieval results, scanning through long displays, interrupting output, increasing inadequate search results, finding the correct subject term, entering commands, selecting from a list of choices, and waiting for the computer to respond. Compared to respondents from other participating libraries, MELVYL users find it easier to conduct searches of all kinds (particularly subject searches), to understand bibliographic displays, instructions and explanations, and to reduce large search results. For the most part, users of Lookup Mode have more serious problems than Command Mode users. Many users complain about inadequate response times, but analysis shows that the users' attitudes are more strongly related to the search mode they use than to the actual system responses they experience (Section V).

In assessing problems with library support services, MELVYL users have more than average difficulty finding a free terminal, and two-thirds report that writing space at the terminal is inadequate. Most users claim that they either did not get help while conducting their search, or received help online (Section VI).

About 31 percent of MELVYL users found nothing that they were looking for in their most recent computer search, and a similar number of respondents found their last search unsatisfactory. This result can be attributed in large part to the fact that the prototype database includes records for only about seven percent of UC's bound volumes, and includes nothing cataloged after 1980. Nonetheless, almost half the respondents found some things of interest during their search that they were not specifically looking for. Despite a relatively high degree of dissatisfaction with search results, over 90 percent have a favorable attitude toward MELVYL in general, and over two-thirds prefer MELVYL to the card catalog; only 14 percent thought the card catalog was better, and only 7 percent expressed an unfavorable attitude toward MELVYL (Section VII).

When asked how they would like to see MELVYL improved, a majority of users expressed interest in being able to view a list of words related to their search terms, and in having information about the circulation status of materials. The ability to search a book's table of contents or index, and the ability to print search results are also popular improvements. When asked how the library could improve MELVYL support, users said they wanted more terminals, both within and outside the library. Among improvements to the database, addition of serial titles was most popular, followed by added monographic records, government documents, newspapers, and dissertations. Most classes of material were wanted by at least 20 percent of respondents, and only about 4 percent said they were satisfied with the present database (Section VIII).

In reviewing the findings from this study, we observed first that our interpretations of the data were dominated by the limitations of the database (which affect retrieval results and satisfaction) and the current distribution of terminals (which affects user characteristics and searching patterns). Despite the serious limitations imposed on the analysis by the prototype nature of MELVYL at the time of this study, it is possible to make some general observations.

The first group of observations confirm the results of earlier analysis of a wide variety of online catalogs:

- Most users (over 90 percent) like online catalogs; MELVYL is no exception.
- Most have discovered MELVYL by seeing terminals in the library; the UC libraries have been quite effective in making the prototype system visible and accessible to the public.
- The demand for additional terminals is great, both to reduce waiting time and to provide convenient access to the catalog from locations other than the library.
- Not enough attention has been given to terminal furniture; two-thirds of MELVYL users complain about insufficient writing space.
- There is substantial demand for printing capabilities.

- There is substantial demand for augmenting the database, both through addition of monograph records and inclusion of other forms of material.
- Subject searching predominates in MELVYL as in other online catalogs, and subject searching problems appear to be important. Even though subject access appears easier in MELVYL than in most other systems, attempts to improve users' success in subject searching, both through user training and system improvements, should be a high priority.
- Most users want to get circulation status information from the online catalog.
- Most users do not express a need for detailed bibliographic information. It would be best to provide very brief displays as defaults, and make it easy for users who want additional information to get it through optional displays.

A few additional observations about MELVYL users are not explicitly validated by previous findings, but appear to merit consideration and discussion.

- For most of the online catalogs studied, the majority of users are men, and men are both more successful and more satisfied with the online catalog than women, according to their own reports. In MELVYL, we found that men outnumbered women by two to one in the survey sample, and males are more likely to be users of Command Mode than are females.
- MELVYL users claim to be using the online catalog to find "another library that has a book, journal or magazine that I want" at a somewhat higher rate than do users of other online catalog systems. Over 10 percent of respondents gave this answer, suggesting a substantial demand for inter-institutional bibliographic access and intercampus lending services.
- The analysis of MELVYL responses lends additional weight to the belief that menu-driven systems are not necessarily easier to use than systems requiring mastery of a command language. Lookup Mode users generally had more difficulty and were less satisfied than users of Command Mode.
- We discovered that attitudes about computer response time had more to do with the user's search mode than with actual system response, suggesting that users' expectations are at least as important as actual response in determining the "adequacy" of response time. Lookup Mode users, for instance, are quite satisfied with response times twice as long as those experienced in Command Mode.

Because improving response time often requires significant financial outlays, it would seem that this area should be a high priority for further study.

- It is evident that when extensive online assistance is provided it will be used; MELVYL users said they used online assistance to learn how to search and to get assistance during a search at about twice the rate reported by users of other systems. We find no grounds for debate about whether online help will be used; the next frontier is to evaluate the teaching effectiveness of online help systems and develop designs for their improvement (Section IX).

SECTION I: BACKGROUND

In early 1981 the Council on Library Resources funded five organizations to conduct a coordinated study of user and non-user responses to public online catalogs. For a detailed account of the history and organization of the Public Access Project sponsored by the Council on Library Resources, the reader is referred to an article by Douglas Ferguson, *et al.*, "The CLR Public Online Catalog Study: An Overview," *Information Technology and Libraries,* June 1982, pages 84–97.

The University of California and Its Libraries

The University of California consists of nine campuses located throughout the state of California with a total enrollment of over 127,000 undergraduate, graduate, and professional students, and over 19,000 academic personnel (see Table 1). Instruction is offered in more than 100 schools

Table 1. UC Student Enrollment and Staff: 1979-80

CAMPUS	Students			Staff		
	Under-grad	Grad-uate	Total	Academic	Other	Total
Berkeley	20,714	8,801	29,515	4,091	6,238	10,329
Davis	12,659	4,888	17,547	2,786	7,022	9,812
Irvine	7,390	2,314	9,704	1,459	4,817	6,276
Los Angeles	20,076	11,525	31,601	4,334	12,350	16,684
Riverside	3,096	1,390	4,486	802	1,638	2,440
San Diego	8,495	2,297	10,792	1,875	6,127	8,002
San Francisco	375	3,380	3,755	1,935	6,017	7,952
Santa Barbara	12,347	1,916	14,263	1,271	2,141	3,412
Santa Cruz	5,563	386	5,949	642	1,251	1,893
TOTAL	90,715	36,897	127,612	19,768	49,249	69,017

and colleges offering undergraduate, graduate, and professional degree programs. In addition, organized research is conducted in approximately 150 specialized laboratories, institutes, and research centers and stations on the campuses and in other locations in the state. Training and research in the health sciences is offered in fourteen professional schools on six campuses. (The San Francisco campus is devoted entirely to the health sciences.) Three separate UC laboratories conduct basic and applied research in nuclear science, energy production, national defense, and environmental and health issues. Twenty-six natural land and water reserve sites provide opportunities for teaching and research in field biology and related subjects. Agricultural research is carried out at three of the campuses and at nine field stations. Through University Extension, more than 10,000 credit and noncredit courses, workshops, seminars, and conferences are attended by over 350,000 students as part of the university's continuing education service.

Each of the nine campuses has its own main library which is supplemented by specialized branches (over 100 branches are located throughout the university). The combined collections of the UC library system total over 19 million bound volumes (see Table 2), and include special collec-

Table 2.   UC Library Collections and Records Contributed to
MELVYL, 1981–82

CAMPUS	MELVYL Records[1]		Bound Volumes[2]		Records per Bound Volume (%)
	Number	%	Number	%	
Berkeley	181,677	14.2	6,117,424	32.2	3.0
Davis	192,301	15.1	1,753,213	9.2	11.0
Irvine	234,098	18.3	1,023,518	5.4	22.9
Los Angeles	176,389	14.0	4,882,164	25.7	3.6
Riverside	94,415	7.4	1,075,123	5.7	8.8
San Diego	239,091	18.7	1,507,875	7.9	15.9
San Francisco	6,619	0.5	500,514	2.6	1.3
Santa Barbara	64,767	5.1	1,473,308	7.7	4.4
Santa Cruz	83,538	6.5	678,725	3.6	12.3
Other	4,505	0.4			
TOTAL[3]	1,277,400	100.2	19,011,864	100.0	6.7

Notes:
[1] As reported in the MELVYL HELP screen, "*Help Contents.*"
[2] Source: University of California, Office of the Assistant Vice President—Library Plans and Policies, *University of California Library Statistics, July 1982.* This count includes some libraries that are not part of the General Library system at UC; many of these "unaffiliated libraries" have contributed or will contribute records to MELVYL. The count includes bound volumes of periodicals as well as monographs.
[3] Percentages may not sum to 100 due to rounding.

tions, original manuscripts, documents, and research materials. Interlibrary loan service is provided for all campuses. In order to make the extensive resources of the UC library system available to all students, faculty, and staff of the university, it is the university's policy to provide comprehensive bibliographic access to the entire collection. Realization of this potential was the goal of the library development plan adopted by the university in 1977.[2] A key element in that plan is an extensive program of library automation. As part of this program, development and production of the University of California online union catalog was begun in 1979.

The MELVYL Online Catalog

The University of California online union catalog, known as MELVYL, provides access to recently acquired books in the University of California libraries. At this time, the catalog is offered in a prototype version containing approximately 733,000 records, representing 1.3 million books in the combined collections of all the campuses. This is only a small fraction of the total number of books in the entire university, and represents only items catalogued between about 1976 and December 1980. Table 2 shows the number of MELVYL records by campus and compares MELVYL representation to total bound-volume holdings. The production version of MELVYL, with new capabilities and a regularly-updated database, is scheduled to be available in the fall.

Only books are included in the catalog. There are no records for journals, music scores, phonograph records, maps, audio-visual materials, or other types of material.

Presently there are 86 MELVYL terminals available for public access.[3] The terminals are distributed among the nine UC campuses, located in both main and branch libraries (see Table 3). Terminals are concentrated in general research libraries, chiefly serving scholars and students in the arts and humanities; 35 terminals (41 percent) are in main campus libraries. An additional 19 terminals (22 percent) are in locations that serve mostly undergraduate students (counting all Santa Cruz terminals in this category; see Table 1, above). Medical and health science libraries (including all of the San Francisco campus) have 11 terminals, and physical and biological science libraries also have 11 terminals. The other 10 terminals (13 percent) are located in branches representing a variety of other academic disciplines. The number of terminals per campus will be increased when MELVYL goes into the production version.

MELVYL is designed to be used by patrons who are not familiar with computers. If the user needs assistance, he can type HELP, press the return key, and MELVYL will respond with instructions and suggestions.

Table 3. MELVYL Terminal Locations at UC Libraries

CAMPUS	BRANCH	NUMBER OF TERMINALS	
Berkeley	Main	5	
	Co-op. Services; Biology; Education-Psychology; Law; Engineering; Library School; Inst. of Transporation Studies—1 each	7	
	Moffitt (Undergraduate)	2	
	TOTAL		14
Davis	Main	5	
	Health Sciences; Law; Physical Science—1 each	3	
	TOTAL		8
Irvine	Main	6	
	Biological Sciences	1	
	Physical Sciences	1	
	TOTAL		8
Los Angeles	Main (URL Reference)	2	
	Architecture & Urban Planning; Biomedical; Chemistry; College (Undergraduate)—1 each	4	
	Engineering & Math. Sciences	2	
	TOTAL		8
Riverside	Main	5	
	Bio-Agriculture	2	
	Physical Science	1	
	TOTAL		8
San Diego	Central	4	
	Cluster	8	
	Biomedical	1	
	Science and Engineering	2	
	Scripps Inst. of Oceanography	1	
	TOTAL		16
San Francisco	Main		8
Santa Barbara	Main		8
Santa Cruz	Main		8
TOTAL			86

MELVYL will also notify the user if it cannot process a request, and will usually suggest what to do.

MELVYL features two search modes: Lookup Mode and Command Mode. In Lookup Mode, MELVYL gives complete instructions and asks the user to make choices or supply information. This is useful to users who are unfamiliar with the catalog and who do not want to learn the command language. Only limited features of the catalog are available in Lookup Mode: selection of library or group of libraries (e.g. by campus or by region); selection of type of search (author/title or subject); and display format (brief, long, etc.). Lookup Mode dialogues are menu-driven; that is, each screen presents the user with instructions and a list of numbered options from which to choose. The user responds by typing the number of one selection or the information requested, such as the author's name. The user may type HELP at any point to receive full instructions.

In Command Mode, the user can take full advantage of MELVYL's capabilities. MELVYL waits for the user to type in commands. The user can learn the command language online, by typing HELP after selecting Command Mode, and then following the instructions that appear on the screen. A search may be conducted using an author name (personal or corporate), a title or uniform title, a series name, or a subject. MELVYL will respond to all keywords that are entered regardless of the order. Spelling, however, must be exact. Books may be searched for by any combination of search terms using the conjunction AND in the initial FIND command. MELVYL will report the number of books in the catalog that fulfill the search request. If only one book is found, its record will be displayed automatically. If more than one book is found, the user must issue a DISPLAY command in order to see the records. The user can specify the number and format of the records he wishes to see.

Searches may be limited or expanded in a variety of ways. The truncation feature allows the user to broaden his search by specifying only the first few letters of a keyword. In this way the user may request that MELVYL retrieve all records which include words beginning with this root regardless of plural endings, verb conjugation, tense, etc. At the time of the study, truncation was available in both Lookup and Command Modes, though users in Lookup were not informed of this. In Command Mode, the conjunctions AND, OR, and AND NOT may be used with the indexes (author, title, etc.) to modify the results of a previous search. AND NOT will eliminate certain records, OR will include other records, and AND will select specific combinations from the records already retrieved. Searches may also be limited by date of publication using the conjunction AND DATE as a modification. MELVYL also provides a means of canceling a modification and returning to the original search results. This can be done using the BACKUP command.

The BROWSE command allows the user to review the access fields in each of the indexes that can be searched. The user may then SELECT from this list the particular terms he wishes to search, and MELVYL will search for records with those headings. The user must then issue a DIS-

PLAY command in order to see the actual records. Optionally, the user may choose to specify that only selected parts of a record be displayed (e.g. author, title, publisher, etc.).

Both Command Mode and Lookup Mode will issue HELP screens upon request at any time during the search. In Lookup Mode, the user merely types in HELP. MELVYL will respond with a message that applies to the situation at hand, referring to the last command issued, the index searched, and the results. In Command Mode, users may request HELP alone, or they may type in HELP plus a keyword to receive detailed information and instruction on practically every aspect of the catalog. HELP GLOSSARY will retrieve a list of over 100 keywords that may be used with HELP.

In Command Mode the user may set and reset both the libraries searched and the display format, and may switch from Command Mode to Lookup Mode at any time. Lookup Mode users may switch modes, but while in Lookup, cannot change their library setting after their initial choice has been made. They may choose to see other display formats after a search is completed (if more than one book is retrieved, Lookup automatically displays in Review format), but only when prompted.

Examples of MELVYL searches are provided in Appendix B.

The Report

This report discusses findings from analyses of user questionnaires from University of California respondents and selected data from the MEL-VYL transaction logging subsystem. Section One is introductory. Section Two describes the two cycles of data collection, development and revision of the data collection process and instruments, the administration of the questionnaires, and the specific sources of UC data: the Online Questionnaire and the transaction log system. In Section Three, characteristics of users of the online catalog are discussed. Sections Four through Eight deal with use and evaluation of the online catalog, its features, and the library environment. Section Four focuses on characteristics of online catalog searches, describing the types of information people bring to the search and how this information is used. Section Five examines use of features and problems encountered by users, while Section Six focuses on problems users experience with various aspects of the library environment, including instruction and terminal availability. User evaluations of particular searches and of the catalog as a whole are discussed in Section Seven. Section Eight describes improvements and additions to the catalog suggested by users. Section Nine presents some concluding observations.

SECTION II: DATA

This chapter describes the general methodology used in the CLR Public Access Project and the University of California Online Questionnaire as a data collection instrument.

The CLR Questionnaires

The questionnaires were designed to capture particular information about users and non-users of online catalogs.[4] Elements of the user interface were identified, and questions were developed to elicit information on five separate issues:

- Search methods and uses.
- Problems with the system and its features.
- Problems with library support for users of the online catalog.
- Improvements and additions to the online catalog.
- Demographic characteristics of users.

The User Questionnaire is included as Appendix A.

The University of California Online Questionnaire

The Online Questionnaire Subsystem

The University of California online catalog is equipped with a questionnaire subsystem capable of controlling the administration of questionnaires, displaying questions, and recording user response. The software for administration of the questionnaire was developed as a subsystem of the user interface of the catalog called Lookup Mode. Lookup Mode provides a simple menu selection and 'fill-in-the-blanks' approach to the catalog for inexperienced users. It already included much of the software required to implement the questionnaire online.

The CLR Public Access Project was the first application of the questionnaire subsystem. Each question of the CLR User Questionnaire was stored as an individual 'screen' in the MELVYL screen file. A sampling routine in the logon software of the catalog permitted a request for questionnaire participation to be issued to only a fixed proportion of users initiating a catalog session. The logic of the questionnaire subsystem is described in section 4 of the Phase I Final Report.[5]

The MELVYL Transaction Log Subsystem

During the normal operation of the MELVYL system, a software monitor incorporated into the patron interface generates log records of virtually every event taking place (e.g., indexes searched, requests for help, etc.). This capability made it possible to monitor the search session which preceded the administration of the online questionnaire. These transaction records can be linked to questionnaire data, and a new record for each questionnaire created. Thus, the linked questionnaire/transaction file provides data for comparing user response to the questionnaire with the actual session at the catalog.

Administering the CLR Questionnaire

At UC, every 25th user, regardless of campus location or time of day, was selected. A request for participation in the study was issued at the beginning of the MELVYL session. If a user agreed to participate, the questionnaire appeared after the search session was completed. Detailed description of the online questionnaire subsystem can be found in the Phase I report.[6]

Responses to the Cycle 2 Questionnaire

Table 4 shows the number of online questionnaires completed (entirely or in part) by users at each UC campus.

Table 4. Final Questionnaire Returns

CAMPUS	Number	Percent
Berkeley	232	18.5
Davis	145	11.5
Irvine	62	4.9
Los Angeles	186	14.8
Riverside	67	5.3
Santa Barbara	163	13.0
Santa Cruz	83	6.6
San Diego	299	23.8
San Francisco	18	1.4
Other	4	0.4
TOTAL	1,259	100.0

SECTION III: USERS OF MELVYL

General

Figure 1 lists the text of questions related to use of the library and its catalogs. Figure 4 lists the questions about personal characteristics asked of respondents, and Figure 9 lists the questions pertaining to academic level and affiliation.

Use of the Library and Its Catalogs

MELVYL users are frequent users of the library: 85.2 percent use the library at least once a week and 42 percent use it daily (Table 5). There is no significant difference among University of California campuses. In

48. I come to the library:
a. Daily
b. Weekly
c. Monthly
d. About four times a year
e. About once a year
f. Not before today

49. I use this computer catalog:
a. Every library visit
b. Almost every visit
c. Occasionally
d. Rarely
e. Not before today

50. I use this library's book, card or microfilm catalog :
a. Every library visit
b. Almost every visit
c. Occasionally
d. Rarely
e. Not before today

51. I use a computer system other than the library's computer catalog:
a. Daily
b. Weekly
c. Monthly
d. About four times a year
e. About once a year
f. Never

52. I first heard about this computer catalog from: (Mark *ONE* only)
a. Noticing a terminal in the library
b. Library tour, orientation or demonstration
c. An article or written announcement
d. A course instructor
e. A friend or family member
f. Library staff

53. I learned how to use this computer catalog: (Mark *ALL* that apply)
a. From a friend or someone at a nearby terminal
b. Using printed instructions
c. Using instructions on the terminal screen
d. From the library staff
e. From a library course or orientation
f. From a slide/tape/cassette program*
g. By myself without any help

* Not included in the UC Online Questionnaire.

Figure 1. Library and Catalog Use Questions

Table 5.   Library Use

Question 48: *I come to this library:*

	UC	All[1]
a. Daily	42.3%	25.8%
b. Weekly	42.9	42.4
c. Monthly	8.8	18.4
d. Four times a year	2.8	7.4
e. Once a year	1.2	1.7
f. Not before today	1.9	4.3

[1] All participating libraries, including UC.

April and May of 1982, only 9.2 percent of MELVYL users were first-time users (Table 6). The card catalog[7] still appears to be used more frequently by online catalog users, but MELVYL is remarkably popular, given its limitations. In fact, the proportion of respondents who use MELVYL on *at least* most library visits (48.0 percent) slightly exceeds the proportion who use the card catalog with similar frequency (46.0 percent).[8]

Tables 5, 7 and 8 contrast use of catalogs and libraries by UC respondents with use by all respondents to Project questionnaires. MELVYL users do not consult the online catalog as frequently as online catalog users in other participating organizations (Table 7). They are, however, much more frequent users of the card catalog (Table 8) and the library (Table 5). The frequency of MELVYL use does not differ significantly among campuses.

Frequency of use of MELVYL differs by search mode. Command Mode users use it more frequently than Lookup Mode users (Table 9). This could be a self-fulfilling prophecy, because the introductory MELVYL

Table 6.   Relative Use of Computer and Card Catalogs: UC Libraries

Question 49: *I use this computer catalog:*
Question 50: *I use this library's book, card or microfilm catalog:*

	Computer Catalog	Card Catalog
a. Every visit	13.9%	16.6%
b. Most visits	34.1	29.4
c. Occasionally	35.6	38.0
d. Rarely	7.2	11.1
e. Not before today	9.2	4.9

Table 7. Computer Catalog Use—Comparison

Question 49: *I use this computer catalog:*

	UC	All
a. Every visit	13.9%	21.1%
b. Most visits	34.1	36.9
c. Occasionally	35.6	26.8
d. Rarely	7.2	5.5
e. Not before today	9.2	9.8

Table 8. Other Catalog Use—Comparison

Question 50: *I use this library's book, card or microfilm catalog:*

	UC	All
a. Every visit	16.6%	12.4%
b. Most visits	29.4	21.2
c. Occasionally	38.0	34.4
d. Rarely	11.1	21.3
e. Not before today	4.9	10.7

Table 9. Frequency of MELVYL Use by Search Mode of Respondent

Question 50: *I use this library's book, card or microfilm catalog:*

	Command Mode	Lookup Mode
a. Every visit	15.4%	13.0%
b. Most visits	41.4	29.4
c. Occasionally	35.9	35.4
d. Rarely	3.2	10.0
e. Not before today	4.1	12.2

screen describes Lookup Mode as being designed for "new and occasional users" (Appendix B).

In this connection, though, it is interesting to note that, of 79 first-time users, 14 (17.7 percent) were using Command Mode (Figure 2).

Online Catalog Users Are Not Necessarily Users of Other Computers

MELVYL users are not significantly different from other questionnaire respondents in terms of computer experience (Table 10). Many users (34.2 percent) have never used another terminal. However, almost the same amount, 34.1 percent, use another terminal weekly or daily. There is no significant difference among campuses.

Most Users Discover the Catalog by Seeing It in the Library

As Table 11 shows, 81 percent of MELVYL users first discover the online catalog by seeing it in the library. Family and friends rank second (7.6 percent), followed by organizational sources like tours, library staff, and course instructors. Discovering the online catalog by seeing a terminal in the library is more common at the University of California than among other libraries in the Public Access Project.

Respondents Learn to Use the Catalog from a Variety of Sources

Although MELVYL users report using a variety of sources in learning to use the online catalog, a majority claim to have used instruction provided by MELVYL itself. The proportion of MELVYL users who learned from online aids is nearly twice that of all other Public Access Project respondents (Table 12).

Almost 30 percent said they learned to use the online catalog without any help, about twice the proportion who said they learned without help in the Public Access Project as a whole, and almost twice the proportion of ARL respondents who so claimed. It should be noted that many who

Table 10. Experience with Other Computer Systems

Question 51: *I use a computer system other than the library's computer catalog:*

	UC	All
a. Daily	14.0%	13.0%
b. Weekly	20.1	16.7
c. Monthly	11.2	13.0
d. About 4 times a year	12.5	11.9
e. About once a year	7.9	9.1
f. Never	34.2	36.3

```
* * * * * * * * * * * * * * CROSSTABULATION OF * * * * * * * * * * * * * * * * * * * * * * * * * *
* * * * *   RQ49      I USE THIS COMPUTER CATALOG   BY SRCHMOD2
* * * * * * * * * * * * * * * * * * * * * * * * * * * * * * * * * * * * * * * * * * * * * * * * * *
```

	SRCHMOD2		
COUNT ROW PCT COL PCT TOT PCT	COMMAND 1.	LOOK UP 2.	ROW TOTAL
RQ49			
1. EVERY VISIT	53 43.4 15.4 6.1	69 56.6 13.0 7.9	122 13.9
2. MOST VISITS	143 47.8 41.4 16.3	156 52.2 29.4 17.8	299 34.1
3. OCCASIONALLY	124 39.7 35.9 14.2	188 60.3 35.4 21.5	312 35.6
4. RARELY	11 17.2 3.2 1.3	53 82.8 10.0 6.1	64 7.3
5. NOT BEFORE TODAY	14 17.7 4.1 1.6	65 82.3 12.2 7.4	79 9.0
COLUMN TOTAL	345 39.4	531 60.6	876 100.0

```
CHI SQUARE =    38.52187 WITH    4 DEGREES OF FREEDOM    SIGNIFICANCE = 0.0000
CRAMER'S V =    0.20970
CONTINGENCY COEFFICIENT =    0.20524
LAMBDA (ASYMMETRIC) =    0.03369 WITH RQ49     DEPENDENT     = 0.0    WITH SRCHMOD2 DEPENDENT.
LAMBDA (SYMMETRIC) =    0.02090
UNCERTAINTY COEFFICIENT (ASYMMETRIC) =    0.01683 WITH RQ49 DEPENDENT.     = 0.03558 WITH SRCHMOD2
DEPENDENT.
UNCERTAINTY COEFFICIENT (SYMMETRIC) =    0.02285
KENDALL'S TAU B =    0.15410    SIGNIFICANCE = 0.0000
KENDALL'S TAU C =    0.18117    SIGNIFICANCE = 0.0000
GAMMA =    0.26247
SOMERS'S D (ASYMMETRIC) =    0.18973 WITH RQ49 DEPENDENT.     = 0.12516 WITH SRCHMOD2 DEPENDENT.
SOMERS'S D (SYMMETRIC) =    0.15082
```

Figure 2. Computer Catalog Use—Comparison by Search Mode.

Table 11.   Means of First Discovering the Computer Catalog

Ranked by Frequency of Response

Question 52: *I first heard about this catalog from:*

	UC	All
a. Noticing a terminal in the library	81.0%	63.6%
e. A friend or family member	7.6	9.3
b. Library tour, orientation or demonstration	4.2	10.2
f. Library staff	3.0	9.0
d. A course instructor	2.4	4.2
c. An article or writtern announcement	1.8	3.7

said they learned "by themselves" may have benefited from online assistance without consciously crediting this source of aid.

The other side of this coin is that only 5.4 percent of respondents said they learned how to use the catalog from library staff. This is only about ⅙ as many as learned from staff on the Public Access Project generally (Table 12).

Library staff play a more prominent role at Riverside (10.9 percent), San Diego (10.2 percent), Santa Barbara (8.0 percent) and Davis (6.5 percent). Library courses are relatively important at Berkeley (6.6 percent). At Irvine, the use of online instruction (30.6 percent) is exceeded by self-teaching (50 percent) and use of printed instruction (41.7 percent); at Riverside, the amount of online instruction (39.1 percent) is equaled by reliance on self-instruction (Figure 3).

Table 12.   Methods of Learning to Use the Computer Catalog

Ranked by Frequency of Response[1]

Question 53: *I learned how to use this computer catalog: (Mark ALL that apply)*

	UC	All	ARL
c. Using instructions on the terminal screen . .	56.4%	29.0%	25.7%
b. Using printed instructions	31.0	53.3	62.2
g. By myself without any help	29.9	19.8	18.4
a. From a friend or someone at a nearby terminal	8.3	15.5	16.8
d. From the library staff	5.4	29.6	24.4
e. From a library course or orientation	2.0	6.2	8.5
f. From a slide/tape/cassette program	[2]	0.2	0.0

[1] Percentages sum to more than 100 due to legitimate multiple responses.
[2] Response category not offered in the UC Online Questionnaire.

FILE   FINAL   (CREATION DATE = 08/03/82)
* CROSSTABULATION *
RQUEST53 (TABULATING   1) I LEARNED HOW TO USE THIS COMP CAT:
BY TERMLOC2
* PAGE 1 OF 1

TERMLOC2

RQUEST53	COUNT ROW PCT COL PCT TAB PCT	BERKE-LEY 1	DAVIS 2	IRVINE 3	LA 4	RIVER-SIDE 5	SANTA BARBARA 6	SANTA CRUZ 7	SAN DIEGO 8	SAN FRAN-CISCO 9	ROW TOTAL
RQ53A FROM A FRIEND		7 10.1 4.6 0.8	11 15.9 10.2 1.3	0 0.0 0.0 0.0	8 11.6 6.7 0.9	6 8.7 13.0 0.7	12 17.4 10.6 1.4	5 7.2 7.5 0.6	19 27.5 10.2 2.3	1 1.4 6.7 0.1	69 8.2
RQ53B BY PRINTED INSTR		41 15.5 27.0 4.9	40 15.1 37.0 4.7	15 5.7 41.7 1.8	37 14.0 30.8 4.4	12 4.5 26.1 1.4	31 11.7 27.4 3.7	18 6.8 26.9 2.1	67 25.3 35.8 7.9	4 1.5 26.7 0.5	265 31.4
RQ53C BY INSTR ON TERMINAL		86 18.3 56.6 10.2	65 13.8 60.2 7.7	11 2.3 30.6 1.3	66 14.0 55.0 7.8	18 3.8 39.1 2.1	60 12.7 53.1 7.1	49 10.4 73.1 5.8	107 22.7 57.2 12.7	9 1.9 60.0 1.1	471 55.8
RQ53D FROM LIBRARY STAFF		2 4.3 1.3 0.2	7 14.9 6.5 0.8	2 4.3 5.6 0.2	3 6.4 2.5 0.4	5 10.6 10.9 0.6	9 19.1 8.0 1.1	0 0.0 0.0	19 40.4 10.2 2.3	0 0.0 0.0	47 5.6
RQ53E FROM LIBRARY COURSE		10 58.8 6.6 1.2	1 5.9 0.9 0.1	0 0.0 0.0	0 0.0 0.0	1 5.9 2.2 0.1	0 0.0 0.0	2 11.8 3.0 0.2	3 17.6 1.6 0.4	0 0.0 0.0	17 2.0
RQ53G BY MYSELF		44 17.4 28.9 5.2	34 13.4 31.5 4.0	18 7.1 50.0 2.1	37 14.6 30.8 4.4	18 7.1 39.1 2.1	35 13.8 31.0 4.1	13 5.1 19.4 1.5	49 19.4 26.2 5.8	5 2.0 33.3 0.6	253 30.0
COLUMN TOTAL		152 18.2	108 12.8	36 4.3	120 14.2	46 5.5	113 13.4	67 7.9	187 22.2	15 1.8	884 100.0

PERCENTS AND TOTALS BASED ON RESPONDENTS
844 VALID CASES   415 MISSING CASES

Figure 3.   Methods of Instruction—Comparison by Campus.

103

```
54. My age group is:
    a. 14 and under              e. 35-44 years
    b. 15-19 years               f. 45-54 years
    c. 20-24 years               g. 55-64 years
    d. 25-34 years               h. 65 and over

55. I am:
    a. Female                    b. Male

56. Mark your current or highest educational level:
       (Mark ONE only)
    a. Grade School or Elementary School
    b. High School or Secondary School
    c. Some College or University
    d. College or University Graduate
```

Figure 4.   User Characteristics Questions

Demographic Characteristics

Questions related to the general demographic characteristics of online catalog users are displayed in Figure 4.

Age

The MELVYL user population is younger than the aggregate population (Table 13). Most MELVYL users (71.9 percent) are under 24 years of age. The largest category is the 20–24 age group, and the percentage for this group is significantly higher than for the aggregate.

Sex

Almost 60 percent of MELVYL users are male (Table 14). The difference between the proportion of male and female users is even greater at

Table 13.   Users by Age Group

Question 54: *My age group is:*

	UC	All
a. 14 and under	1.7%	1.8%
b. 15–19 years	23.4	19.6
c. 20–24 years	46.8	37.8
d. 25–34 years	18.8	26.6
e. 35–44 years	5.4	9.1
f. 45–54 years	1.7	3.0
g. 55–64 years	0.8	1.3
h. 65 and over	1.4	0.8

Table 14. Sex of Online Catalog Users

Question 55: *I am: (a) Female (b) Male*

	Female	Male
All Libraries	40.1%	59.9%
ARL Libraries	39.1	60.9
Univerity of California	33.1	66.9

UC than for the aggregate sample and other ARL libraries. Female users are in the minority at all UC campuses, though the percentage varies from 22.5 percent at Los Angeles to 43.5 percent at Davis. Berkeley and Santa Barbara also have a slightly higher than average percentage of female users, and Riverside and San Francisco have a higher than average percentage of male users (Figure 5).

These differences between campuses may be attributable to differences in campus populations. As was discovered in the aggregate report,[9] however, the propensity of male users is probably not a demographic accident: women are significantly less likely to be users of an online catalog than men. Distribution also differs greatly by mode. Seventy-five percent of command mode users are male, while only 61.9 percent of Lookup Mode users are male (Figure 6).

Educational Levels

More than half of MELVYL users have at least some college education, and 33.1 percent are college graduates (Table 15). Level of education differs significantly by campus. Excluding San Francisco (where all MEL-VYL users are college graduates), Berkeley has the highest percentage of users who are graduates: 42.4 percent. At Santa Cruz and San Diego, 76.1 and 72.5 percent, respectively, have had some college or university education (Figure 7). This distribution is consistent with the makeup of the student body at each campus, and is further affected by terminal distribution, especially by the large concentration of San Diego terminals at the Cluster Undergraduate Library (Tables 1 and 3, Section 1).

The breakdown by mode shows that Command Mode users tend to have more education than Lookup Mode users, though the difference is not large (Figure 8).

Academic Characteristics of Respondents

Figure 9 lists the text of questions related to the academic characteristics of respondents.

FILE   FINAL   (CREATION DATE = 08/03/82)
* CROSSTABULATION OF *
RQ55   SEX   BY TERMLOC2
* PAGE 1 OF 1

TERMLOC2

RQ55	COUNT ROW PCT COL PCT TOT PCT	BERKE- LEY 1.	DAVIS 2.	IRVINE 3.	LA 4.	RIVER- SIDE 5.	SANTA BARBARA 6.	SANTA CRUZ 7.	SAN DIEGO 8.	SAN FRAN- CISCO 9.	ROW TOTAL
FEMALE	1.	59 21.1 39.3 7.0	47 16.8 43.5 5.6	11 3.9 30.6 1.3	27 9.6 22.5 3.2	12 4.3 25.5 1.4	43 15.4 37.7 5.1	19 6.8 29.2 2.3	58 20.7 31.4 6.9	4 1.4 26.7 0.5	280 33.3
FEMALE	2.	91 16.3 60.7 10.8	61 10.9 56.5 7.3	25 4.5 69.4 3.0	93 16.6 77.5 11.1	35 6.3 74.5 4.2	71 12.7 62.3 8.5	46 8.2 70.8 5.5	127 22.7 68.6 15.1	11 2.0 73.3 1.3	560 66.7
	COLUMN TOTAL	150 17.9	108 12.9	36 4.3	120 14.3	47 5.6	114 13.6	65 7.7	185 22.0	15 1.8	840 100.0

CHI SQUARE = 17.32753 WITH 8 DEGREES OF FREEDOM   SIGNIFICANCE = 0.0269
CRAMER'S V = 0.14362
CONTINGENCY COEFFICIENT = 0.14217
LAMBDA (ASYMMETRIC) = 0.0 WITH RQ55 DEPENDENT = 0.00153 WITH TERMLOC2 DEPENDENT.
LAMBDA (SYMMETRIC) = 0.00107
UNCERTAINTY COEFFICIENT (ASYMMETRIC) = 0.01644 WITH RQ55 DEPENDENT. = 0.00518 WITH TERMLOC2 DEPENDENT.
UNCERTAINTY COEFFICIENT (SYMMETRIC) = 0.00788
KENDALL'S TAU B = 0.05627 SIGNIFICANCE = 0.0310
KENDALL'S TAU C = 0.06929 SIGNIFICANCE = 0.0310
GAMMA = 0.09120
SOMERS'S D (ASYMMETRIC) = 0.04062 WITH RQ55 DEPENDENT = 0.07795 WITH TERMLOC2 DEPENDENT.
SOMERS'S D (SYMMETRIC) = 0.05341
ETA = 0.01463 WITH RQ55 DEPENDENT = 0.06642 WITH TERMLOC2 DEPENDENT.
PEARSON'S R = 0.06643 SIGNIFICANCE = 0.0271

NUMBER OF MISSING OBSERVATIONS = 419

Figure 5. Sex of Online Catalog Users—Comparison by Campus.

```
SEARCH MODE CROSSTABS
FILE   LINKQST (CREATION DATE = 01/26/83)
* * * * * * * * * * * * * * * * * * * * * * CROSSTABULATION OF * * * * * * * * * * * * * * * * * * * * * * * * * * * *
      RQ55    Sex                                   BY SRCHMOD2
* * * * * * * * * * * * * * * * * * * * * * * * * * * * * * * * * * * * * * * * * * * * * * * * * * PAGE 1 OF 1

                         SRCHMOD2
                COUNT  │
                ROW PCT│COMMAND LOOK UP    ROW
                COL PCT│                  TOTAL
                TOT PCT│   1.       2.
        RQ55           ├────────┼────────┤
                       │    85  │   200  │   285
          FEMALE    1. │  29.8  │  70.2  │  32.8
                       │  24.8  │  38.1  │
                       │   9.8  │  23.0  │
                       ├────────┼────────┤
                       │   258  │   325  │   583
          MALE      2. │  44.3  │  55.7  │  67.2
                       │  75.2  │  61.9  │
                       │  29.7  │  37.4  │
                       └────────┴────────┘
             COLUMN        343      525       868
             TOTAL        39.5     60.5     100.0


CORRECTED CHI SQUARE  = 16.07690 WITH 1 DEGREE OF FREEDOM.    SIGNIFICANCE = 0.0001
     RAW CHI SQUARE   = 16.67513 WITH 1 DEGREE OF FREEDOM.    SIGNIFICANCE = 0.0000
   PHI    =  0.13860
CONTINGENCY COEFFICIENT  =   0.13729
LAMBDA (ASYMMETRIC) =  0.0     WITH RQ55      DEPENDENT    =  0.0    WITH SCHMOD2 DEPENDENT.
LAMBDA (SYMMETRIC) =  0.0
UNCERTAINTY COEFFICIENT (ASYMMETRIC) =  0.01549 WITH RQ55. DEPENDENT.    = 0.01461 WITH SRCHMOD2
   DEPENDENT.
UNCERTAINTY COEFFICIENT (SYMMETRIC) =   0.01504
KENDALL'S TAU B =  -0.13860    SIGNIFICANCE = 0.0000
KENDALL'S TAU C =  -0.12729    SIGNIFICANCE = 0.0000
GAMMA  =   -0.30262
SOMER'S D (ASYMMETRIC) = -0.13314 WITH RQ55    DEPENDENT.    = -0.14429 WITH SRCHMOD2 DEPENDENT.
SOMER'S D (SYMMETRIC) = 0.13849
ETA  = 0.13860 WITH RQ55   DEPENDENT.      =  0.13860 WITH SRCHMOD2 DEPENDENT.
PEARSON'S R = -0.13860  SIGNIFICANCE =   0.0000

NUMBER OF MISSING OBSERVATIONS =    391
```

Figure 6. Sex of Online Catalog Users—Comparison by Search Mode.

107

Academic Disciplines of MELVYL Users

MELVYL users, like users in the aggregate sample, come from a wide distribution of academic disciplines. The highest percentage of MELVYL users are in the Arts and Humanities. Similarly, the highest percentage of aggregate users are also in the Arts and Humanities. The second largest category of MELVYL users is significantly different from other sample groups: 22.7 percent come from Physical/Biological Sciences, whereas only 11.6 percent of users from the aggregate sample are in this category. The percentage of UC users is somewhat higher than the aggregate in the Social Sciences, but much lower in Business/Management (see Table 16).[10]

The frequency distribution of users by discipline differs from campus to campus. MELVYL users at Berkeley and Santa Cruz are predominantly from Arts and Humanities and the Social Sciences. Users at Davis, Irvine, and Riverside are primarily in the Physical/Biological Sciences. Users at Santa Barbara and San Diego are more evenly distributed, though for both of these campuses, a higher percentage of users come from Physical/Biological Science as well (Figure 10).[11]

Academic Status of Users

As Table 17 shows, 16 percent of MELVYL users are not students, faculty, or staff. Most of these non-affiliated users come from Berkeley, Los Angeles, and San Diego campuses. Of those users affiliated with the University, most are undergraduates: 39 percent juniors and seniors, and 23.2 percent freshmen and sophomores. Graduate students, including those in professional school, account for 15.9 percent of users at UC, whereas at other libraries, they make up 30.6 percent of the user population. A high percentage of undergraduate users come from Santa Cruz

Table 15.   User Educational Levels

Question 56: *Mark your current or highest educational level:*	UC	All
a. Grade School or Elementary School	2.6%	1.0%
b. High School or Secondary School	4.9	9.0
c. Some College or University	59.5	46.2
d. College or University Graduate	33.1	43.8

FILE   FINAL   (CREATION DATE = 08/03/82)
* CROSSTABULATION OF *
RQ56   CURENT OR HIGHEST GRADE COMPLETED BY TERMLOC2

TERMLOC2

RQ56	COUNT ROW PCT COL PCT TOT PCT	BERKE-LEY 1.	DAVIS 2.	IRVINE 3.	LA 4.	RIVER-SIDE 5.	SANTA BARBARA 6.	SANTA CRUZ 7.	SAN DIEGO 8.	SAN FRAN-CISCO 9.	ROW TOTAL
GRADE SCHOOL 1.		5 23.8 3.3 0.6	2 9.5 1.9 0.2	0 0.00 0.00 0.0	1 4.8 0.8 0.1	3 14.3 6.4 0.4	1 4.8 0.9 0.1	3 14.3 4.5 0.4	6 28.6 3.2 0.7	0 0.00 0.00 0.0	21 2.5
HIGH SCHOOL 2.		4 9.3 2.6 0.5	4 9.3 3.7 0.5	7 16.3 19.4 0.8	10 23.3 8.3 1.2	6 14.0 12.8 0.7	2 4.7 1.8 0.2	1 2.3 1.5 0.1	9 20.9 4.8 1.1	0 0.00 0.00 0.0	43 5.1
SOME COLLEGE 3.		78 15.4 51.7 9.2	67 13.2 62.0 7.9	23 4.5 63.9 2.7	60 11.9 50.0 7.1	22 4.3 46.8 2.6	68 13.4 59.6 8.0	51 10.1 76.1 6.0	137 27.1 72.5 16.2	0 0.00 0.00 0.0	506 59.7
COLLEGE GRADUATE 4.		64 23.1 42.4 7.6	35 12.6 32.4 4.1	6 2.2 16.7 0.7	49 17.7 40.8 5.8	16 5.8 34.0 1.9	43 15.5 37.7 5.1	12 4.3 17.9 1.4	37 13.4 19.6 4.4	15 5.4 100.0 1.8	277 32.7
COLUMN TOTAL		151 17.8	108 12.8	36 4.3	120 14.2	47 5.5	114 13.5	67 7.9	189 22.3	15 1.8	847 100.0

14 OUT OF 36 (38.9%) OF THE VALID CELLS HAVE EXPECTED CELL FREQUENCY LESS THAN 5.0.
MINIMUM EXPECTED CELL FREQUENCY = 0.372
CHI SQUARE = 106.31560 WITH 24 DEGREES OF FREEDOM SIGNIFICANCE = 0.0000
CRAMER'S V = 0.20455
CONTINGENCY COEFFICIENT = 0.33395
LAMBDA (ASYMMETRIC) = 0.04399 WITH RQ56 DEPENDENT = 0.04255 WITH TERMLOC2 DEPENDENT.
LAMBDA (SYMMETRIC) = 0.04304
UNCERTAINTY COEFFICIENT (ASYMMETRIC) = 0.06804 WITH RQ56 DEPENDENT = 0.03089 WITH TERMLOC2 DEPENDENT.
UNCERTAINTY COEFFICIENT (SYMMETRIC) = 0.04249
KENDALL'S TAU B = -0.07277 SIGNIFICANCE = 0.0062
KENDALL'S TAU C = -0.06540 SIGNIFICANCE = 0.0062
GAMMA = -0.10673
SOMERS'S D (ASYMMETRIC) = -0.05754 WITH RQ56 DEPENDENT. = -0.09204 WITH TERMLOC2 DEPENDENT.
SOMERS'S D (SYMMETRIC) = -0.07081
ETA = 0.24497 WITH RQ56 DEPENDENT. = 0.10465 WITH TERMLOC2 DEPENDENT.
PEARSON'S R = -0.07092 SIGNIFICANCE = 0.0195

NUMBER OF MISSING OBSERVATIONS =   412

Figure 7.   User Education Levels—Comparison by Campus.

FILE   LINKQST (CREATION DATE = 01/26/83) CROSSTABULATION OF * * * * * *
* * * * * * * * * * * * * * * *
     RQ56   CURRENT OR HIGHEST GRADE COMPLETED   BY SRCHMOD2
*   PAGE 1 OF 1

| | SRCHMOD2 | | |
RQ56	COUNT ROW PCT COL PCT TOT PCT	COMMAND 1.	LOOK UP 2.	ROW TOTAL
GRADE SCHOOL 1.		3 / 13.0 / 0.9 / 0.3	20 / 87.0 / 3.8 / 2.3	23 / 2.6
HIGH SCHOOL 2.		16 / 37.2 / 4.6 / 1.8	27 / 62.8 / 5.1 / 3.1	43 / 4.9
SOME COLLEGE 3.		200 / 38.3 / 57.6 / 22.8	322 / 61.7 / 60.8 / 36.7	522 / 59.5
COLLEGE GRADUATE 4.		128 / 44.3 / 36.9 / 14.6	161 / 55.7 / 30.4 / 18.4	289 / 33.0
COLUMN TOTAL		347 / 39.6	530 / 60.4	877 / 100.0

CHI SQUARE =   9.90622 WITH   3 DEGREES OF FREEDOM   SIGNIFICANCE = 0.0194
CRAMER'S V =   0.10628
CONTINGENCY COEFFICIENT =   0.10569
LAMBDA (ASYMMETRIC) =   0.0 WITH RQ56 DEPENDENT   = 0.0   WITH SRCHMOD2 DEPENDENT.
LAMBDA (SYMMETRIC) =   0.0
UNCERTAINTY COEFFICIENT (ASYMMETRIC) =   0.00684 WITH RQ56 DEPENDENT.   = 0.00935 WITH SRCHMOD2 DEPENDENT.
UNCERTAINTY COEFFICIENT (SYMMETRIC) =   0.00790
KENDALL'S TAU B =   -0.07972   SIGNIFICANCE =   0.0075
KENDALL'S TAU C =   -0.08058   SIGNIFICANCE =   0.0075
GAMMA =   -0.15744
SOMERS'S D (ASYMMETRIC) =   -0.08425 WITH RQ56 DEPENDENT.   = -0.07544 WITH SRCHMOD2 DEPENDENT.
SOMERS'S D (SYMMETRIC) =   -0.07960
ETA =   0.09537 WITH RQ56 DEPENDENT.   = 0.10628 WITH SRCHMOD2 DEPENDENT.
PEARSON'S R =   -0.09536 SIGNIFICANCE =   0.0024
NUMBER OF MISSING OBSERVATIONS =   382

Figure 8.   User Education Levels— Comparison by Search Mode.

57. The category that best describes my academic area is: (Mark *One* only)

a. Arts and Humanities
b. Physical/Biological Sciences
c. Social Sciences
d. Business/Management
e. Education
f. Engineering
g. Medical/Health Sciences
h. Law
i. Major not declared
j. Interdisciplinary

58. The main focus of my academic work at the present time is: (Mark *All* that apply)

a. Course work
b. Teaching
c. Research

59. My present affiliation with this college or university is:

a. Freshman/Sophomore
b. Junior/Senior
c. Graduate—masters level
d. Graduate—doctoral level
e. Graduate—professional school
f. Faculty
g. Staff
h. Other

Figure 9. Questions Regarding Academic Characteristics of Users

Table 16. Academic Disciplines of Users

Ranked by Frequency of Response

Question 57: *The category that best describes my academic area is:*[1]

	UC	All
a. Arts and Humanities	24.2%	26.1%
b. Physical/Biological Sciences	22.7	11.6
c. Social Sciences	19.3	17.6
f. Engineering	14.1	11.9
g. Medical/Health Sciences	5.8	5.6
d. Business/Management	4.7	13.3
i. Major not declared	4.0	3.4
h. Law	2.9	2.0
e. Education	2.0	5.5
j. Interdisciplinary	0.2	3.1

[1] Answered only at college and university sites.

TERMLOC2

RQ57	COUNT ROW PCT COL PCT TOT PCT	BERKE-LEY 1.	DAVIS 2.	IRVINE 3.	LA 4.	RIVER-SIDE 5.	SANTA BARBARA 6.	SANTA CRUZ 7.	SAN DIEGO 8.	SAN FRAN-CISCO 9.	ROW TOTAL
1. ART AND HUMANITI		51 25.1 33.6 6.0	24 11.8 22.0 2.8	6 3.0 16.7 0.7	29 14.3 24.4 3.4	8 3.9 17.0 0.9	27 13.3 23.7 3.2	19 9.4 28.8 2.2	35 17.2 18.5 4.1	4 2.0 28.6 0.5	203 24.0
2. PHYS–BIO SCIENCE		23 11.9 15.1 2.7	36 18.7 33.0 4.3	11 5.7 30.6 1.3	17 8.8 14.3 2.0	15 7.8 31.9 1.8	30 15.5 26.3 3.5	11 5.7 16.7 1.3	50 25.9 26.5 5.9	0 0.0 0.0	193 22.8
3. SOCIAL SCIENCES		37 22.6 24.3 4.4	22 13.4 20.2 2.6	7 4.3 19.4 0.8	28 17.1 23.5 3.3	5 3.0 10.6 0.6	22 13.4 19.3 2.6	17 10.4 25.8 2.0	25 15.2 13.2 3.0	1 0.6 7.1 0.1	164 19.4
4. BUSINESS–MANAGEM		8 19.5 5.3 0.9	5 12.2 4.6 0.6	0 0.0 0.0	10 24.4 8.4 1.2	4 9.8 8.5 0.5	4 9.8 3.5 0.5	2 4.9 3.0 0.2	8 19.5 4.2 0.9	0 0.0 0.0	41 4.8
5. EDUCATION		2 11.8 1.3 0.2	4 23.5 3.7 0.5	0 0.0 0.0	0 0.0 0.0	2 11.8 4.3 0.2	5 29.4 4.4 0.6	3 17.6 4.5 0.4	1 5.9 0.5 0.1	0 0.0 0.0	17 2.0
6. ENGINEERING		15 12.7 9.9 1.8	8 6.8 7.3 0.9	6 5.1 16.7 0.7	16 13.6 13.4 1.9	5 4.2 10.6 0.6	14 11.9 12.3 1.7	6 5.1 9.1 0.7	48 40.7 25.4 5.7	0 0.0 0.0	118 13.9

112

	C1	C2	C3	C4	C5	C6	C7	C8	C9	ROW TOTAL
7. MEDICAL–HEALTH S	5 / 10.4 / 3.3 / 0.6	5 / 10.4 / 4.6 / 0.6	3 / 6.3 / 8.3 / 0.4	10 / 20.8 / 8.4 / 1.2	3 / 6.3 / 6.4 / 0.4	2 / 4.2 / 1.8 / 0.2	2 / 4.2 / 3.0 / 0.2	10 / 20.8 / 5.3 / 1.2	8 / 16.7 / 57.1 / 0.9	48 / 5.7
8. LAW	3 / 11.5 / 2.0 / 0.4	1 / 3.8 / 0.9 / 0.1	2 / 7.7 / 5.6 / 0.2	6 / 23.1 / 5.0 / 0.7	1 / 3.8 / 2.1 / 0.1	8 / 30.8 / 7.0 / 0.9	2 / 7.7 / 3.0 / 0.2	2 / 7.7 / 1.1 / 0.2	1 / 3.8 / 7.1 / 0.1	26 / 3.1
9. MAJOR UNDECLARED	7 / 20.6 / 4.6 / 0.8	4 / 11.8 / 3.7 / 0.5	1 / 2.9 / 2.8 / 0.1	3 / 8.8 / 2.5 / 0.4	4 / 11.8 / 8.5 / 0.5	2 / 5.9 / 1.8 / 0.2	3 / 8.8 / 4.5 / 0.4	10 / 29.4 / 5.3 / 1.2	0 / 0.0 / 0.0 / 0.0	34 / 4.0
10. INTERDISCIPLINAR	1 / 50.0 / 0.7 / 0.1	0 / 0.0 / 0.0 / 0.0	0 / 0.0 / 0.0 / 0.0	0 / 0.0 / 0.0 / 0.0	0 / 0.0 / 0.0 / 0.0	1 / 50.0 / 1.5 / 0.1	0 / 0.0 / 0.0 / 0.0	0 / 0.0 / 0.0 / 0.0	0 / 0.0 / 0.0 / 0.0	2 / 0.2
COLUMN TOTAL	152 / 18.0	109 / 12.9	36 / 4.3	119 / 14.1	47 / 5.6	114 / 13.5	66 / 7.8	189 / 22.3	14 / 1.7	846 / 100.0

45 OUT OF 90 (50.0%) OF THE VALID CELLS HAVE EXPECTED CELL FREQUENCY LESS THAN 5.0
MINIMUM EXPECTED CELL FREQUENCY = 0.033
CHI SQUARE = 191.92705 WITH 72 DEGREES OF FREEDOM SIGNIFICANCE = 0.0000
CRAMER'S V = 0.16840
CONTINGENCY COEFFICIENT = 0.43002
LAMBDA (ASYMMETRIC) = 0.07154 WITH RQ57 DEPENDENT = 0.06240 WITH TERMLOC2 DEPENDENT.
LAMBDA (SYMMETRIC) = 0.06692
UNCERTAINTY COEFFICIENT (ASYMMETRIC) = 0.04845 WITH RQ57 DEPENDENT = 0.04595 WITH TERMLOC2 DEPENDENT.
UNCERTAINTY COEFFICIENT (SYMMETRIC) = 0.04717
KENDALL'S TAU B = 0.07576 SIGNIFICANCE = 0.0021
KENDALL'S TAU C = 0.07144 SIGNIFICANCE = 0.0021
GAMMA = 0.08998
SOMERS'S D (ASYMMETRIC) = 0.07454 WITH RQ57 DEPENDENT. = 0.07699 WITH TERMLOC2 DEPENDENT.
SOMERS'S D (SYMMETRIC) = 0.07575
ETA = 0.14859 WITH RQ57 DEPENDENT. = 0.16390 WITH TERMLOC2 DEPENDENT.
PEARSON'S R = 0.10297 SIGNIFICANCE = 0.0014

NUMBER OF MISSING OBSERVATIONS = 413

Figure 10. Academic Disciplines of Users—Comparison by Campus.

113

CLR USER QUESTIONNAIRE: LIBRARY TYPE COMPARISON XTABS
FILE   FINAL   (CREATION DATE = 08/03/82)   04/04/83   PAGE 125
* * * * * * * * RQ59   PRESENT AFFILIATION   * * * * * CROSSTABULATION OF * * * * * * * * * * * * * * * *
* BY TERMLOC2 * * * * * * * * * * * * * * * * * * PAGE 1 OF 2

TERMLOC2

RQ59	COUNT / ROW PCT / COL PCT / TOT PCT	BERKE-LEY 1.	DAVIS 2.	IRVINE 3.	LA 4.	RIVER-SIDE 5.	SANTA BARBARA 6.	SANTA CRUZ 7.	SAN DIEGO 8.	SAN FRAN-CISCO 9.	ROW TOTAL
1. FRESHMAN-SOPHOMO		32 / 15.9 / 21.5 / 3.8	26 / 12.9 / 24.1 / 3.1	8 / 4.0 / 22.2 / 1.0	26 / 12.9 / 22.4 / 3.1	12 / 6.0 / 25.5 / 1.4	17 / 8.5 / 15.2 / 2.0	18 / 9.0 / 26.9 / 2.2	62 / 30.8 / 33.5 / 7.4	0 / 0.0 / 0.0 / 0.0	201 / 24.1
2. JUNIOR-SENIOR		49 / 15.2 / 32.9 / 5.9	44 / 13.6 / 40.7 / 5.3	17 / 5.3 / 47.2 / 2.0	33 / 10.2 / 28.4 / 4.0	14 / 4.3 / 29.8 / 1.7	55 / 17.0 / 49.1 / 6.6	35 / 10.8 / 52.2 / 4.2	75 / 23.2 / 40.5 / 9.0	1 / 0.3 / 6.7 / 0.1	323 / 38.7
3. GRADUATE-MASTERS		9 / 17.6 / 6.0 / 1.1	8 / 15.7 / 7.4 / 1.0	0 / 0.0 / 0.0 / 0.0	13 / 25.5 / 11.2 / 1.6	6 / 11.8 / 12.8 / 0.7	6 / 11.8 / 5.4 / 0.7	2 / 3.9 / 3.0 / 0.2	7 / 13.7 / 3.8 / 0.8	0 / 0.0 / 0.0 / 0.0	51 / 6.1
4. GRADUATE-DOCTORA		18 / 29.5 / 12.1 / 2.2	10 / 16.4 / 9.3 / 1.2	2 / 3.3 / 5.6 / 0.2	6 / 9.8 / 5.2 / 0.7	5 / 8.2 / 10.6 / 0.6	11 / 18.0 / 9.8 / 1.3	1 / 1.6 / 1.5 / 0.1	5 / 8.2 / 2.7 / 0.6	3 / 4.9 / 20.0 / 0.4	61 / 7.3
5. GRADUATE-PROFESS		3 / 17.6 / 2.0 / 0.4	3 / 17.6 / 2.8 / 0.4	0 / 0.0 / 0.0 / 0.0	2 / 11.8 / 1.7 / 0.2	0 / 0.0 / 0.0 / 0.0	1 / 5.9 / 0.9 / 0.1	0 / 0.0 / 0.0 / 0.0	4 / 23.5 / 2.2 / 0.5	4 / 23.5 / 26.7 / 0.5	17 / 2.0
6. FACULTY		6 / 22.2 / 4.0 / 0.7	3 / 11.1 / 2.8 / 0.4	1 / 3.7 / 2.8 / 0.1	5 / 18.5 / 4.3 / 0.6	0 / 0.0 / 0.0 / 0.0	7 / 25.9 / 6.3 / 0.8	1 / 3.7 / 1.5 / 0.1	4 / 14.8 / 2.2 / 0.5	0 / 0.0 / 0.0 / 0.0	27 / 3.2

114

	Col 1	Col 2	Col 3	Col 4	Col 5	Col 6	Col 7	Col 8	Col 9	ROW TOTAL
STAFF 7.	3 15.0 2.0 0.4	4 20.0 3.7 0.5	1 5.0 2.8 0.1	4 20.0 3.4 0.5	0 0.0 0.0 0.0	2 10.0 1.8 0.2	1 5.0 1.5 0.1	2 10.0 1.1 0.2	3 15.0 20.0 0.4	20 2.4
OTHER STATUS 8.	29 21.5 19.5 3.5	10 7.4 9.3 1.2	7 5.2 19.4 0.8	27 20.0 23.3 3.2	10 7.4 21.3 1.2	13 9.6 11.6 1.6	9 6.7 13.4 1.1	26 19.3 14.1 3.1	4 3.0 26.7 0.5	135 16.2
COLUMN TOTAL	149 17.8	108 12.9	36 4.3	116 13.9	47 5.6	112 13.4	67 8.0	185 22.2	15 1.8	835 100.0

36 OUT OF 72 (50.0%) OF THE VALID CELLS HAVE EXPECTED CELL FREQUENCY LESS THAN 5.0
MINIMUM EXPECTED CELL FREQUENCY = 0.305
CHI SQUARE = 157.64360 WITH 56 DEGREES OF FREEDOM SIGNIFICANCE = 0.0000
CRAMER'S V = 0.16423
CONTINGENCY COEFFICIENT = 0.39851
LAMBDA (ASYMMETRIC) = 0.00586 WITH RQ59 DEPENDENT = 0.04154 WITH TERMLOC2 DEPENDENT.
LAMBDA (SYMMETRIC) = 0.02582
UNCERTAINTY COEFFICIENT (ASYMMETRIC) = 0.04686 WITH RQ59 DEPENDENT. = 0.03816 WITH TERMLOC2 DEPENDENT.
UNCERTAINTY COEFFICIENT (SYMMETRIC) = 0.04207
KENDALL'S TAU B = -0.06796 SIGNIFICANCE = 0.0064
KENDALL'S TAU C = -0.06235 SIGNIFICANCE = 0.0064
GAMMA = -0.08431
SOMERS'S D (ASYMMETRIC) = -0.06394 WITH RQ59 DEPENDENT. = -0.07224 WITH TERMLOC2 DEPENDENT.
SOMERS'S D (SYMMETRIC) = -0.06784
ETA = 0.20316 WITH RQ59 DEPENDENT. = 0.13053 WITH TERMLOC2 DEPENDENT.
PEARSON'S R = -0.06193 SIGNIFICANCE = -0.0368

NUMBER OF MISSING OBSERVATIONS = 424

Figure 11. Academic Status of Users—Comparison by Campus.

CLR USER QUESTIONNAIRE: LIBRARY TYPE COMPARISON XTABS   04/04/83   PAGE 123
FILE   FINAL   (CREATION DATE = 08/03/82)
* CROSSTABULATION *
    RQEST58 (TABULATING   1) THE MAIN FOCUS OF MY ACADEMIC WORK IS:
BY TERMLOC2
*   PAGE 1 OF 1

TERMLOC2

RQUEST58	COUNT ROW PCT COL PCT TAB PCT	BERKE- LEY 1	DAVIS 2	IRVINE 3	LA 4	RIVER- SIDE 5	SANTA BARBARA 6	SANTA CRUZ 7	SAN DIEGO 8	SAN FRAN- CISCO 9	ROW TOTAL
COURSE WORK	RQ58A	95 16.0 64.2 11.4	80 13.5 74.1 9.6	26 4.4 72.2 3.1	78 13.2 67.2 9.4	31 5.2 67.4 3.7	71 12.0 65.1 8.5	49 8.3 74.2 5.9	154 26.0 81.9 18.5	9 1.5 60.0 1.1	593 71.3
TEACHING	RQ58B	13 20.3 8.8 1.6	8 12.5 7.4 1.0	3 4.7 8.3 0.4	9 14.1 7.8 1.1	2 3.1 4.3 0.2	16 25.0 14.7 1.9	5 7.8 7.6 0.6	8 12.5 4.3 1.0	0 0.0 0.0 0.0	64 7.7
RESEARCH	RQ58C	64 21.5 43.2 7.7	39 13.1 36.1 4.7	15 5.1 41.7 1.8	42 14.1 36.2 5.0	20 6.7 43.5 2.4	45 15.2 41.3 5.4	19 6.4 28.8 2.3	47 15.8 25.0 5.6	6 2.0 40.0 0.7	297 35.7
	COLUMN TOTAL	148 17.8	108 13.0	36 4.3	116 13.9	46 5.5	109 13.1	66 7.9	188 22.6	15 1.8	832 100.0

PERCENTS AND TOTALS BASED ON RESPONDENTS
832 VALID CASES   427 MISSING CASES

Figure 12. Focus of Academic Work—Comparison by Campus.

Table 17.   Academic Status of Respondents to the User Questionnaire

Ranked by Frequency of Response

Question 59: *My present affiliation with this college or university is:*[1]

	UC	All
b. Junior/Senior	39.0%	34.1%
a. Freshman/Sophomore	23.2	25.7
h. Other	16.1	8.0
d. Graduate—doctoral level	7.6	9.7
c. Graduate—masters level	6.4	13.4
f. Faculty	3.2	4.0
g. Staff	2.6	2.8
e. Graduate—professional school	1.9	2.3

[1] Answered only at college and university sites.

(79.1 percent) and San Diego (74.0 percent). Santa Barbara and Irvine also have a high percentage of undergraduate users (Figure 11).[12]

Focus of Academic Work

Table 18 compares respondents' focus of academic work at UC with the focus at all other academic libraries. There is not much difference in the responses to this question except that MELVYL users tend to check fewer response categories. This explains why the percentages for MEL-VYL users in the table are slightly lower than for all other libraries. The highest percentage of users whose focus is course work come from San Diego (81.9 percent). Santa Barbara accounts for the highest percentage of users whose focus is teaching (14.7 percent) and Riverside accounts for the highest percentage of users whose focus is research (43.5 percent), closely followed by Berkeley (43.2 percent) (Figure 12).[13]

Table 18.   Focus of Academic Work

Question 58: *The main focus of my academic work at the present time is: (Mark ALL that apply)*[1]

	UC	All
a. Course work	71.4%	74.4%
b. Teaching	7.5	9.5
c. Research	35.6	37.7

[1] Answered only at college and university sites.

SECTION IV: CHARACTERISTICS OF ONLINE CATALOG SEARCHES

General

The first four questions on the User Questionnaire deal with characteristics of the search just completed by the respondent:

- The kind and amount of *bibliographic information* brought to the search
- The *bibliographic task* to be performed, e.g., to find a known item, perform a subject search, or verify bibliographic information
- The *search method* used, as reflected by the bibliographic access points used in the search (subject, author, etc.)
- The *application*, the reason for which the search was performed.

```
1. I came to this computer search with (Mark ALL that apply)
a. A complete author's name     e. A topic word or words
b. Part of an author's name     f. A subject heading or headings
c. A complete title             g. A complete call number
d. Part of a title              h. Part of a call number

2. By searching this computer catalog I was trying to find:
   (Mark ALL that apply)
a. A specific book, journal or magazine
b. Books, journals or magazines on a topic or subject
c. Books by a specific author
d. Information such as publisher, date, spelling of a name etc.
e. If a book that I know the library has is available for my use
f. Another library that has a book, journal or magazine that I
   want

3. I searched for what I wanted by: (Mark ALL that apply)
a. A complete author's name     e. A topic word or words
b. Part of an author's name     f. A subject heading or headings
c. A complete title             g. A complete call number
d. Part of a title              h. Part of a call number

4. I need this information for: (Mark ALL that apply)
a. Recreational uses
b. Making or fixing something
c. My work or job
d. Personal interest
e. A hobby
f. Class or course reading
g. A course paper or report
h. A thesis or dissertation
i. Writing for publication
j. Teaching or planning a course
k. Keeping up on a topic or subject
```

Figure 13.   Questions Regarding Characteristics of the Online Catalog Search

Table 19. Bibliograpic Information Brought to Online Catalog Searches

Comparison of UC Data with Aggregate Data[1]

Question 1: *I came to this computer search with: (Mark* ALL *that apply)*

	University of California	All Respondents
f. A subject heading or headings	49.0%	44.4%
a. a complete author's name	35.3	41.9
e. A topic word or words	34.0	28.7
c. A complete title	27.0	39.3
b. Part of an author's name	12.4	12.7
d. Part of a title	9.9	10.9
g. A complete call number	2.0	5.0
h. Part of a call number	1.3	1.1

[1] Percentages sum to more than 100 due to legitimate multiple responses.

Questions about search characteristics in the User Questionnaire are displayed in Figure 13.

Bibliographic Information

Most Users Come with Subject-Related Information

As Table 19 shows, most MELVYL users come to the online catalog search with information about topics or subjects: 49.0 percent with "complete subject headings" and 34.0 percent with "a topic word or words." These figures are significantly higher than the aggregate figures.

Table 20 shows the responses to Question 1 reclassified into Author,

Table 20. Classes of Information Brought to the Search by Users

Ranked by Frequency of Response

Category of Information[1]	UC	All
Subject	47.0%	36.2%
Author	13.7	10.8
Author-Title	13.2	21.6
Author-Title-Subject	10.9	11.9
Title	6.3	9.0
Author-Subject	5.4	5.7
Title-Subject	3.5	4.8

[1] Derived from User Question 1 (Figure 13). Users who came *only* with call number information are excluded.

Title, and Subject categories. Note that this information is not constructed from the information in Table 19, but is computed from the raw questionnaire responses in order to fully account for multiple responses.

Table 20 shows that almost one-half of MELVYL users come to the online catalog with *only* subject information. The next-ranking category, users with author information, is considerably smaller.

About Thirty Percent of Users Bring Only "Known Item" Information

Another way to look at the importance of subject information in online catalog use is to differentiate between users who come only with information about authors and titles (which we will refer to here as "known item" information, recognizing that we include tasks of the "any book by a specific author" category under this label) and users who come with some topical information as well. Table 21 reveals this dichotomy, showing that 66.8 percent of MELVYL users bring a topical interest to their search, and that 33.2 percent bring only "known-item" information.

Many Users Come with More than One Kind of Information

There is another interesting contrast between users bringing only one element of information to the search and users bringing more than one. Table 22 shows that 67 percent of MELVYL users come with *only* author or title or subject information, while the remaining 33 percent come with more than one item of data. Even if we assume (perhaps correctly) that users making author-title searches are in possession of "one item" of

Table 21. "Known Item" and Subject Information Brought to the Search by Users

Category of Information[1]	UC	All
Author	13.7	10.8
Title	6.3	9.0
Author-Title	13.2	21.6
Subtotal, Known Items	*33.2%*	*41.4%*
Subject	47.0	36.2
Author-Subject	5.4	5.7
Title-Subject	3.5	4.8
Author-Title-Subject	10.9	11.9
Subtotal, Subject Information	*66.8%*	*58.6%*

[1] Derived from User Question 1 (Figure 13). Users who came *only* with call number information are excluded.

Table 22.   Number of Information Elements Brought to the Search by Users

Category of Information[1]	UC	All
Author	13.7%	10.8%
Title	6.3%	9.0%
Subject	47.0	26.2
Subtotal, Single Element	*67.0%*	*56.0%*
Author-Title	13.2	21.6
Author-Subject	5.4	5.7
Title-Subject	3.5	4.8
Author-Title-Subject	10.9	11.9
Subtotal, Multiple Elements	*33.0%*	*44.0%*

[1] Derived from User Question 1 (Figure 13). Users who came *only* with call number information are excluded.

information about a desired known item, there remain about 20 percent of users who come with some unspecified (and perhaps complex) mix of author, title and subject information.

Table 22 also shows that MELVYL users are more likely to bring single elements of information to the search than are users in the aggregate sample. The difference is accounted for by a significantly larger incidence of author and subject information among MELVYL users.

Table 23.   Bibliographic Tasks for which the Online Catalog is Used

Comparison of UC and Aggregate Data[1]

Question 2: *By searching this computer catalog I was trying to find: (Mark ALL that apply)*

	UC	All
b. Books, journals or magazines on a topic or subject	59.5%	53.44%
a. A specific book, journal or magazine	36.4	50.11
c. Books by a specific author	24.6	23.66
e. If a book that I know the library has is available for my use	11.7	16.77
f. Another library that has a book, journal or magazine that I want	10.7	7.44
d. Information such as publisher, date, spelling of a name etc.	4.2	5.33

[1] Percentages sum to more than 100 due to legitimate multiple responses.

CLR USER QUESTIONNAIRE: LIBRARY TYPE COMPARISON XTABS
FILE   FINAL   (CREATION DATE = 08/03/82)
* CROSSTABULATION * * * * * * * * * *
RQEST2 (TABULATING 1) IN THIS SEARCH I WAS TRYING TO FIND:
BY TERMLOC2

04/04/83   PAGE 16

* PAGE 1 OF 1

TERMLOC2

RQUEST2	COUNT / ROW PCT / COL PCT / TAB PCT	BERKELEY 1	DAVIS 2	IRVINE 3	LA 4	RIVERSIDE 5	SANTA BARBARA 6	SANTA CRUZ 7	SAN DIEGO 8	SAN FRANCISCO 9	ROW TOTAL
RQ2A SPECIFIC BOOK ETC		84 / 22.2 / 44.0 / 8.0	38 / 10.1 / 30.9 / 3.6	17 / 4.5 / 35.4 / 1.6	50 / 13.2 / 32.7 / 4.8	21 / 5.6 / 36.2 / 2.0	51 / 13.5 / 36.7 / 4.9	25 / 6.6 / 35.2 / 2.4	86 / 22.8 / 35.0 / 8.2	6 / 1.6 / 33.3 / 0.6	378 / 36.1
RQ2B BOOKS ON TOPIC		97 / 15.5 / 50.8 / 9.3	86 / 13.7 / 69.9 / 8.2	34 / 5.4 / 70.8 / 3.2	93 / 14.9 / 60.8 / 8.9	35 / 5.6 / 60.3 / 3.3	85 / 13.6 / 61.2 / 8.1	44 / 7.0 / 62.0 / 4.2	143 / 22.8 / 58.1 / 13.7	9 / 1.4 / 50.0 / 0.9	626 / 59.8
RQ2C BOOKS BY SPEC AUTHOR		56 / 22.1 / 29.3 / 5.3	26 / 10.3 / 21.1 / 2.5	10 / 4.0 / 20.8 / 1.0	29 / 11.5 / 19.0 / 2.8	14 / 5.5 / 24.1 / 1.3	37 / 14.6 / 26.6 / 3.5	19 / 7.5 / 26.8 / 1.8	56 / 22.1 / 22.8 / 5.3	6 / 2.4 / 33.3 / 0.6	253 / 24.2
RQ2D PUB-DATE-SPELLING		13 / 31.0 / 6.8 / 1.2	2 / 4.8 / 1.6 / 0.2	4 / 9.5 / 8.3 / 0.4	9 / 21.4 / 5.9 / 0.9	1 / 2.4 / 1.7 / 0.1	2 / 4.8 / 1.4 / 0.2	3 / 7.1 / 4.2 / 0.3	8 / 19.0 / 3.3 / 0.8	0 / 0.0 / 0.0 / 0.0	42 / 4.0
RQ2E IF BOOK IS AVAILABLE		17 / 14.3 / 8.9 / 1.6	11 / 9.2 / 8.9 / 1.1	6 / 5.0 / 12.5 / 0.6	20 / 16.8 / 13.1 / 1.9	7 / 5.9 / 12.1 / 0.7	20 / 16.8 / 14.4 / 1.9	9 / 7.6 / 12.7 / 0.9	27 / 22.7 / 11.0 / 2.6	2 / 1.7 / 11.1 / 0.2	119 / 11.4
RQ2F OTHER LIBRARY W BOOK		22 / 20.4 / 11.5 / 2.1	7 / 6.5 / 5.7 / 0.7	7 / 6.5 / 14.6 / 0.7	15 / 13.9 / 9.8 / 1.4	7 / 6.5 / 12.1 / 0.7	15 / 13.9 / 10.8 / 1.4	9 / 8.3 / 12.7 / 0.9	24 / 22.2 / 9.8 / 2.3	2 / 1.9 / 11.1 / 0.2	108 / 10.3
COLUMN TOTAL		191 / 18.2	123 / 11.7	48 / 4.6	153 / 14.6	58 / 5.5	139 / 13.3	71 / 6.8	246 / 23.5	18 / 1.8	1047 / 100.0

PERCENTS AND TOTALS BASED ON RESPONDENTS
1047 VALID CASES   212 MISSING CASES

Figure 14. Bibliographic Tasks—Comparison by Campus.

122

Bibliographic Tasks

Table 23 shows that most users are seeking books, journals or magazines on a topic. At the University of California, the percentage of users seeking information on a topic is larger than for the aggregate sample. MELVYL users are less likely to be searching for specific items or to be interested in availability of an item.[14] Instead, they are more interested in finding out if the item is available through another library.[15] Analysis of data by UC campus shows that users from different campuses are looking for different kinds of information. At Berkeley, 44 percent of users were interested in locating a specific item, whereas 51 percent were interested in books on a topic. At both Irvine and Davis users were most interested in locating books on a specific topic (70.8 percent and 69.9 percent respectively). Users from Berkeley and San Francisco were more interested than users from other campuses in finding books by specific authors. Interest in availability, while not high at any of the campuses, is higher at Santa Barbara, Los Angeles, and Santa Cruz. Interest in display of bibliographic information was highest at Irvine and Berkeley (Figure 14).

Search Methods

Most Users Search by Subject or Topic

Table 24 shows that most MELVYL users use subject headings or topic words in their search: 47.9 percent "searched by subject headings" and 36.4 percent "searched by topic word or words."

Table 24. Methods of Searching Used with the Online Catalog

Comparison of UC and Aggregate Data[1]

Question 3: *I searched for what I wanted by: (Mark ALL that apply)*

	UC	All
f. A subject heading or headings	47.9%	43.4%
e. A topic word or words	36.4	29.9
a. A complete author's name	32.9	38.0
c. A complete title	25.3	35.5
b. Part of an author's name	15.1	15.0
d. Part of a title	11.3	14.2
g. A complete call number	[2]	4.4
h. Part of a call number	[2]	0.8

[1] Percentages sum to more than 100 due to legitimate multiple responses.
[2] Response category not offered at UC.

CLR USER QUESTIONNAIRE: LIBRARY TYPE COMPARISON XTABS
FILE   FINAL   (CREATION DATE = 08/03/82)
* CROSSTABULATION * * * * * * * * * * * * * * * * * *
    RQUEST3 (TABULATING 1) I SEARCHED FOR WHAT I WANTED BY:
BY TERMLOC2
* PAGE 1 OF 1

TERMLOC2

RQUEST3	COUNT ROW PCT COL PCT TAB PCT	BERKE-LEY 1	DAVIS 2	IRVINE 3	LA 4	RIVER-SIDE 5	SANTA BARBARA 6	SANTA CRUZ 7	SAN DIEGO 8	SAN FRAN-CISCO 9	ROW TOTAL
RQ3A COMPLETE AUTHOR		70 20.9 38.3 6.8	35 10.4 28.7 3.4	18 5.4 36.7 1.8	45 13.4 29.8 4.4	18 5.4 31.0 1.8	45 13.4 32.4 4.4	28 8.4 38.9 2.7	72 21.5 30.5 7.0	4 1.2 23.5 0.4	335 32.6
RQ3B PART AUTHOR'S NAME		38 24.8 20.8 3.7	13 8.5 10.7 1.3	9 5.9 18.4 0.9	17 11.1 11.3 1.7	8 5.2 13.8 0.8	27 17.6 19.4 2.6	9 5.9 12.5 0.9	27 17.6 11.4 2.6	5 3.3 29.4 0.5	153 14.9
RQ3C COMPLETE TITLE		42 16.4 23.0 4.1	30 11.7 24.6 2.9	9 3.5 18.4 0.9	35 13.7 23.2 3.4	16 6.3 27.6 1.6	47 18.4 33.8 4.6	19 7.4 26.4 1.9	53 20.7 22.5 5.2	5 2.0 29.4 0.5	256 24.9
RQ3D PART TITLE		23 20.5 12.6 2.2	16 14.3 13.1 1.6	7 6.3 14.3 0.7	12 10.7 7.9 1.2	7 6.3 12.1 0.7	17 15.2 12.2 1.7	4 3.6 5.6 0.4	24 21.4 10.2 2.3	2 1.8 11.8 0.2	112 10.9
RQ53E TOPIC WORD OR WORDS		62 16.5 33.9 6.0	42 11.2 34.4 4.1	24 6.4 49.0 2.3	62 16.5 41.1 6.0	19 5.1 32.8 1.9	51 13.6 36.7 5.0	22 5.9 30.6 2.1	88 23.5 37.3 8.6	5 1.3 29.4 0.5	375 36.5
RQ3F SUBJECT HEADINGS		75 15.2 41.0 7.3	62 12.5 50.8 6.0	33 6.7 67.3 3.2	73 14.7 48.3 7.1	31 6.3 53.4 3.0	64 12.9 46.0 6.2	36 7.3 50.0 3.5	114 23.0 48.3 11.1	7 1.4 41.2 0.7	495 48.2
COLUMN TOTAL		183 17.8	122 11.9	49 4.8	151 14.7	58 5.6	139 13.5	72 7.0	236 23.0	17 1.7	1027 100.0

PERCENTS AND TOTALS BASED ON RESPONDENTS
1027 VALID CASES   232 MISSING CASES

Figure 15. Methods of Searching—Comparison by Campus.

Table 25.   Types of Searches Conducted on Online Catalogs

Ranked by Frequency of Response

Type of Search[1]	UC	All
Subject	44.5%	34.1%
Author	15.2	13.8
Author-Title	11.7	17.5
Author-Title-Subject	9.3	10.1
Title	8.8	12.3
Author-Subject	7.0	6.5
Title-Subject	3.5	5.8

[1] Derived from User Question 3 (Figure 13). Users who conducted *only* call number searches are excluded.

Search methods differ somewhat among the UC campuses. At Irvine, 49 percent of users said they searched by topic and 67.3 percent searched by subject headings. A high percentage of users at Berkeley use complete author (38.3 percent) or part author (20.8 percent) information in their searches, while a lower than average percentage use subject or topic information (Figure 15).

As we did with bibliographic information in a previous section, we can separate out from Question 3 the issues of the kind and amount of information used in the search. Once again, subject searching is most common in the MELVYL system, constituting 44.5 percent of all searches. Table 25 shows the results when search methods are classified into Author, Title and Subject categories.

Table 26.   "Known Item" and Subject Searches in Online Catalogs

Type of Search[1]	UC	All
Author	15.2%	13.8%
Title	8.8	12.3
Author-Title	11.7	17.5
Subtotal, Known Items	*35.7%*	*43.6%*
Subject	44.5	34.1
Author-Subject	7.0	6.5
Title-Subject	3.5	5.8
Author-Title-Subject	9.3	10.1
Subtotal, Subject Information	*64.3%*	*56.5%*

[1] Derived from User Question 3 (Figure 13). Users who conducted *only* call number searches are excluded.

Table 27. MELVYL Compared to Other Catalogs with Subject
Search Capability

Type of Search[1]	UC	Others
Author	15.2%	13.6%
Title	8.8	12.0
Author-Title	11.7	15.6
Subtotal, Known Items	*35.7%*	*41.2%*
Subject	44.5	35.5
Author-Subject	7.0	6.8
Title-Subject	3.5	6.0
Author-Title-Subject	9.3	10.5
Subtotal, Subject Information	*64.3%*	*48.8%*

[1] Derived from User Question 3 (Figure 13). Users who conducted *only* call number searches are excluded.

Over Sixty Percent of Online Catalog Searches Involve Subjects

As Table 26 shows, 64.3 percent of MELVYL searches involve subject searching; 35.7 percent are "known item" searches. Subject searching is more prevalent in MELVYL than in the aggregate sample, even when systems without subject searching capabilities have been excluded, as shown in Table 27.

Multiple Access Points Are Used in About Thirty Percent of Searches

As Table 28 shows, over 60 percent of reported searches involve use of only one kind of heading index—either author, title, or subject.[16] Again,

Table 28. Number of Access Points Used in Online Catalog Searches

Type of Search[1]	UC	All
Author	15.2%	13.8%
Title	8.8	12.3
Subject	44.5	34.1
Subtotal, Single Element	*68.5%*	*60.2%*
Author-Title	11.7	17.5
Author-Subject	7.0	6.5
Title-Subject	3.5	5.8
Author-Title-Subject	9.3	10.1
Subtotal, Multiple Elements	*31.5*	*39.9%*

[1] Derived from User Question 3 (Figure 13). Users who conducted *only* call number searches are excluded.

Table 29. Reasons for Conducting the Online Catalog Search

Comparison of UC and Aggregate Data[1]

Question 4: *I need this information for: (Mark* ALL *that apply)*

	UC	All
g. A course paper or report	38.6%	38.6%
f. Class or course reading	28.4	28.7
d. Personal interest	27.9	29.9
a. Recreational uses	17.4	16.8
k. Keeping up on a topic or subject	14.7	14.2
c. My work or job	12.3	16.9
h. A thesis or dissertation	11.2	9.7
e. A hobby	10.0	7.7
i. Writing for publication	7.5	7.2
j. Teaching or planning a course	4.5	4.6
b. Making or fixing something	3.2	3.2

[1] Percentages sum to more than 100 due to legitimate multiple responses.

the relative weighting toward single-index searches is chiefly accounted for by author and subject searches, although MELVYL users appear slightly more disposed to conduct combined author-subject searches as well.

Applications

In Table 29 we see that most users search the online catalog to find materials for class reading, papers, or personal interest. A second tier of responses is associated with vocational or recreational uses (work or job, "keeping up" on a topic, or recreation). Responses from MELVYL users do not differ greatly from the aggregate responses in most categories, though the percentage seeking information for vocational use is slightly lower. Users from different campuses consult the computer catalog for different reasons. At Davis, 48.4 percent of respondents say that they need information for course papers or reports. Users at Irvine conducted searches for personal interest (34.0 percent), recreational uses (26.0 percent), or for hobbies (22 percent). More than half (52.9 percent) of the users at San Francisco were seeking information for vocational purposes (Figure 16).[17]

On the Relationship Between Bibliographic Information and Search Method

Table 30 compares the search information brought by MELVYL users (Table 20) and the methods used by them (Table 25). There are noticeable

CLR USER QUESTIONNAIRE: LIBRARY TYPE COMPARISON XTABS
FILE   FINAL   (CREATION DATE = 08/03/82)   04/04/83   PAGE 18
* CROSSTABULATION * * * * * * * * * * * * * * * * * *
  RQUEST4 (TABULATING 1) I NEED THIS INFORMATION FOR:
BY TERMLOC2
*   PAGE 1 OF 2

TERMLOC2

RQUEST4	COUNT ROW PCT COL PCT TAB PCT	BERKE- LEY 1	DAVIS 2	IRVINE 3	LA 4	RIVER- SIDE 5	SANTA BARBARA 6	SANTA CRUZ 7	SAN DIEGO 8	SAN FRAN- CISCO 9	ROW TOTAL
RQ4A RECREATIONAL USES		22 12.5 11.9 2.1	18 10.2 14.5 1.7	13 7.4 26.0 1.3	29 16.5 19.2 2.8	8 4.5 14.3 0.8	20 11.4 14.4 1.9	10 5.7 13.7 1.0	54 30.7 22.7 5.2	2 1.1 11.8 0.2	176 17.0
RQ53B MAKE-FIX SOMETHING		7 20.6 3.8 0.7	4 11.8 3.2 0.4	1 2.9 2.0 0.1	3 8.8 2.0 0.3	1 2.9 1.8 0.1	4 11.8 2.9 0.4	0 0.0 0.0 0.0	13 38.2 5.5 1.3	1 2.9 5.9 0.1	34 3.3
RQ4C WORK OR JOB		24 19.0 13.0 2.3	14 11.1 11.3 1.4	6 4.8 12.0 0.6	26 20.6 17.2 2.5	4 3.2 7.1 0.4	16 12.7 11.5 1.5	6 4.8 8.2 0.6	21 16.7 8.8 2.0	9 7.1 52.9 0.9	126 12.2
RQ4D PERSONAL INTEREST		55 19.0 29.7 5.3	31 10.7 25.0 3.0	17 5.9 34.0 1.6	36 12.5 23.8 3.5	17 5.9 30.4 1.6	38 13.1 27.3 3.7	20 6.9 27.4 1.9	70 24.2 29.4 6.8	5 1.7 29.4 0.5	289 28.0
RQ4E HOBBY		20 18.9 10.8 1.9	10 9.4 8.1 1.0	11 10.4 22.0 1.1	14 13.2 9.3 1.4	7 6.6 12.5 0.7	9 8.5 6.5 0.9	7 6.6 9.6 0.7	26 24.5 10.9 2.5	2 1.9 11.8 0.2	106 10.3
RQ4F CLASS-COURSE READING		52 17.7 28.1 5.0	28 9.6 22.6 2.7	19 6.5 38.0 1.8	46 15.7 30.5 4.5	18 6.1 32.1 1.7	32 10.9 23.0 3.1	25 8.5 34.2 2.4	68 23.2 28.6 6.6	5 1.7 29.4 0.5	293 28.4

	1	2	3	4	5	6	7	8	9	ROW TOTAL
RQ4G COURSE PAPER—REPORT	65 16.2 35.1 6.3	60 15.0 48.4 5.8	17 4.2 34.0 1.6	48 12.0 31.8 4.6	26 6.5 46.4 2.5	52 13.0 37.4 5.0	30 7.5 41.1 2.9	99 24.7 41.6 9.6	4 1.0 23.5 0.4	401 38.8
RQ4H THESIS-DISSERTATION	25 22.1 13.5 2.4	9 8.0 7.3 0.9	6 5.3 12.0 0.6	15 13.3 9.9 1.5	6 5.3 10.7 0.6	23 20.4 16.5 2.2	9 8.0 12.3 0.9	17 15.0 7.1 1.6	3 2.7 17.6 0.3	113 10.9
RQ4I PUBLICATION	19 24.1 10.3 1.8	10 12.7 8.1 1.0	6 7.6 12.0 0.6	7 8.9 4.6 0.7	5 6.3 8.9 0.5	11 13.9 7.9 1.1	3 3.8 4.1 0.3	14 17.7 5.9 1.4	4 5.1 23.5 0.4	79 7.6
RQ4J TEACHING A COURSE	10 21.3 5.4 1.0	1 2.1 0.8 0.1	4 8.5 8.0 0.4	10 21.3 6.6 1.0	1 2.1 1.8 0.1	9 19.1 6.5 0.9	6 12.8 8.2 0.6	4 8.5 1.7 0.4	2 4.3 11.8 0.2	47 4.5
RQ4K KEEP UP ON TOPIC	24 15.7 13.0 2.3	18 11.8 14.5 1.7	10 6.5 20.0 1.0	24 15.7 15.9 2.3	5 3.3 8.9 0.5	24 15.7 17.3 2.3	9 5.9 12.3 0.9	33 21.6 13.9 3.2	6 3.9 35.3 0.6	153 14.8
COLUMN TOTAL	185 17.9	124 12.0	50 4.8	151 14.6	56 5.4	139 13.5	73 7.1	238 23.0	17 1.6	1033 100.0

PERCENTS AND TOTALS BASED ON RESPONDENTS
1033 VALID CASES   226 MISSING CASES

Figure 16. Reasons for Conducting the Online Search—Comparison by Campus.

129

Table 30.   Information Brought to and Used in MELVYL Searches

Category[1]	Information Brought[2]	Access Points Used[3]
Subject	47.0%	44.5%
Author	13.7	15.2
Author-Title	13.2	11.7
Author-Title-Subject	10.9	9.3
Title	6.3	8.8
Author-Subject	5.4	7.0
Title-Subject	3.5	3.5
TOTAL[4]	100.0	100.0

[1] Derived from User Questions 1 and 3 (Figure 13). Users who came with or searched by call number information *only* are excluded.
[2] From Table 20.
[3] From Table 24.
[4] Totals may deviate from 100 percent due to rounding.

differences in the two distributions. In Tables 31 and 32, we compare the information brought and the information used in terms of "known item" vs. subject searching and in terms of the number of information items (or access points) involved.

As Table 31 shows, users do not always apply the subject information they claim to bring to the search: known-item searching exceeds known-item information by a small amount. The principal contributor to this shift

Table 31.   "Known Item" and Subject Information Brought to and Used in MELVYL Searches

Category[1]	Information Brought[2]	Information Used[3]
Author	13.7	15.2
Title	6.3	8.8
Author-Title	13.2	11.7
Subtotal, Known Items	*33.2%*	*35.7%*
Subject	47.0	44.5
Author-Subject	5.4	7.0
Title-Subject	3.5	3.5
Author-Title-Subject	10.9	9.3
Subtotal, Subject Information	*66.8%*	*64.3%*

[1] Derived from User Questions 1 and 3 (Figure 13). Users who came with or searched by call number information *only* are excluded.
[2] From Table 21.
[3] From Table 26.

Table 32.   Number of Information Elements Brought to and Used in MELVYL Searches

Category[1]	Information Brought[2]	Information Used[3]
Author	13.7	15.2
Title	6.3	8.8
Subject	47.0	44.5
Subtotle, Known Items	*67.0%*	*68.5%*
Author-Title	13.2	11.7
Author-Subject	5.4	7.0
Title-Subject	3.5	3.5
Author-Title-Subject	10.9	9.3
Subtotal, Subject Information	*33.0%*	*31.5%*

[1] Derived from User Questions 1 and 3 (Figure 13). Users who came with or searched by call number information *only* are excluded.
[2] From Table 22.
[3] From Table 28.

is the subject category. Apparently some users bring only subject information, but search using only author and title information. It seems likely that this observation represents only a small internal inconsistency in questionnaire responses.

A similar, but smaller, discrepancy between information brought and information used appears in Table 32, where single-element searching is more prevalent than single-element information. This, again, may be attributable to inconsistent responses. Other possible causes are discussed in our report on the aggregate findings.[18]

Another source for the apparent discrepancies in Tables 30 to 32 may lie in the search strategies of MELVYL users; perhaps users who come with subject information are led by their search results to do additional

Table 33.   Keyword Indices Actually Used by MELVYL Users

Index	Search Mode		
	All	Command	Lookup
Personal Author	44.0%	40.6%	45.9%
Corporate Author ...	3.1%	6.5%	1.1%
Title	36.2%	38.3%	35.0%
Subject	68.1%	61.7%	71.7%
Series	1.5%	4.0%	0.1%
Uniform Title	0.5%	1.5%	0.0%

Note: Percentages sum to more than 100 due to legitimate use of multiple indices.

Table 34. A Comparison of Questionnaire Responses and Indices
Actually Used

Type of Search	Responses to Question 3	Search Mode (Transaction Log)		
		All	Command	Lookup
Author	15.2%	12.0%	15.4%	10.1%
Title	8.8%	6.1%	11.1%	3.4%
Au-Ti	11.7%	13.6%	11.6%	14.8%
Subject	44.5%	43.8%	38.3%	46.8%
Au-Su	7.0%	7.8%	7.3%	8.0%
Ti-Su	3.5%	4.6%	7.1%	3.2%
Au-Ti-Su	9.3%	12.1%	9.3%	13.6%
TOTAL	100.0	100.0	100.0	100.0

author-title searches, for example. This possibility merits further exploration.

Transaction Log Data

Data from the transaction logs can be used to further describe questionnaire respondents' sessions at the computer catalog. Table 33 lists the
indices actually accessed during the questionnaire search session, and
shows the percentage of respondents that used each index.[19] Percentages
sum to more than 100 since a user may have used one or more of the
indices more than once during a session. The first column shows data for
all UC respondents, the second for Command Mode users, and the third
for Lookup Mode. The major difference between Lookup and Command
Modes is that Lookup Mode respondents use the subject index more than
do Command Mode users.

Table 34 classifies Question 3 into author, title, and subject searches,
and compares these responses to transaction log data about indices used.
Responses to Question 3 are fairly consistent with actual indices. The
differences, though small, do suggest some inconsistencies in user responses or occasional misunderstandings of the terms used in the CLR
User Questionnaire, but the magnitude of the differences shows that the
problem is not methodologically important.

SECTION V: CATALOG FEATURES AND PROBLEMS

Problems with Catalog Features

The questionnaire has 28 questions about how users evaluate various
catalog features. Only 27 of these were asked of MELVYL users: Ques-

tion 14, regarding searching by call number, was excluded from the Online Questionnaire, as MELVYL does not offer this feature (Figure 17).

On Positively and Negatively Phrased Questions

Figure 17 shows that some questions were phrased *positively* (e.g., ". . . is easy . . ."), and some were phrased *negatively* (e.g., ". . . is difficult . . . ," "too slow," "too long," or "too much time,"). Dr. Paul Kantor, a consultant to the project has demonstrated that:

- Positive and negative questions appear to have different "average"

Response categories for all the following questions were:

STRONGLY AGREE	AGREE	NEITHER AGREE NOR DISAGREE	DISAGREE	STRONGLY DISAGREE	DOES NOT APPLY
1	2	3	4	5	6

11. A computer search by title is difficult.
12. A computer search by author is easy.
13. A computr search by subject is difficult.
14. A computr search by call number is easy.
15. A computer search by combined author/title is difficult.
16. Remembering commands in the middle of the search is easy.
17. Finding the correct subject term is difficult.
18. Scanning through a long display (forward or backward) is easy.
19. Increasing the result when too little is retrieved is difficult.
20. Reducing the result when too much is retrieved is easy.
21. Understanding explanations on the screen is difficult.
22. Using codes or abbreviations for searching is easy.
23. Abbreviations on the screen are easy to understand.
24. Locating call numbers on the screen is difficult.
25. Searching with a short form of a name or a word (truncation) is easy.
26. Using logical terms like AND, OR, NOT is difficult.
27. Remembering the exact sequence or order of commands is easy.
28. Understanding the initial instructions on the screen is difficult.
29. Understanding the display for a single book, journal or magazine is easy.
30. Understanding the display that shows more than a single book, journal or magazine is difficult.
31. Interrupting or stopping the display of information is easy.
32. Typing in exact spelling, initials, spaces and hyphens is difficult to do.
33. Knowing what is included in the computer catalog is easy to remember.
34. The order in which items are displayed is easy to understand.
35. Displayed messages are too long.
36. Selecting from a list of choices takes too much time.
37. Entering commands when I want to during the search process is difficult.
38. The rate at which the computer responds is too slow.

Figure 17. Catalog Features Questions on the User Questionnaire

responses, because respondents appear more likely to agree to a positively-phrased question than to disagree with a negatively-phrased one.[20]

- Therefore, the two groups of questions, positive and negative, should be treated separately in analysis and presentation.
- Negative questions particularly should not be mathematically transformed to "point in the same direction" as positive questions.

Following Dr. Kantor's advice, the two sets of questions will be treated separately in this section.

Responses to Positively-Phrased Questions

Tables 35 and 36 show the median and mean responses of users to 13 positively-phrased questions about system features and problems. A positive mean or median response here indicates that the majority of respondents *agreed* to a positively-phrased question about the online cat-

Table 35. Median Responses to Positively-Phrased Questions About System Problems

Ranked in Order from Greatest to Least Reported Difficulty

	UC	All
33. Knowing what is included in the computer catalog is easy to remember	−0.20	−0.0
25. Searching with a short form of a name or a word (truncation) is easy	0.2	0.3
20. Reducing the result when too much is retrieved is easy	0.3	0.3
18. Scanning through a long display (forward or backward) is easy	0.4	0.6
31. Interrupting or stopping the display of information is easy	0.6	0.6
27. Remembering the exact sequence or order of commands is easy	0.6	0.7
16. Remembering commands in the middle of the search is easy	0.6	0.8
22. Using codes or abbreviations for searching is easy	0.8	0.8
34. The order in which items are displayed is easy to understand	0.9	0.9
23. Abbreviations on the screen are easy to understand	1.0	0.8
14. A computer search by call number is easy	[1]	0.8
29. Understanding the display for a single book, journal or magazine is easy	1.2	1.0
12. A computer search by author is easy	1.3	1.1

[1] This feature is not available in MELVYL; the question was deleted in the final version of the Online Questionnaire.

Table 36. Mean Responses to Positively-Phrased Questions About System Problems

Ranked in Order from Greatest to Least Reported Difficulty

	UC	All
33. Knowing what is included in the computer catalog is easy to remember	−0.13	−0.02
25. Searching with a short form of a name or a word (truncation) is easy	0.22	0.19
18. Scanning through a long display (forward or backward) is easy	0.23	0.30
20. Reducing the result when too much is retrieved is easy	0.25	0.19
31. Interrupting or stopping the display of information is easy	0.33	0.38
16. Remembering commands in the middle of the search is easy	0.39	0.55
27. Remembering the exact sequence or order of commands is easy	0.46	0.50
22. Using codes or abbreviations for searching is easy	0.64	0.58
34. The order in which items are displayed is easy to understand	0.79	0.68
23. Abbreviations on the screen are easy to understand	0.90	0.60
14. A computer search by call number is easy	[1]	0.65
12. A computer search by author is easy	1.07	1.02
29. Understanding the display for a single book, journal or magazine is easy	1.09	0.89

[1] This feature is not available in MELVYL; the question was deleted in the final version of the Online Questionnaire.

alog.[21] The larger the value, the more respondents agreed or strongly agreed, i.e., the fewer indicated that they had a problem. The questions in Tables 35 and 36 are therefore ranked from negative measures to positive ones, so that the most serious problems appear at the top of the list. The most serious problem in the group appears to be "remembering what is included in the computer catalog"—the median score indicates that a majority of users found this difficult. For the remaining questions in this group, the majority of users who provided valid responses appeared not to have problems (median scores in Table 35 are positive). The next four most serious problems, in rank order, are:

- Using truncation
- Reducing the result when too much is retrieved
- Scanning through a long display
- Interrupting the display.

Rankings by mean and by median differ somewhat for UC libraries.

The differences do not affect the "top five" list, but change the ranking among the five problems somewhat.

Comparing the mean scores for UC and aggregate responses in Table 36 suggests that MELVYL users experience greater than average problems in the following areas:[22]

- Knowing what is included in the computer catalog
- Scanning through a long display (forward or backward)
- Interrupting or stopping the display of information
- Remembering commands in the middle of the search
- Remembering the exact sequence or order of commands.

Conversely, MELVYL users apparently found the following easier than do those using many other online catalogs:

- Searching with a short form of a name or a word (truncation)
- Reducing the result when too much is retrieved
- Using codes or abbreviations for searching
- The order in which items are displayed

Table 37.   Median Responses to Negatively-Phrased Questions About System Problems

Ranked in Order from Greatest to Least Reported Difficulty	UC	All
19. Increasing the result when too little is retrieved is difficult	0.6	0.4
17. Finding the correct subject term is difficult	0.6	0.1
37. Entering commands when I want to during the search process is difficult	−0.1	−0.5
38. The rate at which the computer responds is too slow	−0.3	−0.6
36. Selecting from a list of choices takes too much time	−0.6	−0.7
26. Using logical terms like AND, OR, NOT is difficult	−0.7	−0.5
13. A computer search by subject is difficult	−0.7	−0.6
32. Typing in exact spelling, initials, spaces and hyphens is difficult to do	−0.7	−0.8
35. Displayed messages are too long	−0.7	−0.8
30. Understanding the display that shows more than a single book journal or magazine is difficult	−1.0	−0.9
24. Locating call numbers on the screen is difficult	−1.1	−1.0
15. A computer search by combined author/title is difficult . . .	−1.2	−1.0
11. A computer search by title is difficult	−1.2	−1.1
28. Understanding the initial instructions on the screen is difficult	−1.3	−0.9
21. Understanding explanations on the screen is difficult	−1.3	−1.0

- Abbreviations on the screen
- A computer search by author
- Understanding the display for a single book, journal or magazine.

Responses to Negatively-Phrased Questions

Table 37 lists the median responses to 15 negatively-phrased questions about system features, and Table 38 contains mean responses to these questions. In these tables, the meaning of positive and negative signs is reversed from Tables 35 and 36. A positive score indicates that a majority *agreed* with a *negative* statement about the catalog, i.e., they had a problem. Scores in Tables 37 and 38 are therefore ordered from positive to negative, with the largest positive scores denoting the most common problems.

Tables 37 and 38 both show that the "top 5" problems in this group of questions are:

- Increasing the search result
- Finding the correct subject term
- Entering commands when I want to

Table 38. Mean Responses to Negatively-Phrased Questions About System Problems

Ranked in Order from Greatest to Least Reported Difficulty	UC	All
19. Increasing the result when too little is retrieved is difficult	0.38	0.23
17. Finding the correct subject term is difficult . . . . , ...	0.34	0.08
37. Entering commands when I want to during the search process is difficult	−0.05	−0.27
38. The rate at which the computer responds is too slow	−0.13	−0.27
36. Selecting from a list of choices takes too much time	−0.41	−0.45
32. Typing in exact spelling, initials, spaces and hyphens is difficult to do	−0.47	−0.55
35. Displayed messages are too long	−0.47	−0.70
13. A computer search by subject is difficult	−0.48	−0.36
26. Using logical terms like AND, OR, NOT is difficult	−0.54	−0.40
30. Understanding the display that shows more than a single book journal or magazine is difficult	−0.90	−0.79
24. Locating call numbers on the screen is difficult	−0.92	−0.82
11. A computer search by title is difficult	−0.96	−0.91
15. A computer search by combined author/title is difficult . . .	−0.97	−0.85
28. Understanding the initial instructions on the screen is difficult	−1.10	−0.76
21. Understanding explanations on the screen is difficult	−1.14	−0.83

- Slow computer responses
- Time required to select from a list of choices.

For the first two items, increasing the search result and finding the correct subject term, a majority of users expressed difficulty (Table 37).

Table 38 shows that in seven of these 15 areas, MELVYL users may have greater than average difficulty:[23]

- Increasing the result when too little is retrieved
- Finding the correct subject term
- Entering commands when I want to during the search process
- The rate at which the computer responds
- Selecting from a list of choices
- Typing in exact spelling, initials, spaces and hyphens
- Displayed messages are too long.

By contrast, MELVYL users apparently experience less serious problems in the following areas:

- A computer search by subject
- Using logical terms like AND, OR, NOT
- Understanding the display that shows more than a single book, journal or magazine
- Locating call numbers on the screen
- A computer search by title
- A computer search by combined author/title
- Understanding the initial instructions on the screen
- Understanding explanations on the screen.

Lookup Mode Users Have More Serious Problems

In 14 of the 27 Likert-scale questions about system problems, respondents who were using MELVYL's Lookup Mode offered responses that were statistically different from those of Command Mode users. Table 39 lists these 14 questions in descending order according to the strength of the difference. In this case, the strength of difference is measured by the Pearson correlation between the search mode of the session and the response to the Likert question, and the largest correlation is listed first in the table.

It is notable that the user's search mode is not a strong contributor to the user's response; the largest correlation reported in Table 39 is 0.20, a relatively mild relationship.

Table 39. Significant Differences in System Problems by Search
Mode

Ranked in Order from Greatest to Least Difference

	"Problem" Mode[1]	*Correlation*[2]
22. Using codes or abbreviations for searching is easy . . .	L	.20
25. Searching with a short form of a name or a word (truncation) is easy	L	.15
26. Using logical terms like AND, OR, NOT is difficult	L	.13
37. Entering commands when I want to during the search process is difficult	L	.13
20. Reducing the result when too much is retrieved is easy	L	.10
30. Understanding the display that shows more than a single book journal or magazine is difficult	L	.10
11. A computer search by title is difficult	L	.09
31. Interrupting or stopping the display of information is easy	L	.09
18. Scanning through a long display (forward or backward) is easy	C	.08
27. Remembering the exact sequence or order of commands is easy	L	.07
28. Understanding the initial instructions on the screen is difficult	L	.07
36. Selecting from a list of choices takes too much time	C	.05
21. Understanding explanations on the screen is difficult	L	.02

[1] Denotes the mode of respondents reporting the greatest difficulty on each question. "L" is Lookup Mode, "C" is Command Mode.
[2] Pearson product moment correlation between question response and search mode; only the absolute value of the correlation coefficient is reported.

In all but two cases, Lookup users appear to have more difficulty than users of Command Mode. In the two cases where Command Mode presents greater problems, the relationship is weak (correlations equal 0.08 and 0.02 respectively). Command Mode users indicate problems with "scanning through a long display" (Question 18) and the time required for "selecting from a list of choices" (Question 36), both areas in which Command Mode would be expected to perform better than Lookup. One explanation for the "long display" problem is that users of Command Mode are presented by default with the "brief" display format, a paragraph display, while Lookup Mode users get the "review" format, a one- or two-line brief record, unless they ask for a fuller display.

The problem with "selecting from a list of choices" may be related to this. If respondents considered selecting from numbered bibliographic items as an aspect of this question, then selecting the desired record from a list of "choices" in brief format would be quite time-consuming for Command Mode users.

While the interpretation of differences for individual questions may be unclear, the evidence taken as a whole suggests that Lookup users have more difficulty using the catalog, although the difference is not great. We cannot, however, be sure whether the difference is attributable to the search modes themselves, or to differences in the skills and attitudes of the users who select one mode over the other.

Transaction Log Data

Data from the transaction logs provides information on types and frequency of user errors and requests for HELP. Frequent errors or requests for HELP may be indications of problems with the computer catalog.

User Errors

Out of the 1,259 sessions for which we have questionnaire data, 326 (25.9 percent) were sessions in which users made errors and were sent error messages. Of these, 147 users made one error, 67 users made 2, 36 made 3, and the rest (76) made 4 or more errors. Error data linked with questionnaire data have been reduced to the number of errors rather than the type of errors for the purposes of this analysis. Detailed data about error situations (including the actual text of the user entries) are available in the computer transaction files. There may be a relationship between types (rather than numbers) of errors committed and reported problems with catalog features, but the necessary classification of errors and analysis of relationships was not feasible for this study.

Users who got help from signs and brochures or from library staff are most likely to commit errors (Table 40); those who either did not obtain help or got it from the computer committed the fewest errors. Those who originally learned to use the catalog from library staff or printed instruc-

Table 40. Sources of Help and User Errors

Ranked in Order of Relative Frequency of Errors

Source of Instruction	Sessions With No Errors	Sessions With One Or More Errors
a. Printed material or signs	62.6%	37.4%
c. Library staff members	65.2	34.8
d. Person nearby	69.0	31.0
b. Instructions on the terminal screen	73.7	26.3
e. I did not get help	78.5	21.5

Table 41. Methods of Learning to Use the Computer Catalog

Ranked in Order of Relative Frequency of Errors

Source of Instruction	Sessions With No Errors	Sessions With One Or More Errors
d. From the library staff	68.8%	31.3%
b. Using printed instructions	70.1	29.9
e. From a library course or orientation	72.2	27.8
c. Using instructions on the terminal screen . .	73.1	26.9
g. By myself without any help	76.1	23.9
a. From a friend or someone at a nearby terminal	80.8	19.2

tions tend to make more errors; users who learned from a friend or took no instruction or assistance make fewer errors (Table 41). It should be pointed out that interpretation of these findings is difficult. It is unclear whether or not the method of instruction or assistance influences error rates, whether errors influence disposition to seek such help (e.g., those who make many errors in a session tend to ask staff for assistance), or whether some predisposition or "external" characteristic influences both factors (e.g., "nervous" users tend to make many errors *and* are reluctant to seek, or fail to understand, online assistance).

Command Mode users make more errors than Lookup Mode users. About half (50.1 percent) of Command Mode users made at least one error in their search, whereas only 10.8 percent of Lookup Mode users made errors. This is not surprising since Lookup Mode doesn't leave much room for users to make explicit errors.[24] Experience with other computer systems does not seem to make users of MELVYL less likely to make errors. In fact, the reverse is true; people who use other systems weekly are more likely than any other group to make errors when using MELVYL. Users who have never used another computer system are least likely to make errors.[25] See Table 42.

Table 42. Experience with Other Computer Systems and User Errors

Frequency of Use of Other Computers	Sessions With No Errors	Sessions With One Or More Errors
a. Daily	75.0%	25.0%
b. Weekly	62.9	37.1
c. Monthly	78.8	21.2
d. About 4 times a year	72.1	27.9
e. About once a year	74.3	25.7
f. Never	81.2	18.8

HELP Requests

HELP, like error messages, is supplied by the MELVYL system to aid users in their searches. HELP is of two sorts. It can be requested by the user, or, in certain situations, is automatically supplied. Users may request assistance by simply typing HELP. HELP messages are designed to respond to the situation at hand.[26] Users may request further assistance by typing HELP plus a keyword, and elicit information on various aspects of MELVYL. The system will also automatically respond with a HELP message if the user makes the same error 3 or more times in a row.

Of the 1,259 questionnaire respondents, 199 (15.8 percent) requested help at some time during their sessions. Of these, 45.2 percent requested help once, 19.1 percent twice, 13.6 percent three times. Help alone was requested by 173 respondents, once by 67.1 percent, twice by 20.2 percent, and 3 times by 6.4 percent. Help with a keyword was requested by 113 respondents at least once, and help was automatically supplied to 12 respondents. Of the people who checked the response category, "I did not get help" for Question 8, 10.4 percent of them actually requested HELP from the system.

More Command Mode users (37.8 percent) use help than do Lookup Mode users (2.0 percent). The use of help for Command Mode users seems to be related to frequency of use; half of the Command Mode users who never used MELVYL before request HELP, while only 25.2 percent who use MELVYL most visits request HELP.

Neither using HELP nor committing errors seems to have an influence on success or satisfaction with the search. In some cases, HELP and errors have a slight relationship with finding other things of interest (question 7) or with finding more or less relevant material. These relationships will require further analysis, and may be related to the kinds of errors users make, or the sort of HELP they have requested. The factors related to user satisfaction with MELVYL will be discussed further in Section VII.

Computer Response Time

As noted earlier, many users perceive that the computer takes too long to respond to their MELVYL search commands. The transaction log linkage allows us to explore the users' perceptions about response times with the actual response times recorded by the system.

For each questionnaire, two response time measures are available:

1. The *total response time*, which is the sum of the response times for all commands entered during a user's session.

2. The *mean response time*, which is the average response time for each command in the session, i.e., the total response time divided by the number of commands.

For respondents to the MELVYL questionnaire, we found that the overall average of total response times was 39.77 seconds, for Command Mode sessions, 37.28 seconds, and for Lookup Mode sessions, 41.30 seconds. The average of mean response times for all respondents was 11.82 seconds, for Command Mode users, 7.77 seconds, and for Lookup Mode users, 14.31 seconds. Thus, the average time for MELVYL to respond to a single Command Mode command is only about half as long as for a single Lookup Mode command; however, Lookup and Command Mode sessions involve about the same total response time (on the average), presumably because Command Mode users enter more commands during their sessions.

Table 43 shows how mean and total response times differ among those who agreed or disagreed with the statement, "the rate at which the computer responds is too slow" (Question 38). In most cases, user responses are at least reasonably consistent with actual system responses; the longer the response time, the more likely the user to agree with the statement

Table 43. Perceived Response Time Problems and Actual Response Times, by Search Mode

	Response to Question 38, *"The Rate at Which the Computer Responds is Too Slow:"*				
	Strongly Disagree	Disagree	Neither Agree Nor Disagree	Agree	Strongly Agree
Average Mean Response Time (seconds)[1]					
All Respondents	8.74	11.44	12.60	12.60	13.65
Lookup Mode	10.39	14.25	14.10	15.19	18.79
Command Mode	4.70	6.62	10.49	8.76	6.43
Average Total Response Time (seconds)[2]					
All Respondents	31.11	35.08	36.90	45.09	57.37
Lookup Mode	33.36	36.75	38.50	48.23	57.51
Command Mode	25.63	32.22	34.67	40.46	57.17

Notes:

[1] Arithmetic mean of all response times in the user's session (sum of response times for all commands divided by the number of commands).

[2] Sum of response times for all commands entered during the user's session.

(i.e., to consider response time a problem). The exception lies with the mean response times of Command Mode users. The largest average mean response time for this group is among users who neither agreed nor disagreed with the statement (10.49 seconds). The mean response times for users who had the most emphatic opinions on *either* side of the response time question were significantly shorter than for this "indifferent" group.

Even though response time patterns for other groups appear to show that perceptions about response time problems are logically related to actual response times, the relationships proved to have little or no statistical significance; in most cases, significant relationships were found only with total response time (a variable whose dimensions are affected by session length and other intervening factors) rather than mean response time (a more direct measure of system response). It was also noted that there was no significant difference between Lookup and Command Mode users with regard to their perceptions of response problems, despite the fact that Command Mode response times are considerably shorter than those for Lookup Mode. These findings caused us to ask whether other characteristics of the MELVYL session might be more influential than measured response time in forming users' attitudes about system response.

To explore this question, regression analyses were constructed using the responses to Question 38 as the dependent variable. Included in the analysis were such factors as the mean and/or total response time, the search mode, the number of items retrieved, the display format used for presentation of results, and the incidence of explicit "long searches," those for which MELVYL notifies the user that extra time will be required.

It was found that only search mode and response time were significantly related to the users' perceptions of response time problems. The results are manifest in two regression models, one including only mean response time and one including only total response time. The findings are shown in Table 44.

The analysis shows four things:

1. Total response time is a slightly better predictor of perceived problems than is mean response time (for Model 2, R^2 is greater, and t-statistics and Beta coefficients indicate a better "fit" to the data). It would appear that the cumulative effects of system response over the course of a session, rather than MELVYL's single-command or "average" performance, has a greater influence on users' attitudes. This finding could be taken to support other research suggesting that *consistency* of response times, rather than their duration, may be more important to users.[27]

Table 44. Determinants of Perceived Response Time Problems

Dependent Variable: Question 38, *"The Rate at Which the Computer Responds is Too Slow:"*

	Variable	Coefficient	Significance of t	Beta Coefficient	R^2
Model 1	Search Mode	−0.276	0.000	0.170	
	Mean Response	0.005	0.032	0.087	0.021
Model 2	Search Mode	−0.283	0.000	0.174	
	Total Response	0.002	0.003	0.114	0.026

2.   Search mode is a more important determinant of user response than is system response time (Beta coefficients[28] are larger for the search mode variable than for the response time variable in both models). It may be that the use of a particular search mode influences (or is influenced by) the users' *expectations* about system response time.

3.   Command Mode users are less satisfied with response time than Lookup Mode users. Despite the fact that Command Mode is faster, the sign of the coefficient on search mode shows that Command Mode users are, *a priori*, more likely to report a problem with response time, regardless of the actual system responses they experience.[29] To the extent that user perception of response problems arises from expectations rather than immediate experience, it would appear that MELVYL users expect very (perhaps unrealistically) fast response times from Command Mode.

4.   Neither search mode nor response time are very successful at predicting users' perceptions. R-square statistics are only in the 0.02 to 0.03 range, indicating that these variables explain only two to three percent of the total variance for Question 38. To a large extent the range of user perceptions about system response remains unexplained by this analysis.

SECTION VI: LIBRARY PROBLEMS

Introduction

Six questions on the User Questionnaire asked how various library services helped users with the online catalog, and what problems they experienced with them. These questions also asked about several aspects of equipment and environment considered to be within the purview of the library, rather than the computer system *per se*. The questions are presented in Figure 18.

8. I got help in doing this computer catalog search from:
(Mark *ALL* that apply)
a. Printed material or signs
b. Instructions on the terminal screen
c. Library staff member
d. Person nearby
e. I did not get help.

Response categories for the following questions were:

STRONGLY AGREE	AGREE	NEITHER AGREE NOR DISAGREE	DISAGREE	STRONGLY DISAGREE	DOES NOT APPLY
1	2	3	4	5	6

39. The availability of signs and brochures is adequate.
40. Signs and brochures are not very helpful.
41. The staff advice is often not helpful.
42. It is hard to find a free terminal.

43. When I use the computer catalog terminal:
(Mark *YES* or *NO*)

	YES	*NO*
a. The keyboard is confusing to use	Y	N
b. There is too much glare on the screen	Y	N
c. The letters and numbers are easy to read	Y	N
d. The lighting around the terminal is too bright .	Y	N
e. There is enough writing space at the terminal	Y	N
f. Nearby noise is distracting	Y	N
g. The terminal table is too high or too low ...	Y	N
h. The printer is easy to use	Y	N

Figure 18. Library Environment Questions on the User Questionnaire

Table 45. Sources of Help Used by Online Catalog Users

Ranked in Order of Frequency of Response[1]

Question 8: *I got help in doing this computer catalog search from (Mark ALL that apply)*

	University of California	All Respondents
e. I did not get help	44.2%	31.0%
b. Instructions on the terminal screen	43.9	32.0
a. Printed material or signs	17.2	40.6
c. Library staff members	4.4	22.2
d. Person nearby	4.0	5.6

[1] Percentages sum to more than 100 due to legitimate multiple responses.

CLR USER QUESTIONNAIRE: LIBRARY TYPE COMPARISON XTABS   04/04/83   PAGE 25
FILE   FINAL   (CREATION DATE = 08/03/82)
* CROSSTABULATION * * * * * * * * * * * * * * *
    RQUEST8 (TABULATING   1) I GOT HELP FROM:
BY TERMLOC2
*   PAGE 1 OF 1

TERMLOC2

RQUEST8 — COUNT / ROW PCT / COL PCT / TAB PCT	BERKE-LEY 1	DAVIS 2	IRVINE 3	LA 4	RIVER-SIDE 5	SANTA BARBARA 6	SANTA CRUZ 7	SAN DIEGO 8	SAN FRAN-CISCO 9	ROW TOTAL
RQ8A PRINTED MATTER-SIGNS	33 19.4 18.3 3.3	23 13.5 19.3 2.3	8 4.7 17.4 0.8	29 17.1 20.0 2.9	12 7.1 21.4 1.2	23 13.5 17.2 2.3	9 5.3 12.7 0.9	31 18.2 13.4 3.1	2 1.2 12.5 0.2	170 17.0
RQ8B TERMINAL SCREEN INST	84 19.3 46.7 8.4	58 13.3 48.7 5.8	15 3.4 32.6 1.5	62 14.3 42.8 6.2	28 6.4 50.0 2.8	63 14.5 47.0 6.3	35 8.0 49.3 3.5	85 19.5 36.8 8.5	5 1.1 31.3 0.5	435 43.6
RQ8C LIBRARY STAFF MEMBER	6 13.6 3.3 0.6	3 6.8 2.5 0.3	3 6.8 6.5 0.3	4 9.1 2.8 0.4	3 6.8 5.4 0.3	5 11.4 3.7 0.5	2 4.5 2.8 0.2	18 40.9 7.8 1.8	0 0.0 0.0 0.0	44 4.4
RQ8D PERSON NEARBY	2 5.0 1.1 0.2	7 17.5 5.9 0.7	2 5.0 4.3 0.2	4 10.0 2.8 0.4	4 10.0 7.1 0.4	6 15.0 4.5 0.6	1 2.5 1.4 0.1	12 30.0 5.2 1.2	2 5.0 12.5 0.2	40 4.0
RQ8E I DID NOT GET HELP	75 16.9 41.7 7.5	45 10.2 37.8 4.5	22 5.0 47.8 2.2	67 15.1 46.2 6.7	18 4.1 32.1 1.8	58 13.1 43.3 5.8	30 6.8 42.3 3.0	119 26.9 51.5 11.9	9 2.0 56.3 0.9	443 44.4
COLUMN TOTAL	180 18.0	119 11.9	46 4.6	145 14.5	56 5.6	134 13.4	71 7.1	231 23.1	16 1.6	998 100.0

PERCENTS AND TOTALS BASED ON RESPONDENTS
998 VALID CASES   261 MISSING CASES

Figure 19. Sources of Help Used—Comparison by Campus.

147

Where Do MELVYL Users Get Help?

As Table 45 shows, 44.2 percent of MELVYL users do not get help in their online searches, and 43.9 percent use instructions on the terminal screen. Both of these figures are considerably higher than those for the aggregate population, where most users get help from printed material or signs. Only 4.4 percent of MELVYL users get help from staff compared to 22.2 percent in the aggregate analysis.

Sources of help vary considerably from campus to campus. Over half of the respondents from both San Diego and San Francisco said they did not get help in their search, and the percentage of those who said they used terminal screen instructions was lower at these campuses than at others. However, a higher percentage of respondents from San Diego said they got help from library staff than at any other campus, though this percentage (7.8 percent) is still much lower than the aggregate response of 22.2 percent. About half of the respondents from Riverside, San Diego, and Davis got help from terminal screen instructions, and use of printed matter and signs was highest at Riverside, Davis, and Los Angeles (Figure 19).

Terminal Availability Is the Most Serious Library Service Problem

Median and mean responses to the four Likert-scale questions about library support services are shown in Tables 46 and 47. The majority of users did not have problems with the services listed. Both median and mean responses show terminal availability to be the most serious matter to respondents. Median responses also show that the majority of MEL-VYL users found terminal availability to be a problem (Table 47). Terminal availability is more of a problem at some campuses than others. It is most serious at Los Angeles, followed by Berkeley and Irvine. At Santa

Table 46. Mean Responses to Questions About Library Service Problems

	UC	All
39. The availability of signs and brochures is adequate	0.35	0.46
40. Signs and brochures are not very helpful . . .	−0.56	−0.68
41. The staff advice is often not helpful	−0.38	−0.85
42. It is hard to find a free terminal	−0.10	−0.29

Table 47.   Median Responses to Questions About Library Service
Problems

	UC	All
39. The availability of signs and brochures is adequate	0.6	0.7
40. Signs and brochures are not very useful . . .	−0.7	−0.9
41. The staff advice is often not helpful	−0.4	−1.0
42. It is hard to find a free terminal	0.1	−0.6

Barbara, San Francisco, San Diego, and Riverside terminal availability
does not present as much of a problem (Figure 20). Responses to Question
41 show that a smaller percentage of MELVYL users disagreed with the
negatively phrased "Staff advice is often not helpful" suggesting that,
although the majority of respondents appreciated the level of staff support
provided, staff advice presents a potential problem for MELVYL users
relative to users at other institutions with computer catalogs.

The Chief Physical Support Problem Is Insufficient Writing
Space at the Terminal

Table 48 shows the responses of MELVYL users to the eight categories
in Question 43 about problems with equipment and the library environment. The most important problem, mentioned by 64.1 percent of respondents, is the lack of adequate writing space around terminals. The

Table 48.   MELVYL User Problems with Library Equipment and
Facilities

Ranked in Order of Frequency of Response[1]

Question 43: *When I use the computer catalog terminal:*

	Problem	Not A Problem
e. There is enough writing space at the terminal	64.1	35.9
c. The letters and numbers are easy to read . . .	32.1	67.9
b. There is too much glare on the screen	11.4	88.6
d. The lighting around the terminal is too bright	10.4	89.6
g. The terminal table is too high or too low	10.3	89.7
f. Nearby noise is distracting	7.4	92.6
a. The keyboard is confusing to use	5.5	94.0

[1] Response percentages are reordered from "YES" and "NO" to "PROBLEM" and "NOT A PROB-
LEM" according to the sense of the question: see Figure 18 for the text of the original question.

```
* * * * * * * * * * * * * * * * * * * * * * CROSSTABULATION OF * * * * * * * * * * * * * * * * *
      RQ42    HARD TO FIND FREE TERMINAL
BY TERMLOC2                                    BY TERMLOC2
* * * * * * * * * * * * * * * * * * * * * * * * * * * * * * * * * * * * * * * * * * * PAGE 1 OF 1
```

TERMLOC2

RQ42	COUNT ROW PCT COL PCT TOT PCT	BERKE- LEY 1.	DAVIS 2.	IRVINE 3.	LA 4.	RIVER- SIDE 5.	SANTA BARBARA 6.	SANTA CRUZ 7.	SAN DIEGO 8.	SAN FRAN- CISCO 9.	ROW TOTAL
STRONGLY DISAGREE	-2.	14 13.7 9.5 1.7	9 8.8 8.6 1.1	5 4.9 13.2 0.6	6 5.9 5.1 0.7	9 8.8 20.5 1.1	20 19.6 18.9 2.4	7 6.9 10.9 0.9	30 29.4 16.0 3.6	2 2.0 15.4 0.2	102 12.4
DISAGREE	-1.	32 14.3 21.6 3.9	22 9.8 21.0 2.7	8 3.6 21.1 1.0	15 6.7 12.8 1.8	14 6.3 31.8 1.7	49 21.9 46.2 6.0	18 8.0 28.1 2.2	60 26.8 31.9 7.3	6 2.7 46.2 0.7	224 27.2
NEITHER A OR D	0.	25 17.2 16.9 3.0	31 21.4 29.5 3.8	5 3.4 13.2 0.6	11 7.6 9.4 1.3	9 6.2 20.5 1.1	19 13.1 17.9 2.3	10 6.9 15.6 1.2	32 22.1 17.0 3.9	3 2.1 23.1 0.4	145 17.6
AGREE	1.	43 22.9 29.1 5.2	23 12.2 21.9 2.8	10 5.3 26.3 1.2	39 20.7 33.3 4.7	6 3.2 13.6 0.7	11 5.9 10.4 1.3	22 11.7 34.4 2.7	34 18.1 18.1 4.1	0 0.0 0.0 0.0	188 22.8
STRONGLY AGREE	2.	34 20.7 23.0 4.1	20 12.2 19.0 2.4	10 6.1 26.3 1.2	46 28.0 39.3 5.6	6 3.7 13.6 0.7	7 4.3 6.6 0.9	7 4.3 10.9 0.9	32 19.5 17.0 3.9	2 1.2 15.4 0.2	164 19.9
COLUMN TOTAL		148 18.0	105 12.8	38 4.6	117 14.2	44 5.3	106 12.9	64 7.8	188 22.8	13 1.6	823 100.0

150

```
  6 OUT OF   45 ( 13.3%) OF THE VALID CELLS HAVE EXPECTED CELL FREQUENCY LESS THAN 5.0
MINIMUM EXPECTED CELL FREQUENCY = 1.611
CHI SQUARE =    122.83266 WITH    32 DEGREES OF FREEDOM    SIGNIFICANCE = 0.0000
CRAMER'S V =    0.19316
CONTINGENCY COEFFICIENT =    0.36037
LAMBDA (ASYMMETRIC) =    0.09516 WITH RQ42    DEPENDENT    = 0.03622    WITH TERMLOC2 DEPENDENT.
LAMBDA (SYMMETRIC) =    0.06483
UNCERTAINTY COEFFICIENT (ASYMMETRIC) =    0.04831 WITH RQ42    DEPENDENT.    = 0.03787 WITH TERMLOC2
  DEPENDENT.
UNCERTAINTY COEFFICIENT (SYMMETRIC) =    0.04246
KENDALL'S TAU B =   -0.13514    SIGNIFICANCE = 0.0000
KENDALL'S TAU C =   -0.13831    SIGNIFICANCE = 0.0000
GAMMA =   -0.16406
SOMERS'S D (ASYMMETRIC) =   -0.13000 WITH RQ42    DEPENDENT.    =   -0.14048 WITH TERMLOC2 DEPENDENT.
SOMERS'S D (SYMMETRIC) =   -0.13504
```

Figure 20. Terminal Availability—Comparison by Campus.

CLR USER QUESTIONNAIRE: LIBRARY TYPE COMPARISON XTABS
FILE   FINAL   (CREATION DATE = 08/03/82)
04/04/83

* * * * * * * * * * * * * * * CROSSTABULATION * * * * * * * * * * * * *
* * * RQUEST43 (TABULATING   1) WHEN I USE THE COMPUTER CATALOG TERMINAL
BY TERMLOC2
* PAGE 1 OF 2

TERMLOC2

RQUEST43 — COUNT / ROW PCT / COL PCT / TAB PCT	BERKE-LEY 1	DAVIS 2	IRVINE 3	LA 4	RIVER-SIDE 5	SANTA BARBARA 6	SANTA CRUZ 7	SAN DIEGO 8	SAN FRAN-CISCO 9	ROW TOTAL
RQ43A KEYBOARD CONFUSING	9 / 20.5 / 6.8 / 1.3	4 / 9.1 / 4.4 / 0.6	2 / 4.5 / 6.9 / 0.3	6 / 13.6 / 6.0 / 0.8	3 / 6.8 / 8.3 / 0.4	4 / 9.1 / 4.4 / 0.6	5 / 11.4 / 8.8 / 0.7	9 / 20.5 / 5.5 / 1.3	2 / 4.5 / 18.2 / 0.3	44 / 6.2
RQ43B GLARE ON SCREEN	21 / 22.8 / 15.8 / 3.0	7 / 7.6 / 7.7 / 1.0	3 / 3.3 / 10.3 / 0.4	17 / 18.5 / 17.0 / 2.4	4 / 4.3 / 11.1 / 0.6	9 / 9.8 / 10.0 / 1.3	14 / 15.2 / 24.6 / 2.0	17 / 18.5 / 10.4 / 2.4	0 / 0.0 / 0.0 / 0.0	92 / 13.0
RQ43C LETTERS EASY TO READ	94 / 17.2 / 70.7 / 13.2	75 / 13.7 / 82.4 / 10.6	24 / 4.4 / 82.8 / 3.4	71 / 13.0 / 71.0 / 10.0	30 / 5.5 / 83.3 / 4.2	76 / 13.9 / 84.4 / 10.7	37 / 6.8 / 64.9 / 5.2	132 / 24.1 / 81.0 / 18.6	8 / 1.5 / 72.7 / 1.1	547 / 77.0
RQ43D LIGHTING TOO BRIGHT	16 / 19.3 / 12.0 / 2.3	8 / 9.6 / 8.8 / 1.1	2 / 2.4 / 6.9 / 0.3	14 / 16.9 / 14.0 / 2.0	4 / 4.8 / 11.1 / 0.6	8 / 9.6 / 8.9 / 1.1	14 / 16.9 / 24.6 / 2.0	16 / 19.3 / 9.8 / 2.3	1 / 1.2 / 9.1 / 0.1	83 / 11.7
RQ43E WRITING SPACE OK	51 / 17.8 / 38.3 / 7.2	38 / 13.2 / 41.8 / 5.4	13 / 4.5 / 44.8 / 1.8	40 / 13.9 / 40.0 / 5.6	13 / 4.5 / 36.1 / 1.8	47 / 16.4 / 52.2 / 6.6	18 / 6.3 / 31.6 / 2.5	64 / 22.3 / 39.3 / 9.0	3 / 1.0 / 27.3 / 0.4	287 / 40.0
RQ43F NOISE DISTRACTING	13 / 22.0 / 9.8 / 1.8	4 / 6.8 / 4.4 / 0.6	4 / 6.8 / 13.8 / 0.6	13 / 22.0 / 13.0 / 1.8	2 / 3.4 / 5.6 / 0.3	10 / 16.9 / 11.1 / 1.4	3 / 3.4 / 3.5 / 0.3	10 / 16.9 / 6.1 / 1.4	1 / 1.7 / 9.1 / 0.1	59 / 8.3
RQ53G TABLE HEIGHT RULE	27 / 31.8 / 20.3 / 3.8	3 / 3.5 / 3.3 / 0.4	7 / 8.2 / 24.1 / 1.0	8 / 9.4 / 8.0 / 1.1	3 / 3.5 / 8.3 / 0.4	9 / 10.6 / 10.0 / 1.3	6 / 7.1 / 10.5 / 0.8	21 / 24.7 / 12.9 / 3.0	1 / 1.2 / 9.1 / 0.1	85 / 12.0
COLUMN TOTAL	133 / 18.7	91 / 12.8	29 / 4.1	100 / 14.1	36 / 5.1	90 / 12.7	57 / 8.0	163 / 23.0	11 / 1.5	710 / 100.0

PERCENTS AND TOTALS BASED ON RESPONDENTS
710 VALID CASES   549 MISSING CASES

Figure 21. Problems with Library Equipment and Facilities—Comparison by Campus

second-ranking problem, mentioned by 32.1 percent of respondents, is legibility of characters on the screen. Glare on the terminal screen is found to be a problem by 11.4 percent of respondents, ambient lighting by 10.4 percent, and terminal table height by 10.3 percent. These problems vary in intensity at the different campuses. At Santa Cruz, glare on the screen, legibility of characters on the terminal screen, and ambient lighting present more of a problem than at other campuses. Respondents at Irvine and Los Angeles find noise to be particularly troublesome, and respondents at Irvine and Berkeley have problems with terminal table height (Figure 21).

SECTION VII: USER SATISFACTION

General

Questions 5 to 7, 9 and 10 of the User Questionnaire address users' satisfaction with the search just completed and with the online catalog in general. These questions are displayed in Figure 22.

```
5. In this computer search I found: (Mark ONE only)
a. More than I was looking for
b. All that I was looking for
c. Some of what I was looking for
d. Nothing I was looking for

6. In relation to what I was looking for, this computer search
   was: (Mark ONE ony)
a. Very satisfactory
b. Somewhat satisfactory
c. Somewhat unsatisfactory
d. Very unsatisfactory

7. I came across things of interest other than what I was
   looking for:
a. Yes
b. No

9. My overall or general attitude toward the computer catalog
   is: (Mark ONE only)
a. Very favorable
b. Somewhat favorable
c. Somewhat unfavorable
d. Very unfavorable

10. Compared to the card, book, or microfiche catalog in this
    library, the computer catlog is: (Mark ONE only)
a. Better
b. About the same
c. Worse
d. Can't decide
```

Figure 22.   User Satisfaction Questions on the User Questionnaire

Evaluation of the Most Recent Search

As Table 49 shows, most users found some relevant material in their searches, though at the University of California, the percentage of users who find more than or all that they were looking for is somewhat lower than for users of online catalogs in general.[30] The percentage of those who found nothing is quite high for MELVYL users, 31.5 percent, though this varies from campus to campus.

At Riverside, 19.3 percent of respondents found more than they were looking for, and at Irvine and San Diego, 16.7 percent and 15 percent of respondents, respectively, found more. At San Diego and Irvine, 19.7 percent and 18.8 percent of respondents found all that they were looking for, and at both Berkeley and San Francisco, 17.6 percent found everything they wanted. These percentages are higher than for other campuses, where more users tended to find only some or none of the information they sought (Figure 23).[31] A slightly higher percentage of Command Mode users found more, all, or some of what they were looking for than did respondents who used Lookup Mode (Figure 24).

Amount retrieved seems to have some relationship with experience with using the online catalog. A much higher proportion of new or infrequent users find nothing or only some of what they are looking for, whereas respondents who use the catalog frequently are much more likely to find some, all or more than they were looking for (Table 50).

Most Users Are Satisfied with Results of the Search

As Table 51 shows, most respondents found their most recent search satisfactory, though again, MELVYL users are less positive than users in general.

Respondents from Davis, Irvine, Riverside, and San Diego reported greater satisfaction with their searches than did respondents from other

Table 49.   Amount of Relevant Material Found in the Online Catalog Search

Question 5: *In this computer search I found: (Mark ONE only)*

	University of California	All Respondents
a. More than I was looking for	11.8%	16.6%
b. All that I was looking for	13.5	27.5
c. Some of what I was looking for	43.2	39.6
d. Nothing I was looking for	31.5	16.3

TERMLOC2

RQ5	COUNT ROW PCT COL PCT TOT PCT	BERKE-LEY 1.	DAVIS 2.	IRVINE 3.	LA 4.	RIVER-SIDE 5.	SANTA BARBARA 6.	SANTA CRUZ 7.	SAN DIEGO 8.	SAN FRAN-CISCO 9.	ROW TOTAL
MORE THAN	1.	21 / 17.8 / 11.5 / 2.1	9 / 7.6 / 7.3 / 0.9	8 / 6.8 / 16.7 / 0.8	15 / 12.7 / 9.9 / 1.5	11 / 9.3 / 19.3 / 1.1	17 / 14.4 / 12.3 / 1.7	2 / 1.7 / 2.7 / 0.2	35 / 29.7 / 15.0 / 3.4	0 / 0.0 / 0.0 / 0.0	118 / 11.5
ALL OR MOST	2.	32 / 23.7 / 17.6 / 3.1	12 / 8.9 / 9.8 / 1.2	9 / 6.7 / 18.8 / 0.9	11 / 8.1 / 7.3 / 1.1	5 / 3.7 / 8.8 / 0.5	11 / 8.1 / 8.0 / 1.1	6 / 4.4 / 8.2 / 0.6	46 / 34.1 / 19.7 / 4.5	3 / 2.2 / 17.6 / 0.3	135 / 13.2
SOME	3.	68 / 15.2 / 37.4 / 6.6	66 / 14.8 / 53.7 / 6.5	21 / 4.7 / 43.8 / 2.1	71 / 15.9 / 47.0 / 6.9	28 / 6.3 / 49.1 / 2.7	58 / 13.0 / 42.0 / 5.7	41 / 9.2 / 56.2 / 4.0	89 / 19.9 / 38.0 / 8.7	5 / 1.1 / 29.4 / 0.5	447 / 43.7
NOTHING	4.	61 / 18.9 / 33.5 / 6.0	36 / 11.1 / 29.3 / 3.5	10 / 3.1 / 20.8 / 1.0	54 / 16.7 / 35.8 / 5.3	13 / 4.0 / 22.8 / 1.3	52 / 16.1 / 37.7 / 5.1	24 / 7.4 / 32.9 / 2.3	64 / 19.8 / 27.4 / 6.3	9 / 2.8 / 52.9 / 0.9	323 / 31.6
COLUMN TOTAL		182 / 17.8	123 / 12.0	48 / 4.7	151 / 14.8	57 / 5.6	138 / 13.5	73 / 7.1	234 / 22.9	17 / 1.7	1023 / 100.0

2 OUT OF 36 (5.6%) OF THE VALID CELLS HAVE EXPECTED CELL FREQUENCY LESS THAN 5.0.
MINIMUM EXPECTED CELL FREQUENCY = 1.961
CHI SQUARE = 57.50038 WITH 24 DEGREES OF FREEDOM   SIGNIFICANCE = 0.0001
CRAMER'S V = 0.13688
CONTINGENCY COEFFICIENT = 0.23069
LAMBDA (ASYMMETRIC) = 0.00694 WITH RQ5 DEPENDENT   = 0.0 WITH TERMLOC2 DEPENDENT.
LAMBDA (SYMMETRIC) = 0.00293
UNCERTAINTY COEFFICIENT (ASYMMETRIC) = 0.02408 WITH RQ5 DEPENDENT.   = 0.01486 WITH TERMLOC2 DEPENDENT.
UNCERTAINTY COEFFICIENT (SYMMETRIC) = 0.01838
KENDALL'S TAU B = -0.01915   SIGNIFICANCE = 0.2257
KENDALL'S TAU C = -0.01940   SIGNIFICANCE = 0.2257
GAMMA = -0.02520
SOMERS'S D (ASYMMETRIC) = -0.01710 WITH RQ5 DEPENDENT.   = -0.02144 WITH TERMLOC2 DEPENDENT.
SOMERS'S D (SYMMETRIC) = -0.01903
ETA = 0.16392 WITH RQ5 DEPENDENT.   = 0.03165 WITH TERMLOC2 DEPENDENT.
PEARSON'S R = -0.02324   SIGNIFICANCE = 0.2288

NUMBER OF MISSING OBSERVATIONS = 236

Figure 23   Amount of Relevant Material Found—Comparison by Campus.

```
SEARCH MODE CROSSTABS
FILE   LINKQST (CREATION DATE = 01/26/83)
* * * * * * * * * * * * * * * * * * * * * * * CROSSTABULATION OF * * * * * * * * * * * * * * * * * * * * * * * * *
*  *  *  *  RQ5    IN THIS SEARCH I FOUND          BY SRCHMOD2
* * * * * * * * * * * * * * * * * * * * * * * * * * * * * * * * * * * * * * * * * * * * * * * * * * * * PAGE 1 OF 1

                    SRCHMOD2
             COUNT  |
            ROW PCT | COMMAND  LOOK UP    ROW
            COL PCT |                    TOTAL
            TOT PCT |    1.        2.
RQ5         --------+-------------------+
MORE THAN      1.   |    51        75   |   126
                    |  40.5      59.5   |  11.9
                    |  12.4      11.6   |
                    |   4.8       7.1   |
                    +-------------------+
ALL OR MOST    2.   |    65        77   |   142
                    |  45.8      54.2   |  13.4
                    |  15.8      12.0   |
                    |   6.2       7.3   |
                    +-------------------+
SOME           3.   |   187       270   |   457
                    |  40.9      59.1   |  43.3
                    |  45.4      41.9   |
                    |  17.7      25.6   |
                    +-------------------+
NOTHING        4.   |   109       222   |   331
                    |  32.9      67.1   |  31.3
                    |  26.5      34.5   |
                    |  10.3      21.0   |
                    +-------------------+
            COLUMN      412       644      1056
            TOTAL      39.0      61.0     100.0


CHI SQUARE    =    8.68651 WITH   3 DEGREES OF FREEDOM    SIGNIFICANCE =  0.0338
CRAMER'S V    =    0.09070
CONTINGENCY COEFFICIENT =    0.09033
LAMBDA (ASYMMETRIC) =    0.0 WITH RQ5       DEPENDENT.    =  0.0       WITH SRCHMOD2 DEPENDENT.
LAMBDA (SYMMETRIC) =    0.0
UNCERTAINTY COEFFICIENT (ASYMMETRIC) =    0.00332 WITH RQ5    DEPENDENT.    =  0.00619 WITH SRCHMOD2
  DEPENDENT.
UNCERTAINTY COEFFICIENT (SYMMETRIC) =    0.00432
KENDALL'S TAU B =    0.07308    SIGNIFICANCE =  0.0053
KENDALL'S TAU C =    0.08328    SIGNIFICANCE =  0.0053
GAMMA =    0.12679
SOMERS'S D (ASYMMETRIC) =  0.08750 WITH RQ5    DEPENDENT.    =  0.06104 WITH SRCHMOD2 DEPENDENT.
SOMERS'S D (SYMMETRIC) =  0.07191
ETA  =  0.06758 WITH RQ5       DEPENDENT.    =  0.09069 WITH SRCHMOD2 DEPENDENT.
PEARSON'S R =  0.06759          SIGNIFICANCE =  0.0140

NUMBER OF MISSING OBSERVATIONS =  203
```

Figure 24.   Amount of Relevant Material Found—Comparison by Search Mode.

156

Table 50.   Retrieval Results and Online Catalog Experience

	I Use This Computer Catalog: (%)				
In This Search I Found:	*Every Visit*	*Most Visits*	*Occasionally*	*Rarely*	*Not Before Today*
More than I was looking for	23.0	11.0	8.0	6.3	9.9
All that I was looking for	12.3	15.3	15.7	10.9	7.4
Some of what I was looking for	45.1	48.8	39.9	34.4	48.1
Nothing I was looking for	19.7	24.9	36.4	48.4	34.6
TOTAL[1]	99.8	100.0	100.0	100.0	100.0

[1] Totals may deviate from 100 percent due to rounding errors.

campuses. At Berkeley and Santa Barbara satisfaction was considerably lower (Figure 25). For MELVYL users, as with the aggregate sample, there is a strong positive relationship between the amount of relevant material retrieved and the level of satisfaction with the search.[32] Because MELVYL's data base is limited to a fairly small percentage of the total holdings of the UC libraries, it is not surprising that fewer respondents were completely satisfied by their searches. The difference between campuses can be partially accounted for by the difference in percentage of holdings represented in the computer catalog. Irvine, Davis, Riverside, and San Diego have a much higher percentage of their libraries' bound volumes in the catalog than do Berkeley and Santa Barbara. (See Table 2, Section I).

Because search satisfaction is related to search results, and search results are related to computer catalog experience, it is not surprising that satisfaction is related to experience with the online catalog. In this case, however, first-time users show themselves to be more satisfied with the online search than experienced users, even though they did not always

Table 51.   Satisfaction with Search Results

Question 6: *In relation to what I was looking for, this computer search was: (Mark ONE only)*

	UC	All
a. Very satisfactory	32.7%	46.5%
b. Somewhat satisfactory	33.5	33.6
c. Somewhat unsatisfactory	14.9	10.4
d. Very unsatisfactory	18.9	9.5

Table 52.   Search Satisfaction and Online Catalog Experience

	I Use This Computer Catalog: (%)				
This Search Was:	*Every Visit*	*Most Visits*	*Occasionally*	*Rarely*	*Not Before Today*
Very Satisfactory	46.7	33.1	28.8	25.0	32.5
Somewhat Satisfactory	27.9	38.5	33.9	31.3	41.3
Somewhat Unsatisfactory	13.1	14.7	17.3	10.9	11.3
Very Unsatisfactory	12.3	13.7	20.1	32.8	15.0
TOTAL[1]	100.0	100.0	100.0	99.9	100.0

[1] Totals may deviate from 100 percent due to rounding errors.

find what they were looking for (Table 52). An expanded discussion of this phenomenon can be found in the aggregate report.[33]

About Half of Users Discover Interesting Material They Were Not Seeking

Almost half of MELVYL respondents (48.6 percent) say they found something of interest other than what they were looking for during the search. As Table 53 shows, this is a slightly lower percentage than for all users.[34]" However, a significantly higher percentage of respondents using Command Mode (54.8 percent) came across other things of interest in their searches than did those respondents using Lookup Mode (44.8 percent) (Figure 26).

"Serendipity," or accidental discovery of interesting material, seems to have an influence on users' ratings of the catalog session. Over 60 percent of respondents who rated the search as satisfactory came across other things of interest, whereas only 20.0 percent of respondents who found the search unsatisfactory had this experience. In general, online catalog experience has an effect on accidental discovery of interesting material, but again, first-time users resemble the most experienced users in this regard.[35]

Table 53.   Serendipity

Question 7: *I came across things of interest other than what I was looking for:*

	UC	All
a. Yes	48.6%	49.8%
b. No	51.4	50.2

CLR USER QUESTIONNAIRE: LIBRARY TYPE COMPARISON XTABS
FILE   FINAL   (CREATION DATE = 08/03/82)
* * * * * * * * * * * * * * * * * * *CROSSTABULATION OF *
* * RQ6   IN REL TO WHAT I WAS LOOKING FOR SEARCH   BY TERMLOC2 * * * * * * * * * * * * * * * * * * *
PAGE 1 OF 1

TERMLOC2

RQ6	COUNT / ROW PCT / COL PCT / TOT PCT	BERKE-LEY 1.	DAVIS 2.	IRVINE 3.	LA 4.	RIVER-SIDE 5.	SANTA BARBARA 6.	SANTA CRUZ 7.	SAN DIEGO 8.	SAN FRAN-CISCO 9.	ROW TOTAL
1. VERY SATISFACTOR		54 / 16.7 / 30.0 / 5.3	34 / 10.5 / 28.1 / 3.4	18 / 5.6 / 37.5 / 1.8	49 / 15.1 / 33.6 / 4.8	21 / 6.5 / 36.8 / 2.1	37 / 11.4 / 27.0 / 3.7	15 / 4.6 / 20.8 / 1.5	93 / 28.7 / 39.7 / 9.2	3 / 0.9 / 17.6 / 0.3	324 / 32.0
2. SOMEWHAT SATISFA		56 / 16.2 / 31.1 / 5.5	50 / 14.5 / 41.3 / 4.9	19 / 5.5 / 39.6 / 1.9	40 / 11.6 / 27.4 / 4.0	20 / 5.8 / 35.1 / 2.0	39 / 11.3 / 28.5 / 3.9	32 / 9.3 / 44.4 / 3.2	82 / 23.8 / 35.0 / 8.1	7 / 2.0 / 41.2 / 0.7	345 / 34.1
3. SOMEWHAT UNSATIS		31 / 20.8 / 17.2 / 3.1	16 / 10.7 / 13.2 / 1.6	3 / 2.0 / 6.3 / 0.3	24 / 16.1 / 16.4 / 2.4	8 / 5.4 / 14.0 / 0.8	32 / 21.5 / 23.4 / 3.2	10 / 6.7 / 13.9 / 1.0	23 / 15.4 / 9.8 / 2.3	2 / 1.3 / 11.8 / 0.2	149 / 14.7
4. VERY UNSATISFACT		39 / 20.1 / 21.7 / 3.9	21 / 10.8 / 17.4 / 2.1	8 / 4.1 / 16.7 / 0.8	33 / 17.0 / 22.6 / 3.3	8 / 4.1 / 14.0 / 0.8	29 / 14.9 / 21.2 / 2.9	15 / 7.7 / 20.8 / 1.5	36 / 18.6 / 15.4 / 3.6	5 / 2.6 / 29.4 / 0.5	194 / 19.2
COLUMN TOTAL		180 / 17.8	121 / 12.0	48 / 4.7	146 / 14.4	57 / 5.6	137 / 13.5	72 / 7.1	234 / 23.1	17 / 1.7	1012 / 100.0

2 OUT OF   36 (5.6%) OF THE VALID CELLS HAVE EXPECTED CELL FREQUENCY LESS THAN 5.0.
MINIMUM EXPECTED CELL FREQUENCY = 2.503.
CHI SQUARE = 39.84010 WITH   24 DEGREES OF FREEDOM   SIGNIFICANCE = 0.0222
CRAMER'S V = 0.11455
CONTINGENCY COEFFICIENT = 0.19462
LAMBDA (ASYMMETRIC) = 0.03148 WITH RQ6 DEPENDENT.   = 0.01542   WITH TERMLOC2 DEPENDENT.
LAMBDA (SYMMETRIC) = 0.02284
UNCERTAINTY COEFFICIENT (ASYMMETRIC) = 0.01492 WITH RQ6 DEPENDENT.   = 0.00986 WITH TERMLOC2 DEPENDENT.
UNCERTAINTY COEFFICIENT (SYMMETRIC) = 0.01187
KENDALL'S TAU B = -0.04147   SIGNIFICANCE = 0.0504
KENDALL'S TAU C = -0.04336   SIGNIFICANCE = 0.0504
GAMMA = -0.05276
SOMERS'S D (ASYMMETRIC) = -0.03823 WITH RQ6 DEPENDENT.   = -0.04499 WITH TERMLOC2 DEPENDENT.
SOMERS'S D (SYMMETRIC) = -0.04133
ETA = 0.13658 WITH RQ6 DEPENDENT.   = 0.05052 WITH TERMLOC2 DEPENDENT.
PEARSON'S R = -0.04546   SIGNIFICANCE = 0.0742

NUMBER OF MISSING OBSERVATIONS =   247

Figure 25. Satisfaction with Search Results—Comparison by Campus.

SEARCH MODE CROSSTABS
FILE LINKQST (CREATION DATE = 01/26/83)
* CROSSTABULATION OF *
       RQ7   CAME ACROSS OTHER THINGS OF INTEREST   BY SRCHMOD2
* PAGE 1 OF 1

		SRCHMOD2		
	COUNT	COMMAND	LOOK UP	ROW
	ROW PCT			TOTAL
	COL PCT			
RQ7	TOT PCT	1.	2.	
YES	1.	223	284	507
		44.0	56.0	48.7
		54.8	44.8	
		21.4	27.3	
NO	2.	184	350	534
		34.5	65.5	51.3
		45.2	55.2	
		17.7	33.6	
COLUMN		407	634	1041
TOTAL		39.1	60.9	100.0

CORRECTED CHI SQUARE =   9.51806 WITH 1 DEGREE OF FREEDOM   SIGNIFICANCE = 0.0020
    RAW CHI SQUARE =   9.91417 WITH 1 DEGREE OF FREEDOM   SIGNIFICANCE = 0.0016
PHI =   0.09759
CONTINGENCY COEFFICIENT =   0.09713
LAMBDA (ASYMMETRIC) =   0.07692 WITH RQ7   DEPENDENT   = 0.0   WITH SRCHMOD2 DEPENDENT.
LAMBDA (SYMMETRIC) =   0.04267
UNCERTAINTY COEFFICIENT (ASYMMETRIC) =   0.00688 WITH RQ7   DEPENDENT.   = 0.00712 WITH SRCHMOD2
    DEPENDENT.
UNCERTAINTY COEFFICIENT (SYMMETRIC) =   0.00700
KENDALL'S TAU B =   0.09759   SIGNIFICANCE = 0.0008
KENDALL'S TAU C =   0.09521   SIGNIFICANCE = 0.0008
GAMMA =   0.19795
SOMERS'S D (ASYMMETRIC) =   0.09996 WITH RQ7   DEPENDENT.   = 0.09527 WITH SRCHMOD2 DEPENDENT.
SOMERS'S D (SYMMETRIC) =   0.09756
ETA = 0.09758   DEPENDENT   = 0.09759 WITH SRCHMOD2 DEPENDENT.
PEARSON'S R = 0.09759   SIGNIFICANCE = 0.0008

NUMBER OF MISSING OBSERVATIONS =   218

Figure 26. Serendipity—Comparison by Search Mode.

Evaluation of the Online Catalog as a Whole

Over 90 Percent of Users Like the Online Catalog

Table 54 shows that most users like the online catalog, and that MEL-VYL users tend to be somewhat more enthusiastic in their response than online catalog users in general. On the whole, MELVYL users are like other Project respondents in that over 90 percent have a favorable attitude toward the online catalog (92.9 percent at UC, 92.4 percent overall). Differences in attitude are not significant from campus to campus, but the choice of search mode seems to have some bearing on the user's overall attitude; 74.9 percent of Command Mode users said their attitude was very favorable, and only 68.2 percent of Lookup Mode users reported a very favorable attitude (Figure 27).

Frequent users are more likely to view the online catalog favorably than are infrequent users, and, as found in other questions relating to satisfaction, most first-time users have a very favorable attitude towards it.

In general, people who found what they were looking for (Question 5) tend to rate the catalog more favorably than those who found nothing, though a surprising number of users who found nothing also rate the catalog positively.[36] Not surprisingly, people who found their searches satisfactory (Question 6) also tend to rate the catalog more favorably than do people who found their searches unsatisfactory.

Most Users Prefer the Online Catalog to the Card Catalog

Table 55 shows that most MELVYL users (68.3 percent) think the online catalog is better than the card catalog, though the percentage is slightly lower than that of the aggregate.[37]

Preference for the online catalog is related to search satisfaction and retrieval results, but even those who had unsuccessful searches seem to prefer the computer catalog. Fifty-three percent of those who found noth-

Table 54.   Overall Satisfaction with the Computer Catalog

Question 9: *My overall or general attitude toward the computer catalog is:*

	UC	All
a. Very Favorable	70.8%	67.0%
b. Somewhat Favorable	22.1	25.4
c. Somewhat Unfavorable	3.2	5.3
d. Very Unfavorable	3.9	2.3

```
SEARCH MODE CROSSTABS
FILE    LINKQST (CREATION DATE = 01/26/83)
* * * * * * * * * * * * * * * * * CROSSTABULATION OF * * * * * * * * * * * * * * * * * * * * * * * *
        RQ9    GENERAL ATTITUDE TOWARD COMPUTER CAT IS    BY SRCHMOD2
* * * * * * * * * * * * * * * * * * * * * * * * * * * * * * * * * * * * * * * * * *  PAGE 1 OF 1
```

```
                SRCHMOD2
           COUNT  |
          ROW PCT | COMMAND  LOOK UP   ROW
          COL PCT |                   TOTAL
          TOT PCT |    1.       2.
RQ9               |
              ----+--------+--------+
VERY FAVORABLE 1. |   299  |   429  |   728
                  |  41.1  |  58.9  |  70.8
                  |  74.9  |  68.2  |
                  |  29.1  |  41.7  |
              ----+--------+--------+
SOMEWHAT FAVORAB 2.|   82  |   147  |   229
                  |  35.8  |  64.2  |  22.3
                  |  20.6  |  23.4  |
                  |   8.0  |  14.3  |
              ----+--------+--------+
SOMEWHAT UNFAVOR 3.|    9  |    23  |    32
                  |  28.1  |  71.9  |   3.1
                  |   2.3  |   3.7  |
                  |   0.9  |   2.2  |
              ----+--------+--------+
VERY UNFAVORA  4. |    9  |    30  |    39
                  |  23.1  |  76.9  |   3.8
                  |   2.3  |   4.8  |
                  |   0.9  |   2.9  |
              ----+--------+--------+
           COLUMN     399      629     1028
            TOTAL     38.8     61.2    100.0
```

```
CHI SQUARE   =    8.04007 WITH  3 DEGREES OF FREEDOM    SIGNIFICANCE = 0.0452
CRAMER'S V   =    0.08844
CONTINGENCY COEFFICIENT =    0.08809
LAMBDA (ASYMMETRIC) =    0.0 WITH RQ9      DEPENDENT.    = 0.0    WITH SRCHMOD2 DEPENDENT.
LAMBDA (SYMMETRIC) =    0.0
UNCERTAINTY COEFFICIENT (ASYMMETRIC) =    0.00505 WITH RQ9    DEPENDENT.    = 0.00613 WITH SRCHMOD2
    DEPENDENT.
UNCERTAINTY COEFFICIENT (SYMMETRIC) =    0.00554
KENDALL'S TAU B =    0.07670    SIGNIFICANCE = 0.0058
KENDALL'S TAU C =    0.07064    SIGNIFICANCE = 0.0058
GAMMA =    0.16940
SOMERS'S D (ASYMMETRIC) =    0.07436 WITH RQ9    DEPENDENT.    = 0.07911 WITH SRCHMOD2 DEPENDENT.
SOMERS'S D (SYMMETRIC) =    0.07666
ETA = 0.08814 WITH RQ9    DEPENDENT.    = 0.08843 WITH SRCHMOD2 DEPENDENT.
PEARSON'S R =    0.08814    SIGNIFICANCE = 0.0023

NUMBER OF MISSING OBSERVATIONS =    231
```

Figure 27. Overall Satisfaction with the Computer Catalog—Comparison by Search Mode.

ing, and 40.5 percent of those who said their search was very unsatisfactory still think the online catalog is better than the card catalog. Again, it is not surprising that users with a favorable attitude towards the online catalog should find it better than the card catalog. What is surprising is that 23.5 percent of users with an unfavorable attitude towards the computer catalog think that it is better than the card catalog.

A Positive Attitude Towards the Computer Catalog Is Influenced by Actual Number of Retrievals

MELVYL transaction logs record the actual number of retrievals per session. This information can be linked to questionnaire data in order to further examine the effect of amount of material retrieved on respondents' attitudes towards the catalog. Transaction log data show sessions with retrievals from 0 to 18,000+ books. Retrievals were categorized and cross-tabulated with Questions 5–7, 9 and 10 of the questionnaire. In general, people who retrieved at least some books in their search sessions say that they were more satisfied with their searches, were favorably disposed towards the computer catalog, and came across more things of interest than people who retrieved nothing during their search sessions. Number of items retrieved had no relationship with responses to Question 10, comparison of the computer and card catalog. For Questions 5 and 6 there is no clear relationship between precise number of books retrieved and levels of satisfaction. For example, 45.5 percent of the people retrieving one book said that in relation to what they were looking for, the search was very satisfactory, 40.7 percent of respondents who retrieved 26–50 books said the search was very satisfactory, and 41.1 percent of those who retrieved 201–400 books found the search very satisfactory. Actual amount retrieved does have a clear relationship with unexpectedly coming across other things of interest, however. As Table 56 shows, the more items users retrieve, the more likely they are to come across other things of interest.

Table 55. User Comparisons of Computer and Card Catalogs

Question 10: *Compared to the card, book, or microfiche catalog in this library, the computer catalog is: (Mark ONE only)*[1]

	UC	All
a. Better	68.3%	74.5%
b. About the same	17.3	16.5
c. Worse	14.4	9.0

[1] Response 10d, "Can't Decide," is excluded from this table.

Table 56. Serendipity and Actual Number of Retrievals

Question 7: *I came across things of interest other than what I was looking for:*

Number of Records Retrieved

	0	1	2–5	6–15	16–25	26–50	51–100	101–200	201–400	401–1000	Over 1000
Yes	42.0%	34.5	35.9	38.1	41.4	54.4	60.0	68.0	67.1	52.4	60.0
No	58.0%	65.5	64.1	61.9	58.6	45.6	40.0	32.0	32.9	47.6	40.0

164

SECTION VIII: IMPROVEMENTS REQUESTED BY USERS

General

Questions 44-46 of the user questionnaire ask users to suggest improvements to the online catalog system in three different areas:

- Features and capabilities to be added to the system
- Service improvements
- Additional kinds of material to be included in the catalog.

44. Select *up to FOUR* features you would like any computer catalog to have:
    a. Providing step by step instructions
    b. Searching by any word or words in a title
    c. Searching by any word or words in a subject heading
    d. Limiting search results by date of publication
    e. Limiting search results by language
    f. Ability to search by journal title abbreviations
    g. Ability to change the order in which items are displayed
    h. Ability to view a list of words related to my search words
    i. Ability to search for illustrations and bibliographies
    j. Ability to search by call number
    k. Ability to print search results
    l. Ability to search a book's table of contents, summary or index
    m. Ability to know if a book is checked out
    n. Ability to tell where a book is located in the library
    o. None

45. Select *up to FOUR* computer catalog service improvements you would like the library to make:
    a. More terminals
    b. Terminals at locations other than near the card catalog
    c. Terminals at places other than library buildings
    d. A chart of commands posted at the terminal
    e. A manual or brochure at the terminal
    f. An instruction manual for purchase
    g. Training sessions
    h. Slide/tape/cassette training program
    i. None

46. Select *up to FOUR* kinds of material you would like to see added to the computer catalog:
    a. Dissertations
    b. Motion picture films
    c. Government publications
    d. Journal or magazine titles
    e. Maps
    f. Manuscripts
    g. Music stores
    h. Newspapers
    i. Phonograph records or tapes
    j. Technical reports
    k. More of the library's older books
    l. None
    m. Other

Figure 28. Questions Regarding Online Catalog Improvements on the User Questionnaire

The questions are displayed in Figure 28. Each question has a list of categories from which respondents are instructed to select up to four improvements or additions.

Improvements to the Catalog System

Question 44 lists fourteen different features and capabilities that could be added to the computer catalog. Response categories deal with several different aspects of the catalog, including search capabilities, provisions for information and instruction, location of wanted items in the library, and manipulation of output. Table 57 shows the categories of question 44 ranked by frequency of response.

The two features most frequently requested by MELVYL users are the ability to view a list of words related to their search terms and the ability to know if a book is checked out. Almost half of UC users indicated a desire for the ability to search a book's table of contents or index. Ability to print search results is seen as a desirable feature by 45.5 percent of all MELVYL users.

Improvements to Library Support Services

Question 45 lists eight service improvements that could be made by the library. Results are shown in Table 58.

In general, the most desired improvements are more terminals, at different locations, and with a chart of commands for easy reference. More

Table 57.   Additional System Features Requested by MELVYL Users

Question 44: *Select up to* FOUR *features you would like any computer catalog to have:*

Ranked by Frequency of Response[1]

h. Ability to view a list of words related to my search words	57.3%
m. Ability to know if a book is checked out	57.0
l. Ability to search a book's table of contents, summary or index	49.3
k. Ability to print search results	45.3
f. Ability to search by journal title abbreviations	26.3
n. Ability to tell where a book is located in the library	24.4
e. Limiting search results by language	20.6
j. Ability to search by call number	20.5
i. Ability to search for illustrations and bibliographies	19.3
d. Limiting search results by date of publication	18.5
g. Ability to change the order in which items are displayed	13.2
o. None	3.2

[1] Percentages sum to more than 100 due to legitimate multiple responses.

Table 58. Library Service Improvements Desired by MELVYL Users

Question 45: *Select up to* FOUR *computer catalog service improvements you would like the library to make:*

Ranked by Frequency of Response[1]

a. More terminals	63.6%
b. Terminals at locations other than near the card catalog	36.9
c. Terminals at places other than library buildings	35.7
d. A chart of commands posted at the terminal	30.7
e. A manual or brochures at the terminal	16.9
i. None	13.6
g. Training sessions	11.5
f. An instruction manual for purchase	10.3
h. Slide/tape/cassette training program	9.3

[1] Percentages sum to more than 100 due to legitimate multiple responses.

terminals is by far the most desired improvement among MELVYL users. This service is an especially high priority among respondents at Berkeley, Davis, Irvine, and Los Angeles (Figure 29).[38] It will be recalled that respondents at Los Angeles, Berkeley and Irvine also indicated that terminal availability was an especially serious problem (Section VI).

Terminals at locations other than near the catalog are wanted by 36.9 percent of the respondents and are a high priority (as indicated by 50 percent of the respondents) at both Irvine and Riverside. Terminals at

Table 59. Additional Kinds of Material Requested by Users

Question 46: *Select up to* FOUR *kinds of material you would like to see added to the computer catalog:*

Ranked by Frequency of Response[1]

a. Journal or magazine titles	64.0%
k. More of the library's older books	39.6
c. Government publications	37.1
h. Newspapers	34.9
a. Dissertations	34.5
j. Technical reports	24.8
b. Motion picture films	24.4
i. Phonograph records or tapes	23.0
g. Music scores	13.5
e. Maps	13.2
f. Manuscripts	10.8
l. None	3.7

[1] Percentages sum to more than 100 due to legitimate multiple responses.

CLR USER QUESTIONNAIRE: LIBRARY TYPE COMPARISON XTABS
FILE   FINAL   (CREATION DATE = 08/03/82)
04/04/83   PAGE 98
* *CROSSTABULATION* * * * * * * * * * * * * * * * *
     RQUEST45 (TABULATING   1) COMPUTER CAT SERVICE IMPROVEMENTS DESIRE
BY TERMLOC2
* PAGE 1 OF 2

TERMLOC2

		BERKE-LEY	DAVIS	IRVINE	LA	RIVER-SIDE	SANTA BARBARA	SANTA CRUZ	SAN DIEGO	SAN FRAN-CISCO	ROW TOTAL
COUNT / ROW PCT / COL PCT / TAB PCT		1	2	3	4	5	6	7	8	9	
RQUEST45											
RQ45A MORE TERMINALS		109 / 20.1 / 70.8 / 12.8	76 / 14.0 / 70.4 / 8.9	27 / 5.0 / 75.0 / 3.2	96 / 17.7 / 80.7 / 11.3	30 / 5.5 / 62.5 / 3.5	51 / 9.4 / 44.7 / 6.0	37 / 6.8 / 56.1 / 4.4	110 / 20.3 / 57.9 / 12.9	6 / 1.1 / 40.0 / 0.7	542 / 63.8
RQ45B TERMS IN OTHER LOCAT		49 / 15.7 / 31.8 / 5.8	41 / 13.1 / 38.0 / 4.8	18 / 5.8 / 50.0 / 2.1	42 / 13.5 / 35.3 / 4.9	24 / 7.7 / 50.0 / 2.8	42 / 13.5 / 36.8 / 4.9	17 / 5.4 / 25.8 / 2.0	73 / 23.4 / 38.4 / 8.6	6 / 1.9 / 40.0 / 0.7	312 / 36.7
RQ45C TERMS OUTSIDE LIBR		47 / 15.6 / 30.5 / 5.5	33 / 11.0 / 30.6 / 3.9	15 / 5.0 / 41.7 / 1.8	37 / 12.3 / 31.1 / 4.4	24 / 8.0 / 50.0 / 2.8	36 / 12.0 / 31.6 / 4.2	35 / 11.6 / 53.0 / 4.1	67 / 22.3 / 35.3 / 7.9	7 / 2.3 / 46.7 / 0.8	301 / 35.4
RQ45D COMMAND CHART POSTED		58 / 21.9 / 37.7 / 6.8	21 / 7.9 / 19.4 / 2.5	10 / 3.8 / 27.8 / 1.2	34 / 12.8 / 28.6 / 4.0	11 / 4.2 / 22.9 / 1.3	37 / 14.0 / 32.5 / 4.4	26 / 9.8 / 39.4 / 3.1	64 / 24.2 / 33.7 / 7.5	4 / 1.5 / 26.7 / 0.5	265 / 31.2
RQ45E MANUAL AT TERMINAL		44 / 30.6 / 28.6 / 5.2	6 / 4.2 / 5.6 / 0.7	1 / 0.7 / 2.8 / 0.1	11 / 7.6 / 9.2 / 1.3	9 / 6.3 / 18.8 / 1.1	18 / 12.5 / 15.8 / 2.1	16 / 11.1 / 24.2 / 1.9	37 / 25.7 / 19.5 / 4.4	2 / 1.4 / 13.3 / 0.2	144 / 16.9
RQ45G MANUAL FOR PURCHASE		23 / 25.6 / 14.9 / 2.7	11 / 12.2 / 10.2 / 1.3	3 / 3.3 / 8.3 / 0.4	13 / 14.4 / 10.9 / 1.5	4 / 4.4 / 8.3 / 0.5	11 / 12.2 / 9.6 / 1.3	3 / 3.3 / 4.5 / 0.4	19 / 21.1 / 10.0 / 2.2	3 / 3.3 / 20.0 / 0.4	90 / 10.6

	C1	C2	C3	C4	C5	C6	C7	C8	C9	ROW TOTAL
RQ45G TRAINING SESSIONS	22 22.7 14.3 2.6	14 14.4 13.0 1.6	2 2.1 5.6 0.2	10 10.3 8.4 1.2	6 6.2 12.5 0.7	22 22.7 19.3 2.6	5 5.2 7.6 0.6	15 15.5 7.9 1.8	1 1.0 6.7 0.1	97 11.4
RQ45H A-V TRAINING PROGR	11 14.3 7.1 1.3	16 20.8 14.8 1.9	1 1.3 2.8 0.1	10 13.0 8.4 1.2	7 9.1 14.6 0.8	7 9.1 6.1 0.8	5 6.5 7.6 0.6	14 18.2 7.4 1.6	6 7.8 40.0 0.7	77 9.1
RQ45I NONE	12 10.8 7.8 1.4	17 15.3 15.7 2.0	5 4.5 13.9 0.6	11 9.9 9.2 1.3	8 7.2 16.7 0.9	22 19.8 19.3 2.6	4 3.6 6.1 0.5	30 27.0 15.8 3.5	2 1.8 13.3 0.2	111 13.1
COLUMN TOTAL	154 18.1	108 12.7	36 4.2	119 14.0	48 5.6	114 13.4	66 7.8	190 22.4	15 1.8	850 100.0

PERCENTS AND TOTALS BASED ON RESPONDENTS
850 VALID CASES   409 MISSING CASES

Figure 29. Library Service Improvements Desired—Comparison by Campus.

169

CLR USER QUESTIONNAIRE: LIBRARY TYPE COMPARISON XTABS   04/04/83   PAGE 100
FILE   FINAL   (CREATION DATE = 08/03/82)
* CROSSTABULATION *
    RQUEST46 (TABULATING   1) ADDITIONAL KINDS OF MATERIALS DESIRED:
BY TERMLOC2
*   PAGE 1 OF 2

TERMLOC2

RQUEST46	COUNT / ROW PCT / COL PCT / TAB PCT	BERKE-LEY 1	DAVIS 2	IRVINE 3	LA 4	RIVER-SIDE 5	SANTA BARBARA 6	SANTA CRUZ 7	SAN DIEGO 8	SAN FRAN-CISCO 9	ROW TOTAL
RQ46A DISSERTATIONS	COUNT	64	36	11	34	16	41	25	60	7	294
	ROW PCT	21.8	12.2	3.7	11.6	5.4	13.9	8.5	20.4	2.4	34.5
	COL PCT	41.3	33.0	31.4	28.6	33.3	35.7	37.3	31.7	46.7	
	TAB PCT	7.5	4.2	1.3	4.0	1.9	4.8	2.9	7.0	0.8	
RQ46B MOTION PICTURE FILMS	COUNT	43	23	7	28	10	26	20	46	3	206
	ROW PCT	20.9	11.2	3.4	13.6	4.9	12.6	9.7	22.3	1.5	24.2
	COL PCT	27.7	21.1	20.0	23.5	20.8	22.6	29.9	24.3	20.0	
	TAB PCT	5.0	2.7	0.8	3.3	1.2	3.1	2.3	5.4	0.4	
RQ46C GOV PUBLICATIONS	COUNT	60	35	15	51	14	43	31	64	7	320
	ROW PCT	18.8	10.9	4.7	15.9	4.4	13.4	9.7	20.0	2.2	37.6
	COL PCT	38.7	32.1	42.9	42.9	29.2	37.4	46.3	33.9	46.7	
	TAB PCT	7.0	4.1	1.8	6.0	1.6	5.0	3.6	7.5	0.8	
RQ46D JOURNAL TITLES	COUNT	95	69	29	77	35	71	39	119	8	542
	ROW PCT	17.5	12.7	5.4	14.2	6.5	13.1	7.2	22.0	1.5	63.6
	COL PCT	61.3	63.3	82.9	64.7	72.9	61.7	58.2	63.0	53.3	
	TAB PCT	11.2	8.1	3.4	9.0	4.1	8.3	4.6	14.0	0.9	
RQ46E MAPS	COUNT	13	11	7	10	3	23	17	30	1	115
	ROW PCT	11.3	9.6	6.1	8.7	2.6	20.0	14.8	26.1	0.9	13.5
	COL PCT	8.4	10.1	20.0	8.4	6.3	20.0	25.4	15.9	6.7	
	TAB PCT	1.5	1.3	0.8	1.2	0.4	2.7	2.0	3.5	0.1	
RQ46F MANUSCRIPTS	COUNT	16	8	5	8	4	14	9	27	2	93
	ROW PCT	17.2	8.6	5.4	8.6	4.3	15.1	9.7	29.0	2.2	10.9
	COL PCT	10.3	7.3	14.3	6.7	8.3	12.2	13.4	14.3	13.3	
	TAB PCT	1.9	0.9	0.6	0.9	0.5	1.6	1.1	3.2	0.2	

RQ46G	22	11	2	12	9	17	15	26	2	116
MUSIC SCORES	19.0	9.5	1.7	10.3	7.8	14.7	12.9	22.4	1.7	13.6
	14.2	10.1	5.7	10.1	18.8	14.8	22.4	13.8	13.3	
	2.6	1.3	0.2	1.4	1.1	2.0	1.8	3.1	0.2	
RQ46H	47	31	13	46	26	38	29	60	6	296
NEWSPAPERS	15.9	10.5	4.4	15.5	8.8	12.8	9.8	20.3	2.0	34.7
	30.3	28.4	37.1	38.7	54.2	33.0	43.3	31.7	40.0	
	5.5	3.6	1.5	5.4	3.1	4.5	3.4	7.0	0.7	
RQ46I	25	21	9	23	17	26	23	54	1	199
RECORDS OR TAPES	12.6	10.6	4.5	11.6	8.5	13.1	11.6	27.1	0.5	23.4
	16.1	19.3	25.7	19.3	35.4	22.6	34.3	28.6	6.7	
	2.9	2.5	1.1	2.7	2.0	3.1	2.7	6.3	0.1	
RQ46J	34	32	6	30	8	29	9	59	4	211
TECHNICAL REPORTS	16.1	15.2	2.8	14.2	3.8	13.7	4.3	28.0	1.9	24.8
	21.9	29.4	17.1	25.2	16.7	25.2	13.4	31.2	26.7	
	4.0	3.8	0.7	3.5	0.9	3.4	1.1	6.9	0.5	
RQ46K	71	41	12	45	18	56	22	59	4	328
MORE OLDER BOOKS	21.6	12.5	3.7	13.7	5.5	17.1	6.7	18.0	1.2	38.5
	45.8	37.6	34.3	37.8	37.5	48.7	32.8	31.2	26.7	
	8.3	4.8	1.4	5.3	2.1	6.6	2.6	6.9	0.5	
RQ46L	3	4	0	1	5	5	2	12	1	33
NONE	9.1	12.1	0.0	3.0	15.2	15.2	6.1	36.4	3.0	3.9
	1.9	3.7	0.0	0.8	10.4	4.3	3.0	6.3	6.7	
	0.4	0.5	0.0	0.1	0.6	0.6	0.2	1.4	0.1	
COLUMN	155	109	35	119	48	115	67	189	15	852
TOTAL	18.2	12.8	4.1	14.0	5.6	13.5	7.9	22.2	1.8	100.0

PERCENTS AND TOTALS BASED ON RESPONDENTS
852 VALID CASES 407 MISSING CASES

Figure 30. Additional Kinds of Material Requested—Comparison by Campus.

locations outside the library are desired by 35.7 percent of UC users and are highly desired among respondents at Santa Cruz and Riverside, where at least 50 percent of the respondents indicated an interest in this feature (Figure 29).

Improvements to the Online Catalog Database

Question 46 lists eleven types of material that could be included in the computer catalog (Table 59). Additional materials in greatest demand by MELVYL users are journal or magazine titles, wanted by 64 percent of the respondents. "More of the library's older books" ranks second, requested by 39.6 percent, "Government publications" ranks third with 37.1 percent. Newspapers and dissertations run a close fourth and fifth place with 34.9 percent and 34.5 percent respectively. Among the campuses, respondents from San Francisco show a high interest in dissertations, Irvine users are especially interested in journal titles, and Santa Cruz respondents expressed a particular interest in music scores. Riverside respondents indicate a special interest in newspapers, and respondents from Berkeley and Santa Barbara expressed greater than average interest in more of the library's older books.[39] Riverside and Santa Cruz expressed high interest in tapes and records (Figure 30).

SECTION IX: CONCLUDING OBSERVATIONS

In reviewing our findings about MELVYL, we found that many of the conclusions we drew from the aggregate data were confirmed, or at least not undermined, by the University of California experience.[40] We discovered the importance of two factors, terminal location and database coverage, in interpreting many of the results found in this study. Despite the limitations imposed by the prototype status of the UC online catalog, we uncovered some findings that are new, or go far beyond the conclusions we were able to reach from the aggregate analysis. We would like to review our findings in each of these categories.

Confirmations of General Findings

There Are No Public Service Barriers to Adopting Online Catalogs

The evidence shows that MELVYL users like the online catalog with about the same frequency as other online catalog users; over 90 percent have a favorable attitude toward the online catalog, and about 85 percent believe it is as good as or better than the card catalog. The aggregate report showed that those who have not used an online catalog like it almost as well. This is not to say that MELVYL cannot be improved: most respondents could think of several changes and improvements they wanted. However, investment in continued improvement and expansion of MELVYL appears amply justified by the users' evaluations of the system.

Make the Catalog Visible

More than at most other institutions, MELVYL users first discover the catalog by seeing a terminal in the library. On the whole, it appears that the libraries have done an exceptionally good job of making terminals visible and accessible to users.

Plan for a Lot of Terminals

Almost two-thirds of UC respondents want more terminals: terminals throughout the library, and terminals in places other than the library. More UC users found terminal availability a problem than was true for survey respondents in general. This problem is created in part by the limited number of terminals presently available. The desire for more terminals, however, seems to extend beyond the irritations of having to wait in line; the data indicate that many users want the convenience of having access to the catalog *where the users are*, rather than where the catalog card cabinet happens to be. In fact, respondents at UC were more likely than the aggregate group to want terminals at library locations other than near the card catalog (36.9 percent vs. 31.4 percent) and terminals at locations outside the library (35.7 percent vs. 34.9 percent).

Provide Lots of Writing Space at the Terminal

Almost two-thirds of UC users complained about the lack of writing space at the terminal, about twice the aggregate rate. It would appear that attention to terminal furniture should be a higher priority for the UC libraries.

Plan to Provide Printers

About 46 percent of UC respondents expressed a desire for the ability to print their search results, a rate about 50 percent greater than the aggregate. Experimenting with various printing arrangements would appear justified by this finding. Additional justification can be found in the aggregate analysis, which showed this feature can help ameliorate a number of searching problems. As a corollary, make sure the printer is easy to use—this was a significant source of complaint among respondents from systems that supported terminal printers.

Plan to Expand the Database

The University of California's ongoing concern with retrospective conversion and additional MELVYL coverage gains added impetus from

MELVYL users: only 4 percent could think of nothing they wanted added to the database. Greatest interest was expressed in continued addition of monographs, and in adding access to serial titles, but high levels of interest were also recorded for other forms of material. In fact, only three generic forms, music scores, maps, and manuscripts, failed to gain the support of at least one-quarter of our respondents. Even in these three cases, interest was generally higher at UC than among the other libraries surveyed in this project. The importance of adding to the database is underscored by the findings that the most serious problem reported by MELVYL users was ''knowing what is included in the computer catalog,'' and that this problem is more serious at UC than among the other institutions surveyed for this project.

Subject Searching Is Important

The aggregate analysis found that most users of online catalogs conduct subject searches, and that subject searching and ''finding the correct subject terms'' were among the most serious problems they experienced. A formal analysis of factors contributing to success and satisfaction showed that problems with subject searching were the most important deterrents to user satisfaction.[41] MELVYL users conduct subject searches at about the same rate as users of other online catalogs (or perhaps a bit more), and have similar difficulties in locating the correct subject terms for their searches: finding the correct subject term was one of the top-ranked system problems, and appeared to affect UC users more seriously than those in the aggregate sample. On the other hand, MELVYL users reported that ''a computer search by subject'' was not difficult, and was less of a problem than at other participating institutions. It may be, then, that the problem with finding correct terms arises more from the limited database than from the design of the system. Because of the importance of subject access to users, however, continued efforts in this area, both to instruct users and to improve the catalog system, seem warranted.

Provide Circulation Status Information

A majority of MELVYL users (57 percent) would like to have information about the availability (circulation) status of books as part of the online catalog, about 50 percent more than want this feature in other systems that do not presently have it. Circulation status information was the second-ranked system improvement among UC respondents.

Provide Brief Displays

The data show that only 4.2 percent of MELVYL users use the online catalog to obtain and record the more technical details of bibliographic information, a smaller percentage than in the aggregate sample. Most users are apparently satisfied with less-than-full bibliographic displays. Our analysis of the finding that Command Mode users have more difficulty managing long displays than Lookup Mode respondents suggested that the problem could be attributable to the use of the MELVYL "brief" (i.e. paragraph) display as a default in Command Mode (Lookup Mode users get the shorter "review" display as a default). Taken together, these findings suggest that a very brief display (like the "review" display in MELVYL) may be sufficient for many users, and highly desirable when more than a few records are retrieved. The capacity to display fuller information for selected records is available in MELVYL; perhaps this feature should be relied upon to a greater degree.

On the Importance of Database Coverage and Terminal Distribution

Even a casual reader of this report will note the frequency with which we refer to matters of terminal location and database coverage to explain apparent differences between campuses or between UC and aggregate data. It is evident that, when terminal access is limited, the characteristics of online catalog users and catalog use will depend to a large extent on where the terminals happen to be located. A different terminal configuration could lead to quite different survey results, not only with respect to the demographic characteristics of users, but also with regard to search patterns, success, and satisfaction. Given the limitations of the database, we can only conjecture about what problems might be ameliorated, and what others increased, as the database grows.

These limitations suggest that it may be difficult to evaluate the MEL-VYL system independently of the influence of terminal location and database coverage. As we have seen above, however, much of what we have found in the UC data confirms findings from a wide variety of other online catalog systems in a wide range of institutional settings. We are therefore reasonably confident that the observations made earlier in this section are reliable regardless of terminal configuration or the current limitations of the database.

We are inclined to believe that the CLR survey instrument and methodology are reasonably robust, and provide reliable and useful data even under very special circumstances, as long as those data are interpreted with the circumstances in mind. In the next section we present some additional observations that have not been validated by other sources and might be influenced by MELVYL's "special circumstances." Being convinced of the robust character of the CLR survey data, however, we believe these findings will withstand the tests of time and change, and therefore offer them for consideration and discussion.

Some Additional Observations on MELVYL Data

Evidence for a Sex Bias in Use of Online Catalogs

Table 14 showed that about one-third of MELVYL users were female, and two-thirds male. Among the ARL libraries in the project and for the aggregate sample, the proportion of female users was significantly higher. This difference could, of course, be attributable to the sex distribution of UC students and staff, but official statistics show that in 1979–80 (the most recent year for which published statistics are available) the student body was about 45 percent female and 55 percent male. This comparison is not conclusive, chiefly because of the influence of terminal distribution: the concentration of terminals in science and engineering libraries, for instance, might influence this result. A more persuasive piece of evidence is the fact that significantly more users of Command Mode are male (75 percent, as opposed to 62 percent for Lookup Mode). The propensity of users to choose Command Mode should not be greatly influenced by terminal location (although there is the possibility that sci/tech users, being more familiar with computers, will tend to choose Command), and we should expect on the whole that men and women would choose to use Command Mode with roughly equal frequencies. The evidence does not support this idea, but provides validation for a finding of the aggregate study, that women are less likely to be users of the online catalog, or to be successful or satisfied in its use.

On Online Union Catalogs

Table 23 showed that over 10 percent of MELVYL respondents used the catalog to find "another library that has a book, journal or magazine that I want." This proportion is larger than the 7 percent figure for the aggregate sample, although not a great deal larger. No doubt the responses in this category are influenced by institutional policy (undergraduates, for example, may not actively seek items from another campus because they believe they are not privileged to order them) as well as database limitations, and the amount of "latent demand" for items held by another library might well be greater. It is nontheless interesting, and perhaps a bit chilling, to contemplate the effect if one of every ten catalog searches resulted in an interlibrary lending request.

On the Disadvantages of a Menu-Driven Interface

The aggregate report presented tentative evidence indicating that menu-driven interfaces for online catalogs were disadvantageous from the point of view of survey respondents.[42] Table 39 demonstrated that at UC Lookup Mode users generally had more serious problems using the catalog than did Command Mode respondents. While it would be premature to try to diagnose the problems of menu systems from the available evidence and analysis, the UC findings add weight to the belief that menus are not necessarily easier to use than command-driven systems, and that menu designs should be studied and tested carefully.

Computer Response Time

The aggregate report concluded that computer response time was an important design consideration, but appeared not to play a predominant role in user satisfaction. Our analysis of actual response times and user reactions (Section V) showed that user attitude was only loosely related to actual response time. Particularly, users of Lookup Mode are generally satisfied with response times twice as long as those experienced by Command Mode users, and regression analysis shows that the user's search mode is a more important determinant of his feeling about computer response time than is the response delay he actually experiences. Where "adequate" response time is an important issue (as it often is when improvements in overall system response can only be obtained at a great cost in equipment and software), it should not be assumed that faster is necessarily better. Clearly, further investigation will be necessary to define and evaluate the "adequacy" of computer response time in bibliographic systems intended for public use.

On the Benefits of Online Assistance

One of the conclusions of the aggregate analysis was that "one factor that ameliorates reliance on both printed aids and staff assistance is online help." Hildreth's comparison of ten online catalogs showed none that exceeded MELVYL's capabilities, or provided more than MELVYL's 155 discrete "help" screens.[43] Evidence from UC data indicates that our conclusion was correct, and an investment in extensive online help pays off. MELVYL users were twice as likely to say they had learned to use the catalog from online instructions as the aggregate respondents, and only one-sixth as likely to have learned from library staff; over 56 percent of MELVYL users say they relied at least in part on online instruction. MELVYL users also are more likely to get searching assistance from the system (44 percent vs. 32 percent for the aggregate sample) and significantly less likely to rely on printed material or staff assistance. It is by no means proven that reliance on online aid is a "good thing," in the sense that it leads to more effective use of the catalog, but it is clear that online assistance *works*: when it is provided, people use it, apparently in preference to alternative sources of instruction and assistance. A significant investment in online assistance therefore seems warranted; the next frontier is to evaluate the effectiveness of such systems and develop improved designs.

APPENDIX A

The User Questionnaire

PART I: ABOUT YOUR MOST RECENT SEARCH

INSTRUCTIONS: Please answer these questions about the computer catalog search you just completed.

1. I came to this computer search with:
(Mark <u>ALL</u> that apply)

a. A complete author's name .... ○
b. Part of an author's name .... ○
c. A complete title .... ○
d. Part of a title .... ○
e. A topic word or words .... ○
f. A subject heading or headings .... ○
g. A complete call number .... ○
h. Part of a call number .... ○

2. By searching this computer catalog I was trying to find:
(Mark <u>ALL</u> that apply)

a. A specific book, journal or magazine ... ○
b. Books, journals or magazines on a topic or subject .... ○
c. Books by a specific author .... ○
d. Information such as publisher, date, spelling of a name, etc. .... ○
e. If a book that I know the library has is available for my use .... ○
f. Another library that has a book, journal or magazine that I want .... ○

3. I searched for what I wanted by:
(Mark <u>ALL</u> that apply)

a. A complete author's name .... ○
b. Part of an author's name .... ○
c. A complete title .... ○
d. Part of a title .... ○
e. A topic word or words .... ○
f. A subject heading or headings .... ○
g. A complete call number .... ○
h. Part of a call number .... ○

4. I need this information for:
(Mark <u>ALL</u> that apply)

a. Recreatinal uses ....
b. Making or fixing something ....
c. My work or job ....
d. Personal interest ....
e. A hobby ....
f. Class or course reading ....
g. A course paper or report ....
h. A thesis or dissertation ....
i. Writing for publication ....
j. Teaching or planning a course ....
k. Keeping up on a topic or subject ....

5. In this computer search I found:
(Mark <u>ONE</u> only)

a. More than I was looking for ....
b. All that I was looking for ....
c. Some of what I was looking for ....
d. Nothing I was looking for ....

6. In relation to what I was looking for, this computer search was:
(Mark <u>ONE</u> only)

a. Very satisfactory ....
b. Somewhat satisfactory ....
c. Somewhat unsatisfactory ....
d. Very unsatisfactory ....

. I came across things of interest other than what I was looking for:

. YES .... ○
. NO .... ○

. I got help in doing this computer catalog search from:
(Mark **ALL** that apply)

. Printed material or signs .... ○
. Instructions on the terminal screen ..... ○
. Library staff member .... ○
. Person nearby .... ○
. I did not get help .... ○

9. My overall or general attitude toward the computer catalog is:
(Mark **ONE** only)

a. Very favorable .... ○
b. Somewhat favorable .... ○
c. Somewhat unfavorable .... ○
d. Very unfavorable .... ○

10. Compared to the card, book, or microfiche catalog in this library, the computer catalog is:
(Mark **ONE** only)

a. Better .... ○
b. About the same .... ○
c. Worse .... ○
d. Can't decide .... ○

PART 2: YOUR EXPERIENCE WITH COMPUTER CATALOG FEATURES

INSTRUCTIONS: Mark the single column for each question that corresponds most closely to how you feel. If the statement does not apply to your experience at the computer catalog, mark the column, "Does Not Apply".

	STRONGLY AGREE	AGREE	NEITHER AGREE NOR DISAGREE	DISAGREE	STRONGLY DISAGREE	DOES NOT APPLY
11. A computer search by title is difficult	O	O	O	O	O	O
12. A computer search by author is easy	O	O	O	O	O	O
13. A computer search by subject is difficult	O	O	O	O	O	O
14. A computer search by call number is easy	O	O	O	O	O	O
15. A computer search by combined author/title is difficult	O	O	O	O	O	O
16. Remembering commands in the middle of the search is easy	O	O	O	O	O	O
17. Finding the correct subject term is difficult	O	O	O	O	O	O
18. Scanning through a long display (forward or backward) is easy	O	O	O	O	O	O
19. Increasing the result when too little is retrieved is difficult	O	O	O	O	O	O
20. Reducing the result when too much is retrieved is easy	O	O	O	O	O	O
21. Understanding explanations on the screen is difficult	O	O	O	O	O	O
22. Using codes or abbreviations for searching is easy	O	O	O	O	O	O
23. Abbreviations on the screen are easy to understand	O	O	O	O	O	O
24. Locating call numbers on the screen is difficult	O	O	O	O	O	O
25. Searching with a short form of a name or a word (truncation) is easy	O	O	O	O	O	O

	STRONGLY AGREE	AGREE	NEITHER AGREE NOR DISAGREE	DISAGREE	STRONGLY DISAGREE	DOES NOT APPLY
6. Using logical terms like AND, OR, NOT is difficult ..	O	O	O	O	O	O
7. Remembering the exact sequence or order of commands is easy	O	O	O	O	O	O
8. Understanding the initial instructions on the screen is difficult	O	O	O	O	O	O
9. Understanding the display for a single book, journal or magazine is easy	O	O	O	O	O	O
0. Understanding the display that shows more than a single book, journal or magazine is difficult	O	O	O	O	O	O
1. Interrupting or stopping the display of information is easy	O	O	O	O	O	O
2. Typing in exact spelling, initials, spaces and hyphens is difficult to do	O	O	O	O	O	O
3. Knowing what is included in the computer catalog is easy to remember	O	O	O	O	O	O
4. The order in which items are displayed is easy to understand	O	O	O	O	O	O
5. Displayed messages are too long	O	O	O	O	O	O
6. Selecting from a list of choices takes too much time.	O	O	O	O	O	O
7. Entering commands when I want to during the search process is difficult	O	O	O	O	O	O
8. The rate at which the computer responds is too slow	O	O	O	O	O	O
9. The availability of signs and brochures is adquate	O	O	O	O	O	O
0. Signs and brochures are not very useful	O	O	O	O	O	O
1. The staff advice is often not helpful	O	O	O	O	O	O
2. It is hard to find a free terminal	O	O	O	O	O	O

YOU ARE MORE THAN HALF-WAY DONE

PART 3: IMPROVING THE COMPUTER CATALOG

INSTRUCTIONS: Select the response or responses that best reflect your views about changes that should be made in the computer catalog.

43. When I use the computer catalog terminal: (Mark YES and NO)

	YES	NO
a. The keyboard is confusing to use	O	O
b. There is too much glare on the screen	O	O
c. The letters and numbers are easy to read	O	O
d. The lighting around the terminal is too bright	O	O
e. There is enough writing space at the terminal	O	O
f. Nearby noise is distracting	O	O
g. The terminal table is too high or too low	O	O
h. The printer is easy to use ..	O	O

44. Select up to FOUR additional features you would like this computer catalog to have:

a. Providing step by step instructions .....O
b. Searching by any word or words in a title ....O
c. Searching by any word or words in a subject heading ....O
d. Limiting search results by date of publication ....O
e. Limiting search results by language .....O
f. Ability to search by journal title abbreviations ....O
g. Ability to change the order in which items are displayed ....O
h. Ability to view a list of words related to my search words ....O
i. Ability to search for illustrations and bibliographers ....O
j. Ability to search by call number ....O
k. Ability to print search results ....O
l. Ability to search a book's table of contents, summary or index ....O
m. Ability to know if a book is checked out ....O
n. Ability to tell where a book is located in the library ....O
o. None ....O

45. Select up to FOUR computer catalog service improvements you would like the library to make:

a. More terminals ....
b. Terminals at locations other than near the card catalog ....
c. Terminals at locations other than library buildings ....
d. A chart of commands posted at the terminal ....
e. A manual or brochure at the terminal ..
f. An instruction manual for purchase ....
g. Training sessions ....
h. Slide/tape/cassette training program ....
i. None ....

46. Select up to FOUR kinds of material you would like to see added to the computer catalog:

a. Dissertations ....
b. Motion picture films ....
c. Government publications ....
d. Journal or magazine titles ....
e. Maps ....
f. Manuscripts ....
g. Music scores ....
h. Newspapers ....
i. Phonograph records or tapes ....
j. Technical reports ....
k. More of the library's older books ......
l. None ....
m. Other ....

47. BRIEFLY DESCRIBE ANY OTHER PROBLEMS WITH THIS COMPUTER CATALOG OR CHANGES YOU WOULD LIKE MADE TO IT:

PART 4: ABOUT YOURSELF

INSTRUCTIONS: Your responses are confidential. Please do not write your name anywhere on this questionnaire.

8. I come to this library:

a. Daily .... ○
b. Weekly .... ○
c. Monthly .... ○
d. About four times a year .... ○
e. About once a year .... ○
f. Noit before today .... ○

9. I use this computer catalog:

a. Every library visit .... ○
b. Almost every visit .... ○
c. Occasionally .... ○
d. Rarely .... ○
e. Not before today .... ○

10. I use this library's book, card or microfilm catalog:

a. Every visit .... ○
b. Almost every visit .... ○
c. Occasionally .... ○
d. Rarely .... ○
e. Never .... ○

11. I use a computer system other than the library's computer catalog:

a. Daily .... ○
b. Weekly .... ○
c. Monthly .... ○
d. About four times a year .... ○
e. About once a year .... ○
f. Never .... ○

52. I first heard about this computer catalog from:
(Mark ONE only)

a. Noticing a terminal in the library .... ○
b. Library tour, orientation or demonstration .... ○
c. An article or written announcement ..... ○
d. A course instructor .... ○
e. A friend or family member .... ○
f. Library staff .... ○

53. I learned how to use this computer catalog: (Mark ALL that apply)

a. From a friend or someone at a nearby terminal .... ○
b. Using printed instructions .... ○
c. Using instructions on the terminal screen .... ○
d. From the library staff .... ○
e. From a library course or orientation ... ○
f. From a slide/tape/cassette program .... ○
g. By myself without any help .... ○

54. My age group is:

a. 14 and under .... ○
b. 15–19 years .... ○
c. 20–24 years .... ○
d. 25–34 years .... ○
e. 35–44 years .... ○
f. 45–54 years .... ○
g. 55–64 years .... ○
h. 65 and over .... ○

55. I am:

a. Female .... ○
b. Male .... ○

56. Mark your current or highest educational level:
(Mark ONE only)

a. Grade School or Elementary School ... ○
b. High School or Secondary School ..... ○
c. Some College or University .... ○
d. College or University Graduate .... ○

If you are not completing this questionnaire at a college or university, please stop here. Thank you.

If you are completing this questionnaire at a college or university, please continue.

57. The category that best describes my academic area is:
(Mark ONE only)

a. Arts and Humanities .... ○
b. Physical/Biological Sciences .... ○
c. Social Sciences .... ○
d. Business/Management .... ○
e. Education .... ○
f. Engineering .... ○
g. Medical/Health Sciences .... ○
h. Law .... ○
i. Major not declared .... ○
j. Interdisciplinary .... ○

58. The main focus of my academic work at the present time is:
(Mark ALL that apply)

a. Course Work ....
b. Teaching ....
c. Research ....

59. My present affiliation with this college or university is:

a. Freshman/Sophomore ....
b. Junior/Senior ....
c. Graduate—masters level ....
d. Graduate—doctoral level ....
e. Graduate—professional school ....
f. Faculty ....
g. Staff ....
h. Other ....

Thank you for participating in this study of the computer catalog. This completes the questionnaire. Please return it.

SUPPLEMENTARY QUESTIONNAIRE ITEMS

60. ○ ○ ○ ○ ○ ○ ○ ○ ○ ○ ○ ○ ○ ○ ○
61. ○ ○ ○ ○ ○ ○ ○ ○ ○ ○ ○ ○ ○ ○ ○
62. ○ ○ ○ ○ ○ ○ ○ ○ ○ ○ ○ ○ ○ ○ ○
63. ○ ○ ○ ○ ○ ○ ○ ○ ○ ○ ○ ○ ○ ○ ○
64. ○ ○ ○ ○ ○ ○ ○ ○ ○ ○ ○ ○ ○ ○ ○

APPENDIX B

A Sample MELVYL Search Session

This appendix contains examples of MELVYL searches using both Command and Lookup Modes, and illustrates the various formats available for retrievals. Messages, instructions, and retrievals are presented in light type. Use responses to prompts are in darker italics. The examples follow the sequence a user would encounter at a terminal. The symbol → is a prompt. Whenever this appears, the computer waits for the user to enter the information requested. All displays are headed with the keywords entered by the user and the number of books retrieved.

In Lookup Mode, the prompt often follows a list of choices to which the user responds by selecting and typing in a number. Keywords, whether author, title, or subject, are merely typed in after the user is prompted for them. The user then requests a particular format by selecting a number, and requests the records to be displayed on the screen. To begin a new search or to end the session, the user types the appropriate number when prompted.

Command Mode is more complicated to use than Lookup. Once the user has selected Command Mode, the prompt → appears with a brief message. The user is expected to type in commands. As shown in the sample, typing in "HELP" will elicit instructions on how to begin a search. Command Mode users must begin each request with a valid command such as "find" or "display", and precede search terms by the proper index, e.g., "su" or "ti". Occasionally, in both Lookup or Command Modes, a request will require a longer search. The user will get a message to inform him of this, and in parentheses, the number of cycles that the search must go through. MELVYL reports back to the user as each cycle is completed, giving the user an idea of how the search is progressing. The user may cancel the long search if desired.

The first example of the Command Mode search in this appendix illustrates the use of "and" to modify an initial search. This creates a long search of 7 cycles. The illustration lists the cycles as they are completed. The search is then limited to the libraries at UC Berkeley with the command "at UCB", and to books published after 1980 with "and date 1980-". Retrievals are requested in MARC format. To continue the display, the user types in "ns" (next screen). The second search illustrates the use of Boolean searching by combining "ti" and "pa" (title and personal author), and retrievals are displayed first in the default format, brief, and then in long format by the user's request. The search is ended by typing "end".

In the Lookup Mode search, the user has selected the northern campus libraries ("nor"), and requested a subject search, using one search term, "online". This retrieves 96 books, displayed in review format. The user begins a second subject search using two terms, "online catalog", and retrieves two books. The user requests to see these displayed in long format, and continues to view screens by typing "1" until there are no more, and then selects "6" to end the search session.

The search session reproduced here was conducted on the prototype MELVYL system on March 3, 1983, for inclusion in this report.

WELCOME TO MELVYL

The University of California's Prototype On–Line Catalog

MELVYL contains 733,412 records representing approximately 1.3 million books in the University of California libraries.

```
* * * * * * * * * * * * * * * * * * * * * * * * * * * * * * * * * * * * * * * * * * * * * * * * * * * * * *
*        This is NOT a complete record of books in the UC libraries.        *
*  CHECK your local catalog if you don't find what you need in MELVYL.  *
* * * * * * * * * * * * * * * * * * * * * * * * * * * * * * * * * * * * * * * * * * * * * * * * * * * * * *
```

- -

** Type the number of the search mode you want, then press RETURN. Or, for more information, type HELP and press RETURN.

1. LOOKUP mode (for new or occasional users)
2. COMMAND mode (for users familiar with COMMAND language)

→ 2

Welcome to Command Mode. You may now begin typing commands. For a brief review of the commands, type HELP and press RETURN.

→ help

To search for books in the catalog, type FIND, followed by the index you wish to search, followed by the keywords you want to search in that index. To search more than one index, continue your search request with a conjunction (AND, OR, or AND NOT), another index name, and more keywords. The index names you may use are:

PA (personal author)   UT (uniform title)
CA (corporate author)   SE (series name)
TI (title)   SU (subject)

After you have retrieved some records, you may display them by typing DISPLAY, followed by the record numbers you want to see, followed by the format in which you want to see them.

The following are all valid search and display commands:

FIND PA JAMES BALDWIN AND TI DEVIL   DISPLAY
FIND PA WILLIAM SHAKESPEARE   DISPLAY ALL BRIEF
FIND SU ATOMIC ENERGY   DISPLAY 1-14 REVIEW

For more detailed instructions, type:

HELP HELP   HELP FIND   HELP DISPLAY

→ *find su online*

Search request: FIND SU ONLINE
Search result: 114 records at UC libraries

→ *and su catalog#*

LONG SEARCH: type YES and press RETURN to continue
             search [7]
             type NO and press RETURN to cancel search
             or type a new search command

→ *yes*

.....[6] more cycles until completion. To cancel search, press BREAK.
.....[5] more cycles until completion. To cancel search, press BREAK.
.....[4] more cycles until completion. To cancel search, press BREAK.
.....[3] more cycles until completion. To cancel search, press BREAK.
.....[2] more cycles until completion. To cancel search, press BREAK.
.....[1] more cycles until completion. To cancel search, press BREAK.

Search request: FIND SU ONLINE AND SU CATALOG#
Search result: 9 records at UC libraries

→ *at ucb*

Search request: FIND SU ONLINE AND SU CATALOG#
Search result: 5 records at Berkeley
     9 records at UC libraries

→ *and date 1980–*

Search request: FIND SU ONLINE AND SU CATALOG# AND DATE 1980-
Search result: 1 record at Berkeley
     1 record at UC libraries

1. Juergens, Bonnie.
 Self-instructional introduction to the OCLC Models 100 and 105
 terminals /by Bonnie Juergens; revised by Michelle Duffy. Rev. ed.
Dallas, Tex.: AMIGOS Bibliographic Council, inc., c1980.
 UCB LibSchLib Z699.4.O42 J83 1980

→ *display marc*

Search request: FIND SU ONLINE AND SU CATALOG# AND DATE 1980-
Search result: 1 record at Berkeley
              1 record at UC libraries

1. U01621159   STA c REC am ENC DCF i   CSC d   ENT
   INT   INX 0 GOV   FSC 0   BIO   CTY txu CON   ILS
   REP   MEI 1 CNF 0 FIC 0   MOD LAN eng   PD. s1980
035      $# 0001 $a BER $e RL18253440 $q 65043157 $z 810411 ⟨BER-G⟩
040   IaU $c IaU ⟨BER-G⟩
090      $# 0001 $a Z699.4.O42 $b J83 1980 $e BER $f CU-LSL $g LibSchLib $z LSL
        ⟨BER-G⟩
100 10 Juergens, Bonnie. ⟨BER-G⟩
245 10 Self-instructional introduction to the OCLC Models 100 and 105
        terminals / $c by Bonnie Juergens ; revised by Michelle Duffy. ⟨BER-G⟩
250   __Rev. ed.__. ⟨BER-G⟩
260 0   Dallas, Tex. : $b AMIGOS Bibliographic Council, inc., $c c1980.
        ⟨BER-G⟩
300   iv, 40 p. ; $c 28 cm. ⟨BER-G⟩
490 1   Amigos training series ; no. 1 ⟨BER-G⟩
610 20 OCLC, inc. ⟨BER-G⟩
650 0 Cataloging $x Data processing. ⟨BER-G⟩
                   (Record 1 continues on the next screen.)
Press RETURN (or type NS) to see the next screen.

→ *ns*

Search request: FIND SU ONLINE AND SU CATALOG# AND DATE 1980-
Search result: 1 record at Berkeley
               1 record at UC libraries

1. (continued)
650   0 Computer input-output equipment. ⟨BER-G⟩
650   0 On-line data processing. ⟨BER-G⟩
700 10 Duffy, Michelle. ⟨BER-G⟩
810 2   Amigos Bibliographic Council. $t Amigos training series ; $v no. 1.
           ⟨BER-G⟩
910      $# 0001 $a 09/08/80 $d 09/15/80 ⟨BER-G⟩
952   cam i ⟨BER-G⟩

There are no more records to display. Type PS to see the previous screen.

→ *find ti automation and pa salmon*

Search request: FIND TI AUTOMATION AND PA SALMON
Search result: 2 records at UC libraries

→ *display*

Search request: FIND TI AUTOMATION AND PA SALMON
Search result: 2 records at UC libraries

1. Preconference Institute on Library Automation, San Francisco, 1967. Library automation: a state of the art review; papers, edited by Stephen R. Salmon.
    Chicago, American Library Association, 1969.
        UCI   Main Lib Z678.9.A1 P7 1967aa
        UCSD S & E   Z678.9.A1 P7 1967aa

2. Salmon, Stephen R.
        Library automation systems / Stephen R. Salmon.
        New York : M. Dekker, c1975.
        UCI   Main Lib Z678.9.S28
        UCSC McHenry Z678.9.S28

→ *display long*

Search request: FIND TI AUTOMATION AND PA SALMON
Search result: 2 records at UC libraries

1.

Author:	Preconference Institute on Library Automation, San Francisco, 1967.
Title:	Library automation: a state of the art review; papers, edited by Stephen R. Salmon. Chicago, American Library Association, 1969.
	ix, 175 p. illus. 28 cm.
Notes:	"Held . . . under the sponsorship of the Information Science and Automation Division of the American Library Association."
	Includes bibliographical references.
Subjects:	Libraries — Automation — Congresses.
Other entries:	Salmon, Stephen R., ed. American Library Association. Information Science and Automation Division.

(Record 1 continues on the next screen.)
Press RETURN (or type NS) to see the next screen.

→ *ns*

Search request: FIND TI AUTOMATION AND PA SALMON
Search result: 2 records at UC libraries

1. (continued)
Call numbers: UCI   Main Lib Z678.9.A1 P7 1967aa (CU-I)
                UCSD S & E   Z678.9.A1 P7 1967aa (CU-SSe)

Press RETURN (or type NS) for the next screen. Type PS for the previous screen.

→ *ns*

Search request: FIND TI AUTOMATION AND PA SALMON
Search result: 2 records at UC libraries

2.
Author: Salmon, Stephen R.
Title: Library automation systems / Stephen R. Salmon.
                New York : M. Dekker, c1975.
             xiii, 291 p. : ill. ; 24 cm.

Series: Books in library and information science ; v. 15

Notes: Includes index.
             Bibliography: p. 245–279.

Subjects: Libraries — Automation.
             Library science — Data processing.

Call numbers: UCI   Main Lib Z678.9.S28 (CU-I)
                UCSC McHenry Z678.9.S28 (CU-SC)

There are no more records to display. Type PS to see the previous screen.

→ *end*

Thanks for using the catalog.

WELCOME TO MELVYL

The University of California's Prototype On-Line Catalog

MELVYL contains 733,412 records representing approximately 1.3 million books in the University of California libraries.

* *
*   This is NOT a complete record of books in the UC libraries.   *
* CHECK your local catalog if you don't find what you need in MELVYL. *
* *

- -
** Type the number of the search mode you want, then press RETURN. Or, for more information, type HELP and press RETURN.

  1. LOOKUP mode (for new or occasional users)
  2. COMMAND mode (for users familiar with COMMAND language)

→ *1*

Welcome to Lookup Mode.
You can search for books at any one of the following campuses or groups of libraries. Select one of the following, and type its code.

	UCD	(Davis)	UCSC	(Santa Cruz)
	UCI	(Irvine)	UCLA	(Los Angeles)
	UCR	(Riverside)	UCSD	(San Diego)
	UCSF	(San Francisco)	UCSB	(Santa Barbara)
	UCB	(Berkeley)		
UC	(all UC libraries)			
HAS	(Hastings law library)			
CLU	(San Diego Cluster library)			
LBL	(Lawrence Berkeley Laboratory)		
LAW	(all UC law libraries)			
MED	(all UC medical libraries)			
NOR	(all northern campuses: UCB, UCD, UCSF, UCSC, HASTINGS)
SOU	(all southern campuses: UCLA, UCSB, UCI, UCR, UCSD)

- -

Type the code for the libraries you want to search, or type HELP, then press RETURN:

→ *nor*

You may search for books in one of two ways:

　　by AUTHOR and/or TITLE
　　or by SUBJECT.

- -

Type the number you want below or type HELP, then press RETURN.

1. AUTHOR/TITLE search.
2. SUBJECT search.

→ *2*

Type SUBJECT words below or type HELP, then press RETURN.

→ *online*

Your search for: subject words ONLINE
retrieved: 96 books from Northern campuses.

1. ACM Symposium on Interactive Systems for Experimental
   Mathematics, . . .
   INTERACTIVE SYSTEMS FOR EXPERIMENTAL
   APPLIED MATHEMATICS; EDITED . . . 1968
2. Atherton, Pauline, 1929- LIBRARIANS AND ONLINE
   SERVICES / by . . . 1977
3. AN AUTOMATED ON-LINE CIRCULATION SYSTEM:
   EVALUATION, DEVELOPMENT, . . . 1973
4. Barwise, T. P. ONLINE SEARCHING : THE IMPACT ON
   USER CHARGES OF THE . . . 1979
5. Bell, M. W. UNIVERSAL PSYCHOLOGICAL INTERFACE /
   M. W. Bell, R. A. . . . 1978
6. BioSciences Information Service. BIOSIS SEARCH GUIDE.
   1979
7. Black, W. Wayne, 1935- AN INTRODUCTION TO ON-LINE
   COMPUTERS BY W. . . . 1971
8. Brignell, John E. LABORATORY ON-LINE COMPUTING :
   AN INTRODUCTION . . . 1975
9. California. Legislature. Assembly. Committee on Efficiency and
   Cost Control.
   A REVIEW OF THE DEPARTMENT OF MOTOR
   VEHICLES ON-LINE ISSUANCE . . . 1972

- -

Type the number you want below or type HELP, then press RETURN.

1. See next screen of this review display.	4. Begin new author/title search.
2. See some records in a brief display.	5. Begin new subject search.
3. See some records in a long display.	6. End the session.

→ 5

Type SUBJECT words below or type HELP, then press RETURN.

→ *online catalog*

Your search for: subject words ONLINE CATALOG
retrieved: 2 books from Northern campuses.

1. Griffith, Jeffrey C. THE USE OF A MICROFICHE CATALOG
   FOR PUBLIC . . . 1976
2. University of California (System). Division of Library Automation.
   UNIVERSITY OF CALIFORNIA PROTOTYPE ON-LINE
   CATALOG : A PROSPECTUS. 1980

- -

Type the number you want below or type HELP, then press RETURN.

1. See some of these records in a BRIEF display.   4. Begin new subject search.
2. See some of these records in a LONG display.   5. End the session.
3. Begin new author/title search.

→ *2*

Type the numbers of the records you want to see in LONG format, or type HELP, then press RETURN. To see current REVIEW screen again, simply press RETURN.

→ *1 2*

Your search for: subject words ONLINE CATALOG
    retrieved: 2 books from Northern campuses.

1.
Author: Griffith, Jeffrey C.
Title: The use of a microfiche catalog for public service and on-line retrieval of bibliographic data / J. C. Griffith, R. M. Hayes.
                [Los Angeles] : Graduate School of Library and Information Science, UCLA ; Arlington, Va. : Prepared by ERIC Document Reproduction Service, 1976.
                74 leaves ; 28 cm.

Series: ERIC reports

Notes: Author's name in "document resume": Griffith, C. C.
                Bibliography: leaves 24-35.
                        (Record 1 continues on the next screen.)

- -

Type the number you want below or type HELP, then press RETURN.

1. See next screen of this display.   4. Begin new author/title search.
2. See other records in LONG format.   5. Begin new subject search.
3. See the review display again.   6. End the session.

→ *1*

Your search for: subject words ONLINE CATALOG
retrieved: 2 books from Northern campuses.

1. (continued)

Subjects: California. University. Libraries.
Library catalogs on microfilm.
Catalogs, Union — California.
On-line data processing.
CARD (Microfiche reader)

Other entries: Hayes, Robert Mayo, 1926-, joint author.

Call numbers: UCB LibSchLib Z699.3.G75 (CU-LSL)

- -

Type the number you want below or type HELP, then press RETURN.

1. See next screen of this display.
2. See previous screen of this display.
3. See different records in LONG format.
4. See the review display again.

5. Begin new author/title search.
6. Begin new subject search.
7. End the session.

→ *1*

Your search for: subject words ONLINE CATALOG
retrieved: 2 books from Northern campuses.

2.
Author: University of California (System). Division of Li-
              brary Automation.
Title: University of California prototype on-line catalog :
              a prospectus. 2nd ed. Berkeley : Division of Li-
              brary Automation, Office of the Assistant Vice
              President, Library Plans and Policies, University
              of California, 1980.
              33 leaves ; 28 cm.

Notes: January 1980.
              Bibliographic footnotes.

Subjects: University of California (System) — Libraries —
              Automation.
                      (Record 2 continues on the next screen.)

- -

Type the number you want below or type HELP, then press RETURN.

1. See next screen of this display.   5. Begin new author/title search.
2. See previous screen of this display.·   6. Begin new subject search.
3. See different records in LONG format.   7. End the session.
4. See the review display again.

→ 1

Your search for: subject words ONLINE CATALOG
retrieved: 2 books from Northern campuses.

2. (continued)

Catalogs, Union — California.
University of California union catalog.

Call numbers: UCB Trans Z678.9 .U56 (CU-IT)

- -

Type the number you want below or type HELP, then press RETURN.

1. See previous screen of this display.
2. See other records in LONG format.
3. See the review display again.

4. Begin new author/title search.
5. Begin new subject search.
6. End the session.

→ 6

Thanks for using the catalog.

NOTES AND REFERENCES

1.   Douglas Ferguson, *et al.*, "The CLR Public Online Catalog Study: An Overview," *Information Technology and Libraries,* June 1982.

2.   University of California, Office of the Executive Director, Library Plans and Policies, *The University of California Libraries: A Plan for Development,* Berkeley, CA: the University, November 1977.

3.   Dialup accounts, provided both for UC libraries and individual users, are not included in this count.

4.   Douglas Ferguson, *et al.*, "The CLR Public Online Catalog Study: An Overview," *Information Technology and Libraries,* June 1982.

5.   Ray R. Larson. *Evaluating Public Access Online Catalogs: Phase I Development and Testing of Data Collection and Analysis Tools. Final Report to the Council on Library Resources.* Berkeley, CA.: University of California, Division of Library Automation, July 1981.

6.   Larson, Evaluating Public Access Online Catalogs.

7.   Throughout this report, the phrase "card catalog" is intended to mean "card, book, or microform" catalog; or, more generally, any traditional form of the catalog, for which the online catalog is a replacement.

8.   This result may be biased somewhat by the large number of responses from the San Diego undergraduate library, where the card catalog is closed (Tables 2 and 4).

9.   See University of California, Systemwide Administration, Division of Library Automation and Library Research and Analysis Group, *Users Look at Online Catalogs: Results of a National Survey of Users and Non-Users of Online Public Access Catalogs,* Berkeley, CA: The University, November 16, 1982 (available from ERIC).

10.   As noted in Section I (see Table 3), about 13 percent of MELVYL terminals are located in science branch libraries, which may explain the high representation of this group relative to other participating institutions. Notably, the branch libraries serving the business and management schools at Berkeley and Los Angeles do not have MELVYL terminals at this time.

11.   This response distribution is undoubtedly influenced by the branch distribution of terminals; see Section I, Table 3.

12.   This distribution is, of course, strongly influenced by the facts that Santa Cruz is chiefly an undergraduate campus (Table 1, Section I) and that half the San Diego terminals are located in the undergraduate library (Table 3, Section I). The relative underrepresentation of graduate students and faculty is similarly influenced by the concentration of terminals in general and undergraduate libraries, rather than discipline-oriented branches (Table 3, Section I).

13.   The focus of work is, of course, related to the academic status of the respondent; the status distribution, in turn, is influenced by terminal location. See the previous note, and Table 3, Section I.

14.   Of course, MELVYL does not provide availability information, as it is not part of, or linked to, a circulation system. This may condition the responses to this question.

15.   Only six of the 15 computer catalog systems (MELVYL, Mankato, ULYSIS [Mission and West Valley Colleges], LCS [Ohio State], OCLC and RLIN II) contain holdings information for multiple library systems.

16.   Various systems define a "heading" in various ways—defining an index to include certain specific MARC fields and subfields, for example. We recognize the wide differences among systems in defining and naming searchable indices; rather than accounting for all the permutations, we will simply refer to them in the terms we used in the questionnaire: author, title and subject.

17.   It will be recalled that the San Francisco campus is devoted entirely to the health sciences. The library use patterns and attitudes of medical researchers, practitioners and students would tend to explain this finding.

18.   University of California, *Users Look at Online Catalogs,*

19.   For subject searches in Lookup Mode, which automatically access both subject and title indices, the data are corrected to remove the title-search component. A similar adjustment was made for the fact that Lookup Mode checks both corporate and personal author indices for author searches unless a number appears in the string, in which case it checks only the corporate author index.

20.   Dr. Paul A. Kantor, personal communication, June 3, 1982.

21.   For purposes of analysis, the original Likert scale, ranging from "1-Strongly Agree" to "5-Strongly Disagree" (Figure 17) was mathematically transferred to a range from " + 2 (Strongly Agree)" to " − 2 (Strongly Disagree)." Respondents in category "6-Does Not Apply" were not included.

22.   With positively-phrased questions, when comparing two *negative* scores, the larger score is the greater problem: more users disagreed that the feature was easy to use. When comparing two *positive* scores, the smaller score indicates the greater problem: fewer respondents agreed that the feature was easy to use.

23.   In comparing mean scores on *negatively-worded* questions, a large positive score denotes a greater problem (more respondents agreed with a negative statement) and a small negative score denotes a greater problem (fewer respondents disagreed with a negative statement).

24.   "Implicit errors," mistaken entries that are nonetheless syntactically correct (i.e., can be interpreted by the system), are probably equally likely in both search modes. It should also be noted that, in Command Mode, pressing "carriage return" to display the next bibliographic screen generates an "error message" when there are no more screens to display. Inasmuch as pressing return can become something of a reflex in Command Mode, it is not surprising that this is the most common form of Command Mode error, and may explain much of the difference in error rates.

25.   This may simply reflect the adventurous spirit of more frequent users, who are probably more likely to use the less restrictive (and more error-prone) Command Mode.

26.   The HELP system, for instance, "knows" what command was entered and what index was searched, and can supply situation-specific help screens without additional prompting from the user.

27.   For additional discussion of this point, see Joseph R. Matthews, *Public Access to Online Catalogs: A Planning Guide for Managers,* Weston, CN: Online, Inc., 1982, p. 53, and Joseph R. Matthews, Gary S. Lawrence, and Douglas K. Ferguson, eds., *Using Online Catalogs: A National Survey,* New York: Neal-Schuman, 1983.

28.   The Beta coefficient, or "normalized regression coefficient", adjusts the "raw" regression coefficients so that they are all measured on a single scale. Thus, Beta coefficients indicate the relative importance of independent variables in explaining the variance of the dependent variable.

29.   The search mode variable was coded "0" for Command Mode and "1" for Lookup Mode; the values of the dependent variable range from + 2 for Strongly Agree (i.e. there is a response time problem) to − 2 for Strongly Disagree. The negative coefficient for search mode, then, shows that as search mode "increases" (that is, for Lookup users), agreement with the statement "decreases" (users are more likely to disagree, i.e., experience no response time problem).

30.   It is estimated that the MELVYL prototype database includes only about seven percent of the bound volumes in UC collections (Table 2, Section I). The amount included in the prototype catalog is significantly less than for most other participating libraries; see

Joseph R. Matthews, Gary S. Lawrence, and Douglas K. Ferguson, eds., *Using Online Catalogs: A Nationwide Study*, New York: Neal-Schuman, 1983.

31.   Table 2 shows that Irvine, Riverside and San Diego have a larger-than-average percentage of their collections in MELVYL (as measured by the ratio of MELVYL records to bound volumes); San Francisco and Berkeley appear to have the smallest amount in the online catalog. Davis and Santa Cruz, the other two "above-average" campuses, both have better coverage than Riverside, but users from these campuses do not report exceptional retrieval results.

32.   See University of California, *Users Look at Online Catalogs*, Chapter 7, for a fuller discussion.

33.   University of California, *Users Look at Online Catalogs*.

34.   This may be largely attributable to the database limitations discussed previously. (See section 7.2.2 of University of California, *Users Look at Online Catalogs*, for a fuller discussion.)

35.   See Sections 7.2.2 to 7.2.6 of University of California, *Users Look at Online Catalogs*, for a discussion of this phenomenon.

36.   See University of California, *Users Look at Online Catalogs*, for a more detailed discussion.

37.   MELVYL database limitations may contribute to this response.

38.   This should not necessarily be construed as suggesting a priority for installation of new terminals. Because the methodology involved surveying users *at the terminal*, the user sample could be somewhat biased toward users who have relatively convenient access.

39.   On the matter of "older" books, it should be noted that the proportions of the collections at Berkeley and Santa Barbara represented in the prototype data base are relatively small; see Table 2, Section I.

40.   University of California, *Users Look at Online Catalogs, op. cit.*

41.   University of California, *Users Look at Online Catalogs*, Chapter 9, and especially pages 144–146.

42.   University of California, *Users Look at Online Catalogs*, Section 5.4, and especially page 74.

43.   Charles R. Hildreth, *Online Public Access Catalogs: The User Interface*, Dublin, OH: OCLC, 1982, Chapter 10, and especially Table 13, page 166.

JOB ANALYSIS:
PROCESS AND BENEFITS

Virginia S. Hill and Tom G. Watson

Of all the tools available to the library manager for facilitating the library staffing process, no other tool is as valuable, indeed as critical, as the job analysis. Not only does it serve as the basis for all other functions of the personnel management process; it may be the single most important defense against staff complaints about discrimination or unfair treatment. With libraries of all kinds facing at worst serious budget reductions and at best budgets which have not kept pace with the recent high inflation, staff reductions have been common. In such a climate of reduction, the risk of challenge by the adversely affected staff, either through the grievance procedures established by the particular library or through the courts is always high, thus requiring library managers to take every reasonable measure to reduce such risks. Of course, there are more positive reasons as well for the importance of job analysis as a personnel management tool. One of the goals of any well run library, in good as well as in bad economic times, is to provide both a high quality and a high quantity of information service, for information is the library's chief product, its pri-

Advances in Library Administration and Organization, Volume 3, pages 209–219.
Copyright © 1984 by JAI Press Inc.
All rights of reproduction in any form reserved.
ISBN: 0-89232-386-8

mary output. A major component in guaranteeing both the desired quality and quantity is the careful matching of people, based on demonstrated skills, aptitude and other significant personal characteristics, with the appropriate jobs, as determined by a clear understanding on the part of management of all the relevant components of those jobs. This is the basic purpose of the job analysis.

Efficiency in manufacturing and other production organizations has been defined by a formula,

$$\frac{OUTPUT}{INPUT} = EFFICIENCY:$$

thus, the objective of productivity becomes increased output per unit of human effort, no matter how each of these factors is measured. If the efficiency formula is converted to dollars, the relationship is clearer:

$$\frac{\$ OUTPUT}{\$ MANHOURS OF WORK} = PRODUCTIVITY$$

A job analysis of the content of the position (and this is both the key element in job analysis as well as the most difficult to perform, even for experienced managers) along with the requirements of skill or education necessary to perform the duties well can increase productivity significantly by helping the manager (1) to determine all of the elements of the job in order (2) to ascertain what specific skills are necessary to perform effectively each of the elements, toward the objective of (3) assigning someone to perform the job, the skills and other qualities of which best match the requirements.

Librarians are not accustomed to thinking in terms of a dollar value on their information product because there are no agreed upon measures for this output, but nonetheless, a dollar value for the service does exist. This fact can be more readily recognized if the above formula is applied to the growing number of information brokering firms which contract to provide information service for a fee.

The following chart partially demonstrates the reason for the extraordinary emphasis accorded the job analysis, not only in selecting and terminating staff, but also in the equally important areas of staff training and job evaluation for the purpose of establishing appropriate compensation ranges and levels. The market establishes a price for both education and skill, but it is a common practice among employers to inflate the wage bill by requiring more qualifications than are really necessary for a particular job or by including in the job responsibilities only a fraction of what it should include.

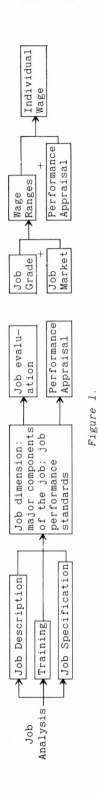

Figure 1.

A recent development in personnel management is the concept of "comparable worth" in determining appropriate compensation, complemented by the law requiring equal pay for equal work. It is instructive to note that a federal district court in Pennsylvania has ruled that discrimination in pay may be inferred from the fact that no evaluation had been undertaken which would have indicated the worth of the jobs to the company.[1] It is uncommon for library managers, particularly in academic libraries, to think in these terms about the positions that make up their organizations. Many of the recent employment laws and regulations have as their basis such concepts as "comparable worth," thus making it necessary for librarians to add new dimensions to their own thinking about personnel decisions and practices. Most decisions about the legality of personnel practices can be made more intelligently, however, by examining, not the laws themselves, but the theories underlying the laws.

EQUAL EMPLOYMENT OPPORTUNITY REQUIREMENTS

Two theories are fundamental in considering the methods of selection, placement, training, promotion, layoff, discipline and termination under the antidiscrimination laws: (1) the theory of disparate treatment and (2) the theory of disparate impact.

Under the first theory, an applicant from one of the protected classes who has been turned down for a position for which he or she has applied must establish an intent on the part of management to discriminate by actively seeking and/or hiring people from outside the protected classes, even though the applicant from the protected class was fully qualified. Another application of the theory involves the disciplining of a member of a protected class for violating a job–related rule or policy when others in the organization have not been punished for the same kind of infraction. Because of the more obvious nature of the violations involving the theory of disparate treatment, and because of the priority that the American Library Association and other professional library organizations have given in recent years to adherence to equal employment laws and regulations, such violations in libraries today ought to be infrequent.

The theory of disparate impact, however, may be both more serious and more significant to the organization because of its potentially wider impact on the organization. A violation involving this theory is likely to involve many staff members in a class action suit because it concerns selection methods which may have substantial adverse impact on a protected group as a whole, not just on one individual staff member or potential staff member. It is more difficult for a manager to guard against this kind of problem because many jobs in a library, particularly at the professional level, are complex or comprised of many types of skills and job elements, so that the manager often is unaware that there are elements in the job which could create problems. What is required is that there be a high degree of correlation between the criteria used for any personnel action and the job to which that personnel action is directly related. A fairly simple example, and one that should be familiar to all librarians, will suffice to illustrate. If policy in an academic library requires that any professional librarian must have a second master's degree in a subject discipline, a review of the content of the librarian position should immediately and clearly demonstrate the need for the more specialized knowledge for that particular position. The recent concern by the library profession about what constitutes the minimum competencies a beginning professional librarian should have is a further illustration of the importance of this theory. Does the content of the job that the typical entry level librarian is hired to do really require the specialized skills and knowledge which are usually acquired through master's level work in library and/or information science? This critical issue, which is far from being resolved by the profession, can be at least partially addressed by the job analysis process.

LEARNING THE LANGUAGE

The terms job description and job analysis are frequently used interchangeably by many managers, but the two terms are not synonymous. Job descriptions are usually one or two page descriptions of the various activities which a job requires a person to perform, including specific functions or areas in the organization for which a person holding the job may be responsible. They may also include some information about basic skills necessary to perform the activities, and they frequently include a description of the other people or positions within the organization with whom the person normally will need to interact or communicate. Ideally, all of the elements in a job description will be drawn from information gleaned in preparing a job analysis.

A number of the terms which have specific meanings in the field of personnel administration frequently occur in other disciplines and contexts with quite different meanings. Specifically, there are five basic terms which have special meanings as they are used in understanding and performing job analyses: element, task, function, position and job. Each of these terms will be defined and examined separately as a preliminary to a discussion of how a job analysis is performed and how it may be used in a library setting.

The *element* is the smallest step or increment into which it is possible to subdivide a work activity without getting into an analysis of motions, movements or specific thought processes involved in performing the work activity. The use of the term element in this context is analagous to its use in chemistry, to denote building blocks of which specific forms of matter are composed, and hence the various parts to which matter can be reduced. In their personnel context, elements are constant over time and from place to place, even though technological innovations may occur which change the method by which a specific element of a task is performed. Thus, not only is it the smallest step or increment of a work activity, but it is also fundamental and necessary to that activity. In this regard, task elements are analogous to the elements of mathematics which are constant through time and without regard to location, although the method of solving mathematical problems, and perhaps even the problems themselves, may be quite different.

A *task* is a discreet unit of work which an individual performs to accomplish a specific purpose. It usually consists of more than one element and it in turn, along with other tasks, makes up a function (to be defined later). A task usually has several characteristics. It has an identifiable beginning and conclusion. It consists of an action and something on which the action is performed. It frequently occurs with considerable uniformity. It is easier to identify tasks in activities that are physical in nature than in those that are primarily mental in nature, though it is no less important in a job analysis which involves a large component of mental activity, such as supervision or planning. To illustrate how the two terms are related, in the task of circulating a library book to a borrower, there are a number of elements, including determining the date due on the item borrowed, noting that date on the item, making a record of the transaction, and storing the record in some manner so that it can be easily retrieved when the item is returned.

A *function* is a larger segment of work which the worker performs on no regular cycle and for which there are considerable variety and flexibility in the way it is performed. For example, the function of supervision may include selection, training and discipline of staff and appraising staff performance, among many other responsibilities.

A *position* is a collection of tasks and/or functions which comprise the total work of one worker. Each worker in the organization occupies a position, and a position exists whether or not anyone is filling it.

A *job* is a group of positions which are made up primarily of the same major tasks or functions. They should be sufficiently similar to be dealt with as a unit in a job analysis. In a larger organization, there may be several people who are described as having essentially the same job. For example, secretaries, catalog assistants, circulation clerks, and reference librarians are all employed in respective positions made up of almost identical tasks.

PERFORMING THE JOB ANALYSIS

The first step in performing a job analysis is accurately and precisely to identify the tasks or functions (the *what* of the job) and the elements (the *how* of the job). Determining the job limits by identifying and charting the starting point and concluding point of a job, as illustrated in Figure 2, is useful for coordinating analysis activities among several positions.

Generally, in describing the tasks and elements, that is, the procedures which make up a job, the first step is to list all elements and tasks which can be identified as part of the job. Next, to achieve a better understanding of the job being analyzed, the tasks and elements should be grouped according to the following categories: routine or daily tasks or functions, periodic tasks or functions, and irregular tasks or functions. The job of secretary to the director of the library provides a good example of how the classification process works. Routine tasks for the typical secretary include routing mail, making appointments, taking and transcribing dictation, and filing and retrieving documents. Periodic functions include such tasks as arranging committee meetings, compiling information for regular administrative reports or for budget preparation and reporting, and distributing internal management information to appropriate departments. Irregular functions might include assembling, classifying and summarizing budget data; compiling and organizing data for preparing grant requests; and assisting the director in special administrative assignments which may be delegated to him or her from time to time by his or her supervisor. Of course, jobs at this level may also include supervision of other positions, depending upon the size and complexity of the library and the number of other office staff necessary for the effective operation of the director's office. These supervisory duties would be classified along with the other duties.

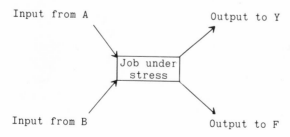

Figure 2.

A single job analysis should describe only one job as it exists and is normally performed in the organization. Temporary assignments which are not a part of the regular job should not be included in the analysis. One advantage of the job analysis is that it is one way a manager can be alerted to the fact that a staff member is frequently overburdened with elements or tasks. Assuming that the staff member is competent and conscientious, this situation should be a clear signal to the manager that the general work flow and the specific job need to be carefully examined to see if procedures have multiplied or overlapped. The position may need to be redefined or reorganized, or perhaps the creation of an additional position may actually be in order.

There are four basic methods of collecting the job data in a job analysis: administering questionnaires to a person or persons performing the job, interviewing a person in a job, observing a person as he or she performs the various aspects of his or her job, and having the person keep a diary or log detailing the job elements and tasks. Some examples of forms which might be adapted to a library setting for each of these methods are available in several sources.[2] Depending on the complexity and level of the job, a combination of the methods may be appropriate. But regardless of the method used to collect the information, the basic data required for the analysis are the same:

1. Routine tasks or functions
2. Periodic tasks or functions
3. Irregular tasks or functions
4. Equipment required
5. Environmental conditions, such as excessive noise, heat or cold
6. Emotional demands, such as monotony (as in shelving), pressure of time, and interaction with the public
7. Physical demands such as lifting or prolonged use of a video terminal
8. Specialized knowledge requiring special skills or special training
9. Education required to do the job
10. Work place location such as outdoors or in remote areas of the building

All of the data summarized above have some relevance to the library setting, but will vary from library to library and from position to position. Some will likely be less critical to libraries, such as the work place location and environmental conditions, unless the library building is poorly designed or has badly deteriorated over time.

The process of gathering the necessary data should heavily involve both the employee and the supervisor since together their input will be able to provide the most thorough and accurate information about the job being analyzed. It is critical that there be agreement between the employee and the staff member about the nature, elements and complexity of the job. In fact, one benefit of such a process is that inevitably both the employee and the supervisor derive a better understanding of the job itself, as well as a greater appreciation for each other's respective roles in the work place.

ORGANIZING THE DATA

After all the necessary information has been assembled, the next step is to draft a job description or a general statement of the essential duties required of the person assigned to the job. The distinction between the job description and the job analysis has been explained earlier in this article. The job description is not useful in the training process nor is it an acceptable device for determining what qualifications a person should have to do the job effectively. Furthermore, the elements of the task, that is, the *how* of the job, are omitted in the job description. The description, however, normally does serve as the basic document for purposes of job performance evaluation.

The job analysis should include the detailed elements of each task or function for any position, as well as the knowledge, skills and training required to perform the job adequately. Of course, library work has as its aim to provide a service in which there is no production of a tangible product. This does not mean, however, that the job analysis process cannot be applied in the library setting because many of the jobs in a library do involve a tangible outcome, i.e., the production of catalog cards, ordering library materials, stack maintenance, checking in and processing serials, and production of non–print materials. The job analysis process is highly applicable to such jobs. However, the applicability of the process to the work of the professional staff is less readily apparent. This intangibility of the work of librarians is a characteristic libraries share with all other service organizations. Therefore, it is important to recognize that in service occupations, there are certain refinements which must be made to the procedures.

The most appropriate method of organizing the data for librarians is a two–column chart, one column identified as the *doing,* that is, the task or function, and the other identified as *knowing,* that is, the actual knowledge required for the job, the level of skill necessary to perform it and the education which is a requisite to the job.[3] See Figure 3.

When the doing column has been completed, the specifications for the minimum entry level requirements for the job under study should be read-

Job Title _____ Date _____	
Doing	Knowing

1. Task
  a. Elements
  b. or
  c. Procedures
2. Task
  Elements
	Level of education, skill,
	special knowledge (by
	experience or prior
	training)

Figure 3.

ily apparent. Although the accurate identification of all the tasks which should be included in the doing column is critical in producing a usable job analysis, the procedure itself is a relatively uncomplicated one. However, establishing the appropriate level of education, skill and special knowledge for the knowing column is considerably more complex. It is in this area that the profession has been facing challenges in recent years by those contending that either the minimum entry level for beginning librarians has been set too high by the profession as a whole or that there are alternate routes to graduate study to attain these minimum competencies. The job analysis holds significant promise for helping to resolve this critical issue.

To complete the chart, a summary of all extraordinary physical or emotional demands; unpleasant or hazardous working conditions, if any, should be provided. These elements are necessary so that when the job is evaluated for compensation purposes, these factors can be considered as a basis for extra renumeration.

The purpose of this article has not been to provide detailed, step–by–step instructions on how to do a job analysis, but rather to present an overview of the process, an understanding of the essential components, and a discussion of its importance in the library setting. The job analysis process is obviously a complex one, and in large libraries which have a separate personnel office, the function will normally be performed by the personnel officer. However, the job analysis is no less important to small libraries, and the techniques for performing a job analysis can be learned by any competent librarian. It is just one more valuable tool for the library manager who values improved organizational life, improved service and good management.

There is ample evidence that a majority of companies which are not service organizations consider the use of job analysis to be an essential part of their personnel programs. One study, for example, places the figure at 75% of all companies.[4] In recent years the library profession has successfully adapted many management practices developed by industry; job analysis is just one more of these tools which can enhance the quality of information service which libraries provide.

NOTES AND REFERENCES

1. Taylor v. Charley Bros. Co., 25 FEP Cases 602. Reported in *Labor Relations Reporter,* Vol. 106, No. 31 (April 20, 1971).

2. As one example, see Ernest J. McCormick, *Job Analysis: Methods and Applications* (New York: AMACOM, 1979).

3. Verne C. Fryklund, *Occupational Analysis: Techniques and Procedures* (New York: The Bruce Publishing Company, 1970).

4. Jean J. Jones, Jr., and Thomas A. DeCottis, "Job Analysis: National Survey Findings." *Personnel Journal* 48 (October 1969): 805.

COLLEGE LIBRARY USERS AND NONUSERS

Nurieh Musavi and John F. Harvey

INTRODUCTION

As a result of rapid social changes and enrollment increase, the double decade, 1960–80, was an outstanding period in academic library history. Student dissatisfaction with the education system, which reflected that social change, was a significant aspect of widespread campus unrest and brought many protests against old policies and patterns.[1] Consequent reevaluation included extensive demand for improvement in course content and the relationship between education patterns and social change.[2] Many attempts were made to improve the entire education system. Sanford said, "The primary aim of education is the fullest possible development of the individual."[3]

Higher education changes did not lessen the library's importance. It was still regarded as a resource center in which individuals could expand their subject knowledge. In seeking to achieve the education systems'

Advances in Library Administration and Organization, Volume 3, pages 221–240.
ISBN: 0-89232-386-8

new objectives, both administrators and librarians believed that it could play a dynamic role. While the library was still considered indispensable, integration with the curriculum had not yet been achieved, nor had utilization for personal satisfaction been realized by a majority of students.[4] The library was also forced to recognize the new challenges and demands.[5] Four factors impacted strongly on library organization and functions:

1. Changes in educational objectives, or, at least, in methods of achieving these objectives
2. Proliferation of the new information media and of data base services
3. Rapid growth in human knowledge and the number of resulting publications
4. Government fund availability

With the 1970s financial stringency and inflation, but also rapidly changing educational objectives, continuous international publication increases and flourishing interdisciplinary programs, libraries could not meet all of the demands made upon them. Thus, library development slowed down and existing functions—especially collection development programs and public service—received extensive criticism. A short summary of this dissatisfaction will offer an insight into the library's most critical problem, lack of user attention, and illuminate the need for our present study.[6]

The major thrust of this study is that the opinions of higher education and library specialists should not form the sole basis for developing library service; other factors should also be considered. The academic library's main function is to supply information. Since, in the past, considerable evidence indicated that only a narrow fraction of the information supplied was used, many persons doubted that library service could be cost effective, justified, or indeed, ever be performed effectively. Poole said:

> It is a well-known fact and one regretted by the wisest educators, that the great majority of the college and university students graduate with very little knowledge of books and their use. How the evil can be remedied is a question easier to ask than to answer.[7]

Although depicted as "the heart of the college," studies have shown that a large undergraduate ratio seldom uses the library.[8] Perhaps because of the wisespread idea that teaching faculty members bear primary responsibility for stimulating library use, librarians are negligent in ascertaining student characteristics and needs.[9] Eaton emphasized a need for this user information: "the characteristics of students, scholastic aptitude and achievement, cultural background and interests, high school library orientation, and access to good public library facilities."[10] Mendelson and Wingard complained:

> There is not only a woeful lack of information available to policy makers on the use of libraries, or even on what constitutes their use, but even less has been published regarding the reasons for nonuse.[11]

In 1963, a National Advisory Commission study inquired into student needs, due to library inadequacies in meeting them.[12] In 1968, the National Advisory Commission undertook a large use study "to provide adequate library service for formal education at all levels."[13] Findings (Dougherty and Bloomquist, 1974) emphasized infrequent use and inadequate resources to rectify the situation. They found that library expansion impacted little on use:

> Academic libraries have traditionally functioned as passive service agencies; that is, they have served people who have initiated the effort to receive their services, but have made little effort to seek out those who may have information needs but have not sought satisfaction in libraries.[14]

Growing demand, high cost, dissatisfaction with the library function, storage and retrieval mechanism improvement, rapid human knowledge increase and publication growth made imperative librarians' awareness of potential users' needs and characteristics prior to new investment planning. Dougherty wrote: " . . . we are concerned about developing library services which will change current user antipathies."[15]

User studies were valueless in identifying potential users and their environments:

> The most common criticism of user studies is that they study users, the people who actually come into the library; the real question is that of the potential population. The user implies that there are also nonusers. Why do nonusers not use the system? What is the difference between users and nonusers? What are the characteristics of these people?[16]

Regarding user population analyses, Olson said, "The emphasis should be on factors the library probably is not aware of . . ."[17] Nonuser studies have been very limited; yet they must be carried out widely to facilitate research result generalization. In comparison with other information system types, academic libraries were less attentive to planning foundations. Current user feedback was needed to assist in correcting operational deviations and developing new plans.[18]

> There are many values to be obtained from performing a user study as a basis for library planning. First, it enables decisions to be based on an objective market analysis of the needs, habits and desires of the intended recipients of the service. Although

an individual may feel that he has a good grasp of his audience's preferences from less formal means of analysis, his beliefs and recommendations will have a sounder foundation and will be more readily accepted by others if they arise from an organized user study.[19]

Information center design, according to Peter Urbach (1967), should be based on " . . . studies of the users' habits and interaction with the existing system."[20] Lucas (1974) moved a step further: "Creative systems design emphasizes the user's role; we shall suggest that the user should actually design the system himself."[21] The National Commission on Libraries and Information Science (NCLIS) attempted to expand user need understanding; Cuadra wrote, " . . . there has been a dearth of serious solid effort to identify and articulate user needs."[22] NCLIS further emphasized the need for knowing potential users:

> The Commission's working philosophy is user–oriented. It is the Commission's intent that information users, including potential as well as current, should be the principal focus of a national program.[23]

Library performance must be permanently monitored. If system objectives are not obtained at a satisfactory level, deviations must be detected and correction steps taken. A satisfactory performance level cannot be achieved unless a feedback mechanism is devised to function as a controller before performance deviates significantly. Without potential user input, it is impossible to evaluate performance and design a satisfactory system. System evaluation should be based on users' use and satisfaction. Certain marketing concepts are appropriate for improving library performance. In marketing, performance is optimized through market place feedback. Not only must operation efficiency be considered but cost effectiveness as well for determining acceptable standards. A poorly used library is not cost effective and its potential users must be unaware of resources and ignorant of use techniques or for some reason dislike or perceive no need to use them.

When system users are reached (in the library), their satisfaction with services and resources can be measured. However, since nonusers are not found there, their attitudes and resource use skill should be investigated separately. A library can reach its objectives only by serving all potential users. The following model was constructed to improve library performance for effective utilization by the entire student body:

a. Setting library objectives and goals
b. Collecting all relevant data about potential users' needs and characteristics
c. Designing a new system or altering the existing one to provide

    resources and services matching system objectives with potential user needs and expectations

d. Publicizing resources and services
e. Giving instruction for utilizing resources and services
f. Providing the loan unit with a mechanism to identify infrequent users
g. Planning the following surveys:
    Attitudes
    Use skills
    Awareness levels
h. Based on findings, changing plans, services and resources
i. Revising the instruction method, if necessary, as well as changing user relations and revising staff behavior
j. Planning follow–up surveys
k. Making necessary changes

USER STUDIES

Only a sampling of academic library user studies can be highlighted here, but all which gave close attention to nonusers have been included. A 1932 University of Minnesota investigation by Eurich was one of the oldest.[24] He found library users' scholarship standing to be significantly higher than that of nonusers. He did not, however, find a statistically significant relationship between grade point average and extent of use. McDiarmid's 1935 study is still valuable and could be used as a model. He believed that "a continuous survey of students' needs and interests" formed a vital element in library function planning. He found four parameters to influence student reading: sex, class, scholarship and institutional environment, and he commented: "The fact that most library reading is curricular does not mean that the librarian has nothing to do with it."[25]

In 1940, Harvie Branscomb conducted a famous study.[26] His findings, relating library use to class standing, sex and grade point average, were later confirmed by Knapp and Lane.[27,28] They discovered that a library use increase occurred between the freshman and sophomore and the junior and senior years: students with lower grades withdrew less material and females withdrew more books than males. Knapp's Knox College study indicated that "differences in sex, scholastic aptitude and scholastic achievement had little or no connection with tendency toward or away from library use."[29] Lane's study revealed 63% of male University of Delaware students to have checked out no books during a two year period, and use increased progressively from the freshman through the senior year.[30]

Clayton found that parents' occupation type and education level had little impact on student use.[31] Students from low income families used the library more than others and secondary school size correlated with library use. Based on circulation data, the findings disclosed that a high percentage of students used no library facilities.

Jain conducted a 1966 Purdue University Library study.[32] His findings agreed with those of Knapp who indicated that 90% of Knox's circulation was course–related and 25% of the courses accounted for 90% of the circulation. Hostrop found that instructors, rather than student characteristics, were the chief student–use determinants. Term paper and speech assignments were the primary factors activating use.

In the entire sample, 6.7% of the 419 students were responsible for more than half of the reserve loans; 4.3% for more than half of the periodical loans; 12.7% for more than half of the general collection loans; and 17.4% for more than half of the total loans. The College Library nonuser is more likely to be a male than a female, and probably is slightly older than the mean. He is more likely to be living away from home than with his family. He is somewhat less able than the student body as a whole in scholastic aptitude, high school scholastic achievement and college record.[33]

Mendelsohn and Wingard reported

That fewer than 30% of the students were found using library facilities during a given week and that the majority of the men sampled withdrew no material from the general collection during a given semester have important implications for curriculum and library planning. That the general collection is not widely used and that its use does not have a significant relationship to academic achievement suggests that an evaluation of library usefulness in terms of collection alone would be most inadequate. The finding that few students use the library for recreational reading raises questions about maintaining relatively high proportions of literature and recreational collections. In addition, a large proportion of (users) bring their own material.[34]

Lubans studied Rensselaer Polytechnic Institute nonusers:

One of the major findings . . . is that library use, especially in the eyes of the nonuser, is strictly course–related and unless he is guided in this manner, the inspiration, inclination or time are not there for the student to extend himself. A subjective conclusion is that use or nonuse is not based on intellectual capacity or quality point average.[35]

In 1974 Lubans conducted another study "to provide input from library users/nonusers into library instruction." Out of 370 questionnaires, 37.6% implied that the respondent was a non or infrequent user. One major nonuse reason was a perceived lack of need, another was ignorance about the extent of service and material available.[36] Lubans strongly confirmed Taylor's opinion that nonuse depended on "a whole range of attitudes and environmental factors":

> Pre–college experience with libraries, failure of instructors to utilize the library except as a glorified reserve collection, the failure of librarians to respond to existing needs, and librarians' lack of understanding that, to an outsider, a library is a complex and frequently frustrating system to use. Today, particularly, the user is offered many more options and channels for information needs than the library presently offers.[37]

Another Colorado survey reported:

> Among college students, research or reference was the primary service used. Less frequently mentioned were circulation services or using the library as a work atmosphere. (Nonusers) gave a number of reasons—being a part–time student, taking extension courses, or being enrolled but attending another school—mostly related to the library not being available or convenient.[38]

Among these investigations, only Lubans' two studies gave nonusers close attention. Tobin, who attempted to give a total international user study picture in all library types also found a paucity on nonusers:

> Of the 477 user studies indexed . . . only five were on nonusers. Since nonusers generally outnumber users, the total of 1% of the world's use studies devoted to nonusers would seem to be inadequate.[39]

While academic library user studies have continued to be completed and reported, the present nonuser study is the only one which could be identified in recent years. The foremost center of user study information is the Centre for Research on User Studies, University of Sheffield, Sheffield, United Kingdom. An ongoing Centre study is the Information Needs of Undergraduates Project which has reported very brief preliminary findings, including nonuser information.[40] Apparently, more attention has been paid recently to nonusers in other library types. For instance, the public library field contains several interesting studies, but the carryover value for academic libraries is hard to calculate and probably limited.[41] Special and school libraries are also represented but the same limitation applies.[42]

STUDY DESIGN

As one approach to library performance measurement, this study has sought to compare library attitudes, skills and awareness of users with nonusers. A primary concern was to establish feedback from all potential users and to facilitate user vs. nonuser comparison. It was based on students' self assessment shown in questionnaire results. No objective device, such as a test, was applied to measure skills, awareness or attitudes.

Definitions:

1. User: A student library material borrower during the term under study
2. Nonuser: A student who checked out no items
3. Attitude: "An attitude is a relatively enduring organization of beliefs around an object or situation predisposing one to respond in some preferential manner."[43] "An attitude represents integration of thought, feeling and deed."[44]

Primary aims for which users were hypothesized to score higher than nonusers:

1. To compare levels of user and nonuser awareness of library services and resources
2. To compare levels of user and nonuser skills in utilizing library resources and services
3. To compare approval levels of user and nonuser attitudes toward libraries and librarians

The universe under investigation comprised an entire college student body. From each group, users and nonusers, seventy students were selected by random sampling. With his approval, Lubans' questionnaires were combined in revised form, together with additional questions to make the instrument more appropriate. The questionnaire contained thirty–four questions and 126 variables and was pretested before use. Table preparation and statistical testing, such as t–test and Chi–Square administration, was accomplished through utilization of the SPSS package at the University of Pittsburgh Computer Center. All findings discussed here were determined to be statistically significant at satisfactory probability levels.

Each questionnaire was individually delivered to the student and completed on the spot. Explanations were given readily and useful information recorded while the conversation progressed. Certain students were approached at their homes and others in the college dormitory thru prior appointments. Some students were eager to discuss their answers and libraries at length.

Greater difficulty was experienced in making appointments with and obtaining reliable information from nonusers than users. Nonusers tried to hide the truth more often than did users. Normally, the questionnaire took 45–50 minutes to complete, but several nonusers gave it much less time. Often, their lack of interest, cooperation, truthfulness or respect for the higher education system was apparent in their comments. Responses which disagreed with library or other records or were internally inconsistent were discarded. In spite of the great difficulty in locating many of them, fifty users and fifty nonusers were eventually identified, found, and interviewed, and they gave dependable replies.

CARLOW COLLEGE AND GRACE LIBRARY

Carlow (formerly Mount Mercy) College, Pittsburgh, Pennsylvania, USA, was founded in 1929. Its primary purpose is to promote women's education and status and to encourage lifelong learning. The College offers a "truly liberalizing and humanizing education." By integrating liberal arts and professional programs, the College provides opportunities not only for women to improve their knowledge but also to enter professional fields. Carlow has commendable facilities, charges a high tuition rate, and is affiliated with the Roman Catholic Church.

Enrollment numbered 750 full- and 250 special and part–time students. They came from several Eastern and Middle Atlantic states but mostly from Western Pennsylvania and Eastern Ohio. Ten percent of them belonged to ethnic minorities, and 3% were males. There were 45 full and 40 part–time faculty members representing a 1:14 ratio with students.

At the time of the study, Carlow awarded the Bachelor of Arts degree in sixteen and the Bachelor of Science in three academic areas. The college occupies a thirteen acre campus in Oakland, Pittsburgh's civic and cultural center. Having easy access to so many nearby cultural facilities is probably the main reason that Carlow students in the study had a higher library service awareness level than did students in previous investigations. Carlow's Grace Library is located centrally in a 1969 campus building. It is attractive and modern and has comfortable and colorful facilities.

Five hundred thirty Fall Term students check out 5849 items. This was a mean of 11.0 or a median of 5.3 items per student user and a mean of

Table 1. Grace Library Statistics, Fall Term, 1975

Collection		Staff	
Book volumes	82810	FTE Librarians	4
Periodical volumes	13376	FTE Support Staff	7
Total volumes	96186	Student aids	25
Book titles	66869	Weekly service hours	66
Titles added 1974–75	2278		
Media items added 1974–75	618	Term Circulation	
Periodical subscriptions	450	Volumes loaned to students	5849
Newspaper subscriptions	12	Volumes loaned to faculty/staff	371
Microfilms	9929	Total	6220

Table 2.   Library Circulation Frequency

Number of Students	Number of Books Checked Out	% of Users
88	1	17%
187	2–5	35
140	6–10	26
78	11–20	15
26	21–30	5
5	31–40	1
4	41–50	1
1	57	0
1	102	0
530		100%

5.8 or a median of 0.3 items per student body member. Faculty use was low; only seven faculty members borrowed books, one of them checking out 53 books, 14% of the total. Table 2 shows the student use pattern for borrowed books. Reserved book loan was not included; only a few items were on reserve and use was low.

Two hundred seventy five students checked out five or fewer books. They constituted 52% of the borrower total and could be grouped as infrequent or low users. Students who borrowed more than five and less than twenty books could be grouped as medium users and constituted 41% of the total. Thirty seven students or 7% were grouped as high users. If the data is analysed differently, another conclusion can be obtained. Five hundred thirty students, or 53% of the entire student body, used the library. Forty seven percent of the students checked out no books. If we add the nonusers, 470, to the low users, 275, then 745 students, or almost 75%, fell into the low or nonuser group. In contrast, thirty seven students distinguished as high users comprised only 3.7% of the student body but were responsible for more than 20% of student circulation.

Equal numbers of total students came from each of the four class levels. Freshmen were the most frequent users. Thirty two percent of all users were freshmen, 26% sophomores, 24% seniors and 18% juniors. The reverse order applied to nonborrowers. We can argue that seniors must have had a three year library service exposure, so they could be expected to have better use skill and resource awareness than freshmen, but their use did not reflect it.

Among users, 40% were commuters. Fortunately, 75% of this group completed questionnaires. Among nonusers, 53% were commuters and 62% of this group were reached. Most commuters were married, had children, and were somewhat older than dormitory students. In addition, the number of male nonusers was three times that of male users. These findings were consistent with those of similar studies, as far as sex and age variables were concerned. The user sample contained one Black student, whereas the nonuser group contained eight.

USERS VS. NONUSERS

Library Awareness

If no differences were detected between users and nonusers in the length or amount of student exposure to different kinds of libraries, if the two groups revealed similar demands for library resources, and if the faculty had informed them both about these services and resources, then the two groups would be equally aware of them. The groups had had almost equal access to grade and high school libraries; about 90% of each group had had both grade and high school library experience. College library use, however, differed sharply between them. The question, "Do you use your college library?", elicited affirmative responses from 100% of the user group but from only 22% of the nonuser group (whose use did not involve borrowing material).

Nonusers gave the following nonuse reasons: "no need" 34% "poor collection" 30%, "using another library" 28% and no answer 8%. "Poor collection," however, was not a reasonable excuse if not used regularly; how could a nonuser evaluate the collection? Most students who considered the collection poor used other libraries instead. The question, "Do you use other academic libraries in this area?", offered another perspective. Eighty–eight percent of users and 72% of nonusers stated that they did. Though users used other academic libraries more, the proportion who evaluated Grace Library as "poor" was higher in the nonuser group. Why had the nonusers formed such a negative opinion?

Of the total, 75% used the University of Pittsburgh Central Library (Hillman); 19%, Carnegie–Mellon University Library (Hunt); 22% Falk Medical and the Western Psychiatric Institute Libraries and 2% University of Pittsburgh departmental libraries. Only 39% used other academic libraries because of "better collections." None mentioned closeness or convenience. Then why did so many students use another library? Administrative officers commented that, since the College was overwhelmingly female, male students might have attracted Carlow coeds to nearby campuses.

The interviews revealed that neither users nor nonusers had borrowed books from other libraries, nor were they aware of interlibrary loan policies. More users than nonusers were specific about resource use in nearby libraries. Almost all users had used other libraries' periodical collections, 60% had used the reference collection, and 25% the book collection. Among nonusers, 30% used periodicals and 17% the reference collection.

Whereas 68% of users used the public library also, only 28% of nonusers did so. Commuters were more often nonusers than users. It was natural to assume that they would use their own community public libraries but they did not. They used the Carnegie Public Library, Pittsburgh, instead. "Better collection" and not "closeness" was the reason given for public library use. Sixty percent of users and 42% of nonusers indicated that the faculty reserved material in Grace Library, and 52% of users and 30% of nonusers had had assignments requiring library use. Other use studies also found a strong class assignment and use association.

Asked to suggest new or different kinds of resources to improve the collection, a smaller proportion of nonusers than users had suggestions or even indicated that resources had been useful. Books were the most important resource and periodicals second. Twice as many users as nonusers asked for "computerized reference services."

Although not large, the two groups' difference on library awareness as a whole proved to be statistically significant. The user group use frequency for all libraries was much higher than that of the nonuser group. A higher proportion of users than nonusers was aware of various resources. And a larger number of users than nonusers had been informed by the faculty of reserve collections and had received library use assignments. In the interviews, on the other hand, discounting actual use, users and nonusers demonstrated equal library awareness. They had almost equal knowledge of what they could find in libraries.

Library Skill Knowledge

Necessary assumptions were that if the students in each group had obtained equal use instruction, had equivalent experience with different libraries and had equal confidence in their ability to use resources, then their skills would be considered equal.

The two groups had had similar experience in using high school libraries for assigned and recreational reading. They had had equal amounts of library resource use instruction, and 80% of users and 74% of nonusers had perceived a need for "recorded information" to fulfill college assignments. Yet, despite these similarities, a significant usage difference remained between the two groups.

Only 22% of nonusers had used the college library, most of them in response to a specific assignment. Obviously, then, students did not consider the library to be the prime choice as a recorded information source. Instead, 48% indicated that they would go to faculty members for guidance, while 44% preferred classmates. Of the 67% who would go to librarians for guidance, only 24% named them as the first choice. Obviously, the potential of the most expensive resource, librarians, was not fully utilized.

Significant group differences were revealed in three Grace Library use questions. The first one, "to do your assignment," was checked by 72% of users but only 18% of nonusers. For the second one, 96% of users but only 12% of nonusers had used the library "to do research." The students who went "to borrow books or other material," included 88% of users but only 18% of nonusers.

Nonusers consistently showed a lower skill level than users in library resource use. Consequently, more nonusers than users expressed the need to learn more about resource use. The groups demonstrated equal interest, however, in learning "government document," "audio–visual material," and "interlibrary loan" use. Special collections were unknown to 72% of the users and 86% of nonusers. Fifty-two percent of users and 78% of nonusers did not know how to use indexes and abstracts. The proportion of nonusers unfamiliar with reference book use, 62%, was much higher than that for users, 36%. In card catalog use, shelf arrangement familiarity and library procedures, users' greater skill was evident. Test results showed a significant difference between users and nonusers in utilizing library resources and library skill knowledge generally, in favor of users.

Attitudes Toward Libraries and Librarians

The most interesting result was observed in data collected to measure student attitudes toward libraries and librarians. The main assumption made was that as negative attitudes increased, library utilization would decrease. Students' library perceptions as well as library evaluations were investigated. It was assumed that students who used Grace Library little or not at all and who did not know other academic libraries well had a poor basis for reasoned evaluation, since responses could only reflect personal feelings.

Only 2% of nonusers evaluated the college library as very good. Whereas 50% of users believed the library was good, only 18% of nonusers thought so. The largest difference was between nonusers and users evaluating the library as poor, 32% to 6%. When asked why, most nonusers complained about too few reserve book copies or too many books missing or on loan. Nonusers had a low frustration threshold. Although frustrated only a few times, still they were convinced that they would never find what they needed. While explaining these problems, some nonusers became emotional and upset.

Nonusers avoided revealing how they managed course work and suggested that textbook reading had enabled them to pass examinations and acquire good grades. Some thought the library was too quiet and boring, but almost the same number complained about library noise. Most nonusers believed that their postgraduation jobs would not be affected by the extent of their college studies and that whatever they studied could not help them in many practical life situations. Forty percent of them had very little hope of finding a post–graduation job that they would like. By contrast, only 10% among users held similar views. Most nonusers believed that a college education was not necessary in order to get a well paid job. Apparently, they had gone to college primarily because their parents wanted them to do so.

Nonusers indicated frequently that social problems reduced college education value. Attempts to elicit their ideas about pursuing a college education to improve the mind and help improve social conditions showed that none of them had these ideas. They had not come to college to improve themselves and believed that there was no need to come for that purpose. Asked, had they not come to college, how would they have improved their minds, none of them mentioned library use, or any other source for that matter.

Not surprisingly, the users group was fully aware of library problems, but had not ceased to go there. They did not believe, however, that these inconveniences were the librarians' fault and strongly believed that the entire student body should be well informed about the library. Frequently, they lamented the lack of a system to provide easy access to all library material. Users showed their awareness that Grace Library had a limited budget and that multiple copies and a large periodical collection could not possibly be provided. They had justified these problems to themselves, but hoped the library could obtain a larger budget in the future. It was at this point that a personality difference became apparent between users and nonusers.

More nonusers than users commented negatively about the library and librarians. Moreover, it appeared often that nonusers could not reasonably discriminate between what they believed and wanted. While 34% believed knowing how to use the library had been overrated, 42% rated the orientation program as effective. Significantly, almost twice as many users as nonusers considered the orientation program to be effective. Commenting upon perceived faculty attitudes, 14% of the nonusers believed that "faculty do not place value on the library," and 28% believed that "faculty are noncommittal," whereas only half as many users expressed these beliefs.

Regarding faculty responsibilities for library utilization, in classwork more nonusers had had library use assignments and said the faculty recommended the library highly than had used it. In contrast, about half of the users had had library use assignments and said that faculty recommended the library highly, but 100% used it. At the same time, one third of the high users indicated no recorded information needed, yet borrowed more than twenty one books apiece. Was it possible that faculty assignments had little student library utilization impact? Perhaps use depended on the kind of assignment and the way faculty integrated the library with course work.

Only a third of the students said they thought the faculty recommended the library highly; almost the same proportion stated that faculty made library use assignments. Consequently, student need for recorded information could apparently be met without library use. When the faculty gave assignments, they did not in fact commit students to library use. Most nonusers perceived a need for library use but not a strong enough need to assure use. Therefore, unless faculty urged students very strongly, a large percentage of them did not use the library to complete assignments.

Reviewing student feelings toward librarians, the findings were clear-cut; frequent users were more positive. The number of nonusers with negative feelings was five times greater than the number of users. As usage level decreased, the unfavorable attitude level increased. However, when the nonuser category differences were tested, the majority of nonusers held favorable attitudes toward librarians. Whereas 10% of nonusers and 2% of users believed that their grade school librarians were cruel, 34% of nonusers and 48% of users found them to have been kind. Incidentally, all Black nonusers held extremely negative attitudes toward librarians. When asked, "What do you think about the librarians in your grade school?", most of them said that they had been cruel. Only 22% of nonusers and 4% of users thought that librarians knew nothing and were resentful toward helping them. In total, 71% of the students were favorable toward librarians.

Most nonusers believed that Grace Library did not hold a strong collection and could not be considered a good library. They stopped using the library and did not refer to another library for needed information as frequently as users did. Only 6% of nonusers believed the library to be "the heart of the college," whereas 38% of the users believed in this idea. Most nonusers said they could get along without a library, so the library's role and importance were entirely concealed from them.

In conclusion, those students who used Grace Library during the term, the users, possessed significantly higher degrees of favorable attitudes toward the library and librarians than did the nonusers.

As a final summary of the findings in the three major categories—awareness, skills and attitudes—significant differences between all three of them were shown to exist between Carlow College Library users and nonusers. Their views differed so it was not surprising that their library use differed. Nonusers were a different kind of person and deserved additional study.

OBSERVATIONS AND CONCLUSIONS

Many researchers believe the reasons for a low use rate can be sought inside the academic library. Perhaps librarians discourage students somewhere along the line and this discouragement results in apathy toward libraries. The data revealed in our study, however, showed various aspects of student life which challenged this opinion. Close and extensive student behavior observations and discussions in a variety of situations over time provided many student life insights.

These observations revealed that the conceptual framework from which nonusers viewed such matters differed from that of users. Perceptions of the education and social affairs system were different. What is more, the two groups differed in their manners, clothing and the order in which they kept their dormitory rooms. Their personalities and behavior seemed dissimilar. Academic library utilization is not an isolated phenomenon. During the study, it was impossible to identify completely the factors determining student use without considering the social and environmental conditions which shaped student behavior.

Library nonusers could as well be called college nonusers. After his nonuser investigation, Lubans commented that nonusers did not need to use the library.[45] The nonuser's primary characteristic seemed to be that she had no library use motivation. A motivating situation consists of two sides: "The subjective side is a condition in the individual which is called need. The objective side is an object outside the individual which may be called incentive or goal."[46] Two explanations for the situation can be given:

a.   Most nonusers, in comparison with most users, appeared to lack strong motivation to gain a college education. They were either pushed by parents or certain other social factors had driven them to college. They seemed to lack special objectives or goals.

b.   College resources such as buildings, faculty, classes, laboratories and equipment were equally underutilized by certain student groups. Library resources were not unique in this respect. Different student groups utilized those college resources which related directly to their goals. The number of students who used most or all resources was very small.

A group of students has always been dissatisfied, passive and reluctant to learn, the college–facilities–and–resources nonusers. The generation of the sixties which challenged the social system changed to a passive generation that saw vanity in everything.[47] Most Grace Library nonusers apparently developed the attitudes of indifference, insecurity, noninvolvement, and lack of specific motivation or goals. they showed dissatisfaction with many education and social system elements but at the same time seemed reluctant to learn the reasons for these difficulties. The Carnegie Commission on Higher Education recommended reducing the number of "reluctant attenders" between 5% and 15%.[48]

A student's motivation for learning, her background and personality are the primary factors leading her to enter a college such as Carlow. Her continuation and success are based on personal or academic motivations. The Carlow catalog of 1975 said, "The role of the faculty is clearly that of catalyst, model, consultant, questioner. The motivation for learning must come from within the individual student."

Recognition for the importance of information flow and stored knowledge as the infrastructure of social improvement and progress has led to deep concern for providing comprehensive knowledge sources for academic institution constituencies. Various attempts have been made to satisfy all potential users. Collection expansion, new information media introduction, modern building and equipment provision, and increased emphasis on curriculum integration with library service are evidences that many responsible officials believed libraries should play an active education system role.

Despite the past decade's improvements, use problems have remained serious. The need for ascertaining potential users' interests and characteristics has been asserted by various consultants. An appropriate activity is to study the local nonuser and user situation with the aim of understanding it thoroughly. Continuous student need, interest and characteristics surveys are a vital library function planning element. Based on an understanding of potential user characteristics, certain nonusers could be transformed into users through close cooperation among librarians, teaching faculty, psychological consultants and students. The investigation's experimental methodology demonstrated academic library user study potential. Since mail questionnaires cannot provide reliable data for such research, structured, tactful interviews and systematic observations should be the basis for investigating potential user characteristics.

While a librarian can do little to attract students to the library unless they already have some personal and academic motivation, many steps can be taken to improve the situation if the librarian wishes to share the academic responsibility and teaching load. No matter what the librarian's subject background, he/she can constantly keep abreast of the social changes which affect education systems and student interests. Therefore, librarians should keep aware of the social trends which directly or indirectly affect libraries and potential users. They should know the different means of learning and teaching. Public service librarians, especially, should learn to work with many other modern campus service centers and to understand their important roles.

Instead of waiting for students to come to the library, another step is for librarians to go to them. A key word is "publicizing." A permanent and active campaign to publicize information resources among teaching staff and students must be launched. Various means, devices and methods must be used. New concepts from other fields should be applied to library service public relations. Educating potential users in resource use is desirable. These steps will not replace self motivation and need but will help all users to take advantage of the library's potential usefulness. And finally, they will enable the librarian to become a full faculty partner in taking responsibility for stimulating dynamic library use.

ACKNOWLEDGMENTS

The authors would like to thank Professors Jay Daily and Allen Kent, Donald Shirey, James Williams, Glenora Rossell, Marcy Murphy, Eleonore Dym and Howard Boksenbaum of the University of Pittsburgh, Sister Patricia Hodge of Carlow College and Elena Mavridou of Nicosia, Cyprus, for assistance.

NOTES AND REFERENCES

1. Eldred R. Smith, "Changes in Higher Education and the University Library," in *New Dimensions for Academic Library Service,* edited by E. J. Josey (Metuchen N. J.: Scarecrow Press, Inc., 1975), p. 37.

2. R. J. Blakely, "Developing General Understanding of Library Potential," in *Student Use of Libraries: An Inquiry into the Needs of Students, Libraries and the Educational Process* (Chicago: American Library Association, 1964), p. 106.

3. Nevitt Sanford, "Unrest in College," *School and Society* 95 (April, 1967), p. 246.

4. L. Wilson, "Library Roles in American Higher Education," *College and Research Libraries* 31 (March 1970), p. 98.

5. Guy R. Lyle, *The Administration of the College Library* (New York: H. W. Wilson Company, 1974), p. 5.

6. Adapted from Nurieh Musavi, "Users and Non-Users of College Libraries," (Unpublished Ph.D. Dissertation, University of Pittsburgh, 1977).

7. William Poole, "The University Library and the University Curriculum," *Library Journal* 14 (November 1893), p. 470.

8. L. Jolly, "The Function of the University Library," *Journal of Documentation* 18 (September 1962), p. 140.

9. Leon Carnovsky, "Self-Evaluation (Or How Good is My Library)," *College and Research Libraries* 3 (September 1942, p. 309.

10. A. J. Eaton, "Success and Failure in Library Use," *College and Research Libraries* 24 (May 1963), p. 202.

11. Harold Mendelsohn and Karen Wingard, *The Use of Libraries and the Conditions That Promote Their Use*. Report to the National Advisory Commission on Libraries (New York: Academy for Educational Development, 1967), p. 2.

12. *Student Use of Libraries: An Inquiry into the Needs of Students, Libraries and the Educational Process* (Chicago: American Library Association, 1964), p. ix.

13. Douglass M. Knight and E. Shepley Mourse, *Editors, Libraries at Large: Tradition, Innovation and the National Interest* (New York: R. R. Bowker Company, 1969), p. 496.

14. Richard M. Dougherty and Laura L. Bloomquist, *Improving Access to Library Resources: The Influence of Organization of Library Collections and Of User Attitudes Toward Innovative Services* (Metuchen, N. J.: Scarecrow Press, Inc., 1974), p. 7.

15. Richard Dougherty, "The Unserved, Academic Library Style," *American Libraries* 2 (November 1971), p. 1057.

16. Irene Braden Hoadley and Alice S. Clark, *Editors, Quantitative Methods in Librarianship: Standards, Research, Management; Proceedings and Papers of an Institute Held at Ohio State University, August 3–16, 1969* (Westport, CT: Greenwood Press, 1972), p. 4.

17. Edwin Olson, "Research in the Policy Process," in *Quantitative Methods in Librarianship; Standards, Research, Management,* edited by Irene Braden Hoadley and Alice S. Clark (Westport, CT: Greenwood Press, 1972), p. 48.

18. Philip M. Morse, *Library Effectiveness: A System Approach* (Cambridge, MA: M.I.T. Press, 1968), p. 2.

19. Robert S. Meyer and Gerhard M. Rostvald, *The Library and the Economic Community; A Market Analysis of Information Needs of Business and Industry in the Communities of Pasadena and Pomona, California* (Walnut Creek, CA, 1969), p. 71.

20. Peter Urbach, "User Reaction as a System Design Tool at CFSTI," in *Information Retrieval: The User's Viewpoint (An Aid to Design),* edited by Albert Tonik (Philadelphia: International Information, Inc., 1967), p. 7.

21. Henry C. Lucas, *Toward Creative Systems Design* (New York: Columbia University Press, 1974), p. 18.

22. National Commission on Libraries and Information Science, *Library and Information Service Needs of the Nation* (Washington, D. C.: Government Printing Office, 1974), p. 1.

23. National Commission on Libraries and Information Science, *A National Program for Library and Information Services,* 2nd draft (Washington, D. C.: Government Printing Office, 1974), p. 3.

24. A. C. Eurich, "The Significance of Library Reading Among College Students," *School and Society* 35 (1932), p. 9288.

25. E. W. McDiarmid, "Conditions Affecting Use of the College Library," *Library Quarterly* 5 (January 1935), p. 68.

26. H. Branscomb, *Teaching With Books: A Study of College Libraries* (Chicago: Association of American Colleges, 1940), pp. 30–36.

27. Patricia Knapp, "The Role of the Library of a Given College in Implementing the Course and Non–Course Objectives of that College," (Unpublished Ph.D. Dissertation, University of Chicago, 1957).

28. G. Lane, "Assessing the Undergraduate's Use of the University Library," *College and Research Libraries* 27 (July 1966): 277–82.

29. Knapp, *op. cit.*

30. Lane, *op. cit.,* p. 278.

31. Howard Clayton, "Investigation of Various Social and Economic Factors Influencing Student Use of One College Library," (Unpublished Ph.D. Dissertation, University of Oklahoma, 1965), p. 90.

32. A. K. Jain, "Sampling and Short–Period Usage in the Purdue Library," *College and Research Libraries* 27 (May 1965): 211–18.

33. M. W. Hostrop, "The Relationship of Academic Success and Selected Other Factors to Student Use of Library Materials at College of the Desert," (Unpublished Ph.D. Dissertation, University of California, Los Angeles, 1966), p. 148.

34. Mendelsohn and Wingard, *op. cit.*, pp. 1–38.

35. John Lubans, "On Non–Use of An Academic Library: A Report of Findings," in *Proceedings of the New York Library Association, College and University Libraries Section,* "Use, Mis–Use and Non–Use of Academic Libraries," (Watertown: Jefferson Community College, 1970), pp. 47–70.

36. John Lubans, "Library–Use Instruction Needs From the Library Users'/Non-Users' Point of View: A Survey Report," in *Educating the User* (New York: R. R. Bowker Company, 1974), pp. 401–9.

37. Robert Taylor, "Orienting the Library to the User," in *Proceedings of the New York Library Association, College and University Libraries Section* (Watertown: Jefferson Community College, 1970), p. 9.

38. *A Survey of the Attitudes, Opinions and Behavior of Citizens of Colorado With Regard to Library Services* (Denver: Colorado State Library, 1973), Vol. 2, p. 1.

39. T. C. Tobin, "Study of Library Use Studies," *Information Storage and Retrieval* 10 (March–April 1974), p. 102.

40. See Cherry Harrop, "The Information Needs of Undergraduates Project: Some Preliminary Findings," *CRUS News*, Number 11 (July, 1981): 2–6. Cherry Harrop, "The Information Needs of Undergraduates Project: Library Use By Some First Year Social Science Students," *CRUS News*, Number 12 (November 1981): 5–10.

41. See George D'Elia, "A Procedure for Identifying and Surveying Potential users of Public Libraries," *Library Research* 2 (Fall 1980): 239–49. Charles Whitney Evans, "The Attitudes of Adults Toward the Public Library and Their Relationship To Library Use," (Unpublished Ph.D. Dissertation, University of California, Berkeley, 1969). The Gallop Organization, Inc. "Book Reading and Library Usage; A Study of Habits and Perceptions." (Princeton, N. J.: 1978). M. Madden, "Library User/Non-User Lifestyles," American Libraries 10 (February 1979): 78–81. M. B. Rees, "Social and Psychological Predictors of Adult Information Seeking and Media Use," Adult Education 19 (1968): 11–29. D. L. Zweizig, "Public Library Use, Users, Uses: Advances in Knowledge of the Characteristics and Needs of the Adult Clientele of American Public Libraries," *Advances in Librarianship* 7 (1977): 231–55.

42. See Sister Mary Peter Claver Ducat, "Student and Faculty Use of the Library in Three Secondary Schools," (Unpublished D. L. S. Dissertation, Columbia University, 1960). M. Slater, *The Neglected Resource: Non–Usage of Library and Information Services in Industry and Commerce* (London: ASLIB, 1980).

43. *International Encyclopedia of the Social Sciences* (New York: Macmillan, 1968), Vol. 1, p. 449.

44. *The Encyclopedia of Education* (New York: Free Press, 1971), Vol. 1, p. 397.

45. Lubans, "Library–Use Instruction Needs . . . ," *op. cit.*, pp. 401–409.

46. N. R. F. Mair, *Psychology in Industry* (Boston: Houghton Mifflin, 1965), p. 412.

47. Adam Ulum, *The Fall of the American University* (New York: Library Press, 1972), p. 125.

48. The Carnegie Commission on Higher Education, *The More Effective Use of Resources; An Imperative for Higher Education; A Report and Recommendations* (New York: McGraw-Hill Book Company, 1972), p. 16.

DAVID MILFORD HUME, M.D.
1917–1973: A BIBLIOGRAPHY AND A
BIOGRAPHICAL SKETCH

Mary Ellen Thomas and B. W. Haynes, Jr., M.D.

PREFACE

In the spring of 1978, I was searching for a project that would be both useful and absorbing. Many experiences over much of my lifetime inclined me toward a subject related to medicine. Not the least of these was the memory of the years from 1958 to 1964 when I worked at the Tompkins–McCaw Library of the Medical College of Virginia, now Virginia Commonwealth University–Medical College of Virginia (VCU–MCV). During those years there was much comment on Dr. David Milford Hume, the forceful and energetic Chairman of the Surgery Department, and his pioneering research efforts in the area of renal homotransplantation. I never met Dr. Hume, but a surgeon of such skill, a scientist of such scholarship and such singleness of purpose, and a character so colorful and so con-

Advances in Library Administration and Organization, Volume 3, pages 241–268.
Copyright © 1984 by JAI Press Inc.
All rights of reproduction in any form reserved.
ISBN: 0-89232-386-8

troversial is of interest to most of us, and I am no exception. Thus, at the Tompkins–McCaw Library, when archivist Nancy Summers suggested that a bibliography of Dr. Hume's publications would be of value, the work was begun.

VCU–MCV Surgery Department staff members, Arlene Steinberg and Joyce Mealy, secured copies of Dr. Hume's Curriculum Vitae and furnished all available reprints of his publications that were still stored in the department. Dr. Hyung M. Lee, VCU–MCV Surgery Department, was most helpful with identifying several citations, as was Dr. Heber H. Newsome, VCU–MCV Surgery Department.

In addition to books or portions of books and to journal articles, effort was made to include government reports and selected discussions in which Dr. Hume took part. All those discussions which were indexed in *Science Citation Index* are included. Some additional ones in which he participated are included, if it was felt their content might be of particular significance.

The reader may note the absence of items for the years 1957, 1976 and 1978. This was not an oversight, but rather no titles were found which were published during those years.

During the course of the work, it became appealing to have biographical information included along with the bibliography; or possibly the bibliography should serve as an appendix to a festschrift. Conversations then took place with several members of the surgical staffs of VCU-MCV and of the McGuire Veterans Administration Hospital. It was discovered that a festschrift honoring Dr. Hume, at least in the area of his major thrust, had been sufficiently done by the good efforts of Dr. Walter Lawrence, Jr., VCU–MCV Surgery Department, and others, with the publication of *The David Milford Hume Memorial Symposium on Transplantation* (New York: Grune & Stratton, 1974). Although interest was expressed in the writing of new biographical material, no currently practicing surgeon who was approached could devote the time to the extensive research necessary for presenting a balanced view. With that fact established, the pursuit of such newly written material was temporarily abandoned.

At my request, Dr. B. W. Haynes, Jr., VCU–MCV Surgery Department, granted permission to reprint his sketch written in 1973 at the time of Dr. Hume's death. Of several possible articles, Dr. Haynes' seemed particularly appropriate because of his mention of Dr. Hume as " . . . a prolific and lucid writer, publishing over two hundred scientific papers. . . ." I am grateful to him and to the Lippincott/Harper Company.

Given the stature and personality of the subject, the amount of biographical information available is just enough to whet one's appetite, in spite of interesting brief sketches such as those by Drs. Moore, Merrill and Murray, appearing on pages 153–163 of the memorial symposium mentioned above. I would therefore offer a plea to any of those persons with a firsthand knowledge of Dr. Hume as a colleague, family member, student or friend, for some record of his life. Photographs and other memorabilia would also be desirable. For such materials to be deposited in the medical libraries of VCU–MCV, Harvard University or the University of Chicago would be of certain value. The usefulness of such materials to future medical historians is supported by the statement of one Richmond surgeon who predicted that "150 to 200 years from now, if they're still publishing medical journals the way they are today, they're going to be talking about him."

In addition to those already mentioned, I acknowledge the encouragement, suggestions or criticisms of the following individuals, none of whom are responsible for any errors or omissions here: Gerard B. McCabe, Director of University Libraries, VCU–MCV; Dr. Lauren A. Woods, Dr. Lazar J. Greenfield, Dr. Walter Lawrence, Jr., Dr. L. Gregg Halloran and James J. Dwyer, all of VCU–MCV; Dr. Hunter H. McGuire, Jr., McGuire Veterans Administration Hospital; Dr. Peter D. Olch and Manfred J. Waserman, National Library of Medicine; Richard J. Wolfe, Rare Books Librarian, Countway Library of Medicine, Harvard University; Dr. Dora B. Weiner, editor, medical historian and faculty member of Manhattanville College; Martha Bell Conway, Administrator of Grants and Contracts, VCU–MCV; Dr. Ray O. Hummel, Jr., Scholar–in–Residence, James Branch Cabell Library, VCU; Mrs. Louise W. Morton, retired staff member, Tompkins–McCaw Library; staff of the Library of Congress, Science and Technology Division; and members of the Reference Department of the James Branch Cabell Library, including department head, Carol Parke. These fellow workers patiently endured my almost incessant and often uninvited reports on the progress of this project for more than a year.

Mary Ellen Thomas

DAVID MILFORD HUME
1917–1973

Isolated events often serve to characterize the essence of a man. I saw Dave one evening about 11:00 P.M. on his way to the operating room. While trying to hurry the elevator, and in his usual forceful and energetic manner, he related that he was about to re–do a clotted arterial graft, make ward rounds, finish an article for publication which was overdue and pressing, and added, as a smiling afterthought, that he had to catch an early morning plane. As he grew impatient waiting for the elevator and took the stairs, I realized how sharply the encounter had etched his character. In a few moments he had shown his boundless unidirectional energy, an extraordinary sense of responsibility and devotion to patients and to surgical education, his unwillingness to compromise with total effort in achieving difficult objectives, and through it all, an unflagging cheerful optimism.

David Hume was born in Muskegon, Michigan on October 21st, 1917. During his undergraduate period at Harvard University he became interested in hypothalamic–pituitary relationships and laid the foundation for what was to be a continued and dedicated interest in surgical endocrinology. Upon graduation from Harvard in 1940, he entered the University of Chicago School of Medicine where he developed further interests in hypothalamic control of pituitary–adrenocortical secretion under the tutelage of Dr. William Bloom. In addition to his usual studies, he utilized stereotactic localization and remote stimulation of the brain to study control of adrenocortical function. It was during this period that he first became interested in renal homotransplantation, its potential and possibilities. Receiving his M.D. degree in 1943, David went to the Peter Bent Brigham Hospital as Surgical Intern to begin a long and fruitful association with that institution. His progression through the residency was interrupted by a year spent in the Navy at Pearl Harbor from 1945 to 1946. Appointed Harvey Cushing Fellow in Surgery in 1948, he continued his work and interest in pituitary adrenal interrelationships and further efforts at renal homotransplantation. Upon completion of his chief resident year in 1951, he began an intense effort in clinical renal homotransplantation in association with Dr. John Merrill, Dr. Joseph Murray, Dr. George Thorn, and Dr. J. Hartwell Harrison. In the period 1951 to 1953, nine cadaver renal homotransplants in patients with terminal renal failure were performed. Four of these grafts were the first organ transplants in man to show sufficient function to maintain the life of the host, and one untreated transplant functioned for six months. Early attempts at immunosuppression with corticosteroids were frustrated by limited supplies of the drug. Recalled to the Navy in 1953, he spent two years at the Naval Medical Research Institute in Bethesda where continued active interest in the pituitary hypothalamic adrenocortical relationships was pursued and further studies on renal homotransplantation and rejection were completed. In 1956, he accepted the Stuart McGuire Professorship of Surgery and the Chairmanship of the Department of Surgery at the Medical College of Virginia, a post which he distinguished for seventeen years.

In 1957, he performed the first twin transplant at the Medical College of Virginia, and launched the renal transplant program which subsequently grew into an internationally recognized clinical and research center providing a major force in the development of clinical homotransplantation. The years that followed were busy ones for, with characteristic energy and enthusiasm, he involved himself not only with the Department of Surgery, his students, and especially his surgical housestaff, but also with the problems of the medical school as well. Aptly characterized by Dr. Francis Moore as a "restless genius," his interest led him to explore any area that might further his basic goal: to improve education of students and house–officers and to further progress in the science and art of surgery. He was a prolific and lucid writer, publishing over two hundred scientific papers on endocrine, transplant, and other surgical subjects, including chapters for textbooks of surgery. He was co–editor of *Principles of Surgery*, a leading medical best–selling text.

Because of his pioneering efforts in renal homotransplantation, many honors came to him. He received the Francis Amory Award of the American Academy of Arts and Sciences in 1962, the Valentine Award of the New York Academy of Medicine in 1970, the University of Chicago's Distinguished Service Medal in 1971, and in 1972 the Distinguished Achievement Award from Modern Medicine. In addition, he received the award as outstanding Harvard Alumnus of the State of Virginia in 1968, the Humanitarian Award by the Richmond Chapter of the Hadassah in 1971, a Special Award for contributions to renal transplants and vascular surgery by the Chamber of Commerce of Richmond in 1972, and was recognized by Governor Linwood Holton of Virginia with the Distinguished Citizens Award in 1972.

Because of his close personal relationship with his surgical housestaff, he especially enjoyed attending annual meetings of the Humera Society, an organization of his former residents who sought annual reunion with him as their leader, counselor, and friend.

A few years before his death, he became interested in flying. With accustomed thoroughness, he took lessons and became expert at piloting his own plane which was a source of excitement and challenge. He was described as careful and thorough by pilots who had flown with him. On Saturday, May 19th, 1973, he took off from Van Nuys alone at 7:00 P.M. planning to fly to Richmond. A few miles from the airport his aircraft struck a mountain, ending his life as he had lived it: following his own critical judgment, self–reliant, self–confident.

He is survived by his wife, Martha, and four children, Susan, Joan, Martha, and Jeffrey. David was buried in a peaceful glen at Woods Hole, a short distance from a family summer home. His restless genius has come to rest.

B. W. Haynes, Jr., M.D.

DAVID MILFORD HUME, M.D., 1917–1973

ACKNOWLEDGMENT

Reprinted from *Transactions of the Southern Surgical Association*, (1973) 83:316–317, by permission of the Lippincott/Harper Company.

DAVID MILFORD HUME, M.D.
1917–1973
A BIBLIOGRAPHY

1949

1. Hume, D. M. "The Role of the Hypothalamus in the Pituitary–adrenal Cortical Response to Stress" (abstract), *Journal of Clinical Investigation* 28(1949):790. Abstract also appears in *Digest of Neurology and Psychiatry* 18(1950):5.

1950

2. Hume, D. M., and Wittenstein, G. J. "The Relationship of the Hypothalamus to Pituitary–adrenocortical Function," in *Proceedings of the 1st Clinical ACTH Conference*, Chicago, 1949, edited by J. R. Mote, pp. 134–47. (Philadelphia: Blakiston, 1950.)
3. Recant, L., Hume, D. M., Forsham, P. H., and Thorn, G. W. "Studies on the Effect of Epinephrine on the Pituitary–adrenocortical System," *Journal of Clinical Endocrinology* 10(1950):187–229.

1951

4. Hume, D. M. "Release of Adrenocorticotropic Hormone from the Pituitary," U.S. Patent Application 159,648, *Official Gazette* 652(1951):1182.
5. Hume, D. M., and Moore, F. D. "The use of ACTH, Cortisone, and Adrenal Cortical Extracts in Surgical Patients," in *Proceedings of the 2d Clinical ACTH Conference*, Chicago, 1950, edited by J. R. Mote, vol. 2, pp. 289–309. (New York: Blakiston, 1951.)

1952

6. Hume, D. M. "The Relationship of the Hypothalamus to the Pituitary Secretion of ACTH," in *Ciba Foundation Colloquia on Endocrinology*, edited by G. E. W. Wolstenhome, vol. 4, "Anterior Pituitary Secretion and Hormonal Influences in Water Metabolism," part 2, pp. 87–102. (New York: Blakiston, 1952).
7. Hume, D. M. "Role of the Hypothalamus in Release of ACTH," in *The Biology of Mental Health and Disease: the Twenty–seventh Annual Conference of the Milbank Memorial Fund*, by the Fund, pp. 273–76. (New York: Paul B. Hoeber, 1952.)
8. Hume, D. M., Merrill, J. P., and Miller, B. F. "Homologous Transplantation of Human Kidneys" (abstract), *Journal of Clinical Investigation* 31(1952):640.

1953

9. Hawn, C. V. Z., Hume, D. M., Merrill, J. P., and Miller, B. F. "Pathologic Changes in Eight Human Renal Homotransplants" (abstract), *Federation Proceedings* 12(1953):391.

10. Haynes, F. W., Forsham, P. H., and Hume, D. M. "Effects of ACTH, Cortisone, Desoxycorticosterone and Epinephrine on the Plasma Hypertensinogen and Renin Concentration of Dogs," *American Journal of Physiology* 172(1953):265–75.

11. Hume, D. M., Discussion at the Tissue Transplantation Conference, *Journal of the National Cancer Institute* 14(1953):685.

12. Hume, D. M. "The Neuro–endocrine Response to Injury: Present Status of the Problem," *Transactions of the 73rd Meeting of the American Surgical Association* 71(1953):258–67. Also published in *Annals of Surgery* 138(1953):548–57.

1954

13. Cowie, A. T., Ganong, W. F., and Hume, D. M. "The Eosinopenic Response to Graded Doses of Hydrocortisone in the Adrenalectomized Dog With and Without Surgical Trauma," *Endocrinology* 55(1954):745–50.

14. Dammin, G. J., Hume, D. M., Merrill, J. P., Miller, B. F., and Thorn, G. W. "Renal Homotransplantation in Man: Case with Unusually Long Functional Survival" (abstract), *Journal of Laboratory and Clinical Medicine* 44(1954):784–85.

15. Ganong, W. F., Fredrickson, D. S., and Hume, D. M. "Depression of the Thyroidal Iodine Uptake by Hypothalamic Lesions" (abstract), *Journal of Clinical Endocrinology and Metabolism* 14(1954):773–74.

16. Ganong, W. F., and Hume, D. M. "Absence of Stress–induced and 'Compensatory' Adrenal Hypertrophy in Dogs with Hypothalamic Lesions," *Endocrinology* 55(1954):474–83.

17. Hume, D. M. and Nelson, D. H. "Corticoid Output in Adrenal Venous Blood of the Intact Dog" (abstract), *Federation Proceedings* 13(1954):73.

18. Liddle, G. W., Rinfret, A. P., Island, D., Nelson, D. H., Wexler, B., Hume, D. M., and Forsham, P. H. "A Potent Steroidogenic Anterior Pituitary Fraction which is Poor in Adrenal Ascorbic–acid Depleting Activity" (abstract), *Journal of Clinical Endocrinology and Metabolism* 14(1954):808–809.

19. McArthur, J. W., Gautier, E., Swallow, K. A., Godley, A., MacLachlan, E. A., Terry, M. L., Hume, D. M., Crépeaux, J., Simeone, F. A., Keitel, H., and Berman, H. "Studies Concerning the Role of the Adrenal Cortex in the Pathologic Physiology of Diabetic Acidosis. II. The Identification of Adrenal-conditioned Factors in the Physiologic Reaction to the Stress of Insulin Deprivation," *Journal of Clinical Investigation* 33(1954):437–51.

20. Nelson, D. H., and Hume, D. M. "New Method for the Determination of ACTH in Blood" (abstract), *Journal of Clinical Endocrinology and Metabolism* 14(1954):781.

1955

21. Egdahl, R. H., and Hume, D. M. "Kidney Transplantation," *Transplantation Bulletin* 2(1955):53–4.

22. Egdahl, R. H., and Hume, D. M. "Nonsuture Blood Vessel Anastomosis; An Experimental Study Using Polyethylene as the Prosthetic Material," *NMRI Naval Medical Research Institute, National Naval Medical Center, Bethesda, Maryland* 13(1955):153–66. Research Report, Project NM–007–081.19.01. (Available from the National Technical Information Service as PB160–151.) Also published in *A.M.A. Archives of Surgery* 72(1956):232–40.

23. Egdahl, R. H., Hume, D. M., and Schlang, H. A. "Plastic Venous Prostheses," *Surgical Forum* 5(1954):235–41. (Published in 1955.)

24. Egdahl, R. H., Nelson, D. H. and Hume, D. M. "Adrenal Cortical Function in Hypothermia," *NMRI Naval Medical Research Institute, National Naval Medical Cen-*

ter, Bethesda, Maryland 13(1955):651–62. Research Report, Project NM–007–081.22.03. (Available from the National Technical Information Service as PB160–188.) Also published in *Surgery, Gynecology and Obstetrics* 101(1955):715–20.

25. Egdahl, R. H., Nelson, D. H., and Hume, D. M. "Effect of Hypothermia on 17-hydroxycorticosteroid Secretion in Adrenal Venous Blood in the Dog," *Science* 121(1955):506–507.

26. Egdahl, R. H., Richards, J. B., and Hume, D. M. "The effect of Chlorpromazine on Pituitary ACTH Secretion in the Dog," *NMRI Naval Medical Research Institute, National Naval Medical Center, Bethesda, Maryland* 13(1955):545–52. Research Report, Project NM–007–081.22.04. (Available from the National Technical Information Service as PB160–225.)

27. Fredrickson, D. S., Ganong, W. F., and Hume, D. M. "Thyroid Uptake of Radioactive Iodine in the Dog: Effect of Diet, Hypophysectomy, and TSH Administration," *Proceedings of the Society for Experimental Biology and Medicine* 89(1955):416–19.

28. Ganong, W. F., Fredrickson, D. S., and Hume, D. M. "The Effect of Hypothalamic Lesions on Thyroid Function in the Dog," *Endocrinology* 57(1955):355–62.

29. Ganong, W. F., Gold, N. I., and Hume, D. M. "The Effect of Hypothalamic Lesions on Plasma of 17-hydroxycorticoid Response to Immobilization in the Dog" (abstract), *Federation Proceedings* 14(1955):54.

30. Ganong, W. F., and Hume, D. M. "Effect of Hypothalamic Lesions on Steroid-induced Atrophy of Adrenal Cortex in the Dog," *Proceedings of the Society for Experimental Biology and Medicine* 88(1955):528–33.

31. Ganong, W. F., and Hume, D. M. "Effect of Partial Hypophysectomy on Adrenocortical, Thyroidal and Gonadal Function in the Dog" (abstract), *Journal of Clinical Endocrinology and Metabolism* 15(1955):843.

32. Hume, D. M., and Egdahl, R. H. "Kidney Transplantation," *Transplantation Bulletin* 2(1955):54.

33. Hume, D. M., and Egdahl, R. H. "Progressive Destruction of Renal Homografts Isolated from the Regional Lymphatics of the Host," *NMRI Naval Medical Research Institute, National Naval Medical Center, Bethesda, Maryland* 13(1955):913–42. Research Report, Project NM–007–081.21.02. (Available from the National Technical Information Service as PB160–104.) Also published in *Surgery* 38(1955):194–214.

34. Hume, D. M., Merrill, J. P., Miller, B. F., and Thorn, G. W. "Experiences with Renal Homotransplantation in the Human: Report of Nine Cases," *Journal of Clinical Investigation* 34(1955):327–82.

35. Hume, D. M., and Nelson, D. H. "Adrenal Cortical Function in Experimental Shock, Measured by Adrenal Venous Blood Corticosteroid Secretion," *NMRI Naval Medical Research Institute, National Naval Medical Center, Bethesda, Maryland* 13(1955):167–76. Research Report, NM–007–081.22.01. (Available from the National Technical Information Service as PB160–187.)

36. Hume, D. M., and Nelson, D. H. "Adrenal Cortical Function in Surgical Shock," *Surgical Forum* 5(1954):568–75. (Published in 1955.)

37. Hume, D. M., and Nelson, D. H. "The Effect of Hypothalamic Lesions on Blood ACTH Levels and 17-hydroxycorticosteroid Secretion Following Trauma in the Dog" (abstract), *Journal of Clinical Endocrinology and Metabolism* 15(1955):839–40.

38. Nelson, D. H., Egdahl, R. H., and Hume, D. M. "Corticosteroid Secretion in the Adrenal Vein of Dogs Exposed to Cold" (abstract), *Journal of Clinical Endocrinology and Metabolism* 15(1955):889.

39. Nelson, D. H., and Hume, D. M. "Corticosteroid Secretion in the Adrenal Venous Blood of the Hypophysectomized Dog as an Assay for ACTH," *Endocrinology* 57(1955):184–92.

1956

40. Bethune, J. E., Ganong, W. F., Hume, D. M., and Nelson, D. H. "Plasma Levels of ACTH in Normal Subjects and Addisonian Patients Following Corticosteroid Administration" (abstract), *Journal of Clinical Endocrinology and Metabolism* 16(1956):913.

41. Egdahl, R. H., and Hume, D. M. "Immunologic Studies in Renal Homotransplantation," *Surgery, Gynecology and Obstetrics* 102(1956):450–62.

42. Egdahl, R. H., and Hume, D. M. "Secondary Kidney Homotransplantation," *Surgical Forum* 6(1955):423–27. (Published in 1956.)

43. Egdahl, R. H. and Hume, D. M. "Studies on Kidney Homotransplant Rejection Using a Cross–circulation Technique," in "Second Tissue Homotransplantation Conference," *Annals of the New York Academy of Sciences* 64(1956):950–57. Abstract appears in *Transplantation Bulletin* 3(1956):71.

44. Egdahl, R. H., Hume, D. M., and Richards, J. B. "Tolerance of the Dog to Extreme Cold Exposure," *NMRI Naval Medical Research Institute, National Naval Medical Center, Bethesda, Maryland* 14(1956):389–94. Research Report, Project NM–007–081.22.10.

45. Egdahl, R. H., Richards, J. B., and Hume, D. M. "Effect of Reserpine on Adrenocortical Function in Unanesthetized Dogs," *Science* 123(1956):418.

46. Ganong, W. F., and Hume, D. M. "Concentration of ACTH in Cavernous Sinus and Peripheral Arterial Blood in the Dog," *Proceedings of the Society for Experimental Biology and Medicine* 92(1956):621–24.

47. Ganong, W. F., and Hume, D. M. "The Effect of Graded Hypophysectomy on Thyroid, Gonadal, and Adrenocortical Function in the Dog," *Endocrinology* 59(1956):293–301.

48. Ganong, W. F., and Hume, D. M. "The Effect of Unilateral Adrenalectomy on Adrenal Venous 17-hydroxycorticosteroid Output in the Dog," *Endocrinology* 59(1956):302–305.

49. Hume, D. M. "Primary and Secondary Renal Transplant Rejection in Man and Dogs," in *Proceedings of the Seventh Annual Conference on the Nephrotic Syndrome*, edited by J. Metcoff, pp. 116–27. (New York: The National Nephrosis Foundation, 1956.)

50. Hume, D. M., Egdahl, R. H., and Nelson, D. H. "The Effect of Hypothermia on Pituitary Corticotropin (ACTH) Release and on Adrenal Cortical and Medullary Secretion in the Dog," in *The Physiology of Induced Hypothermia*. National Academy of Sciences-National Research Council, Publication Number 451:170–74, published in 1956.

51. Hume, D. M., and Ganong, W. F. "A Method for Accurate Placement of Electrodes in the Hypothalamus of the Dog," *Electroencephalography and Clinical Neurophysiology* 8(1956):136–40.

52. Hume, D. M., Nelson, D. H., and Miller, D. W. "Blood and Urinary 17-hydroxycorticosteroids in Patients with Severe Burns," *NMRI Naval Medical Research Institute, National Naval Medical Center, Bethesda, Maryland* 14(1956):87–105. Research Report, Project NM–007–081.22.07. Also published in *Annals of Surgery* 143(1956):316–29.

53. Nelson, D. H., Egdahl, R. H., and Hume, D. M. "Corticosteroid Secretion in the Adrenal Vein of the Non-stressed Dog Exposed to Cold," *NMRI Naval Medical Research Institute, National Naval Medical Center, Bethesda, Maryland* 14(1956):381–87. Research Report, Project NM–007–081.22.06. Also published in *Endocrinology* 58(1956):309–14.

1958

54. Egdahl, R. H., and Hume, D. M. "Bibliography of Kidney Transplantation," *Transplantation Bulletin* 5(1958):37–38.
55. Hume, D. M. "Hypothalamic localization for the control of various endocrine secretions," in *Reticular Formation of the Brain*, Henry Ford Hospital International Symposium, Detroit, 1957, edited by H. H. Jasper, et al, pp. 231–48. (Boston: Little, Brown, 1958.)
56. Hume, D. M. "The Method of Hypothalamic Regulation of Pituitary and Adrenal Secretion in Response to Trauma," in *Pathophysiologia Diencephalica*, an International Symposium, Milan, 1956, edited by S. Curri and L. Martini, pp. 217–28. (Vienna: Springer–Verlag, 1958.)
57. Hume, D. M. "The Secretion of Epinephrine, nor-epinephrine and Corticosteroids in the Adrenal Venous Blood of the Dog Following Single and Repeated Trauma," *Surgical Forum* 8(1957):111–15. (Published in 1958.)

1959

58. TrybusHume, D. M. Discussion of Studies by Dr. James D. Hardy (et al, on catechol amine metabolism), *Annals of Surgery* 150(1959):682–83.
59. Hume, D. M. "Homotransplantation of the Kidney: Experimental and Clinical Studies," *Bulletin de la Societé Internationale de Chirurgie* 18(1959):572–79 (English); 580–87 (German); 587–94 (Spanish); 594–601 (French); 601–607 (Italian); 608–14 (Russian). Also published in *Khirurgiia* (Moscow) 35(1959):103–107 (Russian).
60. Hume, D. M. "Experimental and Clinical Homotransplantation of Kidney," in *Transplantation of Tissues: Skin, Cornea, Fat, Nerves, Teeth, Blood Vessels, Endocrine Glands, Organs, Peritoneum, Cancer Cells*, edited by L. Peer, vol. 2, part 9, "Organs," pp. 484–540. (Baltimore: Williams and Wilkins, 1959.)
61. Hume, D. M. "Experimental Transplantation of Lung, Heart, Liver, and Spleen," in *Transplantation of Tissues: Skin, Cornea, Fat, Nerves, Teeth, Blood Vessels, Endocrine Glands, Organs, Peritoneum, Cancer Cells*, edited by L. Peer, vol. 2, part 9, "Organs," pp. 473–83. (Baltimore: Williams and Wilkins, 1959.)
62. Hume, D. M. and Bell, C. C., Jr. "The Secretion of Epinephrine, Nor–epinephrine, and Corticosteroid in the Adrenal Venous Blood of the Human," *Surgical Forum* 9(1958):6–12. (Published in 1959.)
63. Hume, D. M., and Egdahl, R. H. "Effect of Hypothermia and of Cold Exposure on Adrenal Cortical and Medullary Secretion," in "Hypothermia," *Annals of the New York Academy of Sciences* 80(1959):435–44.
64. Hume, D. M., and Egdahl, R. H. "The Importance of the Brain in the Endocrine Response to Injury," *Transactions of the 79th Meeting of the American Surgical Association* 77(1959):359–74. Also published in *Annals of Surgery* 150(1959):697–712.
65. Hume, D. M., and Jackson, B. T. "Adrenal Output of Corticosteroids in the First 14 Days After Hypothalamic Destruction in the Dog," (abstract), *Federation Proceedings* 18(1959):481.
66. Hume, D. M., and Jackson, B. T. "The Early and Late effects of Hypothalamic Destruction or Removal on Pituitary-adrenal Activity" (abstract), paper presented at the Endocrine Society, 41st Meeting, 1959.
67. Hume, D. M., Jackson, B. T., Kupfer, H. G., Ham, W. T., and Egdahl, R. H. "Fetal Hematopoietic Tissue Transplantation Following Lethal Whole Body Irradiation in Dogs, and a Consideration of its Clinical Use" (abstract), *Journal of Clinical Investigation* 38(1959):1013–1014.

1960

68. Bell, C. C., Jr., Haynes, B. W., Jr., Hume, D. M., and Egdahl, R. H. "Clinical and Experimental Studies in Fetal Skin Homografting," *Surgical Forum* 10(1959):857–60. (Published in 1960.)

69. Bell, C. C., Jr., Hume, D. M., and Egdahl, R. H. "The Importance of Avoiding Bacterial Contamination in Metabolic Studies," *Surgical Forum* 11(1960):91–93.

70. Ginn, H. E., Jr., Unger, A. M., Hume, D. M., and Schilling, J. A. "Human Renal Transplantation; An Investigation of the Functional Status of the Denervated Kidney After Successful Homotransplantation in Identical Twins," *Journal of Laboratory and Clinical Medicine* 56(1960):1–13.

71. Hume, D. M. "Pheochromocytoma in the Adult and in the Child," *American Journal of Surgery* 99(1960):458–96.

72. Hume, D. M., Jackson, B. T., Zukoski, C. F., Lee, H. M., Kauffman, H. M., and Egdahl, R. H. "The Homotransplantation of Kidneys and of Fetal Liver and Spleen After Total Body Irradiation," *Transactions of the 80th Meeting of the American Surgical Association* 78(1960):12–31. Also published in *Annals of Surgery* 152(1960):354–73.

73. Jackson, B. T., Melby, J. C., Hume, D. M., and Egdahl, R. H. "Maturation of Adrenal Cortical and Medullary Function in the Dog" (abstract and paper) for presentation at the Endocrine Society, 42d Meeting, 1960.

74. Zukoski, C. F., Egdahl, R. H., and Hume, D. M. "Bibliography of Kidney Transplantation," *Transplantation Bulletin* 26(1960):158–59.

75. Zukoski, C. F., Jackson, B. T., Egdahl, R. H., and Hume, D. M. "The Effect of Donor and Host Irradiation on the Renal Homograft Reaction" (abstract), *Federation Proceedings* 19(1960):358(1 Part 1).

76. Zukoski, C. F., Lee, H. M., and Hume, D. M. "The Prolongation of Functional Survival of Canine Renal Homografts by 6-mercaptopurine," *Surgical Forum* 11(1960):470–72.

1961

77. Hume, D. M. Discussion of papers by Dr. Irvine H. Page, in "Some Neurohumoral and Endocrine Aspects of Shock; Proceedings of a Conference on Recent Progress and Present Problems in the Field of Shock," *Federation Proceedings* 20(1961):87–97 (2 Part 3, Supplement 9).

78. Hume, D. M. Editorial Comments (on the present status of renal homotransplantation), in *Yearbook of Urology* (1960–1961 Year Book series), edited by W. W. Scott, pp. 135–43. (Chicago: Year Book Medical Publishers, 1961.)

79. Kauffman, H. M., Egdahl, R. H., and Hume, D. M. "Bibliography of Kidney Transplantation. Addendum No. 2 (1959–1961)," *Transplantation Bulletin* 28(1961):128–30.

80. Sacks, J. H., and Hume, D. M. "Studies of Liver Cell Function in Cirrhosis," *Surgical Forum* 12(1961):343–45.

81. Zukoski, C. F., Lee, H. M., and Hume, D. M. "The Effect of Antimetabolites on Prolonging Functional Survival of Canine Renal Homografts: 6-mercaptopurine, 8-azaguanine" (abstract), *Federation Proceedings* 20(1961):34(1 Part 1).

82. Zukoski, C. F., Lee, H. M., and Hume, D. M. "Effect of Hypothalamic Stimulation on Gastric Secretion and Adrenal Function in the Dog," *Surgical Forum* 12(1961):282–85. Also appears in *Journal of Surgical Research* 3(1963):301–306.

83. Zukoski, C. F., Lee, H. M., and Hume, D. M. "The Effect of 6-mercaptopurine on Renal Homograft Survival in the Dog," *Surgery, Gynecology and Obstetrics* 112(1961):707–714.
84. Zukoski, C. F., Lee, H. M., and Hume, D. M. "Prolonged Functional Survival of a Secondary Renal Homotransplant in the Dog," *Surgery* 50(1961):926–30.

1962

85. Hume, D. M., Bell, C. C., Jr., and Bartter, F. "Direct Measurement of Adrenal Secretion in Man During Operative Trauma and Convalescence," *Surgery* 52(1962):174–87.
86. Mannick, J. A., Suter, C. G., and Hume, D. M. "The 'Subclavian Steal' Syndrome: A Further Documentation," *JAMA* 182(1962):254–58.
87. Zukoski, C. F., Lee, H. M., and Hume, D. M. "The Effect of Antimetabolites on Prolonging Functional Survival of Canine Renal Homografts," *Journal of Surgical Research* 2(1962):44–48.

1963

88. Egdahl, R. H., and Hume, D. M. "Surgery in Pancreatitis," *American Journal of Surgery* 106(1963):471–75.
89. Haynes, B. W., Jr., Lounds, E. A., and Hume, D. M. "Adrenocortical Function in Severe Burns," presented to the American Association for the Surgery of Trauma, 23rd Session, San Francisco, 1963.
90. Hume, D. M., Magee, J. H., Kauffman, H. M., Jr., Rittenbury, M. S., and Prout, G. R., Jr. "Renal Homotransplantation in Man in Modified Recipients," *Transactions of the 83rd Meeting of the American Surgical Association* 81(1963):296–332. Also published in *Annals of Surgery* 158(1963):608–44.
91. Hume, D. M., and Porter, R. R., "Acute Dissecting Aortic Aneurysms," *Surgery* 53(1963):122–54.
92. Kauffman, H. M., Hume, D. M., and Egdahl, R. H. "Bibliography of Kidney Transplantation. Addendum No. 3," *Transplantation* 1(1963):403–406.
93. Rittenbury, M. S., Hench, M. E., and Hume, D. M. "Bacteriological Evaluation of Skin Disinfectant" (abstract), *Bacteriological Proceedings* (1963):13.
94. Rittenbury, M. S., Hume, D. M., and Hench, M. E. "'Pathogen-free' Patient-care Area," in *Antimicrobial Agents and Chemotherapy—1962; Proceedings of the Second Interscience Conference on Antimicrobial Agents and Chemotherapy*, Chicago, edited by J. C. Sylvester, pp. 51–65. (Ann Arbor: American Society for Microbiology, 1963.)
95. Cleveland, R. J., Lee, H. M., Kauffman, H. M., Dwyer, J. J., and Hume, D. M. "Hypothermia as a Means of Organ Preservation" (abstract), *Virginia Journal of Science* 15(1964):338.
96. Cleveland, R. J., Lee, H. M., Prout, G. R., and Hume, D. M. "Preservation of the Cadaver Kidney for Renal Homotransplantation in Man," *Surgery, Gynecology and Obstetrics* 119(1964):991–96.
97. Hume, D. M. "Current Results of Organ Homotransplantation in Man and Prospects for the Future" (abstract), Lewis A. Conner Memorial Lecture, American Heart Association, *Circulation* 30(1964):37(Supple. 3).
98. Hume, D. M. Discussion (edited by Dr. J. Murray) of data presented at the Human Kidney Transplant Conference, Washington, D. C., 1963. *Transplantation* 2(1964):581–94.

99. Hume, D. M. Discussion on Aneurysm of Abdominal Aorta, *Annals of Surgery* 160(1964):638–39.
100. Hume, D. M. Discussion on Analysis of Mechanism of Immunosuppressive Drugs in Renal Homotransplantation, *Annals of Surgery* 160(1964):471–73.
101. Hume, D. M. Discussion on Renal Heterotransplantation in Man, *Annals of Surgery* 160(1964):408–410.
102. Hume, D. M. "The Regulation of ACTH and Corticosteroid Secretion," in *Hormonal Steroids: Biochemistry, Pharmacology and Therapeutics*, Proceedings of the First International Congress on Hormonal Steroids, Milan, 1962, edited by L. Martini and A. Pecile, vol. 1, pp. 185–198. (New York: Academic Press, 1964.)
103. Hume, D. M., Magee, J. H., Kauffman, H. M., Jr., Bower, J. D., Lee, H. M., Cleveland, R. J., and Prout, G. R., Jr. "Transplantation at the Medical College of Virginia. Summary through September, 1963," Proceedings of the Human Kidney Transplant Conference, Washington, D. C., September 26–27, 1963, *Transplantation* 2(1964):164–165.
104. Hume, D. M., Magee, J. H., Prout, G. R., Jr., Kauffman, H. M., Jr., Cleveland, R. H., Bower, J. D., and Lee, H. M. "Studies of Renal Homotransplantation in Man," in "Sixth International Transplantation Conference," *Annals of the New York Academy of Sciences* 120(1964):578–606(1 Part 2).
105. Jackson, B. T., Egdahl, R. H., and Hume, D. M. "Chronic Pituitary Stalk Section in the Dog" (abstract), *Federation Proceedings* 23(1964):513(2 Part 1).
106. Kauffman, H. M., Clark, R. F., Fisher, L. M., and Hume, D. M. "Lethality of Intravascular Injections of Spleen and Liver Cells," *Annals of Surgery* 159(1964):227–43.
107. Kauffman, H. M., Clark, R. F., Magee, J. H., Rittenbury, M. S., Goldsmith, C. M., Prout, G. R., Jr., and Hume, D. M. "Lymphocytes in Urine as an Aid in the Early Detection of Renal Homograft Rejection," *Surgery, Gynecology and Obstetrics* 119(1964):25–36.
108. Kauffman, H. M., Cleveland, R. J., Lee, H. M., Dwyer, J. J., and Hume, D. M. "Lymphocyturia and Renal Homograft Rejection in Man" (abstract), *Virginia Journal of Science* 15(1964):342–43.
109. Kauffman, H. M., Cleveland, R. J., Lee, H. M., and Hume, D. M. "Significance of Lymphocyturia in Renal Homograft Rejection," *Surgical Forum* 15(1964):168–70.
110. Lee, H. M., Kauffman, H. M., Cleveland, R. J., Dwyer, J. J., and Hume, D. M. "Prolongation of Functional Survival of Renal Homografts by Local Radiation" (abstract), *Virginia Journal of Science* 15(1964):343.
111. Lee, H. M., Kauffman, H. M., Cleveland, R. J., and Hume, D. M. "Selective immunosuppression by local radiation of renal homografts," *Surgical Forum* 15(1964):158–60.
112. Magee, J. H., Hume, D. M., Kauffman, H. M., and Bower, J. D. "Massive Diuresis Following Renal Homotransplantation," *Proceedings of the Society for Experimental Biology and Medicine* 116(1964):480–83.
113. Mannick, J. A., Brooks, J. W., Bosher, L. H., Jr., and Hume, D. M. "Ruptured Aneurysms of the Abdominal Aorta; A Reappraisal," *New England Journal of Medicine* 271(1964):915–20.
114. Mannick, J. A., and Hume, D. M. "Salvage of Extremities by Vein Grafts in Far-advanced Peripheral Vascular Disease," *Surgery* 55(1964):154–64.
115. Prout, G. R., Jr., Hume, D. M., Magee, J. H., Lee, H. M., Bower, J. D., and Cleveland, R. J. "Bilateral Nephrectomy: Its Role in Renal Homotransplantation and the Anephric State in Man" (abstract), *Transactions of the American Urological Association* (1964).

116. Prout, G. R., Jr., Macalalag, E. V., Jr., Denis, L. J., and Hume, D. M. "Renal Homotransplantation: Serum Protein Patterns," *Investigative Urology* 1(1964):457–65.

117. Prout, G. R., Jr., Macalalag, E. V., Jr., and Hume, D. M. "Serum and Urinary Lactic Dehydrogenase in Patients with Renal Homotransplants," *Surgery* 56(1964):283–95.

118. Rittenbury, M. S., Hume, D. M., and Hench, M. E. "A Clinical Bacteriologic Evaluation of Surgical Antiseptics and a Plastic Skin Drape," *Surgery, Gynecology and Obstetrics* 119(1964):568–74.

119. Sacks, J. H., Filippone, D. R., and Hume, D. M. "Studies of Immune Destruction of Lymphoid Tissue: I. Lymphocytotoxic Effect of Rabbit-Anti-Rat-Lymphocyte Antiserum," *Transplantation* 2(1964):60–74.

1965

120. Billingham, R. E., Hume, D. M., Reemtsma, K., and Robin, E. D. "Symposium: Some Problems in Organ Transplantation," *Journal of the Albert Einstein Medical Center* 13(1965):327–53.

121. Bower, J. D., and Hume, D. M. "Experience with the Seattle Hemodialysis System in Renal Homotransplantation," *Transactions of the American Society for Artificial Internal Organs* 11(1965):225–31.

122. Cleveland, R. J., Kauffman, H. M., Graham, W. H., and Hume, D. M. "Prolongation of Renal Homograft Survival by Inhibition of the Afferent Arc of the Immune Response," *Surgical Forum* 16(1965):269–71.

123. Cleveland, R. J., Kauffman, H. M., Graham, W. H., and Hume, D. M. "Studies on the Mechanism by which Local Radiation Prolongs Survival of Kidney Homografts" (abstract), *Virginia Journal of Science* 16(1965):386.

124. Dalton, W. E., Lee, H. M., Kauffman, H. M., and Hume, D. M. "Immunosuppressive Effect of Heterologous Antilymphocyte Serum in Dogs" (abstract), *Virginia Journal of Science* 16(1965):387–88.

125. Dalton, W. E., Millington, G., Lee, H. M., and Hume, D. M. "Comparison of Antibody Response to Sheep Erythrocytes and Response to Skin Homografts in Rats Receiving Appropriate Antiserum," *Surgical Forum* 16(1965):245–47.

126. Hume, D. M. "Catecholamines in Hemorrhagic Shock," in *Symposium on Medical Aspects of Stress in the Military Climate,* sponsored by Walter Reed Army Institute of Research, Walter Reed Army Medical Center, Washington, D. C., 1964, pp. 487–97. (Washington, D. C.: USGPO, 1965.) Superintendent of Documents Classification Number D104.2:St8/2.

127. Hume, D. M. Discussion on Chronic Survival After Human Renal Homotransplantation, *Annals of Surgery* 162(1965):784–85.

128. Hume, D. M. (moderator), "Panel on the Maintenance of Life in Uremia," held at the Second Annual Kidney Symposium, Virginia Chapter of the National Kidney Disease Foundation, Richmond, Virginia, 1964, *MCV/Q; Medical College of Virginia Quarterly* 1(1965):12–18.

129. Hume, D. M., Kauffman, H. M., and Cleveland, R. J. "Renal homotransplantation in man" (scientific exhibit), *Postgraduate Medicine* 38(1965):421–31.

130. Kauffman, H. M., Clark, R. F., and Hume, D. M. "Bone Marrow and Spleen Cell Homotransplantation in Dogs Following Combination Chemotherapy and Total Body Irradiation," *Journal of Surgical Research* 5(1965):2–10.

131. Kauffman, H. M., Clements, A. S., Cleveland, R. J., and Hume, D. M. "Fluorescent Antibody Studies on Renal Homografts" (abstract), *Virginia Journal of Science* 16(1965):392.

132. Kauffman, H. M., Cleveland, R. J., Dwyer, J. J., Lee, H. M., and Hume, D. M. "Prolongation of Renal Homograft Function by Local Graft Radiation," *Surgery, Gynecology and Obstetrics* 120(1965):49–58.

133. Kauffman, H. M., Cleveland, R. J., and Hume, D. M. "Bibliography of kidney transplantation. Addendum No. 4," *Transplantation* 3(1965):278–85.

134. Sharpe, A. R., Jr., King, E. R., and Hume, D. M. "Sequential Response of T½ of 131I Hippuran Renograms in Renal Homotransplantation" (abstract), *Journal of Nuclear Medicine* 6(1965):336.

135. Slapak, M., Dalton, W. E., Lee, H. M., and Hume, D. M. "New Method of Estimating Glomerular Filtration Rate using Cobalt-57 Labelled Vitamin-B12" (abstract), *Virginia Journal of Science* 16(1965):395.

136. Slapak, M., Dalton, W. E., Lee, H. M., and Hume, D. M. "Variations of Glomerular Filtration Rate After Renal Homotransplantation in the Human Being and the Dog as Measured by the Blood Clearance of Co57 Vitamin B12," *Surgical Forum* 16(1965):260–62.

137. Slapak, M., and Hume, D. M. "A New Method of Estimating Glomerular-Filtration Rate by the Use of Diminishing Blood Concentration of Labelled Vitamin B12," *Lancet* 1(1965):1095–97.

138. Wolf, J. S., and Hume, D. M. "Prolongation of Renal Homograft Survival by External Radiation of Renal Arterial Blood" (abstract), *Federation Proceedings* 24(1965):573(2 Part 1). Also published as an abstract in *Virginia Journal of Science* 16(1965):396–97.

139. Wolf, J. S., and Hume, D. M. "Studies of a Method of Inducing Specific Lymphopenia in Dogs," *JAMA; Journal of the American Medical Association* 194(1965):1119–21. Also published as an abstract in *JAMA; Journal of the American Medical Association* 192(1965):553.

140. Wolf, J. S., and Hume, D. M. "Transplant Immunity in Animals with Lymphocytopenia Induced by Indwelling Beta Irradiation," *Surgical Forum* 16(1965):202–204.

1966

141. Hume, D. M. Discussion on Protection of the Donor Kidney During Homotransplantation, *Annals of Surgery* 164(1966):417.

142. Hume, D. M. "Progress in Clinical Renal Homotransplantation," in *Advances in Surgery*, edited by C. E. Welch, vol. 2, pp. 419–98. (Chicago: Year Book Medical Publishers, 1966.)

143. Hume, D. M. "Some Surgical Problems in Diabetic Patients," *MCV/Q; Medical College of Virginia Quarterly* 2(1966):35–36.

144. Hume, D. M., and Kauffman, H. M. "Endocrine Glands," in *Surgical Bleeding; Handbook for Medicine, Surgery and Specialties,* edited by A. W. Ulin and S. S. Gollub, pp. 205–16. (New York: McGraw–Hill, Blakiston Division, 1966.)

145. Hume, D. M., Lee, H. M., Prout, G. R., Jr., Bower, J. D., Wolf, J. S., and Slapak, M. "Renal Homotransplantation in Man: Studies in 63 Cases," in *The Kidney*, by 33 Authors. (International Academy of Pathology, Monographs in Pathology, No. 6), edited by F. K. Mostofi and D. E. Smith, pp. 409–432. (Baltimore: Williams & Wilkins, 1966.)

146. Hume, D. M., Lee, H. M., Williams, G. M., White, H. J. O., Ferré, J., Wolf, J. S., Prout, G. R., Jr., Slapak, M., O'Brien, J., Kilpatrick, S. J., Kauffman, H. M., Jr., and Cleveland, R. J. "Comparative Results of Cadaver and Related Donor Renal Homografts in Man, and Immunologic Implications of the Outcome of Second and Paired Transplants," *Transactions of the 86th Meeting of the American Surgical Association* 84(1966):16–61. Also published in *Annals of Surgery* 164(1966):352–97.

147. Kauffman, H. M., Jr., Cleveland, R. J., Robertshaw, G. E., Graham, W. H., and Hume, D. M. "Inhibition of the Afferent Arc of the Immune Response to Renal Homografts by Local Graft Radiation," *Surgery, Gynecology and Obstetrics* 123(1966):1052–56.

148. Kauffman, H. M., Jr., Fisher, L. M., and Hume, D. M. "Kidney Transplantation," in *Surgical Bleeding: Handbook for Medicine, Surgery, and Specialities,* edited by A. W. Ulin and S. S. Gollub, pp. 409–18. (New York: McGraw–Hill, Blakiston Division, 1966.)

149. O'Brien, J. P., and Hume, D. M. "Membranous Glomerulonephritis in Two Human Renal Homotransplants," *Annals of Internal Medicine* 65(1966):504–10.

150. O'Brien, J. P., Sharpe, A. R., Jr., and Hume, D. M. "Insulin I-131 Kinetics Following Renal Homotransplantation" (abstract), *Clinical Research* 14(1966):384. Also published as abstract under the title, "Iodine-131 Insulin Kinetics Following Renal Homotransplantation," *Journal of Nuclear Medicine* 7(1966):363.

151. Sharpe, A. R., Jr., King, E. R., Hume, D. M., Lee, H. M., Kauffman, H. M., and Rittenbury, M. S. "Sequential Response of the Iodine-131 Hippuran Renogram in Renal Homotransplantation," *Journal of Nuclear Medicine* 7(1966):556–63.

152. White, H. J. O., Ferré, J., and Hume, D. M. "Perfusion of the Extracorporal Canine Liver under Physiological Conditions" (abstract), *Virginia Journal of Science* 17(1966):354.

153. Wolf, J. S., Lee, H. M., and Hume, D. M. "Mixed Lymphocyte Cultures in Patients Undergoing Renal Homotransplantation" (abstract), *Federation Proceedings* 25(1966):295(2 Part 1).

154. Wolf, J. S., Lee, H. M., O'Foghludha, F. T., and Hume, D. M. "Effect of Circulating Blood Radiation with an Extracorporeal Strontium-90 Shunt on Transplantation Immunity in Dogs and Man," *Surgical Forum* 17(1966):245–46.

155. Wolf, J. S., O'Foghludha, F. T., Kauffman, H. M., and Hume, D. M. "Prolongation of Renal Homograft Survival by Indwelling Beta Radiation," *Surgery, Gynecology and Obstetrics* 122(1966):1262–68.

1967

156. Board, J. A., Lee, H. M., Draper, D. A., and Hume, D. M. "Pregnancy Following Kidney Homotransplantation from a Non-twin. Report of a case with concurrent administration of azathioprine and prednisone," *Obstetrics and Gynecology* 29(1967):318–23.

157. Braf, Z. F., Smellie, W. A. B., Williams, G. M., and Hume, D. M. "Preparation of Specific Potent Anti-lymphocyte Serum in the Horse Using Dog Thymocytes," *Surgical Forum* 18(1967):227–29.

158. Harlan, W. R., Jr., Holden, K. R., Williams, G. M., and Hume, D. M. "Proteinuria and Nephrotic Syndrome Associated with Chronic Rejection of Kidney Transplants," *New England Journal of Medicine* 277(1967):769–76. Also published as abstract under the title, "Proteinuria, Nephrotic Syndrome and Chronic Rejection of Human Renal Allografts," *Clinical Research* 15(1967):359. Same authors in different order, same title, variant abstract published in *Clinical Research* 15(1967):77.

159. Hume, D. M. "Adrenal Insufficiency," in *Manual of Preoperative and Postoperative Care,* by the Committee on Pre and Postoperative Care, American College of Surgeons; Editorial Subcommittee: H. T. Randall (Chairman), J. D. Hardy and F. D. Moore, pp. 110–16. (Philadelphia: W. B. Saunders, 1967.)

160. Hume, D. M. Discussion on Recurrent Cushing's Disease and Intermittent Functional Adrenal Cortical Insufficiency Following Subtotal Adrenalectomy, *Annals of Surgery* 166(1967):592–95.

161. Hume, D. M. Discussion on Unrecognized Aspects of Alpha Adrenergic Blockade, *Surgery* 62(1967):101–102.

162. Hume, D. M. "Renal Homotransplantation in Man," in *Annual Review of Medicine* 18(1967):229–68. (Palo Alto, California: Annual Reviews, 1967.)

163. Hume, D. M. "Surgery of the Adrenals," chapter 34 in *Manual of Preoperative and Postoperative Care*, by the Committee on Pre and Postoperative Care, American College of Surgeons; Editorial Subcommittee: H. T. Randall (Chairman), J. D. Hardy and F. D. Moore, pp. 419–34. (Philadelphia: W. B. Saunders, 1967.)

164. Hume, D. M., Williams, G. M., Lee, H. M., White, H. J. O., Ferré, J., and Wolf, J. S. "Experiences with 108 Consecutive Non–twin Renal Homotransplants in Man," in *Proceedings of the Third International Congress of Nephrology*, Washington, D.C., 1966, vol. 3, "Clinical Nephrology," edited by E. L. Becker, pp. 351–64. (Basel and New York: S. Karger, 1967.)

165. Hume, D. M. and Wolf, J. S. "Modification of Renal Homograft Rejection by Irradiation," *Transplantation* 5(1967):1174–91(4 Part 2, Proceedings Suppl.).

166. Lee, H. M., Hume, D. M., Vredevoe, D. L., Mickey, M. R., and Terasaki, P. I. "Serotyping for Homotransplantation. IX. Evaluation of Leucocyte Antigen Matching with the Clinical Course and Rejection Types," *Transplantation* 5(1967):1040–45(Proceedings Supplement).

167. Mannick, J. A., Jackson, B. T., Coffman, J. D., and Hume, D. M. "Success of Bypass Vein Grafts in Patients with Isolated Popliteal Artery Segments," *Surgery* 61(1967):17–25.

168. Morris, P. J., Hume, D. M., and Terasaki, P. I. "The Development of Cytotoxic Antibodies in Renal Transplantation," in *Histocompatibility Testing 1967*. (Report of a Conference and Workshop, held at Torino and Saint–Vincent, Italy), edited by E. S. Curtoni, P. L. Mattiuz and R. M. Tosi, p. 339. (Baltimore: Williams & Wilkins, 1967.)

169. Morris, P. J., Terasaki, P. I., Williams, G. M., and Hume, D. M. "The Development of Cytotoxic Antibodies in Renal Transplantation," *Surgical Forum* 18(1967):270–72.

170. Prout, G. R., Jr., Hume, D. M., Lee, H. M., and Williams, G. M. "Some Urological Aspects of 93 Consecutive Renal Homotransplants in Modified Recipients," *Journal of Urology* 97(1967):409–25.

171. Rapaport, F. T., Dausset, J., Hamburger, J., Hume, D. M., Kano, K., Williams, G. M., and Milgrom, F. "Serologic Factors in Human Transplantation," *Transactions of the 87th Meeting of the American Surgical Association* 85(1967):294–306. Also published in *Annals of Surgery* 166(1967):596–608.

172. Robertshaw, G. E., Kauffman, H. M., Madge, G. E., and Hume, D. M. "Treatment of Renal Homografts with Local Graft Radiation and Actinomycin C or D," *Transplantation* 5(1967):549–51.

173. Robertshaw, G. E., Madge, G. E., Williams, G. M., and Hume, D. M. "Nephrotoxic activity of Hyperimmune Homologous Dog Immune Serum," *Surgical Forum* 18(1967):276–78.

174. Slapak, M., Lee, H. M., and Hume, D. M. "'Transplant Lung' and Lung Complications in Renal Transplantation," in *Advance in Transplantation, Proceedings of the 1st International Congress of the Transplantation Society*, edited by J. Dausset, J. Hamburger and G. Mathe, Section XVI, "Other Problems," pp. 769–76. (Baltimore: Williams and Wilkins, 1967; and Copenhagen: Munksgaard, 1968.)

175. Thomas, P. J., Logue, R. B., Hope, J. W., Sunderman, F. W., Braley, A. E., Prout, G. R., Jr., Hume, D. M., and Ashworth, C. T. "Clinicopathologic Conference," *Texas Medicine* 63(1967):81–88.

176. White, H. J. O., Ferré, J., and Hume, D. M. (R. Y. Calne). "Perfusion of the Extracorporeal Canine Liver under Physiological Conditions" (abstract), *British Journal of Surgery* 54(1967):231.

177. Williams, G. M., Lee, H. M., Weymouth, R. F., Harlan, W. R., Jr., Holden, K. R., Stanley, C. M., Millington, G. A., and Hume, D. M. "Studies in Hyperacute and Chronic Renal Homograft Rejection in Man," *Surgery* 62(1967):204-212.
178. Williams, G. M., Morris, P. J., Harlan, W. R., and Hume, D. M. "Serological Studies in Transplant Recipients with Nephrotic Syndrome," in *Advance in Transplantation, Proceedings of the 1st International Congress of the Transplantation Society*, edited by J. Dausset, J. Hamburger and G. Mathe, Section V, "Organ Transplantation," pp. 373-78. (Baltimore: Williams and Wilkins, 1967; and Copenhagen: Munksgaard, 1968.)
179. Williams, G. M., Stanley, C. M., Millington, G. A., and Hume, D. M. "Serological Reactions Against Particulate Renal Antigen in Renal Transplant Recipients," *Surgical Forum* 18(1967):253-54.
180. Williams, G. M., White, H. J., and Hume, D. M. "Factors Influencing the Long Term Functional Success Rate of Human Renal Allografts," *Transplantation* 5(1967):837-43(Proceedings Supplement).
181. Wolf, J. S., and Hume, D. M. "Alteration of the Immune Response to Transplantation by Beta Irradiation of Circulating Blood," *Bulletin de le Societé Internationale de Chirurgie* 26(1967):433-43.
182. Wolf, J. S., and Hume, D. M. "Hematologic Response to Beta Irradiation of Extracorporeal Blood in Leukemic and Immunosuppressed Patients," *Experimental Hematology* (U.S. National Laboratory, Oak Ridge) No. 12(1967):6-7.
183. Wolf, J. S., McGavic, J. D., and Hume, D. M. "Inhibition of the Effector Mechanism in Transplant Immunity by Local Graft Irradiation," *Surgical Forum* 18(1967):249-50.

1968

184. Ferré, J., and Hume, D. M. "La Catalasa Urinaria en las Crisis de Rechazo en Homoinjertos Renales Humanos," ("Urinary Catalase Activity in the Rejection Crisis of Human Kidney Allografts"), *Revista Clinica Española* (Madrid) 108(1968):18-21.
185. Gayle, W. E., Jr., Williams, G. M., and Hume, D. M. "Control of Hepatic Sphincters by Sympathetic Amines: Beta Receptors," chapter 60 in *Organ Perfusion and Preservation*, edited by J. C. Norman, J. Folkman, et al, pp. 805-19. (New York: Appleton-Century-Crofts, 1968.)
186. Hall, M. C., and Hume, D. M. "Bone Changes in Patients with Renal Transplants," *Journal of the American Medical Women's Association* 23(1968):1040-47.
187. Hall, M. C., Irby, R., Elmore, S. M., Pierce, J. C., Bright, R. W., and Hume, D. M. "Skeletal Problems Encountered in a Series of Human Renal Allografts" (abstract), *Arthritis and Rheumatism* 11(1968):486.
188. Hume, D. M. "Kidney Transplantation," chapter 10 in *Human Transplantation*, edited by F. T. Rapaport and J. Dausset, pp. 110-150. (New York: Grune & Stratton, 1968.)
189. Hume, D. M. "Organ Transplants and Immunity," *Hospital Practice* 3(1968):27-35.
190. Hume, D. M. "Pheochromocytoma," chapter 7 in *Clinical Endocrinology*, edited by E. B. Astwood and C. E. Cassidy, vol. 2, pp. 519-51. (New York: Grune & Stratton, 1968.)
191. Irby, R. and Hume, D. M. "Joint Changes Observed Following Renal Transplants," *Clinical Orthopedics and Related Research* 57(1968):101-14.
192. Irby, R., and Hume, D. M. "Synovial Reactions and Bone Changes Observed Following Renal Transplantation and Immunosuppressive Therapy" (abstract), *Arthritis and Rheumatism* 11(1968):104.

193. Linehan, J. D., Lee, H. M., and Hume, D. M. "Adrenocortical Responsiveness in Patients with Renal Transplants Receiving Prednisone," *Surgical Forum* 19(1968):217–19.

194. Moore, T. C., Chang, J. K., and Hume, D. M. "Urinary Excretion of Histamine in Renal Transplant Patients," *Surgery, Gynecology and Obstetrics* 127(1968):1023–32.

195. Morris, P. J., Hume, D. M., and Terasaki, P. "A Study of Serological Tissue Typing in Renal Transplantation and the Importance of Preexisting Cytotoxins in Donor Selection" (abstract), Proceedings of the Australasian Society of Nephrology, Ordinary Meeting, Melbourne, 1967, *Australasian Annals of Medicine* 17(1968):83.

196. Morris, P. J., Williams, G. M., Hume, D. M., Mickey, M. R., and Terasaki, P. I., "Serotyping for Homotransplantation: XII. Occurrence of Cytotoxic Antibodies Following Kidney Transplantation in Man," *Transplantation* 6(1968):392–99.

197. Pierce, J. C., and Hume, D. M. "The Effect of Splenectomy on the Survival of First and Second Renal Homotransplants in Man," *Surgery, Gynecology and Obstetrics* 127(1968):1300–1306.

198. Rolley, R. T., Williams, G. M., and Hume, D. M. "Distribution of Leucocyte Antigens in Human Tissues," *Surgical Forum* 19(1968):241–43.

199. Semb, B. K. H., Williams, G. M., and Hume, D. H. [i.e., D. M.]. "The Effect of Allogenic Lymphocytes on the Isolated Perfused Kidney," *Transplantation* 6(1968):977–85.

200. Slapak, M., Lee, H. M., and Hume, D. M. "Transplant Lung—A New Syndrome," *British Medical Journal* 1(1968):80–84(5584).

201. Smellie, W. A. B., Vinik, M., Freed, T. A., and Hume, D. M. "Pertrochanteric Venography in the Study of Human Renal Transplant Recipients," *Surgery, Gynecology and Obstetrics* 126(1968):777–80.

202. Task Group I. "Transplant Science: Present Status of Transplantation of Organs Other than the Heart," D. M. Hume (Chairman), *American Journal of Cardiology* 22(1968):899–904.

203. Williams, C., Jr., Bryson, G. H., and Hume, D. M. "Islet Cell Tumors and Hypoglycemia," *Transactions of the Southern Surgical Association* 80(1968):127–43. Reprinted in *Annals of Surgery* 169(1969):757–73.

204. Williams, G. M., Hume, D. M., Hudson, R. P., Jr., Morris, P. J., Kano, K., and Milgrom, F. " 'Hyperacute' Renal–Homograft Rejection in Man," *New England Journal of Medicine* 279(1968):611–18.

205. Williams, G. M., Hume, D. M., Kano, K., and Milgrom, F. "Transplantation Antibodies in Human Recipients of Renal Homografts," *JAMA* 204(1968):119–22.

206. Williams, G. M., Lee, H. M., and Hume, D. M. "Advances in Renal Transplantation" (abstract), *Virginia Journal of Science* 19(1968):207.

207. Williams, G. M., Rolley, R. T., and Hume, D. M. "A Comparison of Lymphocyte and Kidney Cell Typing in Eleven Patients," *Surgical Forum* 19(1968):209–210.

1969

208. Braf, Z. F., and Hume, D. M. "Prolongation of Functional Survival of Second-set Canine Renal Homografts Using Antithymocyte Serum: Preliminary Report," *Surgery* 66(1969):594–96.

209. Braf, Z. F., Smellie, W. A. B., Williams, G. M., and Hume, D. M. "Evaluation of Antithymocyte in the Treatment of Canine Renal Homografts," *Surgery, Gynecology and Obstetrics* 129(1969):71–78.

210. Gayle, W. E., Jr., Williams, G. M., and Hume, D. M. "Heterologous (Chimera) Cross Circulation for Hepatic Failure," *Review of Surgery* 26(1969):368–70.

211. Gayle, W. E., Jr., Williams, G. M., and Hume, D. M. "Immunologic Consequences of Human Being and Baboon Cross Circulation," *Surgical Forum* 20(1969):354–55.

212. Hall, M. C., Elmore, S. M., Bright, R. W., Pierce, J. C., and Hume, D. M. "Skeletal Complications in a Series of Human Renal Allografts," *JAMA; Journal of the American Medical Association* 208(1969):1825–29.

213. Hume, D. M. Discussion on Anti–serum to Cultured Human Lymphoblasts: Preparation, Purification and Immunosuppressive Properties in Man, *Annals of Surgery* 170(1969):630–32.

214. Hume, D. M. "Prospects of Kidney Transplantation," in *Organ Transplantation Today;* Symposium Held on the Occasion of the Official Opening of the Sint Lucas Ziekenhuis, Amsterdam, 1968, edited by N. A. Mitchison, J. M. Greep and J. C. M. Hattinga–Verschure, (Excerpta Medica Monograph), pp. 311–330. (Baltimore: Williams & Wilkins, 1969; and Amsterdam: Excerpta Medica Foundation, 1969.)

215. Hume, D. M., Gayle, W. E., Jr., and Williams, G. M. "Cross Circulation of Patients in Hepatic Coma with Baboon Partners Having Human Blood," *Surgery, Gynecology and Obstetrics* 128(1969):495–517.

216. Hume, D. M., Leo, J., Rolley, R. T., and Williams, G. M. "Some Immunological and Surgical Aspects of Kidney Transplantation in Man," *Transplantation Proceedings* 1(1969):171–77.

217. Leo, J. R., Kilpatrick, S. J., Jr., DePlanque, B. A., Williams, G. M., and Hume, D. M. "A Genetic Model of Human Histocompatibility Based on the Results of Double Cadaver 218. Renal Homografts," *Transplantation Proceedings* 1(1969):379–81.

218. Linehan, J. D., Jr., Lee, H. M., Robertshaw, G. E., and Hume, D. M. "Suppression of Homograft Immunity with Thiocymetin," *Surgical Forum* 20(1969):270–72.

219. Moore, T. C., and Hume, D. M. "The Period and Nature of Hazard in Clinical Renal Transplantation: I. The Hazard to Patient Survival," *Annals of Surgery* 170(1969):1–11.

220. Moore, T. C., and Hume, D. M. "The Period and Nature of Hazard in Clinical Renal Transplantation: II. The Hazard to Transplant Kidney Function," *Annals of Surgery* 170(1969):12–24.

221. Moore, T. C., and Hume, D. M. "The Period and Nature of Hazard in Clinical Renal Transplantation: III. The Hazard to Transplant Kidney Survival," *Annals of Surgery* 170(1969):25–29.

222. Pierce, J. C., and Hume, D. M. (Project Directors). "The Procurement and Characterization of Post Renal Transplant Rejection Serum; Annual Report, 1969" to D. C. Kayhoe (Chief), Transplantation Immunology Branch, National Institutes of Health, 1969. 37 pp. (Available from the Library of Congress Photoduplication Service as PB190–596.)

223. Robertshaw, G. E., Madge, G. E., Williams, G. M., and Hume, D. M. "Hyper–acute Rejection of Dog Renal Auto Grafts," *Surgical Forum* 20(1969):291–92.

224. Rolley, R. T., Williams, G. M., Lerner, R. A., Hanscom, G., and Hume, D. M. "Characterization of Antibodies Following Human Renal Homograft Rejection," *Transplantation Proceedings* 1(1969):275–78.

225. Schwartz, S. I. (editor–in–chief); Hume, D. M., Lillehei, R. C., Shirer, G. T., Spencer, F. C., and Storer, E. H. (associate editors). *Principles of Surgery* (New York: McGraw–Hill, Blakiston Division, 1969). Contributions by D. M. Hume to Part 1, "Basic Considerations": Chapter 1, "Endocrine and Metabolic Responses to Injury," by DMH, pp. 3–45; Chapter 10, "Transplantation," by DMH and R. R. Lower, pp. 259–340. Contributions by D. M. Hume to Part 2, "Specific Organ Systems": Chapter 36, "Pituitary and Adrenal," by DMH, pp. 1217–85; Chapter 37, "Thyroid and Parathyroid," by S. I. Schwartz and DMH, pp. 1286–1369.

226. Smellie, W. A. Vinik, M., and Hume, D. M. "Angiographic Investigation of Hypertension Complicating Human Renal Transplantation," *Surgery, Gynecology and Obstetrics* 128(1969):963–68.

227. Tucker, H. S., Jr., Estep, H. L., Hume, D. M., Vinik, M., and Kay, S. "Cushing's Syndrome with Nodular Adrenal Hyperplasia," *Transactions of the American Clinical and Climatological Association* 80(1969):37–49.

228. Vinik, M., Smellie, W. A. B., Freed, T. A., Hume, D. M., and Weidner, W. A. "Angiographic Evaluation of the Human Homotransplant Kidney," *Radiology* 92(1969):873–79.

229. Vinik, M., Smellie, W. A. B., Freed, T. A., Hume, D. M., and Weidner, W. A. "Renal Ischemia and Homograft Rejection. Preliminary Angiographic Data in the Dog," *Investigative Radiology* 4(1969):252–63.

230. Weymouth, R. J., Lee, H. M., Hume, D. M., and Williams, G. M. "Renal Transplantation: An Electron Microscopic Study of the Glomerulus in Man" (abstract), *Anatomical Record* 163(1969):284.

231. Williams, G. M., DePlanque, B., Lower, R., and Hume, D. M. "Antibodies and Human Transplant Rejection," *Annals of Surgery* 170(1969):603–616.

232. Williams, G. M., Lee, H. M., and Hume, D. M. "Renal Transplants in Children," *Transplantation Proceedings* 1(1969):262–66.

233. Wolf, J. S., Fawley, J. C. and Hume, D. M. "In Vitro Interaction of Specifically-sensitized and Non–sensitized Lymphocytes with Kidney Cells from Human Renal Homografts, "*Transplantation Proceedings* 1(1969):328–30.

234. Wolf, J. S., Fawley, J. C., and Hume, D. M. "Quantitative Evaluation of Lymphocyte Cytotoxicity to Kidney Cells from Rejected Human Renal Homografts" (abstract), *JAMA* 208(1969):1481.

235. Wolf, J. S., Gayle, W. E., Braf, Z., Robertshaw, G., O'Foghludha, F. T., and Hume, D. M. "Experimental and Clinical Studies of Extracorporeal Blood Irradiation in Transplantation," in *Dialysis and Renal Transplantation* (Proceedings of the European Dialysis and Transplant Association, vol. 5), edited by D. N. S. Kerr, D. Fries and R. W. Elliott, pp. 125–27. (Amsterdam: Excerpta Medica Foundation, 1969.)

236. Wolf, J. S., McGavic, J. D., and Hume, D. M. "Inhibition of the Effector Mechanism of Transplant Immunity by Local Graft Irradiation," *Surgery, Gynecology and Obstetrics* 128(1969):584–90.

237. Wolf, J. S., O'Foghludha, F. T., Braf, Z. F., and Hume, D. M. "Design and Evaluation of Beta Emitting Radio Applicators in Studies of Transplantation Immunity in Dogs and Man" (abstract), *British Journal of Haematology* 17(1969):412.

1970

238. Dalton, W. E., Lee, H. M., Williams, G. M., and Hume, D. M. "Pancreatic Pseudocyst Causing Hemobilia and Massive Gastrointestinal Hemorrhage," *American Journal of Surgery* 120(1970):106–107.

239. Hall, M. C., and Hume, D. M. "Separation of Massive Avascular Osteocartilaginous Fragment of Femoral Condyle Following Renal Transplantation. Report of two cases," *Journal of Bone and Joint Surgery* 52-A(1970):550–55.

240. Hume, D. M. Brief testimony, Anatomical Gift Act. 91st Congress, 2d Session, February 4, 1970. (Brief testimony at a hearing on S. 2999, to authorize, in the District of Columbia, the gift of all or part of a human body after death for specified purposes.) Superintendent of Documents Classification number Y4.D63/2:An1/2. (Also available: Congressional Information Service, Microfiche Collection, 1970, microfiche number S301-8.3, pp. 14–22.)

241. Hume, D. M. Discussion on Organ Transplantation Between Widely Disparate Species, *Transplantation Proceedings* 2(1970):554–56.

242. Hume, D. M. "The Immunological Consequences of Organ Homotransplantation in

Man," in *The Harvey Lectures,* Series 64, delivered under the auspices of The Harvey Society of New York, 1968–1969, pp. 261–388. (New York: Academic Press, 1970.)

243. Hume, D. M. "Renal Transplantation," *Academy of Medicine of New Jersey Bulletin* 16(1970):149–54.

244. Hume, D. M., Lee, H. M., Wolf, J. S., Pierce, J. C., O'Foghludha, F. T., Rolley, R. T., Gayle, W. E., Levinson, S., Sterling, W., and Newsome, H. H. "Transplantation Immunity: Effect of Radiation and Related Studies; Progress Report, July 1, 1969–June 30, 1970, and Budget and Proposal for Period July 1, 1970–June 30, 1971," 25 pp. [AEC Grant AT (40-1) 2459.] (Available from the Library of Congress Photoduplication Service as TID–25490.)

245. Hume, D. M., Sterling, W. A., Weymouth, R. J., Siebel, H. R., Madge, G. E., and Lee, H. M. "Glomerulonephritis in Human Renal Homotransplants," *Transplantation Proceedings* 2(1970):361–412.

246. Kay, S., Frable, W. J., and Hume, D. M. "Cervical Dysplasia and Cancer Developing in Women on Immunosuppression Therapy for Renal Homotransplantation," *Cancer* 26(1970):1048–52.

247. Pierce, J. C., and Hume, D. M. "Toxicity of Azathioprine," in *La Transplantation Cardiaque; Deuxieme symposium mondial, 1969,* (World Symposium on Heart Transplantation, 2d, Montreal, 1969.) pp. 189–97. (Quebec, Canada: Les Presses de L'Universite Laval, 1970.) Also published in *Laval Medicale* 41(1970):295–303 (English).

248. Slapak, M., Beaudoin, J. G., Lee, H. M., and Hume, D. M. "Auxiliary Liver Homotransplantation. A New Technique and An Evaluation of Current Techniques," *Archives of Surgery* 100(1970):31–41.

249. Smellie, W. A. B., Braf, Z. F., Vinik, M., and Hume, D. M. "Caval Ligation Above Canine Renal Autografts," *European Surgical Research* 2(1970):277–86.

250. Waller, M., Pierce, J. C., Hume, D. M., Mallory, J., and Millington, G. A. "Antihorse Globulin Antibodies in Human Sera," *Clinical and Experimental Immunology* 6(1970):645–53.

251. Weymouth, R. J., Seibel, H. R., Lee, H. M., Hume, D. M., and Williams, G. M. "The Glomerulus in Man One Hour After Transplantation. An Electron Microscopic Study," *American Journal of Pathology* 58(1970):85–104.

252. Wolf, J. S., Fawley, J. C., and Hume, D. M. "Quantitative Evaluation of Lymphocyte Cyto Toxicity to Kidney Cells from Rejected Human Renal Homografts" (abstract), in *Progress in Lymphology; Papers Presented at the Third International Symposium on Lymphology,* Brussels, 1970, edited by J. A. Gruwez, p. 98. (Stuttgart?: G. Thieme? 1970?).

1971

253. Abouna, G. M., Amemiya, H., Fisher, L. M., Still, W. J., Porter, K. A., Costa, G., and Hume, D. M. "Hepatic Support Therapy by Intermittent Liver Perfusions and Exchange Blood Transfusions," *Transplantation Proceedings* 3(1971):1589–96. Reprinted in *Artificial Organs and Cardiopulmonary Support Systems,* edited by F. T. Rapaport and J. P. Merrill. (New York: Grune & Stratton, 1972.)

254. DePlanque, B. A., Williams, G. M., Borst-Eilers, E., and Hume, D. M. "Antibodies and Early Human Transplant Rejection," *Transplantation Proceedings* 3(1971):376–79.

255. Hume, D. M. "Organ Transplants and Immunity," chapter 19 in *Immunobiology; Current Knowledge of Basic Concepts in Immunology and Their Clinical Applications,* edited by R. A. Good and D. W. Fisher, pp. 185–94. (Stamford, Connecticut: Sinauer Associates, 1971).

256. Hume, D. M., Lee, H. M., Pierce, J. C. and Cobb, G. C. "Histocompatibility Con-

comitants of the Clinical Course of Renal Homografts," *Transplantation Proceedings* 3(1971):371–75.

257. Hume, D. M., Lee, H. M., Pierce, J. C., Wolf, J. S., Stickley, E., Newsome, H. H., Bell, C. C., Shanfield, I., and Sterling, W. A. "Transplantation Immunology: Effect of Radiation and Related Studies; Progress Report, July 1, 1970–June 30, 1971," 20 pp. [AEC Grant AT (40–1) 2459.] (Available from the Library of Congress Photo-duplication Service as ORO–2459–379.)

258. Hume, D. M., Mendez–Picon, G., Gayle, W. E., Smith, D. H., Abouna, G. M., and Lee, H. M. "Current Methods for Support of Patients in Hepatic Failure," *Transplantation Proceedings* 3(1971):1525–35. Reprinted in *Artificial Organs and Cardiopulmonary Support Systems,* edited by F. T. Rapaport and J. P. Merrill. (New York: Grune & Stratton, 1972).

259. Pierce, J. C., Cobb, G. W., and Hume, D. M. "Relevance of HL–A Antigens to Acute Humoral Rejection of Multiple Renal Allotransplants," *New England Journal of Medicine* 285(1971):142–46.

260. Pierce, J. C., and Hume, D. M. "Cross–matching for Organ Transplantation. I. The Use of Kidney Cells and Immune Adherence," *Transplantation Proceedings* 3(1971):127–29.

261. Robertshaw, G. E., Mendez–Picon, G., Madge, G. E., and Hume, D. M. "Prolonged Survival of Dog Second Set Renal Homografts Using a Heterologous Anti-antiserum," *Surgical Forum* 22(1971):249–50.

262. Sterling, W. A., Pierce, J. C., Hutcher, N. E., Lee, H. M., and Hume, D. M. "A comparison of Hypothermic Preservation with Hypothermic Pulsatile Perfusion in Paired Human Kidneys," *Surgical Forum* 22(1971):229–30.

263. Sterling, W. A., Pierce, J. C., Lee, H. M., and Hume, D. M. "Rehabilitation of Patients with Renal Failure by Kidney Transplantation" (abstract), The American Society of Nephrology, Abstracts, 1971.

264. Wolf, J. S., Fawley, J. C., and Hume, D. M. "In Vitro Quantitation of Lymphocyte and Serum Cytotoxic Activity Following Renal Homograft Rejection in Man," *Transplantation Proceedings* 3(1971):449–52.

265. Wolf, J. S., Fawley, J. C., Shanfield, I., and Hume, D. M. "Predictability of Successful Human Renal Re-transplantation by In-vitro Methods" (abstract), *European Surgical Research* 3(1971):291.

1972

266. Abouna, G. M., Cook, J. S., Fisher, L. M., Still, W. J., Costa, G., and Hume, D. M. "Treatment of Acute Hepatic Coma by Ex-vivo Baboon and Human Liver Perfusions," *Surgery* 71(1972):537–46.

267. Abouna, G. M., Fisher, L. M., Still, W. J., and Hume, D. M. "Acute Hepatic Coma Successfully Treated by Extracorporeal Baboon Liver Perfusion," *British Medical Journal* 1(1972):23–25.

268. Abouna, G. M., Lim, F., Cook, J. S., Grubb, W., Craig, S. S., Seibel, H. R., and Hume, D. M. "Three-day Canine Kidney Preservation," *Surgery* 71(1972):436–44. Abstract appears in *Transplantation Proceedings* 4(1972):796–97.

269. Bryant, C. P. and Hume, D. M. "Preliminary Observations on 19 Human Renal Transplants; Correlation of Clinical and Immunofluorescent Results" (abstract), *Anatomical Record* 172(1972):280.

270. Calne, R. Y., Hamburger, J., Hume, D. M., Kizer, W., Kountz, S. L. and Mannick, J. A. "Panel Discussion on Recipient Acceptability for Transplantation" (summary), *Transplantation Proceedings* 4(1972):581. Reprinted in *Clinical Transplantation,* p. 155 (see Item #278.)

271. Haesslein, H. C., Pierce, J. C., Lee, H. M., and Hume, D. M. "Leukopenia and Azathioprine Management in Renal Homotransplantation," *Surgery* 71(1972):598–604. Abstract appears in *Transplantation Proceedings* 4(1972):797–98.

272. Hamburger, J., Calne, R. Y., Harris, J., Hattler, B., Hume, D. M., Miller, H., Smith, G. J. V., and Williams, G. M. "Panel Discussion on Anuria, Rejection, and Glomerulonephritis" (summary), *Transplantation Proceedings* 4(1972):679. Reprinted in *Clinical Transplantation*, p. 253 (see Item #278).

273. Hume, D. M. "The operation," *Transplantation Proceedings* 4(1972):625–28. Reprinted in *Clinical Transplantation*, pp. 199–202 (see Item #278).

274. Hume, D. M. (Chairman). Proceedings of the 1st International Symposium on Clinical Organ Transplantation, Richmond, Virginia, 1972, *Transplantation Proceedings* 4(1972):427–798. Reprinted as *Clinical Transplantation*, edited by D. M. Hume and F. T. Rapaport. xii, 370 pp. (New York: Grune & Stratton, 1972, 1973).

275. Hume, D. M. "Present Role of Histocompatibility Matching in Clinical Transplantation," *Transplantation Proceedings* 4(1972):429–32. Reprinted in *Clinical Transplantation*, pp. 3–6 (see Item #278).

276. Hume, D. M., Belzer, F. O., Cerilli, G. J., Kizer, W., Levey, R., Mannick, J. A., Murray, J. E., Penn, I., Shanfield, I., Sheil, A. G. R., Simmons, R., Smith, M. J. V., Texter, J. H., and Williams, G. M. "Panel Discussion on Technical Aspects of Renal Transplantation" (summary), *Transplantation Proceedings* 4(1972):649. Reprinted in *Clinical Transplantation*, p. 223 (see Item #278).

277. Hume, D. M., and Bryant, C. P. "The Development of Recurrent Glomerulonephritis," *Transplantation Proceedings* 4(1972):673–77. Reprinted in *Clinical Transplantation*, pp. 247–51 (see Item #278).

278. Hume, D. M., and Rapaport, F. T., editors. *Clinical Transplantation*. New York: Grune & Stratton, 1972, 1973., xii, 370 pp. *Clinical Transplantation* is reprinted from the December, 1972 issue, volume IV, Number 4, of the quarterly journal, *Transplantation Proceedings*. . . ." (Same as *Clinical Transplantation* cited in Item #274.)

279. Hume, D. M., and Rapaport, F. T. "Introduction" (to Proceedings of the 1st International Symposium on Clinical Organ Transplantation, Richmond, Virginia, 1972), *Transplantation Proceedings* 4(1972):427. Reprinted in *Clinical Transplantation*, p. 1 (see Item #278).

280. Hume, D. M., Wolf, J. S., Lee, H. M., and Abouna, G. "Liver Transplantation," *Transplantation Proceedings* 4(1972):781–84. Reprinted in *Clinical Transplantation*, pp. 355–58 (see Item #278).

281. Lee, B. B., Lee, H. M., Dalton, W. E., and Hume, D. M. "Correlation of Cytophilic Antibody Titre with Efficacy of Anti-skin Sera" (abstract), *Federation Proceedings* 31(1972):933.

282. Lee, B. B., Lee, H. M., Dalton, W. E., and Hume, D. M. "Prolongation of Skin Graft Survival with Homologous Antiskin Hyperimmune Serum in Rats," *Surgical Forum* 23(1972):292–93.

283. Lee, H. M., Linehan, D., Pierce, J. C., and Hume, D. M. "Renal Artery Stenosis and Gastrointestinal Hemorrhage in Human Renal Transplantation," *Transplantation Proceedings* 4(1972):681–83. Reprinted in *Clinical Transplantation*, pp. 255–57 (see Item #278).

284. Lee, H. M., Sulkin, M., and Hume, D. M. "A Standard Technique for Procurement of Cadaver Donor Organs," *Transplantation Proceedings* 4(1972):583–84. Reprinted in *Clinical Transplantation*, pp. 157–58 (see Item #278).

285. Levinson, S. A., and Hume, D. M. "Effect of Exchange Transfusion with Fresh Whole Blood on Refractory Septic Shock," *American Surgeon* 38(1972):49–55.

286. Penn, I., Calne, R. Y., and Hume, D. M. "Panel Discussion on Liver Transplantation" (summary), *Transplantation Proceedings* 4(1972):785. Reprinted in *Clinical Transplantation*, p. 359 (see Item #278).

287. Pierce, J. C., Bach, M., Hume, D. M., Opelz, G., Seigler, H., and Stickel, D. "Panel Discussion on Histocompatibility Matching" (summary), *Transplantation Proceedings* 4(1972):455. Reprinted in *Clinical Transplantation*, p. 29 (see Item #278).

288. Pierce, J. C., Madge, G. E., Lee, H. M., and Hume, D. M. "Lymphoma, a complication of renal allotransplantation in man," *JAMA; Journal of the American Medical Association* 219(1972):1593–97.

289. Seibel, H. R., Weymouth, R. J., Hume, D. M., Lee, H. M., and Sterling, W. A. "Ultrastructural Examination of Homograft Human Renal Biopsies from Anastomosis to Nephrectomy," *Investigative Urology* 9(1972):411–22.

290. Sheil, A. G. R., Condie, R. M., Hume, D. M., Lance, E. M., Mannick, J. A., Monaco, A., Murray, J. E., Pierce, J., Simmons, R., and Starzl, T. S. "Panel Discussion on Suppression or Avoidance of Immune Responses" (summary), *Transplantation Proceedings* 4(1972):507. Reprinted in *Clinical Transplantation*, p. 81 (see Item #278).

291. Sterling, W. A., Bryant, C. P., O'Hanian, S. H., Pierce, J. C., Lee, H. M., Hume, D. M., Weymouth, R. J. and Siebel, H. R. "Evaluation of Renal Transplant Recipients by Immunofluorescent Microscopy," *Surgical Forum* 23(1972):263–65.

292. Sterling, W. A., Pierce, J. C., Lee, H. M., Hume, D. M., Hutcher, N. E., and Mendez–Picon, G. "Renal Preservation by Hypothermic Storage Plus Pulsatile Perfusion," *Surgery, Gynecology and Obstetrics* 135(1972):589–92.

293. Sterling, W. A., Pierce, J. C., Lee, H. M., Hume, D. M., Lee, B. B., Brichta, L. F., Currier, C. B., and Hasegawa, A. "Comparison of Methods of Preservation of Cadaver Kidneys," *Transplantation Proceedings* 4(1972):621–23. Reprinted in *Clinical Transplantation*, pp. 195–97 (see Item #278).

294. Sterling, W. A., Pierce, J. C., Lee, H. M., and Hume, D. M. "Rehabilitation of Retransplant Patients," *Transplantation Proceedings* 4(1972):751–53. Reprinted in *Clinical Transplantation*, pp. 325–27 (see Item #278).

295. Thomas, F., Thomas, J., Wolf, J. S., Schatzki, P., Cohen, C., and Hume, D. M. "Prevention of Hyperacute Kidney Rejection by Early Splenectomy: Etiologic and Therapeutic Implications," *Surgical Forum* 23(1972):261–63.

296. Thomas, J., and Hume, D. M. "A Standardized ALG for Use in Man," *Transplantation Proceedings* 4(1972):477–79. Reprinted in *Clinical Transplantation*, pp. 51–53 (see Item #278).

297. Thomas, J., Thomas, F., Maurer, H., Caul, J., and Hume, D. M. "Platelet Activation by Antihuman Thymocyte Globulin," *Surgical Forum* 23(1972):288–89.

298. Waller, M., Pierce, J. C., Moncure, C. W., and Hume, D. M. "Humoral Responses in Human Organ Transplantation," *Clinical and Experimental Immunology* 11(1972):173–86.

299. Wilson, R. E., Hume, D. M., Kizer, W., Kountz, S. L., Simmons, R., and Penn, I., "Panel Discussion on Long-term Results in Retransplant Patients" (summary), *Transplantation Proceedings* 4(1972):749. Reprinted in *Clinical Transplantation*, p. 323 (see Item #278).

1973

300. Bryant, C. P., Hume, D. M., and Sterling, W. A. "Correlation of Immunofluorescent Observations on Early Post-transplant Biopsies with Graft Survival" (abstract), *Virginia Journal of Science* 24(1973):168.

301. Currier, C. B., Jr., Pierce, J. C., and Hume, D. M. "Canine Renal Allograft Rejection and Antibody Formation Following Blood Transfusions," *Surgical Forum* 24(1973):279–81.

302. Kay, S., and Hume, D. M. (Deceased). "Carcinoma of the Parathyroid Gland: How Reliable are the Clinical and Histologic Features?" *Archives of Pathology* 96(1973):316–19.

303. Levinson, H. J., Thomas, J., Thomas, F., Waller, M., Maurer, H., and Hume, D. M. "Prolongation of Human Skin Graft Survival by Low-dose Rabbit Antithymocyte Globulin," *Surgical Forum* 24(1973):274–76.

304. Levinson, S. A., Levinson, H. J., Halloran, L. G., Brooks, J. W., Davis, R. J., Wolf, J. S., Lee, H. M., and Hume, D. M. "Limited Indications for Unilateral Aortofemoral or Ileofemoral Vascular Grafts," *Archives of Surgery* 107(1973):791–96.

305. Maurer, H. M., Thomas, J., Thomas, F., Caul, J., and Hume, D. M. "Thrombogenic Activity of Anti-human Thymocyte Globulin," *Pediatric Research* 7(1973):358–430.

306. Robertshaw, G. E., Doane, J. C., Madge, G. E., and Hume, D. M. "The Effects of Irradiation on Canine Renal Homografts Placed in the Portal Circulation," *Review of Surgery* 30(1973):69–71.

307. Shanfield, I., Wolf, J. S., Wren, S. F. G., MacLean, L. D., and Hume, D. M. "Mechanism of Permanent Survival of Canine Renal Allografts Following a Limited Course of ALS Treatment," *Transplantation Proceedings* 5(1973):533–34. Reprinted in *Transplantation Today; Proceedings of the 4th International Congress of the Transplantation Society*, San Francisco, 1972, edited by F. T. Rapaport, H. Balner and S. L. Kountz, vol. 2, pp. 533–34. (New York: Grune & Stratton, 1973).

308. Shanfield, I., Young, R. B., and Hume, D. M. "True Hermaphroditism with XX XY Mosaicism: Report of a Case," *Journal of Pediatrics* 83(1973):471–73.

309. Thomas, F., Thomas, J., Millington, M., and Hume, D. M. "Species Variability in Clinical Antihuman Antithymocyte Globulin Production: Rabbit vs. Horse AHTG in primate skin Graft survival," *Surgical Forum* 24(1973):288–90.

1974

310. Dunlap, W. M., James, G. W., III, and Hume, D. M. "Anemia and Neutropenia Caused by Copper Deficiency," *Annals of Internal Medicine* 80(1974):470–76.

311. Halloran, L. G., Hutcher, N. E., Levinson, S. A., Schatzki, P. F., and Hume, D. M. "Morphology of the Liver Before and After Intestinal Bypass for Morbid Obesity," *Surgical Forum* 25(1974):359–61.

312. Hume, D. M., and Rapaport, F. T. *1st International Symposium on Organ Preservation*, Cambridge, England, 1973. *Transplantation Proceedings* 6(1974):235–328.

313. Newsome, H. H., Clements, A. S., and Hume, D. M. "Specificity of Antisera to Aldosterone and Deoxycorticosterone," in *Radioimmunoassay and Related Procedures in Medicine*; Proceedings of a Symposium, Istanbul, Turkey, 1973, edited by A. Ericson, vol. 2, pp. 79–85. (Vienna, Austria: International Atomic Energy Agency, 1974).

314. Schwartz, S. I. (Editor–in–Chief), Lillehei, R. C., Shires, G. T., Spencer, F. C., and Storer, E. H. (Associate Editors). *Principles of Surgery*. 2d edition. (New York: McGraw-Hill, 1974.) Contributions by D. M. Hume to Part 1, "Basic Considerations": Chapter 1, "Endocrine and Metabolic Responses to Injury," by DMH, pp. 1–63. Contributions by D. M. Hume to Part 2, "Specific Organ Systems": Chapter 37, "Pituitary and Adrenal," by DMH and T. S. Harrison, pp. 1363–1427; Chapter 38, "Thyroid and Parathyroid," by S. I. Schwartz, DMH and E. L. Kaplan, pp. 1429–1511.

315. Thomas, J., Millington, M., Volk, M., Thomas, F. and Hume, D. M. "Rabbit Antihuman Thymocyte Globulin (RAHTG): In Vitro and In Vivo Testing," *Transplantation Proceedings* 6(1974):395–98.

1975

316. Hasegawa, A., Smith, M. J. V., Lee, H. M., and Hume, D. M. (Deceased). "Cine–fluoroscopic Studies of Ureteral Function in the Human Renal Transplant," *Journal of Urology* 114(1975):381–84.

317. Hasegawa, A., Volk, M., Lee, H. M., and Hume, D. M. "The Role of Macrophage Cytophilic Antibodies in Kidney Transplant Patients," *Keio Journal of Medicine* 24(1975):73–90.

318. Lee, H. M., and Hume, D. M. "Long–term Results in Renal Transplantation," *Kidney International* 8(1975):498.

319. Lee, H. M., Mendez–Picon, G., Pierce, J. C., and Hume, D. M. "The Course of Renal Artery Stenosis in Transplant Recipients" (abstract), presented to the Western Dialysis and Transplantation Society Meeting, 1975.

320. Thomas, F., Lee, H. M., Wolf, J. S., Pierce, J. C., and Hume, D. M. "Long term (8–12 yr.) prognosis in related and unrelated renal transplant patients," *Transplantation Proceedings* 7(1975):707.

1977

321. Lee, H. M., Mendez–Picon, G., Pierce, J. C., and Hume, D. M. "Renal Artery Occlusion in Transplant Recipients," *American Surgeon* 43(1977):186–92.

1979

322. Hume, D. M. "Early Experiences in Organ Homotransplantation in Man and the Unexpected Sequelae Thereof," *American Journal of Surgery* 137(1979):152–61.

THE ASSOCIATION OF
RESEARCH LIBRARIES
1932–1982
50TH ANNIVERSARY

Scottsdale, Arizona was the scene in May, 1982 of the Association's fiftieth anniversary celebration. Several outstanding papers were presented. The editors of this volume are proud to publish four of these papers, one by a scholar, one by a library educator, one by a retired library director, and one by the Deputy Librarian of Congress.

THE IMPACT OF CHANGES IN SCHOLARSHIP IN THE HUMANITIES UPON RESEARCH LIBRARIES

Ralph Cohen

My remarks are directed to the changes in the study of humanities, es-pecially literature, in the next decade and the effects these changes may have upon research libraries. No matter what changes take place, it should be noted that many scholars will continue to work within the present boundaries and remain resistant to new problems and formulations. Per-haps it is only fair to say that their continuity helps us to detect the discontinuities.

The new directions of humanistic study will, I believe, make consid-erable demands upon research libraries in terms of changes in concepts, equipment, and materials. The concepts that have for many years gov-erned research in the humanities, especially literature, include a canon of books worthy of study and exploration, the relation of these books to

Advances in Library Administration and Organization, Volume 3, pages 271–276.
Copyright © 1984 by JAI Press Inc.
All rights of reproduction in any form reserved.
ISBN: 0-89232-386-8

historical contexts, the belief in individual authorship of these books, and the belief that these books constitute a sound basis for, in the words of the Commission on the Humanities, "the disciplined development of verbal, perceptual, and imaginative skills needed to understand experience." As for the fields encompassed by the term "humanities," the Commission identified languages and literatures, history, and philosophy as the "central humanistic fields," My comments, however, shall be derived primarily from my own field of language and literature.

This field is undergoing conceptual changes though these have not yet ousted the older governing concepts. Rather they exist alongside them, and one of the most obvious examples of conceptual change is in the vocabulary of criticism—the terms "book," "literary work," have been replaced by terms like "text" and "writing" to avoid the metaphysical implications of wholeness and progression. The canon of books worthy of study has now been surrounded by a body of texts formerly ignored or overlooked. In contemporary scholarship the relation of book to historical context has been undermined by a view that avoids the division of writing into literary and nonliterary texts. As Harold Bloom puts it, there is no difference between fictional and critical texts. So, too, the notion of an "historical" context is being replaced by "historical consciousness" because all human actions—and literary texts are such actions—are considered historical in their very existence. As for individual authorship, the concept has been advanced that individuals are shaped by their communities and thus a text is inevitably a consequence of communal behavior. As for the aim of the humanities, the "understanding [of] experience" has been interpreted as a class aim, as imposing ideological views upon readers, not providing some neutral or so-called objective skills to understand "experience."

To what new directions in literary studies do these conceptual changes lead? The canon of books has changed as a direct result of changes in society, especially toward the role of women and blacks. Texts by women have been introduced as forms of gender consciousness and study. The Brontes have, of course, been part of the canon for some time as is the case with Jane Austen, but Aphra Behn, Kate Chopin, Susan Glaspell, and a host of other women writers have now been made part of literary study, and they are accepted figures for further research, So, too, as a result of programs of black studies, works by African as well as American black writers have been introduced into the curriculum and made acceptable for research. This means that library collections will have to be enlarged and that works once considered ephemeral will have to be reclaimed as research materials.

The expansion of the canon and the revision of the curriculum were also the consequence of educational changes aimed at undermining an elite view of education—responsive to the desires of as well as needs of the community at large, courses in popular literature have been introduced. These courses seek to offer an alternative to Matthew Arnold's dictum that the aim of liberal education is to study the best that has been thought and written because this "best," it is held, refers to the interests of a particular class and its desires. Rather, popular culture as an area of study and research seeks to understand and explain how writing functions to give pleasure and ideological direction to the lower classes, those to whom Spenser or Milton or Wordsworth provide neither pleasure nor nourishment for the living of their lives.

Popular works such as ballads and broadsides long ago entered the literary canon of works that might be respectably studied, and there even developed a discipline—folklore—that taught these materials. So, too, conduct and courtesy books were considered—albeit by historians rather than literary scholars—appropriate for research. But cheap paper romances, nineteenth–century rags–to–riches success stories, westerns, detective stories, and children's literature, have until recently been excluded from university study. But not only does there now exist a scholarly *Journal of Popular Culture*, but a number of scholarly studies of popular culture have recently appeared, and Dashiel Hammett and Raymond Chandler have now achieved academic respectability. Courses in romances or the detective story are no longer strangers to the curriculum.

It is not merely that in 1976 Lewis James of the University of Kent published an anthology *English Popular Literature 1819–1851* and that in 1977 Victor E. Neuberg, a British librarian, published a Pelican original called *Popular Literature, a History and a Guide*, but that eminent scholars such as Robert Weimann and Ronald Paulson have turned to this field: Robert Weimann in *Shakespeare and the Popular Tradition in the Theater* (1978) and Ronald Paulson in *Popular and Polite Art in the Age of Hogarth and Fielding*.

The difficulties are going to be serious for librarians selecting, collecting, and storing what had been considered expendable materials. Much of this material is now unrecoverable, but its value for study and for the understanding of our so–called high culture should not be underestimated. These writings helped shape popular attitudes and stereotypes, and in the little research that has been done on these materials, it is apparent that in England, for example, they provided the provinces with ideological views that were the objects of ridicule in the urban centers.

The study of popular culture is, of course, considerably encouraged by the present publication of paperbacks in our country with their exploitation of sex, romance, mystery, and other popular themes. Serious research is only just beginning to inquire into the production, distribution, and audience of popular fiction. The changing nature of library holdings

will include comic books, comic strips, and newspaper ads, for in this
latter category Marshall McLuhan set the model in *The Mechanical Bride*.

I have been enumerating some of the changes in research resulting from
changes in concepts governing the aims of humanistic study. And I have
indicated that these will affect the size and kind of collections. I want
now to turn to another group of studies that involve changes in equipment
leading to changes in literary study and library procedures. I refer to the
technological revolution in which we are all involved. This technological
revolution pertains to computer and duplicating procedures on the one
hand and television and film media on the other. Computer technology
has had relatively little impact on the humanities thus far, but it has altered
and will continue to alter the shape of research library services. Computer
technology makes possible the storage and retrieval of masses of information. At present there exist computer programs for the wholesale production of concordances, and Cornell University has produced a considerable number of these. It is not necessary to speculate that the
quantitative approach to literary study will, in time, reveal connections
within texts and among texts that will change the caliber of true literary
scholarship, whether this pertains to the probability of identifying an author's true text by identifying his vocabulary and sentence construction
or to understanding the hierarchy of words in his vocabulary.

The stylistic study of Michael Riffaterre, for example, relies on a study
of a common period vocabulary, and this can most readily be discovered
through computer techniques. Indeed, any stylistic study which aims at
generalizations based on quantitative studies can best be achieved by
computer technology. Though here, again, one must note the role of research libraries in helping to establish short–title catalogues of all available works—as in the efforts now being undertaken to set up an eight-
eenth–century short–title catalogue. One can point to the immense help
research libraries may be able to provide when they can offer researchers
a printout of all recent articles on a single subject or a list of all the works
of a single writer with locations of these throughout the world.

In another sense, information technology will serve to make humanities
research an international enterprise. The Report of the Commission on
the Humanities stressed the need for the elimination of constraints on
world–wide bibliographical information. Such information crosses national boundaries, and the study of comparative literature requires such
access.

Technological developments have made the collection of oral materials
possible, and thus libraries will be able to store regional songs, stories,
and histories. Research library personnel will be expected to assist scholars in preserving and using new materials. And collections will also include scripts, working scripts, and films.

A study of motion pictures—or as it is referred to in university catalogues, film courses—is developing in universities throughout the country. There are, of course, some special libraries like that of the Museum of Modern Art in New York or the film institutes in Washington and California, but this study is international in scope and interdisciplinary in nature. Research in this area is burgeoning, but the cost of purchasing and reviewing films presents special problems. For example, will it be possible to make such materials available for transmission as books are? Can libraries afford to provide film machines as they do microfilm readers? Perhaps research libraries must draw the line at the materials they purchase, and films should be confined to special libraries.

The study of films and their insight into the relation between the arts of writing, photography, and acting have led a number of philosophers and psychologists to study them: Rudolph Arnheim, Stanley Cavell, Alex Sosonski, Marshall Cohen, Siegfried Krakauer. The film, like the comic strip, involves words and pictures, and the research into the interrelation of the arts, interdisciplinary studies, represent major areas of new research that are now being undertaken in the humanities. The rationale for this research is the development of semiotics—the study of sign behavior. This area of inquiry has made it possible to consider verbal and nonverbal behavior within the same system. Thus a literary text and other forms of behavior are analyzed as parts of a common system governed by a theory of signs. In the work of Thomas Seobeck, of Umberto Eco, of Yury Lotman, the study of literature is merged with that of social and ritual behavior. Indeed, it is sometimes difficult to tell the difference between studies in different disciplines, for example, a collection of essays on metaphor by the anthropologists David Sapir and Christopher Crocker—*The Social Use of Metaphor*—and a symposium on metaphor published in *New Literary History*.

Anyone familiar with research in the humanities is cognizant that it has become increasingly interdisciplinary. Literary study, for example, involves psychoanalytic premises in the work of Murray Schwartz, Norman Holland, and others. It involves economic and sociological premises in such works as Fredric Jameson's *The Political Unconscious* or Terry Eagleton's *Criticism and Ideology*. It involves phenomenological premises in Geoffrey Hartman's *Wordsworth's Poetry 1787–1811* or James Swearingen's *Reflexivity in Tristram Shandy*. I could go on to pursue the interrelations between literary and art study, between the history of literature and the history of science, between religion and literature. But my point is that research libraries will need to reassemble their collections so that key works from nonliterary fields will be available to scholars who are working on literary problems. I realize that this is no simple matter, but it does indicate the need to rethink how best to serve the scholar in consequence of new concepts governing literary study.

I have been discussing some of the changes in scholarship that will lead to changes in library collections and procedures. I am aware that the expansion of resources is an age–old library problem, but I think that changes in scholarship are pointing to more than space within the old boundaries. The very nature of humanistic study will involve, as I pointed out, new interrelations of materials. Whether this means that we need special humanities libraries rather than special English or Philosophy libraries, or whether this means that anthropological and literary materials need to be cross–indexed, my point is that some new thinking on problems of classification and accessibility will have to be undertaken. You know more about how to manage this than I do, but I urge you not to assume that we have here a problem that can be solved in terms of present procedures.

The second problem is one that, for its solution, requires the cooperation of international librarianship. It is probably as much a legal as a library problem. I refer to the setting up of international bibliographical information—the identification in all countries throughout the world of pertinent materials for the study of a subject. One such project is the international Dickens bibliography being prepared by Ada B. Nisbet of UCLA—a project unique in its scope and aim.

The third problem is more one for humanistic scholars than it is for libraries. There is a need to pursue scholarship as teams—groups of scholars working together on a subject and sharing their knowledge, not unlike scientific teams.

I think, finally, that the successful collaboration between research librarians and humanistic scholars must be continued and expanded. Not merely because this partnership is characteristic of a humanistic endeavor, but because decisions about selections, collections, and reorganization of materials should be done jointly. This, too, would be the best way to monitor changes in the field and to make plans to take these into account. And perhaps I should add not merely between scholars and librarians, but among librarians within a country and between countries.

THE ARL AT FIFTY

Stephen A. McCarthy

"Libraries are not made, they grow," according to an obiter dictum of the British Essayist Augustine Birrell. What is true of libraries may not be true of all library organizations, but it is true of the ARL. It has been growing for 50 years, is now 50 years old or young, as you choose, and its best years are ahead of it. I am sure you will agree that this is the case and that you will go on to make it so. As a prelude to these "best years", a backward look may serve a useful purpose. My effort will be to describe briefly and comment on the development of the ARL over these past 50 years.

Since this is the fiftieth anniversary year for the ARL, the first meeting was held in 1932, but just barely. The date was December 29. Dr. James T. Gerould, Librarian of Princeton, was "mainly responsible for the organization of the Association of Research Libraries", according to Wilson and Tauber, who went on to say of Gerould, "He was impressed with the importance of providing a medium through which the problems of research libraries could be considered effectively without involving a large, heterogeneous membership."[1] As would be expected, Gerould called the meeting to order and Edward Henry was appointed temporary

Advances in Library Administration and Organization, Volume 3, pages 277–285.
Copyright © 1984 by JAI Press Inc.
All rights of reproduction in any form reserved.
ISBN: 0-89232-386-8

secretary. The meeting proceeded to adopt a constitution which had been prepared in advance by the organizers. The purpose of the organization was stated in Section 2 of the constitution, which read as follows: "The object shall be by cooperative effort to develop and increase the resources and usefulness of the research collections in American libraries." Membership in the association was institutional and its leadership was placed in an Advisory Committee of five and an Executive Secretary, all of whom were elected for five year terms. The Advisory Committee and the Executive Secretary also served as the Membership Committee. Election of new members was by a ⅔ vote of the members present and those voting by mail and membership could be terminated in the same way. The annual dues were $5 and failure to pay dues for two successive years was cause for termination. I found no record of such action.

It has been remarked of the ARL that it was characterized by its casual attitude on organizational and procedural matters. This quality is evident in the list of original charter members, December 29, 1932, which in addition to the 42 members of that date lists the Boston Public Library with the date October 1933. This informality carried over into the operations of the new organization: the Executive Secretary was a non–salaried officer; the office was the Executive Secretary's brief case; and the clerical and secretarial work was done by the Executive Secretary's secretary. Most meetings in the early years were dinner meetings and there was no formal agenda. The Advisory Committee introduced topics for discussion and individual members could make suggestions by communicating with the Executive Secretary in advance, or could raise questions or offer comments at the meeting. It was customary to hold the meetings in conjunction with the ALA meetings, as a matter of convenience and economy for the Association and for the members.

I am indebted to Frank McGowan and his dissertation on the ARL for the following analysis of the initial membership: "Inclusion of twenty–nine libraries as charter members of the Association was based upon membership in the American Association of Universities. Eight additional academic institutions were considered suitable by the organizing committee as were five non–academic research libraries."[2] In this connection it should be noted that both graduate study and research in those pre–war years were much more highly concentrated in a relatively small number of institutions than has been the case in the decades following the war.

Among the topics which interested the ARL in the first years of its existence were the bibliographical control of dissertations, the strengthening and use of the Union Catalog at the Library of Congress as a clearing house for interlibrary loan requests, German scientific periodicals which were increasing in cost and deteriorating in physical condition and the service basis pricing of the indexing publications of the H. W. Wilson

Company. With the cooperation of the AAU, the Executive Secretary of the ARL became editor of the annual publication *Doctoral Dissertations Accepted by American Universities* which was published by the H. W. Wilson Co. Members of the ARL were major contributors to the Union Catalog at the Library of Congress as well as active users of this catalog as an aid in securing interlibrary loans. At that time the Union Catalog compiled a list of unlocated titles which was distributed to ARL libraries for checking and reporting back to the Library of Congress. In this connection a forerunner of the New Federalism appeared in April 1936 when Mr. Kletsch of the Union Catalog wrote the Executive Secretary and requested "an appropriation from the ARL for the purchase of some duplicating machine, possibly a secondhand mimeograph, in order to extend the service of the clearing house to all American libraries." The ARL did not rush to the rescue. Instead it noted that the added load coming from ARL members had not been demonstrated. The propriety of spending ARL funds for equipment to be used by the Union Catalog was also questioned.

Another machine note from the 1936 meeting was the request made by Dean Louis R. Wilson of the Graduate Library School of the University of Chicago that he be informed of any application of business machines, particularly the Hollerith tabulator, to library procedures. He noted the interest of a graduate student in this equipment and its use by Donald Coney for the analysis of circulation records.

Since ARL members were large libraries they were charged the highest prices for the Wilson indexes purchased on the service basis. The view of the membership was that smaller libraries voted for the inclusion of additional periodical titles to be indexed and this increased the cost to ARL libraries. It was also noted that some state institutions might be acting illegally if they paid more for a given product than other purchasers. This led to a long, detailed, exhaustive study of the Wilson service basis pricing by Miles O. Price, Law Librarian at Columbia, and his wife on behalf of the ARL with the cooperation of Mr. H. W. Wilson. Because the Price study was so thorough and so lengthy it has been alleged that no one ever read it. In any case it was decided to engage a consultant to evaluate the study and then negotiate with the Wilson Company. It turned out that Mr. Wilson was a better salesman than the consultant. The outcome was a clarification of the elements of the service basis and its acceptance, with reluctance, I suppose, by the ARL.

In the late thirties there was discussion of the desirability of publishing the catalog of the Library of Congress. At the outset the Library of Congress was not interested but with the passage of several years the view changed and the LC was receptive to the project. The ARL was the principal promoter, securing subscription orders and working with LC and the publisher to get the production underway. There was a problem about the title of the catalog because it could not be the finished bibliographic publication that LC wanted and thus it could not be called "The Library of Congress Catalog". It was finally agreed that the title should be *A Catalog of Books Represented by Library of Congress Printed Cards*. Once published, of course, it was promptly called "The Library of Congress Catalog." It was the first of the many published catalogs reporting the general collections of the Library of Congress.

The membership of the ARL remained approximately the same during the first twenty years of the organization's existence. There were, however, some changes over the years through the election of new members, the withdrawal of several others and the voting out of a total of eight members. In 1952 there were 45 members as compared with the 42 or 43 charter members.

This constancy of membership reflected the point of view that seems to have been dominant among the founders of the ARL to the effect that a small organization made up of large libraries with common problems was the best instrumentality for solving these problems. Another aspect of this attitude was the view that the ARL should be primarily a high level planning and policy group rather than an operating agency. The ARL did not consider itself to be in competition with any other organization nor did it duplicate the work of any other organization; rather it sought only to do things that needed doing and were not being done.

Although membership was controlled and not open, the Association had not developed and disclosed a set of clear, objective criteria for membership. There had been at least one instance of a membership based on the personality of the librarian, rather than on the status of the institution's library, certainly a curious anomaly in an organization composed of institutions. It was thought, rumored and said that the ARL was a club, not a professional library organization and that institutional membership was a cloak that was used to cover friends and exclude others. Let's face it: there was lots of criticism and some of it was deserved.

In fairness, however, it can certainly be argued that the object of the founding group was not to be small, selective and, if you will, elite, solely for the sake of being small, selective and elite. Instead, the objective was that stated in the constitution—"to develop and increase the resources and usefulness of the research collections in American libraries through cooperative effort." The best mechanism for achieving this objective was an organization of modest size made up of institutions that faced common problems, many of which could best be dealt with by a shared and concerted effort. If one recalls the conditions of 1932 generally and the prevailing situation in higher education and research, it seems to me that the position of the organizers of the ARL becomes clearer and its justification sound. We all know from experience that it is easier to work with a small, cohesive group than with a large one. In a small group participants are more likely to accept responsibility, to express themselves freely and to carry through an agreed action. Beyond this there is the economy of time and money. All of these factors plus admittedly a high level of self–appreciation on the part of the founders led to the conclusion that a small, high quality ARL was the desideratum.

However, by the mid–fifties, after the passage of more than twenty years, many changes had occurred in research libraries, their parent institutions and academic research. Not only were the numbers of students greatly increased, but so was the number of institutions of collegiate and university level and the number offering advanced graduate work. The new emphasis on graduate study represented a significant change from the pre–war years. These many new factors called for appropriate changes in organizations that undertook to assist research libraries in meeting their obligations to the scholarly community. But the ARL Membership Committee in 1956 saw it differently and announced what they chose to call "a return to first principles." As a result of the Committee's work four new members were added to the ARL. The Committee's action very probably no longer represented the prevailing view of the membership, but several more years were to pass before action was taken to adjust the ARL to the new postwar world.

In keeping with the objective to increase research library resources and after several years of discussion, the ARL in 1947/48 embarked on the Farmington Plan. This project arose out of the wartime experience which showed that the nation's libraries were deficient in their holdings of important publications issued in foreign countries. To correct this situation, the Farmington Plan was designed as a program that would insure the acquisition and prompt cataloging of at least one copy of every important publication which appeared any where in the world. The plan invited libraries to commit themselves to accept all publications in a selected subject field and language as they were supplied by the designated dealers. The plan was first applied in Europe. At a later date publications from other countries were acquired by libraries at whose institutions special area teaching and research programs were carried on. There were of course countless difficulties and problems. They arose on all sides. There was the need to identify competent, responsible dealers who were prepared, able and willing to undertake the work of selection and supply on the one hand, and on the other there were the participating libraries each with its own expectations of what the plan would produce and each struggling to modify its acquisition and cataloging procedures to conform to the requirements of the new program. Those responsible for the program established a reporting procedure in order that an evaluation of the project might be undertaken at a later date. This led to the publication of the *Farmington Plan Newsletter* which later became the *Foreign Acquisitions Newsletter*, published by the ARL until its recent discontinuance.

The Farmington Plan may, I think, be properly regarded as the forerunner and exemplar of several other cooperative acquisition programs which have been carried on in the past 25 or 30 years. These programs have been financed in part by the federal government largely through the provision of soft currencies made available for the purchase of foreign publications for American research libraries. The National Program for Acquisition and Cataloging at the Library of Congress, now financed by regular Library of Congress appropriations, is the most recent of these programs. In hearings for the establishment of these programs and subsequently for supporting appropriations, the ARL has played a part.

James T. Gerould was not only the leading organizer of the ARL but he was also responsible for what over the years has become one of the most useful services of the Association. As Librarian at the University of Minnesota he began collecting and distributing in a limited way a report called *Statistics of University Libraries*. When he moved on to Princeton the *Statistics* accompanied him. Under the name of *Princeton Library Statistics* it was continued until 1962–63. This compilation of data was taken over as an ARL responsibility in 1963–64 and renamed *Academic Library Statistics*. It is now called *ARL Statistics*. For the group of libraries included from the beginning this is a remarkably long statistical record. For practicing ARL directors the "Statistics" have always been an important tool to evaluate a library's progress, to gauge its status vis-à-vis its peers and to support the case for increased staff, book funds and other library purposes. The expansion of *ARL Statistics* in recent years in its inclusiveness, its analytic tables and its availability on tape in machine readable form—all these make the *ARL Statistics* indispensable for the academic library administrator.

Over the past ten years the ARL has also developed and published the *Annual Salary Survey*, as a means of providing prompt information in this important area. Two useful, special statistical reports have been published during the past year: The *ARL Library Index and Qualitative Relationships in the ARL*; and the *Cumulated ARL University Library Statistics 1962/63–1978/79*. Both reports are available on tape as well as in book form. They represent a significant achievement on the part of the Committee on Statistics as they make useful data readily available for study and analysis.

In its statistical publications as in other areas the ARL has sought to fill a need which no other library organization or government agency was willing or prepared to do. At one time it seemed that the ALA or the Educational Statistics unit of the Office of Education might perform this service. This did not happen, hence the continued and increased ARL activity.

In 1954 the ARL sponsored a conference of librarians and university administrators to discuss the financial problems of research librarians. The conference was designed to respond to a statement which appeared in *Financing Higher Education in the United States* by John D. Millett which said among other things "the librarian profession as such puts little emphasis on economy."[3] The papers and discussions of this conference were published in the following year under the title *Problems and Prospects of the Research Library*. The conclusion of the conference was a recommendation to the Association of American Universities that it appoint a Commission on Research Libraries and that it solicit foundation support for a study of research library problems. The AAU took favorable action on this recommendation. This action was intended to provide the same kind of mechanism that had carried out the study of financing higher education.

The record does not show that this study was ever undertaken. In a sense, this was an effort that failed apparently because the AAU was not successful in obtaining the necessary support. The conference did, however, provide an opportunity for library directors and university administrators to exchange views and get better acquainted with each other. In this respect, at least, the conference was not a failure.

As noted earlier there had been a number of changes in membership during the forties and fifties but in 1956, 24 years after its founding the ARL had only 49 members, six or seven more than at the first meeting in 1932. At the same time the number of higher education institutions had grown dramatically, the programs of graduate study and research had been greatly expanded and the enrollment at all levels of higher education was increasing substantially each year. In the decades following the war there was steady growth in the volume of publication in this country and abroad and American libraries in considerable number were acquiring more publications than ever before. In addition to the normal university programs, many institutions were engaged in government–supported research projects, some of which had substantial library implications. Moreover the National Science Foundation had the responsibility to foster scientific research. This mandate led to investigation and experimentation designed to enhance the quality and availability of scientific information. In order to accomplish this objective the Science Information division of the NSF extended its interest to agencies that were responsible for assembling, organizing and facilitating the use of science information as a significant element in science education and research.

Since the ARL roster included many of the institutions at which research and training sponsored by NSF were underway, its concern for the strength and activities of the Association was to be expected. Discussion between representatives of the NSF and the ARL resulted in a preliminary understanding to the effect that the NSF would be prepared to give favorable consideration to a proposal from the ARL seeking assistance in reorganizing the Association to make it a corporation and more broadly representative of the research library community, with a headquarters office and a commitment to operational activities.

In 1961 the ARL voted that a committee be appointed to take the steps necessary to reorganize the Association. This was done prior to the meetings in January 1962 at which the new constitution and other necessary documents were unanimously approved. This action set the stage for the ARL as it is today. James Skipper accepted appointment as Executive Director and established temporary headquarters at the National Library of Medicine. In the summer of 1963 the new office in the Brookings building was occupied.

At the July 1961 meeting Robert Vosper was asked to report the libraries that might be expected to become members based on five year averages of book funds, Number of Ph.D.'s granted and number of fields in which the Ph.D. was offered. This resulted in a list of thirty potential members. After consideration by the Board of Directors and subsequently by the membership, twenty–two university libraries and the Center for Research Libraries became members, bring the total number to 72.

Since that time there have been further efforts to adapt and reformulate membership criteria for university libraries and to identify and establish suitable criteria for non–academic libraries. The record of the past ten years shows again how difficult it is to set up and maintain equitable criteria. The last effort was made in 1980. It is to be hoped that the new guidelines or criteria may prove more satisfactory over a longer period than has been the case in the past.

After the reorganization of 1960–61 the ARL set about doing the things that were expected of it. It has had a degree of success. With foundation and government support it has undertaken projects and studies of research library problems and published the results, including reports on the use and bibliographic control of microforms, on book storage, on library lighting, on interlibrary loans and interlibrary communication and on a plan to make periodical resources more accessible. It has substantially expanded and strengthened its statistical publications, it has assisted in building up research resources by its role in various cooperative programs and through the establishment of the Center for Chinese Research Materials, it has sponsored the Office of Management Studies with its many activities and publications and it has taken an active part in the effort to assure libraries and their users appropriate access to copyrighted material. No doubt more could have been done, given different circumstances and greater talent, but the record does not call for apologies.

Despite some of the unpleasant connotations of words used to characterize the ARL from time to time, the Association has continued on its way undeterred and, I trust, with serenity. As a small group whose meetings were open only to members and their guests, it was perhaps only natural that there be resentment and criticism. From the perspective of the membership it was a group of libraries that had common problems and this organization was an effective mechanism for solving them. Certainly the ARL started modestly, it grew slowly and it came to maturity in the sixties and seventies. It grew only as its resources and opportunities permitted. Had it begun with a goal of becoming a large organization as quickly as possible, it might have fared better, but there is also the possibility that it might have failed. One can rationalize the preferred conclusion.

The Committee on Research Libraries of the American Council of Learned Societies had this to say in its 1967 report entitled *On Research Libraries*: "Founded in 1932 the Association (of Research Libraries) has had a notable record, not only in diagnosing and prescribing for the ills of research libraries, but in devising projects and programs to enhance the value of library services to the research community."[4]

As it begins the second half of its first century the ARL faces many difficult problems ranging from the need for highly qualified personnel and substantial financial support to the most effective and economical use of computer technology and communications facilities and to the best methods of preserving the records of human achievement. However you may characterize the organization, the ARL has a major job to do.

The ARL cannot solve all the problems, but it can solve some of them if it is determined to do so. Whatever it has been in the past and no matter the criticisms and mistakes, the ARL now and in the years immediately ahead is you—no one else. What will get done is what you do; what you don't do will very probably not get done. I wish you good luck.

NOTES AND REFERENCES

Minutes of the ARL have been used throughout without specific references.

1. Wilson, Louis R., and Tauber, Maurice F. *The University Library* (Chicago: University of Chicago Press, 1945), p. 503.

2. McGowan, Frank M. "The Association of Research Libraries, 1932–1962," Unpublished Ph.D. dissertation. University of Pittsburgh, 1972, p. 57.

3. Association of Research Libraries. *Problems and Prospects of the Research Library*, edited by Edwin E. Williams. (New Brunswick, N.J.: Scarecrow Press, 1955). p. 26, quotation from John D. Millett, *Financing Higher Education in the United States*. (N.Y.: Columbia Univ. Press, 1952), p. 123.

4. American Council of Learned Societies. *On Research Libraries* (Cambridge, MIT Press, 1969), p. 14. (Submitted to the National Advisory Commission on Libraries, Nov. 1967).

ARL/LC: 1932–1982

William J. Welsh

When I was first asked to make a presentation on ARL and the Library of Congress, the task seemed to be an easy one, but I was a victim of my own optimism. Our history is a complicated but fascinating one. Certainly, over the past five decades, ARL has more than fulfilled its original charter that stated, "The object shall be, by cooperative effort, to develop and increase the resources and usefulness of the research collection in American libraries."

Americans' penchants for associations often amuse our foreign friends, but this nation owes it preeminent position in library resources to the likes of the Association of Research Libraries and its early defenders such as Keyes Metcalf, Ralph Ellsworth, Archibald MacLeish, and many others. The dream to acquire and make accessible to scholars every item of research value in the world germinated with the Association of Research Libraries. It began slowly, but as you look back over the minutes of the last 99 meetings of the Association of Research Libraries, you can trace the evolution from dream to reality.

The first major undertaking between ARL and the Library of Congress was the publication of the depository catalog in book form, the *Catalog*

Advances in Library Administration and Organization, Volume 3, pages 287–294.
Copyright © 1984 by JAI Press Inc.
All rights of reproduction in any form reserved.
ISBN: 0-89232-386-8

of Books Represented by Library of Congress Printed Cards up to 1942. At the time, this was a monumental gamble taken on by the Association of Research Libraries. This led to the publication by the Library of Congress of the tome *Cumulative Catalog of Library of Congress Printed Cards*. For the first time there was generally available in convenient form a publication which now lists at frequent intervals a substantial segment of current American and foreign publications.

A 1948 ARL Committee of Research Libraries and the Library of Congress set the stage for the ARL/LC agenda for the next two decades. The Committee was to investigate and report on (1) the bases on which the Library of Congress might make full sets of printed cards available without charge to U.S. libraries, (2) federal subsidy to selected libraries giving service to federal field offices; (3) cooperative cataloging arrangements; (4) inclusion of catalog cards from other libraries in the Cumulative Catalog; (5) interchange of personnel; and (6), the role of the Library of Congress as an informational clearinghouse. At the January 1949 ARL meeting, the Committee reported on their progress: printed cards could be provided to regional depositories under certain conditions. The question of federal support to libraries serving Federal field offices was insoluble at that time in that any intelligent and well–coordinated plan would be hopelessly interferred with by the "logrolling of politicians."

At the January 1949 meeting, cooperative cataloging was studied, and it was recommended that entries be simplified, and that cooperating libraries revise and promulgate cataloging rules and deal with subject cataloging. The demand was present for the inclusion of catalog cards of other libraries in the *Cumulative Catalog* but the cost would be so great as to make it impractical. The response to a questionnaire on exchange of personnel was far from unanimous, and the Committee would consider it further. Finally, the role of the Library of Congress as an informational clearinghouse was still under consideration. During the March 1949 meeting, little progress was reported by the Committee.

In November, 1949, Luther Evans responded to the status of the assignments of the Committee on Research Libraries and the Library of Congress. Problem I, the list of libraries that would receive full sets of cards had been published in an October *Information Bulletin*. As for Problem II, Federal Subsidy to libraries giving extensive service to Federal field offices, Luther expressed his view that the Government has an important responsibility for seeing that the country's leading scholars have easily available all of the intellectual resources they require. He suggested that this responsibility might best be met by some system of Federal grants to research libraries. He noted that for Problem III, Cooperative Cataloging, an LC manual on subject headings was in press. He recommended that a standing committee be constituted to revise cataloging rules. Problem IV—the Cumulative Book Index, was reported as underway. Evans suggested that Problem V, exchange of personnel, should be done through bilateral agreements. Finally, the role of the Library of Congress as an information center needed further study. Evans concluded by recommending that the Committee be dissolved. The Committee concurred in this recommendation and the Association granted the request.

No recapitulation of cooperation projects undertaken by the Library of Congress and ARL would be complete without mention of the Farmington Plan. The indefatigable Keyes Metcalf pursued this project with the fervor of a born again Christian. In an effort to assist in the project's success, LC agreed to take materials in those categories not accepted by other libraries.

In an attempt to acquire U.S. government publications which are not available through normal channels, the Library of Congress joined with 44 other libraries in the Documents Expediting Project. I would like to report that the situation today with respect to government publications has made the continuation of this project unnecessary but I cannot. We now have 125 participating members.

The move toward better organization of Union Catalog activity began with ARL's insistence on coordination and standardization of long–run microfilming of newspapers. Standards were developed and the Library of Congress volunteered to establish in its Union Catalog Division a clearinghouse of information regarding long–run microfilm programs. As a first step, LC prepared and ARL issued *Newpapers on Microfilm: A Union Checklist*. In January 1956, *The Library of Congress Catalog, Books, Authors* contained for the first time the holdings of other libraries. The July issue was renamed *The National Union Catalog*. ARL's persistence brought into being this major U.S. reference tool.

Throughout the 1950's, great effort was spent in improving foreign coverage in American research libraries. A Committee on National Needs was appointed by the Association of Research Libraries. Luther Evans wrote in his 1952 Annual Report, " . . . research libraries have a solemn responsibility to determine what informational needs may prove critical for our national welfare, or even safety, to define their responsibility for meeting those needs, and to take necessary cooperative measures as soon as possible." Recently, at the Library of Congress we conducted a symposium honoring Evan's memory and I was reminded of what remarkable talents, especially in his commitment to a free world being dependent on knowledge, Luther brought to the national library scene at a time when freedom to read and speak were being seriously challenged. He was relentless in his dedication to worldwide acquisition.

With worldwide acquisitions accelerated, the need to develop standardization of cataloging rules for foreign countries became more apparent.

ARL, ALA, and LC joined together for a coordinated effort to obtain standardization and improvement of lists of subject headings.

An internal Committee on Centralized Cataloging was established in LC in January 1953 in response to the report on Centralized Cataloging prepared by Ralph Ellsworth. The feasibility of using cataloging copy prepared abroad was begun with the implementation of the Public Law 480 acquisitions project. [Interestingly enough, the American Council on Learned Societies, led by Mortimer Graves and the United Auto Workers Union, supported legislation and the ARL Shared Cataloging led in efforts to fund the program.] The Library of Congress was authorized to use U.S.–owned foreign currencies for acquisitions to its collection and other research institutions' collections and to catalog materials from countries designated as excess currency areas including Brazil, Egypt, India, Indonesia, Israel, Pakistan, Poland, Spain, and Yugoslavia. LC's initial experience with overseas offices would prove to be fortuitous in the next few years.

For the Library of Congress and the Association of Research Libraries, the 1960's would bring to fruition Charles Coffin Jewitt's plan for centralized cataloging and would see application of automated techniques to library operations. The so–called King Report, *Automation and the Library of Congress*, optimistically concluded that the automation of bibliographic processing, catalog searching, and document retrieval are technically and economically feasible in large research libraries. The die was cast.

Politically, no time could have been riper to launch the most gigantic and most comprehensive cooperative program ever attempted by the library world. Lyndon Johnson sat in the White House and controlled the Congress. Higher education became a popular recipient of federal funds and the "educational industrial complex," as Congresswoman Green later dubbed the Washington lobby, had a heyday. Fortunately for research libraries and scholarship in this nation, libraries had a piece of the action. ARL can be credited with making the proposal in 1965 to Congress to amend the Higher Education Act to give the Librarian of Congress responsibility for acquiring, insofar as possible, all library materials currently published throughout the world which were of value to scholarship, of cataloging them promptly after receipt, and of distributing bibliographic information through printed cards or other means. William Dix, Librarian of Princeton University and the distinguished Chairman of the ARL Committee on Shared Cataloging, outlined the advantages of such legislation before the Subcommittee on Education in the House. He stated that the program would enrich and strengthen the resources of LC, utilize skilled manpower, which is in short supply, more effectively enable libraries to eliminate alarming backlogs of uncataloged books, provide basic elements necessary for automation of bibliographic information, and release for productive use millions of dollars spent in duplicative efforts. With Quincy Mumford's concurrence, the Congress approved the legislation and the National Program for Acquisition and Cataloging came into being. John Cronin and Quincy Mumford can be credited with implementation of this gigantic task with considerable help and assistance from Sir Frank Francis and Josef Stummvoll. Shared Cataloging became the subtitle of the program.

A conference was convened in London in January 1966 attended by the national libraries and the producers of current national bibliographies of England, France, West Germany, Norway, and Austria. It was agreed that it would be desirable for LC to use for cataloging purposes the description of books listed in the national bibliographies of those countries where bibliographies exist and that it was possible for the producers of the bibliographies to supply LC with a copy of the entries prior to publication. A prototype operation was in place in London in June. Subsequently, offices were established in Austria, France, Norway and West Germany and regional acquisitions offices were opened in Brazil and Kenya. Eastern Europe was soon added to the list of cooperating countries.

What had been a dream for over a century took less than a year to put in place. Research libraries were asked to notify LC of their purchase orders and to provide information on materials currently received on an automatic basis to insure that LC would acquire and catalog the material promptly.

The 1967 *Annual Report of The Librarian of Congress* succinctly put the progress of the National Program for Acquisitions and Cataloging in perspective: "Fiscal 1967 was the first full year of operation for the National Program for Acquisitions and Cataloging. At its close the important publications of 21 countries and three continents were covered by NPAC offices in 9 countries, subscriptions had been placed for the bibliographical services of 17 foreign institutions, and 92 American libraries were receiving sets of currently printed cards for about 150,000 publications a year. These cards are also available to other libraries."

Concurrent with the implementation of the National Program for Acquisitions and Cataloging, the Automation Committee of the Association of Research Libraries was working with the Library of Congress on a pilot project to develop procedures and programs for the conversion, file maintenance, and distribution of machine readable cataloging data. LC invited participation in the pilot project and 16 libraries representing all segments of U.S. libraries were chosen to participate. There was general consensus that what became known as MARC served a useful purpose. Encouraged by the enthusiasm of the library community, LC announced that a full–scale operation MARC Distribution Service was in the planning stage. Out of this experimentation and the interest expressed by the British National Bibliography emerged MARC II, the philosophy of which was the design of one format structure capable of containing bibliographic information for all forms of material and related records. Because of the magnitude of the task, MARC II was applied to one form of material at a time. In March 1969, distribution of machine readable tapes for English language monographs began on a weekly basis. I am happy to report that MARC has now been expanded to include all languages except Japanese, Chinese, Korean, Persian, Hebrew, and the Arabic languages. Thus, the products of the National Program for Acquisitions and Cataloging are even more readily available on a timely basis. MARC also covers most formats of materials as well as our authority files. I like to think that Charles Jewitt, who first envisioned centralized cataloging, and Herbert Putman who as you know was responsible for the implementation of the distribution of printed catalog cards would be astounded by our progress.

On occasions like this it is always popular to pat ourselves on the back and look at the accomplishments, which we indeed deserve to do, but at the same time we as administrators and custodians of the nation's storehouse of knowledge—or citadels of freedom—whichever you prefer, have a responsibility to evaluate our shortcomings and find new and innovative ways to cross frontiers heretofore unknown. We have, I believe, two great challenges facing us for the remainder of this century. One is the preservation of the materials acquired with such zeal by our predecessors and the application of new technology to accomplish this, and secondly, I believe it is up to Members of the Association of Research Libraries to insure that library professionals do not become mere information managers in an age when information dominates our economy. We have to do better than IBM, RCA, and Xerox.

I think the path to solving our preservation problems is analogous to that of acquisitions and cataloging. The ARL Committee on Preservation which was formed in 1960 charged Gordon Williams and his Committee with the task of analyzing the preservation problem and formulating possible solutions. Williams' report "The Preservation of Deteriorating Books: An Examination of the Problem with Recommendations for Solutions," was adopted by ARL in 1965. It called for the creation of a federally supported central agency which would (1) undertake the centralized preservation of deteriorating records deposited by libraries; (2) coordinate its own preservation program with local libraries to assure that all significant records would be preserved while avoiding unwilling duplication; (3) assure the ready availability of microform or full size photocopies of deteriorating materials to all libraries; and (4) preserve, in the interest of textual preservation and the ready availability of copies, all microform masters made at its expense or deposited by others and coordinate the preservation of microform masters made by other agencies. LC with more optimism than warranted committed itself to establish a national preservation program. 1967 saw the Brittle Book Project done in cooperation with ARL, LC and CLR. The conclusions of that study were equally rosy—there appeared to be no barrier to the establishment of a national program to identify for preservation best copies of deteriorating materials.

Without being too harsh on LC and ARL, the Williams report did provide a blueprint for a national program but in 1967, LC was in no position to head a national program in either a direct or advisory capacity. Its own shop had to be put in order. Over the next several years, LC established a preservation laboratory, a preservation microfilming office, and a reconstituted restoration office with a unified preservation budget.

Even now LC cannot claim a national program, but the research and testing office's efforts will accrue benefits for all libraries. There is a diethyl zinc program that may do for library preservation what NPAC did for acquisitions and cataloging. With the advent of optical disc technology coupled with massive deacidification efforts, we may be on the threshold of success. I believe our cooperative efforts have led us to this point.

Finally, despite our dependence on a technology, we must not let it overwhelm the profession of librarianship and our true mission to make knowledge readily available. There are many attempts, both nationally and locally to reduce the profession to "information brokers" with no respect for the content of collections or for the longheld American tradition of free library service. Each of us can readily name over a dozen librarians whom we have personally known who are prominent scholars in various subject specialties, many of whom became so in our libraries. These individuals have taken great delight in sharing their knowledge with whoever has ventured into their library. We need to continue to foster the intellectual development of members of our staff and their commitment to the importance of scholarship. We need to reinforce the vocation mentality of the past. Technology cannot replace subject speciality, rather it should enhance that speciality. Our profession must continue to respect scholarship and the free world's absolute dependence on knowledge. We are going to have to be our own press agents if we are to overcome being folded in with the information industry. We are going to have to prove to a wide segment of our population that "cost effectiveness" is not always easily measured in the world of scholarship. Many times the dividends are a long time coming.

Finally, whatever agenda we set for ourselves during the remaining years of this century, we know that continued cooperation as well as the sharing of our intellectual and physical resources will be a necessity. I don't think we should be prophets of gloom and doom but I do believe that we will have to realistically face some difficult times. On the lighter side, we need to remember that ARL emerged during a period of depression in our country and yet its goals have been exceeded by the wildest of expectations. We owe much to the illustrious group of research librarians whose faith, hard work, and dedication brought about phenomenal change during the past half century. We have built a strong foundation from which to grow.

THE INFLUENCE OF ARL ON ACADEMIC LIBRARIANSHIP, LEGISLATION, AND LIBRARY EDUCATION

Edward G. Holley

Only once before have I appeared before the members of the Association of Research Libraries. Ten years ago, following a Council on Library Resources Fellowship, I addressed your meeting in Atlanta on the topic, "Library Governance in Higher Education: What Is Evolving?" At that meeting I remarked to the late Charles Stevens, then Director of the National Commission on Libraries and Information Science, that I found the ARL meeting one of the most stimulating professional conferences I had ever attended. Stevens agreed. He then added that he had always found the ARL meetings the most important of any he attended because the members always discussed major topics of national and international concern. The broad approach, the national perspective, the general lack of a provincial or parochial point of view, all seemed to Stevens a vital testimony to the effectiveness of the Association of Research Libraries.

Advances in Library Administration and Organization, Volume 3, pages 295–305.
Copyright © 1984 by JAI Press Inc.
All rights of reproduction in any form reserved.
ISBN: 0-89232-386-8

As a library historian, I do not find Charles Stevens' comment surprising. Any social organization which consists of the leaders of major research institutions should address matters of significance beyond their local concerns. Moreover, the academic milieu in which ARL directors operate ought to stimulate thinking about the problems of society as a whole and how research libraries affect and are affected by such problems. In the academic tradition of weighing all issues carefully, looking at various alternatives, and making decisions after thoughtful analysis, the ARL director is in a better position not only to make decisions affecting his or her library system but also to consider the impact of those decisions on other libraries and information centers.

Whether such decisions are the actual outcome of such deliberations, of course, the historian or sociologist must ultimately assess. Mere debate and analysis do not always result in action, whether positive or negative. As Louis Kaplan has noted in his own assessment of the Association of Research Libraries, an earlier leadership group, the American Library Institute (1905–1951), testifies to the failure of one library leadership group in our history to achieve laudable goals.[1] Though Kaplan believes ARL has not been "resplendent in the fulfillment of its goals," I believe that objective analysis can lead one to the opposite conclusion.

When I began research for this paper, I had my assistant, Margaret Miles, make a chart of the issues discussed in ARL's *Minutes* and *Newsletters* for the past twenty years. The range is truly impressive, but the major topics have clearly been (1) bibliographic control, in its many formats, including cataloging, support for the Higher Education Act of 1965, Title II–C (both the original and its subsequent revision), out of which emerged the National Program for Acquisitions and Cataloging, CONSER, doctoral dissertations, etc.; (2) relations with the higher education community, especially as that relationship involves financing research and libraries; (3) resource sharing, including such cooperative programs as the Farmington Plan, the Chinese and Slavic Centers, consortia, bibliographic utilities, collection development and management; (4) federal programs, including the aforementioned Higher Education Act but also copyright and other legislation of importance to research; (5) library management (a development of the seventies), including staff participation in governance, staff development, the Management Review and Analysis Program, the establishment of the Office of Management Studies, etc.; (6) technology, which could be listed under any of the above, but not forgetting concern with microforms, MARC records, video discs, and approaches to preservation such as permalife paper and the Barrow experiments, and (7) the ARL itself, its organization and role, the kind of navel–gazing in which most social groups engage from time to time (yours has chiefly related to which institutions we shall let in and which we shall leave out).

Now that is a formidable list by anyone's definition. Not all projects have succeeded, of course, and some probably stayed in place beyond their period of usefulness, e.g., the Farmington Plan. Yet throughout the whole list runs a theme of commitment to cooperative action for solving common problems. In an earlier essay, I noted that the role played by professional organizations in cooperative enterprises is often overlooked.[2] Librarians tend to take their associations for granted. At the same time they expect those associations to be there and provide the organizational framework through which they can discuss future plans, publish the professional literature, promote surveys and research, encourage library development, and lobby for legislative support. Clearly, professional advancement would be seriously handicapped without organizations which develop group consciousness and respond to the public interests in ways which achieve socially desirable goals.

In this general sense the ARL has made a number of important contributions to academic librarianship. Like most organizations, the Association existed for many years with few but important victories. Frank McGowan,[3] ARL's historian for the period 1932–62, gives the Association credit for bibliographic control of doctoral dissertations (with the concomitant publication of dissertations on microfilm by University Microfilms), publication of the 1942 Library of Congress *Catalog*, inauguration of the PL 480 Program, and the development of the Farmington Plan. For much of its first thirty years, ARL was perceived as a clubby little group of administrators who focused on a narrow segment of librarianship and were not very well tuned in to the larger world in which the American Library Association operated. Doubtless that perception was reinforced by the confidentiality of the early *Minutes*, Ralph Ellsworth's characterization of ARL as "a nice fellowship of like–minded men," and the members' refusal to let the editor of the *Library Journal* attend and report on their meetings.[4]

That perception was reinforced by Ellsworth's much–quoted comparison of ARL to ALA in his 1961 "Critique of Library Associations in America," in *Library Quarterly*.[5] Yet Ellsworth's contention that ARL has drained time and talent from ALA and its largest division, ACRL, seems to me not to stand up under serious examination. If Ellsworth is correct in asserting that ARL directors don't want to waste their time on the bureaucratic ALA and that they prefer ARL because of its emphasis on action vs. talk, his assertion must apply only to *some* ARL directors. McGowan points out that nine ARL members served as ALA presidents from 1932–62. An additional five have served in the last twenty years, excluding the speaker who was not a director of an ARL library at the time, but whose background was clearly in that tradition. Moreover, in ACRL's forty–four year history, over half the ACRL presidents have represented their institutions in ARL, including five of the last six ACRL presidents. Their number certainly included ALA's chief critic, Ralph Ellsworth, who served ACRL as president not once but twice! Whatever failures ACRL may have had in the past, they cannot be accounted for by any siphoning off of time and talent by ARL. In addition many members of the ARL have served on important ALA boards and committees, including at least one ARL member on every ALA Committee on Accreditation for the past decade. Thus I can only conclude that the relationship of ARL to ALA, while it may have declined in recent years as ARL has moved from club to a more professional association, has been and is now a rather close one, even if it may have been indirect.

Now let me return to my earlier conversation with Charles Stevens. His off–the–cuff assessment ten years ago seems to me very much on the mark. A major contribution of ARL to academic librarianship has been as a forum for the discussion of major policy issues. In my opinion, there does need to be a forum where national and international issues receive careful study from persons with the background and knowledge to make solid recommendations to appropriate organizations. ARL's discussions have been reported thoroughly in its *Minutes* and represent a significant contribution to our professional literature. As a careful reader of the *Minutes*, I am convinced that Stevens was right. ARL discusses important issues which either are not addressed at all by other associations or which could not receive in other organizations the in–depth attention they deserve.

Despite Ellsworth's encomium, some critics of ARL argue that ARL talks more than it acts. Both Kaplan and McGowan comment that ARL's history represents a mixture of talk and action. In assessing ARL's effectiveness in terms of its stated goals, Kaplan observed that the Association has done little to encourage *research* (emphasis mine) in the problems of ARL libraries or in the education of research librarians.[6] McGowan noted that ARL has ignored more issues than it undertook.[7] On the other hand one might argue reasonably that ARL's history reflects a careful tailoring of priorities to those issues where it can have the greatest influence. To identify issues, to clarify thinking, to develop statements of national policy represent important contributions which any profession neglects at its peril. My own view is that policy analysis, i.e., sophisticated discussions of important issues, may well represent ARL's major contribution to academic librarianship.

Turning now to legislation, my second assigned area, what have been ARL's achievements in this area? Library literature, correctly in my opinion, gives ARL major credit for the National Program of Acquisitions and Cataloging, fathered and nourished by the late William Dix. NPAC, the former Title II–C of the Higher Education Act of 1965, was entirely in the tradition of ARL's major focus on bibliographical control. Dix, as an active member of ALA and soon to be President during that Association's most difficult year, was in an excellent position to push for this legislation. He had his own problems in coping with the cataloging of Arabic and other esoteric materials at Princeton and was keenly aware of the waste involved in cataloging the same title more than once. By any objective assessment, the implementation of this legislation has saved all libraries throughout the country enormous amounts of money. Funds under Title II–C enabled all libraries, through access to increased quantities of Library of Congress bibliographic data, to keep pace with the flooding tide of books and periodicals spawned by increased state and federal support during the late sixties and early seventies.

Legislation, of course, is a sometime thing. Title II–C (NPAC) came into existence during those halcyon days of the Great Society. The smoothness with which the original Title II–C funds were subsequently transferred to LC's operating budget and the substitution of a new Title II–C for Stregthening Research Libraries represent notable successes. Other legislative activities have followed the normal pattern of delay, and, occasionally, defeat. One remembers the long and costly efforts to revise the 1909 Copyright Law. In his remarks on "The Future of ARL," David Weber called this battle "a major defense effort" which was debilitating.[8] As a one–time participant in that fight, I concur with his judgment. That ARL played a major role in the battle for the Copyright Revision Act of 1976, along with ALA and several other library associations, is clear. After one joint meeting of librarians and publishers, I remember one official from a major publishing firm expressing the hope that Steve McCarthy would soon retire so that we could get on with the passage of a "reasonable" law!

ARL's meetings in recent years have concentrated on federal legislation for obvious reasons. Through student aid, research grants, and categorical programs the federal government has become a major factor in higher education's funding. Again, as Weber's speech reminded us, that funding has brought its price in a degree of federal control, even as the old–time opponents of federal aid to education used to remind us thirty years ago. Yet the health of libraries, especially research libraries, depends very much on the health of the parent institution. The financial health of universities is in serious danger of being eroded, not just from federal reductions in library aid but particularly in proposed reductions in student aid, which is even more crucial to private universities and smaller universities than it is in large public universities. ARL, accustomed to thinking in broader terms than just libraries, needs to be sensitive to these developments as I am sure you will be.

One of the problems facing ARL in the legislative arena is the fact that the group is small, unashamedly meritocratic, and poorly dispersed geographically. Those adjectives are not hurtful nor a deterrent when the economy is flourishing, but can be disastrous if not approached judiciously when budgets are tight. Within the ARL itself there has been some infighting over the revised Title II–C and the allocation of grants to a relatively few large institutions. The U. S. Department of Education's policy of making large grants to a very few institutions, incidentally, was one consciously pursued by the former Commissioner of Education, Ernest Boyer. But the complaints about distribution of funds illustrate the difficulty of maintaining a united front. Yet to proceed in the federal legislative arena without a united library front will almost certainly ensure defeat as Lee Jones noted in an article on "The Politics of Consensus" in the *Journal of Academic Librarianship* last year.[9]

Jones used the National Periodicals Center as a major illustration of the need for compromise. The National Periodicals Centers, despite several years of discussion in ARL and other circles, had not elicited much support from the larger library community. By the time Lee Jones, Nancy Gwynn, and Richard De Gennaro appeared at an ALA conference to talk about NPC, some of us could sense that it was already too late to mobilize the library profession behind the plan, especially in the light of opposition from the director of a major public library.

That leads me to an observation about the importance of not becoming isolated from your colleagues in other associations. As the earlier success of HEA Title II-C and the modest success in the Copyright Revision Act of 1976 remind us, we need the support not only of all librarians but also of friends of libraries. We may well have become, as Warren J. Haas says, about the research librarian, "an aggregation of professions," each one with our own specialty, expertise, and interests. Nonetheless, on some matters of common interest, we need to act together and build on strength.

One more footnote on library legislation before I pass on to my final topic. Although I leave the discussion of ARL and LC to William Welsh, I certainly cannot omit from this recital a mention of the Bryant Memorandum on the Library of Congress in 1962. Our professional literature is strangely silent on this matter. Only the *Wilson Library Bulletin* gave it so much as a brief three–page summary. Yet I suspect that LC's responsiveness to the profession's bibliographic needs may have been significantly enhanced by publication of Douglas Bryant's memorandum in the *Congressional Record*. (One of these days I'll have one of my students do a paper on that topic). In the early sixties there was substantial criticism of the Library of Congress by librarians and officials in government agencies like the National Science Foundation. At the request of Senator Claiborne Pell, Douglas Bryant, then Associate University Librarian at Harvard, prepared a hard–hitting memo on the role of the Library of Congress in serving the libraries of the country. Bryant included suggestions for major improvements in role, organization, and bibliographic activities. The Librarian of Congress asked that the memo be put on the ARL agenda for the June, 1962 meeting. At the Miami Beach meeting he asked for ARL suggestions and a list of priorities for LC from the Bryant Memo. From the terse record in the *Minutes*, where a motion for the Board of Directors to consider the topic and adopt an ARL position at that meeting failed for a lack of a second, one can surmise that more was going on here than was ever brought to public attention.[10] Clearly the Memo focused the Librarians' attention in a marvelously constructive way.

When one turns to the topic of "library education," at least in the formal sense, one looks in vain for any direct ARL impact. Kaplan's assessment is correct in pointing to this neglect. Prior to the focus on "Education for Librarianship" at ARL's October, 1980, meeting, the only previous ARL efforts came to an end in the early seventies. An ARL Committee on Training for Research in Librarianship was appointed in 1966 and struggled to secure funding for a study of manpower needs. For several years this committee, chaired by David Kaser, worked with the U.S. Office of Education and Rutgers University to launch a three–phase project to address both training needs and directions for the future. Changes in personnel at USOE and Rutgers apparently doomed the project and the Committee itself disappeared at the time of ARL's experiment with the "Commissions" form of organization. Nonetheless, the Task Force on Library Education, formed in 1980 and now taking a hard look at the education of research librarians, could benefit from consideration of the outline of the earlier committee in its 1966 report.[11]

In order to keep ARL's neglect in perspective one should remember that the library profession in the late sixties was just emerging from a period of staff shortages, that Title II–B funding had provided fellowships for recruiting at the master's and doctoral level which had been enjoyed only once before in the profession's history (the Carnegie Corporation grants in the twenties and thirties), many pinned their hopes on the disappointing Bundy–Wasserman study (funded by USOE), and that the Asheim Library Education and Manpower statement (now the Library Education and Personnel Utilization statement) was in process and would be approved by ALA in 1970.

Nonetheless the profession entered the decade of the seventies with a profound discontent with library education, not unlike, incidentally, the current unrest on the same topic. The editors of *Library Journal* in the

January 1, 1970 issue predicted that "dissatisfaction will grow among a new breed of library school students, with resulting changes in the library school curriculum to include greater emphasis on the content of various literatures, the case method, and a return to some form of internship in the field."[12] Few predictions of *LJ* have been more on target. Curricula did change, new methods developed, and internships are very much a topic of conversation these days, and not just in the ARL Task Force.

Why didn't ARL have more of an impact upon professional education? One can only speculate. The Association certainly did not ignore the problems of library personnel. The landmark Downs–McAnally article on "The Changing Role of Directors of University Libraries," in the March, 1972 *College and Research Libraries*, the Booz Allen and Hamilton Study at Columbia University, and the launching of ARL's Office of Management Studies focused attention on the internal problems of libraries, which were largely related to personnel. Thus issues of governance (one of my own earlier concerns), staff development and utilization, management skills, and leadership training brought forth MRAP, communications networks, management consulting, and a host of other attempts to settle down the troops and get on with the research library enterprise. To quote Ellsworth Mason, it was a time of "off with the heads of heads," but subsequently many staff members complained that the damned director didn't *lead* any more.[13]

Yet I assure you that ARL exercised influence on library education, even if the Association itself was not directly involved in problems of the library training agencies. As a director–turned–dean, I can vouch specifically for the impact of ARL's publications programs. Our students read and studied ARL's *Minutes*, *Newsletters*, MRAP reports (when available), SPEC kits and OMS studies. They also devoured ARL's statistical reports, though ARL directors, like those in every other statistical–gathering organization, often deplored the way in which such reports were used.

Moreover, the ARL group provides an obvious focus for research. Your libraries are relatively homogeneous, the data for them are easily available, and your staffs are remarkably cooperative with students working on master's papers and doctoral dissertations. You often complained about the amount of time questionnaries took, you quarreled with the students' results, and you wondered whether anybody on the faculty understood either research techniques or research libraries. You said all these things, but you normally cooperated. Some of you even served on dissertation committees to keep the rest of us honest! The profession's growing research literature, often more neglected than used, is better because of your cooperation.

Thus I would say the ARL's indirect impact upon library education has been quite significant. No one who expects to practice in this profession can ignore ARL's contributions to bibliographic activities, to national policy formulation, or to personnel studies. Those contributions must be a part of any curriculum in a first–rate library school. One of the functions of a professional school is to develop critical thinking about the profession's overarching problems. ARL has frequently laid out the agenda for discussion of such problems at a very sophisticated level, as I have already noted.

In some ways the ARL and the library schools face an old dilemma, characteristic of all social organizations: "How do we as professionals unite in a common cause while at the same time preserving our focus on a specialized area and enhancing the unique contribution our own institutions make to the general welfare?" Translated into the library educator's dilemma I recently said that the question becomes "How can professional education provide the necessary theoretical base, develop some specializations, introduce the student to practice through an internship, and create a zest for learning that will cover a lifetime of changes?"[14] That question will never be answered to everyone's satisfaction because each generation has to address it in a different context. That ARL has chosen to take the lead in promoting the interaction of those who teach, practice, and research seems to me to augur well for our professional future, yours and mine.

CONCLUSION

Do I have any words of wisdom from my look at ARL's past in the areas of academic librarianship, legislation, and library education? Other than urging you to continue your leadership role in policy making, I have just one: more attention to the user of your resources and services. As a librarian, I understand that your bibliographic and management and legislative activities are not for yourselves but for your users. That is not always apparent to them. We librarians have difficulty remembering why we create structures, devise organizations, and write standards. Perhaps the current moves in higher education to emphasize "outcomes measurement," "effectiveness indicators," and "the student consumer" will force us to re–examine what difference our libraries make in the educational and research process.[15] New attempts to answer the question, "What difference does a college degree make?" is easily translated into a similar question, "What difference does a research library make?" One would hope that such re–examination might lead to the kind of public support necessary for continued viability of the research library community.

No one seems to me to have summed up our dreams better than Jim Haas did seven years ago in a speech on ARL and the Library of Congress. He ended his remarks with the hope that ARL could "in the year 1982, and on the 50th anniversary of ARL, . . . look about and see a sophisticated, reliable, effective and financially viable system for the identification and distribution of recorded information—a system in which technology is effectively employed, social obligations are met, and public comprehension of our goals and efforts are clearly established."[16] As directors on the firing line, you may wonder if Jim's adjectives could be applied to any system for the *identification* much less the *distribution* of recorded knowledge. Struggles to keep our bibliographic utilities afloat make you painfully aware of the difficulties we face.

For my part I do not despair. As a library historian, I am aware of how far we have come as library and information professionals. In our historical record one can trace successes and failures, victories and defeats, but we are not a weak profession, despite the self-abnegation of which we are often, correctly, accused. With a healthy respect for achievements in the past and renewed energy to face the future, the Association of Research Libraries can continue to play a vital role—not just in increasing the usefulness of resources and services of research libraries, but also in providing leadership for your colleagues in other libraries.

NOTES AND REFERENCES

1. Louis Kaplan, "The Association of Research Libraries: A Study of Organizational Effectiveness," *Journal of Academic Librarianship* 1(September, 1975): 11.

2. Edward G. Holley, "The Role of Professional Associations in a Network of Library Activity," *Library Trends* 24(October, 1975):293.

3. Frank M. McGowan, "The Association of Research Libraries, 1932–1962." (Unpublished Ph.D. dissertation, University of Pittsburgh, 1973), pp. 180–194.

4. Ralph Ellsworth to Charles W. David, letter, February 27, 1950, quoted in McGowan, p. 190; Eric Moon "A National Organization or a Private Club?" *Library Journal* 88(April 1, 1963): 1429.

5. Ralph Ellsworth, "Critique of Library Associations in America," *Library Quarterly* 31(October, 1961): 388–389.

6. Kaplan, p. 10.

7. McGowan, p. 189.

8. David Weber, "The Future of ARL; A Charter Member's View," Association of Research Libraries *Minutes* 96th Meeting, May 15–16, 1980, pp. 45–46.

9. C. Lee Jones, "The Politics of Consensus," *Journal of Academic Librarianship* 7(July, 1981): 156–160.

10. "Bryant Memorandum on the Library of Congress," Association of Research Libraries *Minutes* 60th Meeting, June 16, 1962, p. 20; "Bryant Memorandum Answered," *Wilson Library Bulletin* 37(December, 1962): 310–312.

11. "Training Requirements for Research Library Personnel Proposed Outline of Study," Association of Research Libraries *Minutes* 69th Meeting, January 8, 1967, pp. 39–41.

12. "Nearsighted Foresight," *Library Journal* 95(January 1, 1970): 17.

13. Personal letter of Ellsworth Mason to the author.

14. Edward G. Holley, "Extended Library Education Programs in the United States." In *Advances in Librarianship*, edited by Michael Harris. 11: 52. New York: Academic Press, 1981.

15. The Southern Association of Colleges and Schools has underway a major study aimed at revision of its accreditation standards to reflect these concerns.

16. Warren J. Haas, "The Library of Congress and the ARL," Association of Research Libraries *Minutes*, 87th Meeting, October 15–16, 1975, p. 6.

Other Useful Sources

Stephen A. McCarthy, "Association of Research Libraries," in *University and Research Libraries in Japan and the United States*, edited by T. R. Buckman et al. (Chicago: American Library Association, 1972), pp. 250–254.

John G. Lorenz, "The Association of Research Libraries: A Five-Year Review, 1975–1979," in *The Bowker Annal of Library and Book Trade Information* 25th edition, 1980, pp. 140–145.

Edwin E. Williams, "Association of Research Libraries," in *Encyclopedia of Library and Information Science* 2(1969): 51–55.

BIOGRAPHICAL SKETCH OF THE CONTRIBUTORS

Ralph Cohen is Kenan Professor of English at the University of Virginia. His interests include literary theory and criticism and he writes on those subjects. Recently, he was the Northrop Frye Professor of Literary Theory at the University of Toronto.

Andrea Dragon, Assistant Professor in the School of Communication, Information and Library Studies at Rutgers University, lectures and writes on the management and marketing of library services. Recently she spoke on the topic of marketing library information service at a joint meeting of the Special Library Association and the American Society for Information Science.

Vicki Graham, a doctoral candidate in English at the University of California at Berkeley, is a project assistant in the California University system. Her activities include documentation of project resources and the writing and execution of data analysis programs. Formerly, she was an assistant librarian for the Metropolitan Transportation Commission of Berkeley, California.

John F. Harvey is an international Library and Information Consultant. His most recent foreign service was at Mottahedin University in Tehran, Iran. He has been both a library director and dean of a library school. Harvey is both an author and editor of publications in Library Science.

John D. Haskell, Jr., Associate Librarian of the College of William and Mary, has an active scholarly interest in New England history. He has produced several bibliographies in that field. Active in the Association of College and Research Libraries, Haskell also is a reviewer of grant applications for the National Endowment for the Humanities.

Advances in Library Administration and Organization, Volume 3, pages 307–309.
Copyright © 1984 by JAI Press Inc.
All rights of reproduction in any form reserved.
ISBN: 0-89232-386-8

Boyd W. Haynes, Jr., M.D., is Professor of Surgery and Director of the Burn Center, Medical College of Virginia Campus of Virginia Commonwealth University. Haynes writes and speaks on burn therapy and related topics, and is a past president of the American Burn Association. He is a recipient of that association's Distinguished Service Award.

Edward G. Holley, Dean of the School of Library Science at the University of North Carolina, is a prolific author. A former university library director, he is the 1983 winner of the Melville Dewey medal from the American Library Association.

Virginia Swann Hill, Associate Professor of Management at the University of Southern Mississippi, has worked in government and business. She is an accredited Personnel Specialist of the American Society for Personnel Administrators, and is a consultant in industry.

Gary S. Lawrence, Director of the Library Studies and Research Division, University of California System, writes and speaks at professional companies on the subject of online catalogs. His related interests include research on the economics of information and library service and the effects of technology on libraries and library users.

Stephen A. McCarthy, a part-time consultant to the Council on Library Resources, retired from the post of Executive Director of the Association of Research Libraries. During his long distinguished career, he served in several academic libraries including those of Columbia University, the University of Nebraska, and Cornell University. He was Director of Libraries at the two latter institutions, retiring once before from his post at Cornell.

Nurieh Musavi, Assistant Professor, School of Librarianship, Western Michigan University, was chairman of the Mottahedin University's School of Library and Information Science in Tehran, Iran. Musavi's scholarly interests are in information science and management including technical processing.

James G. Neal is Assistant Dean and Head Reference and Instructional Services Division, Pattee Library, Pennsylvania State University. When he wrote this article he was Assistant Director for Memorial Library Public Services at the University of Notre Dame. He moved to Pennsylvania in August, 1983. Active in the American Library Association, Neal writes on library concerns. He is co-editor of a forthcoming new journal, *Financial Management and Planning in Libraries*. His interest includes library history, personnel administration and technology, and organizational changes.

Heather L. Presley, a graduate student in film, works as a research assistant for the University of California system. She reviews professional literature and writes reports on current library issues.

Mary Ellen Thomas, Coordinator of Library Orientation at the James Branch Cabell Library of Virginia Commonwealth University, has had a variety of library reference service in medical, research and general academic libraries. Occasionally, she has worked on the compilation of bibliographies. Her service in a medical library led to her interest in producing the bibliography published here.

Tom G. Watson, Assistant to the Vice Chancellor, University of the South, was formerly university librarian for that institution. He is the first author to have a second article in this annual, his first article having appeared in volume 2. Management of libraries has been a major interest of his and he speaks as well as writes on this subject for professional audiences.

William J. Welsh, Deputy Librarian of Congress, serves as the library's representative in national and international library circles, and shares responsibility for the overall administration of the Library of Congress with the Librarian of Congress. A prolific author and speaker, Welsh's interests range from the historical to the leading edge of modern library technology.

Priscilla C. Yu, Documents Bibliographer at the University of Illinois Library, is active in the American Library Association, with service on committees concerned with exchange of library materials. Yu writes on this subject especially with an interest in China and other Asian countries.

AUTHOR INDEX

American Council of Learned
  Societies, 285
American Library Association, 223
Angle, H., 51
Anthony, Robert H., 26
Association of Research Libraries,
  283, 301
Awad, Elias M., 30

Berkner, Dimity S., 35
Beyer, J., 51
Biskup, Peter, 74, 80, 81
Blakely, R. J., 221
Bloom, Harold, 272
Bloomquist, Laura L., 223
Bluedorn, A. C., 60
Branscomb, H., 225
Broadbent, Kieran P., 10, 17
Bryant, Douglas, 301
Byrd, Cecil K., 76, 77, 79, 80

California, University of,
  Office of the Executive Director,
  Library Plans and Policies, 91
California, University of,
  Systemwide Administration
  Division of Library Automation
  and Library Research and

California, University of (*Continued*)
  Analysis Group, 105, 157,
  158, 161, 172, 174, 176
Carnegie Commission on Higher
  Education, 237
Carnovsky, Leon, 222
Cascio, Wayne F., 30
Chén, Yü-chën, 9
China Society of Library Science,
  12
China Yearbook (*see* Zhongguo
  Niajian Chinese Encyclopedia
  yearbook; see Zhongguo Baike
  Niajian)
Clark, Alice S., 223
Clayton, Howard, 226
Colorado State Library, 227
Commission on the Humanities,
  272, 274
Committee for the Compilation of
  the History of Library
  Service, 5
Coppin, Ann, 76, 77, 78, 79
Cramer, S. A., 80
Crossly, Charles, 79, 81
Cummings, L. L., 30

Danton, J. Periam, 74, 76, 78

SUBJECT INDEX

Advances in
Library Administration and Organization

Edited by **Gerard B. McCabe,** *Director of Libraries, Rena M. Carlson Library, Clarion, University of Pennsylvania* and **Bernard Kreissman,** *University Librarian, University of California, Davis*

REVIEWS: "Special librarians and library managers in academic institutions should be aware of this volume and the series it initiates. Library schools and university libraries should purchase it."
—*Special Libraries*

". . . library schools and large academic libraries should include this volume in their collections because the articles draw upon practical situations to illustrate administrative principles."
—*Journal of Academic Librarianship*

Volume 1, 1982
ISBN 0-89232-213-6

CONTENTS: Introduction, *W. Carl Jackson.* **Continuity or Discontinuity - A Persistant Personnel Issue in Academic Librarianship,** *Allan B. Veaner, University of California, Santa Barbara.* **Archibald Cary Collidge and "Civilization's Diary: Building the Harvard University Library",** *Robert T. Byrnes, Indiana University.* **Library Automation: Building and Equipment Considerations in Implementing Computer Technology,** *Edwin B. Brownrigg, Division of Library Automation, University of California.* **Microforms Facility at the Golda Meir Library of the University of Wisconsin, Milwaukee,** *William C. Roselle, University of Wisconsin, Milwaukee.* **RLIN and OCLC - Side by Side: Two Comparison Studies,** *Kazuko M. Dailey, Jaroff Grazia and Diana Gray, University of California, Davis.* **Faculty Status and Participative Governance in Academic Libraries,** *Donald D. Hendricks, University of New Orleans.*

Volume 2, 1983
ISBN 0-89232-214-4

CONTENTS: Introduction, *Bernard Kreissman.* **Management Training for Research Librarianship,** *Deanna B. Marcum, Program Associate, Council on Library Resources.* **Subject Divisionalism: A Diagnostic Analysis,** *J.P. Wilkinson, University of Toronto.* **Videotext Development for the United States,** *Michael B. Binder, Fairleigh Dickinson University.* **The Organizational and Budgetary Effects of Automation on Libraries,** *Murray S. Martin, Tufts University.* **The Librarian as Change Agent,** *Tom G. Watson, University of the South.* **Satellite Cable Library Survey,** *Mary Diebler, PSSC.* **Deterioration of Book Paper,** *Richard G. King, Jr., University of California.* **Evaluation and the Process of Change in Academic Libraries,** *Delmus E. Williams, Western Illinois University.* **Toward a Reconceptualization of Collection Development,** *Charles B. Osburn, University of Cincinnati.* **Strategies and Long Range Planning in Libraries and Information Centers,** *Michael E.D. Koenig and Leonard Kerson, Columbia University.* **Project Management: An Effective Problem Solving Approach,** *Robert L. White, University of California, Santa Cruz.* **A Preliminary and Selective Survey of Two Collections of Juvenilia,** *Michele M. Reid, New Jersey Institute of Technology.* **Biographical Sketch of the Contributors.**

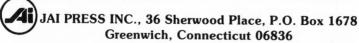JAI PRESS INC., 36 Sherwood Place, P.O. Box 1678
Greenwich, Connecticut 06836
Telephone: 203-661-7602   Cable Address: JAIPUBL

Foundations in
LIBRARY AND INFORMATION SCIENCE

A Series of Monographs, Texts and Treatises

Series Editor: **Robert D. Stueart**
Dean, Graduate School of Library and Information Science
Simmons College, Boston

New!

GOVERNMENT INFORMATION QUARTERLY

An International Journal of Resources Services, Policies, and Practices

Editor: **Peter Hernon**
Graduate Library School, University of Arizona

Associate Editor: **Charles R. McClure**
School of Library Science, University of Oklahoma